Transformational HRM Practices for Hong Kong

Transformational HRM Practices for Hong Kong

Edited by Anna P. Y. Tsui and Wilfred K. P. Wong

Hong Kong University Press
The University of Hong Kong
Pok Fu Lam Road
Hong Kong
https://hkupress.hku.hk

© 2020 Hong Kong University Press

ISBN 978-988-8528-48-6 (*Paperback*)

All rights reserved. No portion of this publication may be reproduced or transmitted in any form or by any means, electronic or mechanical, including photocopying, recording, or any information storage or retrieval system, without prior permission in writing from the publisher.

British Library Cataloguing-in-Publication Data
A catalogue record for this book is available from the British Library.

Digitally printed

Contents

Acknowledgements	vi
List of Contributors	vii

1. Introduction — 1
   Anna P. Y. TSUI and Wilfred K. P. WONG

2. Contexts and Environments of Human Resource Management in Hong Kong — 14
   Anna P. Y. TSUI

3. Talent Acquisition Strategies in the New HR Era — 41
   Jenny W. LAM

4. Talent Assessment Strategies in Hong Kong — 61
   Neil COWIESON, Kit K. W. LAM, and Gloria W. Y. CHAN

5. Learning and Development Strategies in Hong Kong — 90
   Eliza C. P. CHAN

6. Development of the Performance Management System: Evolution or Revolution? — 107
   Wilfred K. P. WONG

7. Managing Total Rewards Strategies in Hong Kong — 129
   Norris Y. W. WONG and Wilfred K. P. WONG

8. Employment-Related Laws and Employee Relations in Hong Kong — 152
   Francis HON

9. Digital Transformation of Human Resource Management in the Era of Disruptive Technology — 170
   Josh BERSIN and Anna P. Y. TSUI

10. Managing Organizational Change in Hong Kong: The Role of Human Resource Management for Success — 191
    Victor M. T. NG, Derek K. H. CHENG, Emily Guohua HUANG, and Michael N. YOUNG

11. Challenges and Future for Human Resource Management in Hong Kong — 212
    Anna P. Y. TSUI

Index — 227

Acknowledgements

We must give heartfelt thanks to many people involved in this book project. We were impressed by the overwhelming support from professionals and companies when the project was kicked off. We thank them for their trust in us and sacrifice of time and effort in contributing the chapters, despite their busy schedules and, in the case of some, lack of familiarity with academic writing. They spent tremendous efforts in gathering ideas, sourcing references, and writing and revising drafts. Not only did they share their experiences and insights, they were willing to promote the field of HRM and wrote with their hearts to benefit others who are not familiar with HRM. Also, we must give tribute to people in the Hong Kong Institute of Human Resource Management and all the respondents in various organizations who gave us valuable information about their HRM experience, practices, and insights.

We express our gratitude to the reviewers of this book for their insightful comments on the early drafts. We must also thank the research assistants at the Chinese University of Hong Kong for their useful support in the process. Finally, we could not have published this book without the editorial assistance of Hong Kong University Press.

Contributors

Josh BERSIN is an independent research and technology analyst. He is the founder of Bersin by Deloitte, provider of global research in human resources. He spent much of his career in technology, sales, marketing, and business leadership and is actively writing about major global trends in HR and talent management. He now runs joshbersin.com and studies all aspects of HR, including business leadership, corporate learning and development, recruiting, and HR technology. He is also a keynote speaker advising HR teams and vendors in the HR space and also serves as an educator, thought leader, and personal coach to HR and business leaders around the world.

Eliza C. P. CHAN started her career in training and development with a British conglomerate, which gave her strong foundation not only in the training and development profession but also exposure to a diverse business environment. She continued progression in learning and development and later joined a global bank. Eliza spent much of her career life in the banking industry, focusing on consumer banking and institutional banking. She left banking for some time, joined a telecommunications organization, and then rejoined banking, moving her career to talent management and development. Unusual for a learning and development practitioner, Eliza coupled her responsibilities in a human resource business partnership role. She reckons that this role has equipped her with a wealth of down-to-earth experience and understanding from multiple perspectives of the organization, managers and employees. After over twenty years in the banking industry, she has recently made a move to a publishing company, in the role of organization development and employee communication.

Gloria W. Y. CHAN is the research consultant of Human Scope Limited. She is a registered psychologist with the Australian Health Practitioner Regulation Agency (AHPRA), having obtained a master's degree in psychology (organizational and human factors) from the University of Adelaide in Australia. She supports the design and delivery of assessment and development centres, and the design and application of psychometric tests. She also plays a lead role in Human Scope's talent development research. Before joining Human Scope, Gloria gained experience working in various industries in Australia, ranging from the Australia public health sector to the defence industry.

Derek K. H. CHENG served previously in various multinational corporations and sizeable firms in Hong Kong and mainland China. He has substantial experience in human resource management at both operational and strategic levels. Since retirement in 2008, he has been very active as a part-time lecturer teaching human resource management subjects at various tertiary educational institutions in Hong Kong. More recently, he has developed intense interests in academic research, particularly in the areas of leadership, high performance work practices, and change management. He holds two MSc degrees, an MBA degree, and a DBA degree.

Neil COWIESON is the founder and executive director of Human Scope Limited. He has been a chartered organizational psychologist for thirty years. He has been based in Hong Kong for over twenty years. In 2005 Neil founded Human Scope, focusing on leadership assessment and development, talent identification, 360-degree feedback, psychometric testing, assessment and development centres, and executive coaching. Before forming Human Scope, Neil was head of HR Development, Asia Pacific for HSBC. He also held positions in SHL as managing director of Greater China and in the Business Psychology Group at BT UK.

Neil co-founded the Division of Industrial and Organizational Psychology of the Hong Kong Psychological Society, serving as president.

Francis HON has degrees in philosophy, law, and social and cultural theory, and is a member of the Society of Trust and Estate Practitioners. He started his career in the HKSAR government's Labour Department and was a conciliation officer of labour disputes. Later, he was the accreditation manager of the Hong Kong Institute of Human Resource Management (HKIHRM) and was responsible for designing the certificate programme in employment law and employee engagement. He also taught employment law at HKIHRM and HKU SPACE. Francis now works as an administrative staff member in the Hong Kong campus of a US university.

Emily Guohua HUANG is an associate professor at Hong Kong Baptist University. Her research interests are in the area of organizational behaviour and human resource management, including workplace uncertainties, job insecurity, emotional intelligence, and counterproductive work behaviours at the individual and group levels. Her work has been published in leading international journals such as the *Journal of Applied Psychology*, *Journal of Management*, and *Human Resource Management*.

Jenny W. LAM is an experienced HR professional in Hong Kong who specializes in recruitment and staffing. A graduate from the Chinese University of Hong Kong with a bachelor's degree in business administration and a master's degree of arts in English studies from the University of Hong Kong, Jenny has worked in various business sectors including banking, search firms, FMCG and luxury retail for years. Her main roles are as a recruiter and an HR business partner to help support line managers with human resource management solutions. Her multifaceted experiences in various industries have provided her a bird's eye view on different industrial hiring trends.

Kit K. W. LAM is the managing director of Human Scope Limited. She is a chartered organizational psychologist, specializing in talent management, leadership assessment and development, and coaching. Since 2006, Kit has supported individuals to achieve their full potential and has focused on nurturing talents and leaders. She has coached and supported over 1,500 individuals globally in their development journeys, including functional leaders and general managers across industries.

Kit previously worked in employee engagement consulting in Hong Kong and China, serving blue-chip global corporations. She actively supports the development of aspiring occupational psychologists. She has been a reviewer for BPS DOP annual conferences and has lectured at the University of Macau.

Victor M. T. NG is a veteran banker with over thirty years of experience in retail, commercial, and corporate banking business management. He worked for Bank of America (Asia) from 1992 to 2006 and assumed senior management positions in diverse capacities. Between fall 2006 and 2007 he spearheaded the acquisition and integration of Bank of America (Asia) by a state-owned bank. He then oversaw the bank's strategic mergers and acquisitions, integrations, and expansion initiatives from 2008 to 2017. Besides being a professional banker, he fulfilled his aspiration to become a scholastic practitioner when he obtained his doctor of business administration in 2013. Soon after his DBA graduation, he began teaching graduate and undergraduate courses in Hong Kong and China. He has been an adjunct associate professor at Hong Kong Baptist University and Hang Seng University of Hong Kong since 2014. His research interests involve employee reactions to corporate mergers and acquisitions, as well as organizational changes.

Anna P. Y. TSUI received her PhD degree from the University of Hong Kong's Faculty of Business and Economics. She is now a senior lecturer in the Department of Management at the Chinese University of Hong Kong and has been in the academic sector for over a decade. She has immense teaching interests in management, business strategy, and human resource management with specialism in general HRM, staffing, and employment practices. In addition, she engages research in the HRM areas of employment law and industrial relations, corporate social responsibility, higher education issues, and other current business topics. She has published a few books, business cases, newspaper articles, and a number of scholarly papers in several journals. Before this book, she had worked with many veteran HR professionals in producing another practical HRM book in 2009, *Professional Practices of Human Resource Management: Linking HRM to Organizational Success*.

From time to time, she also conducts training for organizations on various topics of interest. Before working as an academic, she was a veteran HR professional in different business sectors such as electronics manufacturing, public utility, and hospital organizations. She was mainly a generalist responsible for a wide spectrum of HR activities.

Norris Y. W. WONG is an independent total rewards consultant based in Hong Kong. She obtained a master's degree in business administration from the University of Durham, UK. She is also a certified global remuneration professional with the WorldatWork organization in the US.

Before becoming an independent consultant, Norris was in leadership positions in total rewards function of various global companies, including BP Plc., Prudential Corporation Asia, AIA Group, and State Street Asia.

Wilfred K. P. WONG, JP, is the founder and managing director of RESOLUTIONS HR & Business Consultancy Company. Before founding his consultancy company, he was a senior human resource executive at Cathay Pacific Airways and DFS Group. He obtained a bachelor's degree and a master's degree in business administration from the Chinese University of Hong Kong. And he is a fellow member of the Hong Kong Institute of Human Resource Management and was its council member in the last two decades. He was elected as its president from 2008 to 2010 and is also a full member of the Hong Kong Computer Society. He is an experienced business leader with professional experience in managing business and HR functions.

In recent years, he has been appointed by the HKSAR government as either the chair or a member of many government committees with important responsibilities concerning the local community. For instance, he is the chair of the Pay Trend Survey Committee, a council member of the HKICPA (HK Institute of Certified Public Accountants) and the HKCAAVQ (HK Council for Accreditation of Academic and Vocational Qualifications), and an executive committee member of the Hong Kong Housing Society. With his invaluable community service to society, Mr. Wong has been appointed by the HKSAR government as a Justice of the Peace since 2015.

Michael N. YOUNG is an associate professor at Appalachian State University. Before joining App State, he worked as an academic in Hong Kong for nineteen years. His research interests involve corporate governance, management of Asian firms, state-owned enterprise reforms in China, and financial and organizational economics. He has over a hundred peer-reviewed cases, conference presentations, and journal publications, and over 2,600 citations on Google Scholar. He is an active member of the Academy of Management and has served for seven years as the Hong Kong regional representative for the Business Policy and Strategy Division. He is on the editorial board of *The Journal of Management Studies*, *Management and Organization Review*, and *Journal of World Business*.

1
Introduction

Anna P. Y. Tsui and Wilfred K. P. Wong

> **LEARNING OUTCOMES**
>
> By the end of this chapter, readers should be able to
> - understand the concepts and developments in the field of human resource management;
> - describe the development of HRM in Hong Kong;
> - understand the roles and competencies of HR professionals; and
> - identify the elements and professional standards of HRM in Hong Kong.

Some Background of HRM Development

The role of human resource management (HRM) has been evolving for some time in the West, mainly led by the Anglo-American countries. For example, the shift from 'personnel management' to 'human resource management' was part of the movement to acknowledge the value of employees as an organizational resource, and was an attempt to remove some of the stigma associated with the slow, bureaucratic personnel department. The concept of HRM is able to be more proactive, descriptive, and executive by implying that employees are *resources* of the employer.[1] On the other hand, the behavioural science movement in the 1960s had paid attention to the 'value' aspect of human resource in organizations and a better quality of life for workers. Then, the 'human resource accounting' theory was an outcome of a series of developments in the field of HRM. This view, emphasizing human resource as assets for organizations, began to gain support in the 1980s. Since then, the field of HRM has developed rapidly owing to various factors, such as growing competitions, especially by the Japanese firms; slowing economic growth in some developed economies; research findings of HRM's contributions to firm performance; development of professional organizations and creation of HR specific positions in industry; and introduction of HR curricula in the undergraduate and postgraduate programmes.[2]

At the same time, many scholars have helped set the directions for transformation of HRM through various high-impact HR operating models and concepts, including 'strategic human resource management' that contributes to effective management of human resource, improvement in organizational performance, and the success of a business;[3] 'high performance work system' where organizations would have the best possible fit between their social system (people and how they interact) and technical system (equipment and processes);[4] HRM as means to achieve sustainable competitive advantage owing to its qualities of being valuable, rare, inimitable, and non-substitutable;[5] 'human capital management';[6] and 'talent management'.[7] Studies have also moved on to examine the devolution of HRM to line managers when some assert that line managers with HRM responsibilities can positively influence employee commitment and ultimately the business performance.[8] As a result, definitions of human resource management can vary.[9] The debate about the nature of HRM continues today. But to sum up, HRM involves 'people management functions and practices'.

In parallel, the roles and competencies of HR professionals are transformed. Various typologies and models have been developed in the world. For example, Storey devises a two-dimensional model that highlights the HR tactical versus strategic role and what he describes as 'interventionary' versus 'non-interventionary' HR activities.[10] Other examples come from Lawson and Limbrick, as well as Schoonover.[11] Ulrich, in his early discussion, depicted four roles of HR professionals (i.e. strategic partner, change agent, administrative expert and employee champion) that highlighted a strategic versus an operational focus in addition to HR's propensity to engage with people as opposed to processes.[12] Later, he revisited the framework to reflect changes. The 'employee champion' role is replaced by two distinct roles, 'employee advocate' and 'human capital developer'. The 'administrative expert' has become the 'functional expert', and a new role is added, 'HR leader'. The 'change agent' role is absorbed into the 'strategic partner' concept. In 2017 Ulrich and his team further proposed nine HR competency domains with three core drivers.[13] And the Society of Human Resource Management (SHRM) of the US also defines a set of behaviours and skills associated with success, named as HR success competencies.[14]

Meanwhile, we also note some major transformations in various HR functions in the world. The following highlights some of these features.

Radical changes in talent acquisition and assessment

As jobs and skills are changing, we need to use different strategies and channels to source and recruit talent. Talent acquisition is a very important challenge companies are now facing. They are using HR technologies, social networking, analytics and various cognitive tools (such as artificial intelligence, machine-to-machine learning, robotic process automation, and natural language processing and predictive algorithms) to find people in different new ways. They also attract talents through a distinct brand and determine who will best fit the job, team, and the company. Additionally, candidate experience in the recruitment process is emphasized so as to engage them. Employer branding, applicant tracking system, chatbots, psychometric testing, assessment centre, videos, games, and simulations are adopted as well to attract the candidates while assessing them.

Revamping the performance management and rewards systems

In recent years, companies have been criticized for doing traditional performance management system with infrequent meetings between supervisors and subordinates. The ratings and the forced distribution system are blamed. Instead of motivating their employees and improving performance, both the managers and employees feel unhappy. Some companies are now experimenting with new performance management approaches that emphasize continuous feedback while reducing the focus on appraisal and the associated ratings system. We observe more regular discussions about capabilities and skills, with coaching of the employees using a more forward-looking approach. The focus has shifted from talking *about* people to talking *with* people in open conversations.[15] The development of rewards strategies is also facing changes. We find the importance of total rewards in the workplace and an increasing use of pay for performance and different forms of rewards. Also, the compensation data are more transparent and pay decisions may not be made annually, especially for highly competitive jobs.

Innovations in learning and development

The structure, operations, and mission of 'learning and development' (commonly known as 'training and development') are facing significant changes as well.[16] Today, learning ability has become the most essential competency in our fast-changing environment. And most of the learning can be self-directed. With the development of new technologies and tools, we see the learning function as a highly strategic business area that focuses on innovation and leadership development by delivering a superb learning experience, promoting lifetime learning and bringing multifunctional teams together. There is also a new focus on convergence bringing multi-disciplines of sales, marketing, design, finance, and IT onto cross-functional teams when building products and solutions. Moreover, we notice that no training is offered unless there are data to support that the programme has a positive and measurable impact on employee as well as organizational performance. Learning analytics are important to organizations.

Disruptive HR technology and analytics

HR technology is also a key focus area for HR transformation. We now live in a world flooded with apps, mobile and cloud-based technology, artificial intelligence, cognitive bots, analytics software, as well as virtual reality and augmented reality. These tools have brought new functionalities to the world of HR. Organizations have traditionally used them to automate processes and drive operational efficiencies. But now we can use these enabling technologies to revamp our HR processes (such as in performance management, recruiting, learning and development, succession planning, and important personnel decisions like promotion), enhance our HR roles (i.e. to be more strategic), improve the overall customer experience and foster a more engaged and connected workforce. Besides, we notice that analytics are moving into the mainstream.

Companies that can 'datafy' their HR systems and processes are seeing better results in their quality of hire, leadership pipelines and employee turnover.[17] As a result, HR departments are shifting towards analytics solutions to drive evidence-based decision-making while adding value.

Corporate culture and employee engagement

As younger and more diverse workers enter the workforce, a growing number of business leaders understand that the success of a company or department depends heavily on the people within them and their level of engagement and job satisfaction. Culture is one of the top factors conducive to employee satisfaction. The stronger a culture is, the more likely a staff member is to be satisfied. We must now compete for the best talent based on corporate culture, instead of an organization's profitability. When employee engagement and company culture become a key focus for business, it is often the role of HR to take on these new missions. Its role as 'employee advocate' is therefore to be reinforced.

Strengthening the legal environment

As society progresses, problems are observed in many developed societies—for instance, poverty and inequality. There is a growing pressure to regulate the labour scene with more employment laws assuming that such action can protect the workers and maintain justice. Together with other issues such as ageing, demands for democracy and work-life balance, the governments have introduced more laws in different areas of employment. But some may have received resistance from employers due to extra costs and losing business competitiveness arguments. While we have to strike a nimble balance between the need for protecting workers' rights and business performance, there are important implications for HR professionals to understand when implementing these changes in their organizations.

HRM Development in Hong Kong

Hong Kong's HRM has also evolved tremendously. In particular, it has undergone drastic changes in the light of changing contexts and environments in the last few decades. Businesses are facing issues such as the force of globalization, fluctuating economy, workforce diversity, fierce competition but escalating labour costs, disruptive technology, and political and legislative changes. Hong Kong has transformed from a manufacturing to a service or knowledge-based economy. This new economy is characterized by a decline in manufacturing and a growth in service or knowledge as the core of the economic base. To meet the human capital needs in such a knowledge economy, organizations have to attract, develop, and engage their knowledge workers. But there is a shortage of talent. HR departments have to help business develop effective strategies in order to win the 'war for talent'.

Moreover, organizations are now staffed by members of multiple generations and a diverse workforce, which may differ in terms of their work values, attitudes, and behaviours. HR practices have to be modified so as to allow members of all groups to work together and to achieve workplace diversity and inclusion. In addition, we envisage Hong Kong's change of sovereignty to China for over twenty years. While many Chinese-based companies are set up in Hong Kong which are making significant contributions to the local economy, some HR professionals have closer relationship with their business and HR counterparts in mainland China. They need to know the differences in legal environment, behaviour of people and style of management. All these changes demand a new model for HRM.

In consequence, there is a pertinent need for a business partnership role for HR to support and drive a range of business initiatives in order to make a greater impact on the business activities. A consultancy company has echoed our view by revealing the top five HR jobs in Hong Kong as the workplace environments are changing (Table 1.1). HR as a business partner has topped the list, which is followed by a need for HR in talent acquisition. Expertise in human resource information system and HR technologies is also gaining importance. In reality, we observe major shift of HR role in partnership with other managers (see Box 1.1) and representation on the company board (Box 1.2). HR professionals are seen to support organizational strategies.

Table 1.1: Top 5 HR jobs in Hong Kong

1. HR Business Partner
2. Regional Talent Acquisition
3. Regional Compensation and Benefits
4. HR Shared Services
5. Human Resource Information System

Source: Hudson. (2016). *Human resources Hong Kong market trends*.
Retrieved from https://hudson.hk/insights/infographics/market-trends/human-resources

HRM in Action—Box 1.1

Sukie as a HR Business Partner

HR business partners are HR professionals who work closely with senior leaders to develop an HR agenda that closely supports the overall purpose of the organization. The process of alignment is known as HR business partnering and may involve the HR business partner in strategic activities such as sitting on the board of directors, working closely with the board of directors and senior managers on daily basis, and being close to their customers (i.e. managers and employees, as 'account managers'). The idea of HR business partners is popularized by Professor Dave Ulrich, who sees HR business partners as part of a successful modern HR function, along with shared services and centres of excellence. It is common now as organizations become more people-focused and see the value in aligning HR agendas towards a common business goal. It helps break down the traditional silos and encourages collaboration between departments. And the role of HR is now an adviser to managers to expand the business and achieve work goals through people strategy.

Sukie has worked in the HR field for ten years. She has just joined a famous multinational retail fashion company as an HR business partner. She is required to work closely with the product teams with an overall responsibility for all HR policies and practices within her section. She visits the retail shops every week and works closely with the shop leaders. While listening to their concerns and providing employee relations advice to managers and employees on site efficiently, she offers relevant HR solutions more effectively, in line with the needs of the business. Sukie understands that it is a challenging job. It requires knowledge and experience of retail business and an ability to communicate in business terms so as to gain long-term trusting relationships with her clients and HR colleagues. She has to be flexible, adaptable and solve ad hoc problems satisfactorily.

Source: Interview information; Ulrich, D. (2017, Feb. 14). 7 lessons learned from the HR business partner model. Retrieved from https://www.linkedin.com/pulse/7-lessons-learned-from-hr-business-partner-model-dave-ulrich

HRM in Action—Box 1.2

HR Executive on a Company Board

Company boards are usually composed of experienced senior executives who focus on business or high-level issues such as finance, marketing, and sales and believe that their functions are the foremost way to protect the interests of shareholders. As a result, many company boards do not deal with HR matters—not to mention the presence of an HR representative.

Company A (the Company) was founded in 2000 by the chief executive officer (CEO) with key businesses in trading of commodities and sourcing hard goods for clients. Headquartered in Hong Kong, it had established branch offices in Guangdong, Taipei, and Singapore. More than 200 people were employed, with a majority of them based in Hong Kong.

About six years ago, Peter Wong joined the Company as the head of HR when it decided to establish the branch offices outside Hong Kong. Together with a few senior partners, the CEO formed an executive committee (similar to the board of directors) with a purpose of overseeing the company business direction, strategies, expenditure, and budget, as well as HR issues. The committee met at least once a month. Peter was invited to join the executive committee as the secretary. He was delighted that the profile of the HR profession could be raised as human capital issues would be discussed on the board. He expected the board to grab hold of key strategic HR issues such as succession planning, talent management, and compensation and benefits. He might have opportunities to explain HR policies, programmes, and reports, and would be able to speak his mind. Also, he could offer counsel on employee engagement and human capital development issues that a change of organizational culture would eventually bring about.

Unfortunately, after six months, Peter found that at least 90 per cent of the meeting time in the executive committee was spent on business or operational matters. And he said no more than ten words in the last three meetings. Given the agenda items were initiated by the assistant of the CEO, HR issues were seldom included. In the meetings he could hardly join the partners' discussion. Nobody paid attention to his presence. As the committee secretary, he was always busy with taking minutes of the meetings.

At the end of 2017 the Company noticed that the business results did not meet the target. A negative growth was recorded. In the executive committee meeting, the CEO urged everyone to put forward plans to contain costs and improve sales and profitability. He also asked Peter to freeze hiring for the attrition, and look into the possibility of workforce reduction, particularly those in Hong Kong with less than two years of service. The CEO decided that no extra expense would be incurred on settling the severance payment. On the contrary, Peter made a counterproposal to review the employee performance appraisal records so that underperforming people would be asked to leave. The managing director insisted on his decision, and other members made no objection. Eventually, Peter was instructed to carry out the CEO's directive accordingly.

While contemplating how he should handle the above workforce reduction issue, Peter now pondered how long he could bear the situation (i.e. his role and presence on the company board). Should he stay on the board? If so, how could he join the members' discussion and educate the CEO and members about the importance of HR management? What value could HR add to the board functions? And how could the CEO and board members develop a good understanding of HR and human capital issues?

Indeed, we have seen a rapid and professional development of HRM in Hong Kong in the past decade. Outstanding human resource management practices by the organizations are increasingly recognized. And the number of HR professionals, HRM programmes, and courses is on the rise. For example, it is estimated that the current number of individuals in the HRM sector is more than 133,000.[18] Professional organizations are found, such as the leading Hong Kong Institute of Human Resource Management (HKIHRM) (www.hkihrm.org; see also the previous book),[19] Hong Kong People Management Association (HKPMA) (www.hkpma.net), Hong Kong Management Association (HKMA), (www.hkma.org.hk) as well as HR Magazine (hrmagazine.com.hk). HKIHRM has seen its membership increase from more than 100 to over 5,300 (including 600 corporations) from the 1980s to 2017. HR surveys (such as the Pay Trend and Pay Level Survey, Hong Kong Manpower Statistics Survey, and the Training and Development Needs Survey), forums, reports, and publications have been issued, and a number of HR conferences and seminars have been organized. Recognitions and awards are being given to organizations exhibiting outstanding human resource management practices.[20] Collaborations and partnerships with overseas professional bodies are also being forged. For instance, HKIHRM is a member of the Asia Pacific Federation of Human Resource Management (APFHRM), one of the continental federations under the World Federation of People Management Associations. Their former presidents have served as presidents of APFHRM. HKIHRM has also partnered with HR People and Strategy from the US and signed a memorandum of understanding with the Chartered Institute of Personnel and Development (CIPD) from the UK to strengthen collaboration in training, research, and other HR activities. There is also a reciprocal professional membership recognition arrangement between HKIHRM's professional members (MIHRM (HK)) designation and the Canada-based Human Resource Management Association's certified human resource professional (CHRP) designation.

To enhance the professional status of HRM and prepare students to work as future managers or specialists in the field of HRM, HKIHRM has created an HR Professional Standards Model in 2010. It made references to academic models, competency frameworks, and other HR organizations, as well as the competency requirements of major local companies. Three perspectives have been identified that demonstrate the standards for HR practitioners in the aspects of the Core Professional HR Knowledge; the Work Experience in terms of their roles and responsibilities; and the Capability in terms of competencies demonstrated at work. And five competencies (professional knowledge, business partnership, ethics, customer/user focus, and communication/influence) are distinguished.[21] As of February 2018, a total of twenty-three programmes from seventeen higher education institutions have been endorsed by HKIHRM. This is good news for universities, since it advances the development of their HR curricula for the needs of society and organizations. Students looking for HRM programmes will have a comprehensive source of information.

In August 2014 a Cross-Industry Training Advisory Committee (CITAC) on Human Resource Management was also established by the HKSAR Government Qualification Framework to draw up competency standards (referred to as the Specification of Competency Standards, or SCS) in respect of key functional areas of Hong Kong's HRM.[22] HKIHRM has also identified a HR Career Ladder consisting of associate member, professional member, and fellow member, with descriptions of their respective characteristics and contributions.[23] With these benchmarks, both junior and experienced HR professionals can use this platform to integrate their academic qualifications and work experience in the pursuit of continuing education and development. Organizations can also recruit their HR staff with the right competencies and experiences.[24]

The Rationale and Objectives of the Book

It has been ten years since the first author published a book with other HR practitioners about professional HRM practices in Hong Kong organizations.[25] At that time, we received favourable comments and encouragements from various stakeholders (for example, filling up the gap in the market, meeting the local needs with a practitioner-oriented focus). And the book was adopted as a text for the Executive MBA students in an HRM course in one of the local universities. But in the light of the recent changes in the field, there is an urgent need to update our stakeholders of the current trend, strategies, practices, and various tools in relation to HRM in Hong Kong. We could not find any new publications about the situation of HRM in Hong Kong published in the past decade. Most of the present books about HRM are still dominated by those of Western or Anglo-American origins emphasizing theoretical issues or their cultures. But 'replications' may just oversimplify the managerial realities across different cultures. We therefore decided to pursue this book project. The main focus of this new book is to provide both theory and practice, with a stronger focus on the latter in the context of Hong Kong. Such an approach can communicate hands-on knowledge and ways of practical implementation to local readers. We therefore invited seasoned and experienced human resource professionals in the field as contributors for various book chapters. The HR professionals, line managers involved in HRM, and students taking human resource management courses or programmes in Hong Kong could be a suitable audience. Also, HR professionals and managers who have cross-border business activities in mainland China would find the book useful. Additionally, mainland Chinese managers in Hong Kong would find the contents instructive. They may learn different (both successful and unsuccessful) experiences to deal with the more demanding and challenging work environments they are facing outside mainland China. The book also sets agenda for future directions and implications for HRM professionals in Hong Kong. In sum, the major objectives of this book are:

- to develop a showcase opportunity for HR to drive sustainable business impact and to co-create value to businesses operating in Hong Kong;
- to delineate the underlying factors affecting the implementation of various HR strategies and practices with a view to narrow the gaps between HRM theory and practice;
- to help stakeholders and students of HRM understand the current challenging Hong Kong environment and their implications to HR professionals in organizations;
- to identify the changing roles and functions of HRM;
- to provide up-to-date knowledge and skills with practical guidelines to HR stakeholders on how to implement effective HRM practices in organizations; and
- to identify challenges and future directions and implications of HRM in Hong Kong.

Organization of the Book

We identify the following essential elements of HRM in this book. And in the light of different contexts and environments, we include a chapter about the contextual environments affecting HRM in Hong Kong:

(1) Contexts and environments of HRM in Hong Kong
(2) Acquiring potential employees (talent acquisition strategies)
(3) Assessing candidates and employees (talent assessment strategies)
(4) Learning and development strategies
(5) Performance management system
(6) Managing total rewards strategies
(7) Employment-related laws and employee relations
(8) Digital transformation of HRM due to HR technology
(9) Role of HRM in change management
(10) Challenges and future for HRM in Hong Kong

This book is thus organized into 11 chapters. Chapter 1, the introduction, provides a snapshot with the concepts of human resource management and the present state of HRM development in Hong Kong. We note that professional HRM practices are becoming more prevalent because of changing environment and business needs. There is an increasing number of HR specialists who demonstrate strategic roles and competencies. Especially, some HR executives are on the company boards who help senior managers to make business decisions. We also witness the emergence of HR business partners in organizations. At the same time, there is a membership expansion in professional HR associations, a strong demand for formal HRM education, and establishment of professional HR standards.

Chapter 2 is about the contexts and environments of HRM in Hong Kong. Researchers have argued for the importance of studying HRM in contexts. We therefore need to have an overview of major environmental forces on the HRM practices first. They include the sociocultural, economic, technological and political-legal aspects. We find a more diverse force with a rise of knowledge workers, aged workers, female employees, and the younger generation. In addition, we understand the economic forces arising from globalization and the emergence of different types of organizations. The chapter then gives a glimpse of HR technology and analytics that are currently affecting the ways to carry out HRM activities in organizations. Finally, we discuss the political environment and the change of employment laws and relationships in the increasingly turbulent society of Hong Kong.

In Chapters 3 and 4 we discuss current talent acquisition and assessment strategies in Hong Kong. Chapter 3, 'Talent Acquisition Strategies in the New HR Era', highlights the imbalance between job demand and supply leading to a 'war for talent'. Consequently, there is a need to review current HRM strategies when recruiting the best candidates. Companies are innovating their recruitment process using automation, data analytics, and other advanced tools. The adaptations of new methodologies and mindsets in response to the new HR era are also examined. Chapter 4, 'Talent Assessment Strategies in Hong Kong', highlights the importance of objective, reliable, and fair selection methods to business and ways to implement them. Use of traditional assessment tools such as psychometric tests, assessment centres, leadership assessment, and feedback and coaching are discussed. Then, innovations in the areas of gamification and digital/video interviewing are examined. Organizations would find them useful in the current workplace while exercising judgment and observing professional guidelines when using these tools.

Chapter 5 is about learning and development strategies in Hong Kong. We explain a concept change from 'training and development' (T&D) to 'learning and development' (L&D) in the workplace. This change has underlined a more proactive approach to gaining knowledge nowadays. It expands the scope of this HR function from just a job to support a continuous process of gaining knowledge and growth of workforce. And it adopts a multidimensional approach stressing a link between the learning experience and work performance. It also reflects a stronger emphasis on the responsibility of a learner. For L&D professionals, it then requires different sets of skills and competencies when adopting different learning contents, delivery methods, and technology-supported tools.

Chapters 6 and 7 are about changes of performance management system and rewards management practices. Both discuss the concepts and practices of performance and rewards management in Hong Kong. In particular, Chapter 6, 'Development of the Performance Management System: Evolution or Revolution?', highlights the current debate on the trend of performance management and performance appraisal systems brought about by leading companies in the world. While companies observe the benefits of using performance appraisal as the foundation to motivate employees to work harder, some others comment on its perils leading to poor employee morale and a wastage of time and efforts to managers. But despite the dilemma, we find that organizations would not do away with their performance management system. Instead, companies need to revamp their performance management system to fit into the current business needs. Chapter 7, 'Managing Total Rewards Strategies in Hong

Kong', discusses current rewards management strategies in Hong Kong, including the definitions and strategies of total rewards, recent development, and implementation in the work place. In addition, there is a trend of enhancing employee benefits in areas such as leave entitlements, flexible work arrangement, and employee wellness. We also look at these issues before drawing implications to HR and rewards management professionals.

In Chapter 8, 'Employment-Related Laws and Employee Relations in Hong Kong', we discuss employment-related law and the employment relations scene in Hong Kong. As the society advances, notions of civic pride and demands for rule of law, rights and fairness, as well as democracy are instilled in the minds of many Hong Kong people. They would demand better working conditions such as employment rights protection in terms of minimum wage and maximum working hours, equal employment opportunities, more leave entitlements and holidays, and statutory retirement benefits. Indeed, in recent years, the Hong Kong government has introduced more regulatory and protective employment laws. These issues are covered in this chapter. On the other hand, like their counterparts elsewhere, the role of trade unions in Hong Kong has diminished. Most labour disputes are settled by official channels satisfactorily. In this chapter, we also highlight the concept of employee engagement and its importance of maintaining harmonious employee relations in Hong Kong.

Chapter 9, 'Digital Transformation of Human Resource Management in the Era of Disruptive Technology', covers a hot topic on current HR technology development. Over the years, we have seen an explosion of new technologies and innovations disrupting our business systems and HR processes. Traditional HR functions such as talent acquisition and recruitment, performance management and compensation, and training and development can be transformed. HR activities should be more forward-looking and strategic that they can help organizations make better decisions. However, when we examine the status and extent of adopting HR technology in Hong Kong companies, we find that Hong Kong's HR is still at the early stage of digital maturity—they may be just exploring digital possibility (automating) or extending the current capability of their human resource information system with 'reactive and procedural' or 'functional and fragmented' HR activities. Major objective of using technology is to enhance operational efficiency only. And our HR people are not 'disruptors' yet.

Chapter 10 covers a special topic, 'Managing Organizational Change in Hong Kong: The Role of Human Resource Management for Success'. We discuss an acquisition in the banking industry in Hong Kong. A wholly owned subsidiary licensed bank (Bank B) of a foreign-funded international financial institution was acquired by a Chinese state-owned regional bank (Bank A) in the mid-2000s. Despite the pronouncement by Bank A that Bank B had a well-developed platform, business model and talents for Bank A's future business expansion, abrupt changes had taken place shortly after the acquisition. The performance of the resulting bank, Bank A (Asia), soon deteriorated. And within three years of the acquisition, it recorded an exceptionally high employee turnover rate. The bank subsequently employed consultants to interview the leavers and make important change management initiatives. Essentially, they cover issues in talent retention, a sense of continuity, communication, and the involvement of HRM. The chapter argues that omission of HRM strategically or operationally would undermine an organization's effectiveness in managing change.

Finally, Chapter 11 presents the challenges and future for human resource management in Hong Kong in view of the forthcoming change drivers to business. They provoke changes of business strategies. As a consequence, new HR implications also cause transformation of their HR strategies and practices. New HR skills and competencies are required. An overview of these characteristics is examined at the end of the chapter.

Notes

1. Boxall, P. F. (1992). Strategic human resource management: Beginnings of a new theoretical sophistication? *Human Resource Management Journal, 2*(3), 60–79. Legge, K. (1995). *Human resource management: Rhetorics and realities*. Basingstoke: Macmillan. Storey, J. (Ed.). (2007). *Human resource management: A critical text* (3rd ed.). London: Thomson Learning. Schuler, Randall, S., and Jackson, S. E. (2007). *Strategic human resource management: Global perspectives*. Malden: Wiley.
2. Budhwar, P., and Aryee, S. (2008). An introduction to strategic human resource management. In The Aston Centre for Human Resource (Ed.), *Strategic human resource management: Building research-based perspective* (pp. 9–89). London: CIPD.
3. Budhwar, P., and Aryee, S. (2008). An introduction to strategic human resource management. In The Aston Centre for Human Resource (Ed.), *Strategic human resource management: Building research-based perspective* (pp. 9–89). London: CIPD. There may be three perspectives to describe the contribution of HRM in improving a firm's performance: 'universalistic' perspective (emphasizing the best of HR practices and that business strategies and HRM policies are mutually independent); 'contingency' perspective (the fit between the business strategy and HRM strategies that business strategies establish the pattern of HRM policies); and the 'configurational' perspective (a simultaneous internal and external fit between a firm's external environment, business strategies and HR strategies). We may also have the 'hard' variant (highlighting the 'resource' aspect of HRM) and the 'soft' variant (discussing the 'human' aspect of HRM).
4. Huselid, M. A. (1995). The impact of human resource management practices on turnover, productivity, and corporate financial performance. *Academy of Management Journal, 38*, 635–673. Snell, S. A., and Youndt, M. A. (1995). Human resource management and firm performance: Testing a contingency model of executive controls. *Journal of Management, 21*, 711–737.
5. Barney, J. B. (1991). Firm resources and sustained competitive advantage. *Journal of Management, 17*(1), 99–120.
6. As a type of resource, human capital means that the employee characteristics (in terms of their training, experience, judgment, intelligence, relationships and insights, etc.) can add economic value to the organizations. It thus implies that employees in organizations are not interchangeable or replaceable but the source of success or failure. See, for example, Becker, G. S. (1993). *Human capital: A theoretical and empirical analysis, with special reference to education* (3rd ed.). Chicago: University of Chicago Press.
7. It refers to the anticipation of required human capital for an organization and the planning to meet those needs. The field has increased in popularity after McKinsey's 1997 research and the 2001 book on The War for Talent. See, for example, Michaels, E., Handfield-Jones, Helen., and Axelrod, Beth. (2001). *The war for talent*. Boston: Harvard Business Press. Chambers, E. G. (1997). *The war for talent*. The McKinsey Quarterly. Retrieved from http://www.executivesondemand.net/managementsourcing/images/stories/artigos_pdf/gestao/The_war_for_talent.pdf
8. Budhwar, P. (2000). Strategic integration and devolvement of human resource management in the British manufacturing sector. *British Journal of Management, 11*(4), 285–302.

9. See some examples listed in Tsui, A., and Lai, K. T. (2009). Introduction. In A. Tsui and K. T. Lai (Eds.), *Professional practices of HRM in Hong Kong: Linking HRM to organizational success* (pp. 1–10). Hong Kong: Hong Kong University Press.
10. Storey, J. (1995). *Human resource management: A critical text* (1st ed.). London: Routledge.
11. Lawson, T. E., and Limbrick, V. (1996). Critical competencies and development experiences for top HR executives. *Human Resource Management, 35*(1), 67–85. Schoonover, S. C. (2003). *Human resource competencies for the new century*. Falmouth: Schoonover Associates.
12. Ulrich, D. (1997). *Human resource champions: The next agenda for adding value and delivering results*. Boston: Harvard Business School Press.
13. Ulrich, D. (2017, Feb. 14). *7 lessons learned from the HR business partner model*. Retrieved from https://www.linkedin.com/pulse/7-lessons-learned-from-hr-business-partner-model-dave-ulrich
14. Society for Human Resource Management. (2016). *The SHRM competency model*. Retrieved from https://www.shrm.org/LearningAndCareer/competency-model/PublishingImages/pages/default/SHRM%20Competency%20Model_Detailed%20Report_Final_SECURED.pdf
15. Deloitte. (2017). *Rewriting the rules for the digital age: 2017 Deloitte human capital trend*. Deloitte University Press. Retrieved from https://www2.deloitte.com/content/dam/Deloitte/global/Documents/About-Deloitte/central-europe/ce-global-human-capital-trends.pdf
16. Mustafa, E. (2013). The ten characteristics of world class learning and development. *Human Resource Management International Digest, 21*(6), 3–5.
17. Society for Human Resource Management. (2016). *Use of workforce analytics for competitive advantage*. Retrieved from https://www.shrm.org/foundation/ourwork/initiatives/preparing-for-future-hr-trends/Documents/Workforce%20Analytics%20Report.pdf
18. Hong Kong Institute of Human Resource Management. (2012). *Benchmarking study of HR strategy & practices*. Hong Kong: HKIHRM.
19. Tsui, A., Lai, K. T., and Wong, Isabella, H. M. (2009). The development and current state of HRM in Hong Kong. In A. Tsui and K. T. Lai (Eds.), *Professional practices of HRM in Hong Kong: Linking HRM to organizational success* (pp. 11–26). Hong Kong: Hong Kong University Press.
20. For example, HKIHRM, HKMA, Human Resources Online (https://www.humanresourcesonline.net), the Labour Department of the Hong Kong Special Administrative Region (HKSAR) government, and media such as Classified Post and Career Times have organized competitions and presented awards to organizations with outstanding HR practices.
21. HKIHRM. (n.d.). *Professional standards model*. Retrieved from http://www.hkihrm.org/index.php/ps/professional-standards-model
22. Hong Kong: HKIHRM. The Government of the HKSAR. (n.d.). *HKSAR Government Qualification Framework*. Retrieved from https://www.hkqf.gov.hk/en/itac/index.html
23. HKIHRM. *HR career ladder*. Retrieved from http://www.hkihrm.org/index.php/mb/members-area/student-corner/hr-career-ladder
24. Davis, C. (2017, March). Gearing up for the future of Hong Kong's HRM profession. *Human Resource* (pp. 18–22). The competency standards cover seven functional areas, namely organization development and HR strategy, workforce planning and resourcing, reward management, talent management, HR policies and processes, compliance and risk management as well as employee engagement.
25. Tsui, A., Lai, K. T., and Wong, Isabella, H. M. (2009). The development and current state of HRM in Hong Kong. In A. Tsui and K. T. Lai (Eds.), *Professional practices of HRM in Hong Kong: Linking HRM to organizational success* (pp. 11–26). Hong Kong: Hong Kong University Press.

2
Contexts and Environments of Human Resource Management in Hong Kong

Anna P. Y. Tsui

LEARNING OUTCOMES

By the end of this chapter, readers should be able to

- understand the contexts behind the HRM practices in Hong Kong;
- identify the changes of Hong Kong's population and workforce;
- describe the features of different HR practices under contexts;
- identify the types of companies in Hong Kong and their HRM characteristics;
- acquire an overview of different types of HR technology initiatives; and
- acquire an overview of Hong Kong's employment laws and employee relations.

Introduction

Researchers have argued for the importance of studying HRM in contexts.[1] Therefore, in this chapter, we discuss major contexts and environments on Hong Kong's human resource management today. It begins with an examination of the sociocultural context with an emphasis on the change of the labour force, including the rise of knowledge workers, ageing population, workforce diversity as well as management of the younger generations. Next is a study at the economic environment due to globalization and the emergence of different types of organizations in Hong Kong. The resulting changes of HRM practices are discussed. The chapter will turn to an examination of HR technology and analytics that are currently affecting HRM in organizations. Finally, we look at the legal-political context and explore the change of employment laws and relationship in a more turbulent society of Hong Kong. Figure 2.1 shows the framework of the contexts affecting HRM in Hong Kong.

Figure 2.1: The contexts affecting HRM practices in Hong Kong

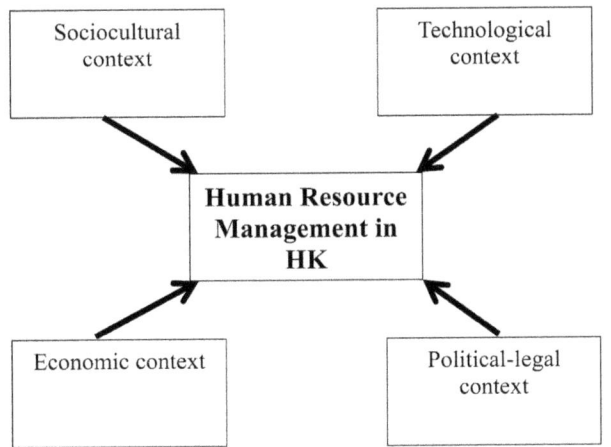

Sociocultural Context for HRM in Hong Kong

By virtue of the ethnicity of over 90 per cent of its population, Hong Kong is a Chinese society. But it is also an 'Asia's world city', a melting pot of Chinese and Western cultures. Most people speak Cantonese, enriched with Western borrowed words or 'verbal armoury of emotions'.[2] Historically, Hong Kong owes its original and subsequent development to a population from the mainland China. After the Second World War, people flocked into Hong Kong were pushed by political crises and upheavals in China. It featured a transient population under a British dependent territory on Chinese soil. A nostalgic label was given, a 'borrowed place living on borrowed time'.[3] Hong Kong is described as a migrant society with people having 'refugee' mentality. Overwhelmed by a cash-neurotic psychology and a visitor mindset, the workforce is hard-working, pragmatic, adaptive, and resilient. Local businesses encountering cyclical ups and downs in the past have been successfully overcome by the help of this workforce.[4] On the other hand, such propensities have generated a transient character to Hong Kong's social structure and class composition. The society is found with a lack of a stable commitment from its local people. Problems of social integration and ambivalence of identities are often revealed, despite its reversion back to China after 1997.[5]

Hong Kong is pluralistic with a diversity of sociocultural patterns of management and business practices, often according to the ethnic background of capital ownership, cultural assumptions and styles of management, as well as other structural variables like firm sizes and types of industry. For example, in the early years of industrialization, with a large supply of unskilled and low-cost labour from mainland China, most of the firms were small Chinese family businesses engaging in low technology, export-oriented, and cost-leadership production. The working conditions of these small factories were generally poor. Common recruitment methods were employee referrals or the use of labour contractors. In contrast, the HRM practices in the larger multinational firms of Anglo-American origins and the public sector organizations were more formalized. While a variety of recruitment methods were adopted, the selection procedures were more stringent than those of the small family-owned businesses.[6]

In this context, despite the popularity of enshrining Confucian culture as a prescription of paternalism to manage people in Hong Kong, its cult of local management practices differs from those found in other Asian countries such as Japan or China.[7] Given the pluralistic nature, values pursued in the Hong Kong firms are not necessary intrinsic to the mainstream of Confucian cultural legacy.[8] Some have argued for a crossvergence between Eastern values and Western-style (mostly from Anglo-Saxon influence) management in Hong Kong based on the influence of multinational corporations and cultures from elsewhere.[9]

Changes in the workforce

The previous section outlines the sociocultural background of the workforce in Hong Kong. This section portrays some changes of the workforce resulting from the complex and more sophisticated background in Hong Kong as its economy is growing.

As a result of globalization and its growing role in the world economy, Hong Kong's labour market has proliferated in occupational and cultural diversity in recent years. One of the major challenges affecting HRM is the transformation from a manufacturing to a service or knowledge-based economy in Hong Kong. This new economy is characterized by a decline in manufacturing and a growth in service or knowledge as the core of the economic base. A knowledge economy is one which is directly based on the production, distribution, and use of knowledge and information.[10] To meet the human capital needs, organizations have to attract, develop, and retain their knowledge workers, who are mainly found in service occupations and high-technology firms.[11]

Apart from changes in the economy, Hong Kong is faced with major shifts in the composition of the population. The proportion of the population aged 65 and over is expected to rise sharply from 16.6 per cent in 2016 to 31.1 per cent in 2036, owing to the longer life expectancy and low fertility rate of the local citizens. The median age will rise from 44 in 2016 to over 50.9 in 2036.[12] As a result of the ageing population, HR professionals are spending time on issues related to planning retirement and re-employing (such as part-time or contractual employment), retraining, and motivating old workers. They have to control the rising costs of healthcare and retirement benefits (for example, changing retirement schemes from pensionable terms or defined benefit to defined contribution or Mandatory Provident Fund (MPF) schemes). On the other hand, these older people often have unique skills and abilities critical to organizational success. They may also want to contribute at work or earn more money. Coupled with a labour shortage problem, Hong Kong society has been actively reviewing the issue of extending the retirement age of the workforce. The government and some public organizations have raised the retirement age of new recruits and extended that of the older employees.[13]

Another issue facing organizations is that they can be staffed by newer generations of the millennials with different work values, attitudes, and behaviours (see Box 2.1). Organizations have to modify their HR practices so as to accommodate these younger generations in terms of autonomy, learning, and experience (for example, providing overseas assignments) which allow faster career advancement.[14]

HRM in Action—Box 2.1
Behaviours of the Millennials

Different terms are used to describe people in different generations. Those who were born between 1946 and 1964 are called the boomers or baby boomers. Generation X employees are those who were born between 1965 and 1981. In general, they place a strong emphasis on hard work, loyalty, and achievement and value intrinsic rewards. In contrast, people of Generation Y (or the millennials) who were born from 1982 to 1999 and those Generation Z born after 2000 are more likely to value extrinsic rewards, freedom and leisure time, career development and promotion opportunities, and work-life balance.* They are sometimes described as belonging to Generation C (denoting 'connected') or iGeneration as most of them are digital natives and tech-savvy.

Below are some anecdotal example behaviours of millennials observed by some HR professionals in Hong Kong:

1. Parental involvement—nowadays, parental influence and control can be strong in different aspects of these people's lives. While some of them are tightly connected with their parents, some parents are described as 'monster' or 'helicopter' parents. In one incident, an HR Officer phoned a candidate named Peter to invite him for an interview. His mother alleged that she was 'Peter' and made an interview appointment. In a subsequent interview arrangement, his mother again insisted that she was 'Peter'. When the real Peter attended the interview, he was found to lack confidence and decision-making ability. Coupled with the 'Peter' factor, he was immediately rejected by the HR department.

2. Spoiled/entitled youngsters—some millennials have a strong sense of entitlement. Parents may coddle their children, constantly telling them how special they are and that anything sought is possible. Parents often reward them easily, simply for participating. For example, an HR professional interviewed a female applicant for a job, project executive. While the candidate had never thought about her career interest, she mentioned that she would open her own business. But she had no idea what kind of business it would be. She only knew that she would soon receive money from her father who owned a business. And of course, the candidate was rejected by the HR department.

3. Poor work ethic—some millennials do see work as a means to enjoy life. But life often comes before work. They may follow a mantra of working smarter, not harder. A Gen Y employee, after being transferred from another department, found that the job was boring to him. He constantly slept in his office. And interestingly, another Gen Y person was constantly absent without reason. Despite his supervisor's warnings, he explained that he had 'jet lag' for several months as he was studying in a foreign country before. Now he was living on his own. Therefore, he woke up late and was absent for work. These two employees were terminated eventually.

4. Little respect for authority—this generation can be independent and are often not afraid to challenge the status quo and their supervisors. For example,

---

* Twenge, J. M., Campbell, S. M., Hoffman, E. J., and Lance, C. E. (2010). Generational differences in work values: Leisure and extrinsic values increasing, social and intrinsic values decreasing. *Journal of Management*, 36(5), 1117–1142.

students may think that they are 'customers'. They want relationships with their teachers and bosses like the ones they have with their parents and friends. At the same time, they may feel that teachers and employers do not respect them. Once, the author had a lunch appointment with a female student. The author was late because of overrunning a class. She received several WhatsApp messages with foul language, expressing the anger of the student. In another incident inside a company, a Gen Y subordinate left office on his own without notifying his supervisor and colleagues when typhoon signal No. 8 was hoisted during office hours. At the time, his supervisor was so worried that the whole department looked for him in the office. When he was reached by phone, he argued that he had the right to leave office when the HK Observatory announced the typhoon signal. He put less value on 'reporting to the boss' as he thought that the corporate culture was too conservative. Instead, he exercised his own judgement to leave his office.

Source: Information from various interviews.

Another change in the Hong Kong workforce is that it is growing more diverse in racial, ethnic, and gender terms. According to the 2016 population by-census, 92 per cent were Chinese (ethnically speaking, Han Chinese), and about 7.8 per cent of the population were non-Chinese (see Table 2.1). The ethnic minorities were growing at an annual average rate of 3.6 per cent over the past fifteen years. And the labour force participation rate of women today is increasing rapidly too (see Table 2.2). Excluding the foreign domestic helpers, ethnic minorities account for about 4 per cent of the population in 2016.[15] These ethnic minorities usually display certain distinctive socioeconomic characteristics different from those of Chinese in Hong Kong. They tend to have larger families with more children. With language and assimilation problems, they are in general less educated. Therefore, they fall below the poverty line with higher unemployment rate than the general population.[16]

Table 2.1: Hong Kong's population by ethnicities

Ethnic group	2006		2016	
	Number	Percentage	Number	Percentage
Chinese	6,522,148	95.0	6,752,202	92.0
Filipino	112,453	1.6	184,081	2.5
Indonesian	87,840	1.3	153,299	2.1
White	36,384	0.5	58,209	0.8
Indian	20,444	0.3	36,462	0.5
Nepalese	15,950	0.2	25,472	0.3
Pakistani	11,111	0.2	18,094	0.2
Thai	11,900	0.2	10,215	0.1
Japanese	13,189	0.2	9,976	0.1
Other Asian	12,663	0.2	19,589	0.3
Others	20,264	0.3	68,986	0.9
Total	6,864,346	100.0	7,336,585	100.0

Source: Census and Statistics Department. (2016). *2016 Population by census*. Retrieved from http://www.bycensus2016.gov.hk/en/bc-mt.html

Table 2.2: Hong Kong population by sex and age groups

Age	Male	Female	Total
0–14	411,600 (51.6%)	385,500 (48.4%)	797,100 (100%)
15–64	2,443,200 (45.5%)	2,925,700 (54.5%)	5,368,900 (100%)
65+	475,900 (46.6%)	545,600 (53.4%)	1,021,500 (100%)

Source: Census and Statistics Department. (2016). *2016 Population by census*. Retrieved from http://www.bycensus2016.gov.hk/en/bc-mt.html

The Economic Context for HRM in Hong Kong

Globalization

A second factor that calls for changes of HR strategies and practices is globalization. Globalization refers to the development of an increasingly integrated global economy marked by free trade, free flow of capital, and the tapping of cheaper foreign labour markets.[17] Global trades are now common, facilitated by free trade agreements between countries and free trade organizations such as the World Trade Organization.[18] Also, e-business and e-commerce are new options nowadays. Amazon, eBay, and Alibaba are famous examples that provide consumer-to-consumer, business-to-consumer, and business-to-business sales and services using web portals.[19] At the same time, firms may have offshoring of their activities by relocating a business process like production, accounting, or customer service to another country. Others may export or import, use licensing or franchising, or set up strategic alliances, joint ventures, or wholly-owned subsidiaries in other developing countries utilizing the cheaper labour or production costs there.[20]

Multinational corporations and small and medium enterprises

The effect of globalization on Hong Kong is much stronger than elsewhere since it has a highly externally oriented and open economy. Its influence in directing HRM development in Hong Kong has been particularly crucial since Hong Kong's industrialization. In particular, multinational corporations (MNCs) are accountable for diffusing their practices from their home countries to firms in Hong Kong. Various perspectives can be used to explain the transfer and diffusion, including resource-based, internationalization, transaction cost, resource dependency, and institutional theories.[21] And their role of HRM is more strategically oriented, since they have brought along more advanced and sophisticated HRM practices than local firms. For instance, American and British firms focus more on psychometric testing and assessment centres, formal performance management systems, and job evaluation methods. They are willing to offer more attractive reward and benefits as well as training and development systems to retain their managers.[22] And they can attract more job seekers thanks to better work-life balance initiatives, employer brand and reputation, resources, and corporate cultures.[23]

But Hong Kong has a dual labour market, comprising a primary sector and a secondary sector. While the former consists of the civil service, MNCs and some large private firms, the latter refers to the small and medium enterprises (SMEs). These SMEs (with fewer than 100 employees in manufacturing and fewer than 50 employees in non-manufacturing firms) constitute the majority of businesses in Hong Kong, accounting for more than 98 per cent (or 320,000 SMEs) of the total business units and provided job opportunities to almost 1.3 million people, or about 46 per cent of total employment in March 2017. Most of them were in import/export trade and wholesale, social and personal services, professional and business services, retail, accommodation, and food services sectors.[24]

Compared with those in the MNCs, HR practices in this sector are ad hoc, informal, or transactional. Traditional recruitment methods (such as newspaper advertising or employee referrals), payroll and benefits administration, and on-the-job training are more likely found. And informal uncoordinated approach of performance appraisal and compensation practices is used. Because of resource constraints, keen competition, and imbalance of power between labour and management, outbursts of disputes and conflicts sometimes take place. Many of them do not have HR departments. Otherwise, HR activities are performed by the administration department or the secretary or personal assistant of the managers. Roles of HR, if present, are described as 'administrative', 'housekeeping', 'fire-fighting to head off problem workers or unions'.[25] In essence, the importance of HRM is greatly dependent on owner-managers' management style and personalities, their recognition of the need for delegation and professionalization of HRM, and the perceived impact of HRM on their business success and survival.[26] Nevertheless, in recent years, HRM in this sector is becoming more sophisticated because of growing complexity of the labour legislation and promotional efforts by the government and professional bodies.[27]

Mainland Chinese companies

Over the past few years, we have witnessed another major source of growth in the economy. There is a rapid expansion of Chinese-headquartered companies battling for talent with other multinational corporations. Table 2.3 gives us a picture of distribution of this type of companies with regional headquarters established in Hong Kong vis-à-vis other MNCs headquartered locally. As seen, their numbers in the former group were increasing while those in the latter groups were either relatively stable or diminishing. Indeed, we now have more than 1,100 Chinese firms, among over 10,000 MNCs in the territory. Many Chinese firms use mergers and acquisitions for quick expansion. They are primarily conglomerates, property developers, banks, and financial services institutions, as well as some wholesale and retail companies. The number had tripled in twenty years and accounted for 64 per cent of the city's stock market capitalization in 2017, up from 15 per cent in 1997.[28]

The mainland economy's growth has far outpaced that in many developed countries, including Hong Kong. Hong Kong's share of combined GDP vis-à-vis China's has fallen from 16 per cent in 1997 to only 3 per cent in 2014. In terms of exports, Hong Kong's share fell from 51 per cent to 17 per cent over the same period.[29] Nevertheless, Hong Kong is playing an important role in connecting mainland China to the rest of the world. The credibility of free economy and free trade, a reliable legal system, and

Table 2.3: Number of regional headquarters in Hong Kong by country (top five) where the parent company was located

Year/ Location of Parent Co.	Total	U.S.	Japan	Mainland China	Britain	Germany
1996	816	188	122	85	90	40
2006	1228	295	212	112	114	76
2010	1285	288	224	96	115	77
2011	1340	315	222	99	113	74
2012	1367	333	219	106	122	86
2013	1379	316	245	114	126	81
2014	1389	310	240	119	120	91
2015	1401	307	238	133	126	87
2016	1379	286	239	137	124	85
2017	1413	283	233	154	122	87

Source: Census and Statistics Department. Companies in Hong Kong with parent companies located outside HK. Retrieved from https://www.censtatd.gov.hk/hkstat/sub/sp360.jsp?tableID=133&ID=0&productType=8

Note: A regional headquarters is an office that has managerial control over offices and/or operations in the region (i.e. Hong Kong plus one or more other places) on behalf of its parent company located outside Hong Kong.

capital markets has given foreign investors a sense of security of doing business with Chinese firms. While Hong Kong provides an invaluable platform from which foreign capital can enter the mainland, its role as an international financial centre can also serve as a springboard for Chinese firms' international expansion and technological and management expertise absorption.

At the same time, HRM practices of Chinese firms on mainland are evolving from being administrative/personnel to becoming more strategic. Some studies have revealed diminishing differences between HRM practices in foreign-invested and Chinese-owned firms, with a level of convergence between Chinese and the Western firms.[30] Some use Western HRM practices such as online recruitment, psychometric tests, assessment centres, performance-based reward systems, employee participation, and coaching and mentoring schemes. Domestic private firms also use commitment-oriented HRM practices.[31] These changes are shaped by the increased marketization of Chinese firms and their need for attracting and retaining talent.[32]

In Hong Kong, we are also witnessing changes of HRM practices in the Chinese firms. Since these companies have to tap into Hong Kong's international talent base, they adapt modern HRM practices. Many, especially large ones, recruit aggressively. Some offer prospective candidates highly attractive compensation packages, including a substantial portion of discretionary bonuses. Top candidates are enticed with ample career development opportunities to join Chinese firms. Some have raised the job titles and responsibilities to secure the best talent. And some recognize the need for other work environment and benefits, such as initiating employer branding efforts, flexi-work arrangements, medical benefits, and parental leave.[33] But despite growing evidence of HRM sophistication, we have to conclude that they are far from being as strategic as their Western counterparts. Many executives and line managers of these Chinese firms may have insufficient understanding of the importance of HRM to business. They perceive their HR department as playing a secondary or supporting role, relative to other departments such as finance and marketing.[34] There could also be an absence of formal HR policies. Otherwise, execution capability is a concern due to limited funding and resources.

Moreover, a number of problems arise for Hong Kong employees working in Chinese companies in terms of adjusting to Chinese work culture and communication style. First is the language hurdle. Most documents are in simplified Chinese that Hong Kong people need to accommodate as they are used to studying or working in an English-oriented environment. Second, differences arise in the communication style. Chinese employees tend to avoid conflicts, in contrast to other cultures that are more direct in their communication. There are also clear differences in attitudes towards hierarchy and authority. Their way of decision-making can vary significantly, particularly with regard to speed. Although many people are employed locally, some employees have to report to senior executives based in China. These people have to be assimilated to Chinese business relationship and communication style. Third, the leadership styles vary. Some top executives in Hong Kong may have received education or work overseas. They have a more open-minded attitude and are willing to adopt more democratic leadership style. However, some executives are transferred from the mainland parent companies. They may use a more directive or task-oriented leadership because they lack people management skills.

HRM in Action—Box 2.2

Chinese Management Style from a Hong Kong Employee's Eyes

David had worked as a loan manager in the commercial banking division of a large famous Chinese bank for three years upon graduating from his university with a master's degree. He had come across ups and downs when working in this bank. Now, he shared some observations of the management culture in this Chinese organization with us.

- Hierarchical structure—being one of the 'big four' state-owned banks, the bank had a strong tendency towards a hierarchical and bureaucratic structure. Senior managers often came from the mainland. Their management style and workplace culture were traditional Chinese. Many documents were written in Chinese language, even in simplified Chinese. Speaking Putonghua was not uncommon. And since many levels of managers or presidents existed (for example, vice president, assistant vice president, general manager, assistant general manager, team head), applications for loans required a series of approvals that took longer to process than was the case among their counterparts in MNCs. Overlapping procedures and reports were found.

  Furthermore, information did not flow freely around a strong hierarchy but followed the hierarchical lines. When a subordinate gave information to his or her boss (who might then pass it to his or her boss), the boss would also pass it horizontally to a counterpart in a different function before it was pushed through the chain again to the relevant party. When the information was sent back, it followed a similar path in reverse direction.

- A strong 'respect' culture—David noted that some senior managers did not expect to be contacted by junior people. Instead, they dealt with the team leaders, whether major or minor issues were concerned. This put extra pressure on team leaders who had to get involved in issues they would normally delegate to junior colleagues. Management style tended towards paternalistic, with managers telling people what to do and subordinates doing what they were told unquestioningly.

  Being a loan manager, David was extremely stressed when organizing meetings between the unit managers and the corporate clients. The meetings of these seniors were often showpiece events. For example, while David had to pre-order the taxi to arrive at the right time and the right place, he had to open the door for his seniors politely. He needed to reserve the table in advance, take care of the seating plan and food, and pay very close attention to his manner of talking. Otherwise, he could easily be reprimanded by his boss. He always behaved subserviently throughout the working lunch.

- Lack of work efficiency—the bank had many long-serving employees. Strong hierarchies led to a lack of initiative of these staff members at the lower levels. Subordinates only performed the tasks told by David and would not do any extra. If the boss wanted something done, he would give an instruction. And if the instruction was not given, the boss obviously would not want the task to be done. To perform an unasked task might be tantamount to insubordination.

- Rewards management—the bank usually paid a lower basic salary than other international banks. But it often offered a higher bonus than its international counterparts, which could be three or four times of a monthly salary depending on an employee's performance. In some cases, especially in the commercial banking division, outstanding employees might receive a bonus equivalent to one year of one's basic salary. If an employee was achievement-driven and hard-working, the overall compensation could be much higher than that in an international bank. Chinese banks also provided various perks on Chinese festive days—for example, giving mooncakes at the Mid-Autumn Festival.

- Career prospect—since the Chinese businesses were performing well in the past few years, career opportunities in these firms could be better than their counterparts in MNCs. Although turnover rate of the fresh graduates was high (could be more than 30 per cent in a year in some divisions), 'survivors' would have good career advancement opportunities. They might become team head in eight to ten years.

Source: Interview information.

Start-Up companies

Hong Kong's economy is also conducive to the development of start-up companies since it has a free economy with low tax. These firms are expanding quickly, which have increased from 998 in 2014 to more than 2,500 in the end of 2016. E-commerce was the dominant start-up sector (25 per cent) followed by SaaS (software as a service—13 per cent) and hardware technology firms (11 per cent).[35] Among them, 57 per cent were set up by local founders. WeLab (which operates WeLend in Hong Kong and WoLaiDai in China)[36] and GoGoVan[37] are named as 'unicorn' (valued at over US$1 billion). In general, a start-up company is defined as an entrepreneurial venture, typically with a newly emerged fast-growing business, aims to fulfil a need by developing a business model using an innovative product, service, process or a platform. It often starts with a small business in the form of a sole proprietorship, partnership, or organization which is scalable to large business. And the ecosystem may consist of individuals (like entrepreneurs, venture capitalists, or angel investors) as well as institutions and organizations like top research universities, business schools, and entrepreneurship programmes, non-profit organizations, or government entrepreneurship programmes and services.[38] Google, Uber, and Airbnb are global success stories. Table 2.4 gives some local start-up examples providing HR services.

Table 2.4: Examples of local start-ups providing HR services

HR Start-up	Activities
TalkPush (https://talkpush.com)	A platform to automate the phone screening of job candidates by improving the process of pre-screening candidates, validating them and enhancing collaboration between decision makers in the hiring process.
JobDoh (https://page.jobdoh.com)	A start-up looking to improve efficiency in the casual labour market by providing a location-based, on-demand mobile application that seeks to match employers with the right job applicants and put them in contact directly.
Jobable (https://www.jobable.com)	A startup helping companies leverage big data in their recruitment process. Using proprietary algorithms and advanced machine learning technology, it enables HR departments to streamline all applications in one place, immediately identifying the most relevant candidates and enabling those responsible for recruitment to spend more time meeting the 'high potentials' who have the best personality and cultural fit for the role.
Freshlinker (https://freshlinker.com)	It positions itself as a centralized, informative one-stop platform for young talents to create a virtual profile and apply for opportunities within seconds. It functions by matching algorithms to create a young talent–centric ecosystem that strategically helps young talent with career planning.
Weesper (https://www.weesper.com)	A talent referral platform that helps companies reach suitable candidates by connecting them to a community of connectors and headhunters. Cash rewards are given with successful referrals.

Start-up companies are usually small without complex organizational structures. And the business model is simple. Often, members do not have job descriptions and need to work flexibly. They focus on activities like developing products, building sales channels, and boosting market share. Accordingly, the HR practices follow the same approach. The systems and processes are simple, lean, and quick in order to support members to achieve high performance and team spirit. The environment emphasizes on delivery of key outputs and is result-driven, motivational, and rewarding (especially when the product is popular or sold to a strategic investor at a later stage). Box 2.3 below provides some insights of HR practices in a local start-up.

HRM in Action—Box 2.3

OnePersonalization's Roadblocks and HR Strategies

OnePersonalization, owned by a team of two directors and other co-founders, delivers custom shoes that are aesthetically pleasing and relatively inexpensive. The idea for the start-up came from a group of Chinese University of Hong Kong (CUHK) students who questioned why people could not buy 'comfortable designer shoes at reasonable price'. They created OnePersonalization Ltd. to fill up this need by using 3D scanning and mobile phone app technologies.

The whole process of development was not entirely smooth. When the start-up was at the CUHK pre-incubation centre and followed by 9/F of Lai Chi Kok's Fashion Farm Foundation in 2014, it had to overcome many obstacles. The team members knew very little about shoemaking and the suppliers. By the referral of a founder's friend, they convinced a professor at Hong Kong Polytechnic University (PolyU) to be their consultant. The professor then taught them how to get the 3D shape of a foot by using a low-cost 3D scanner. The PolyU professor also introduced them to Mr. Poon, an experienced shoemaker who owned his shoe shop in Peninsula Centre in Tsim Sha Tsui. Mr. Poon also helped PolyU students to make shoes based on their designs. Another challenge was that the customers found it inconvenient to visit their outlet on 9/F of Fashion Farm Foundation to measure their feet. So they consulted the Hong Kong Productivity Council to work out a 3D Foot Size mobile phone app to expand their online sales. Additionally, they once had a retail shop in Central. But the rental cost was so high that they closed the shop after one year of operation. Now, they had retail shops in Tsim Sha Tsui and Causeway Bay, manned by two full-time and two part-time retail staff members. They also had two part-time employees in some events such as roadshows or wedding exhibitions.

Nevertheless, OnePersonalization grossed an additional HK$1 million from another investor in 2016. The company was awarded with the Hong Kong Small and Medium Enterprise Innovation Award in 2016, and the 3D Foot Size app won a silver medal in the International Exhibition of Inventions Geneva in 2017. It had also been admitted into the Hong Kong Science & Technology Park in 2016 for the Incu-App programme to develop an even better version 3D Foot Size app. It aimed to be available through the online marketplace in mainland China by the end of 2017.

HR strategies of start-ups are quite different from traditional practices. Basically, the companies have embraced a 'start-up approach'. They are young companies that have sprung up and begun buzzing with new ideas. A new and exciting work culture has been brought up that appeals to the digital natives of the Internet era. The following gives some features of OnePersonalization's HR practices.

- Efficient recruitment through referrals or networks—a robust and efficient recruitment process is a top priority for a start-up. But since the business was unstable, no full-time employees were hired in OnePersonalization in the beginning. It was also difficult to attract candidates because of the limited budget and uncertainty for continuity of employment. Recruitment relied much more on internal referral since use of recruitment agencies could be expensive and they had a limited understanding of the new industry. In 2014 a part-time assistant was hired based on the personal networking of a founding director. And the post did not have a fixed job description. The part-timer was responsible for a full spectrum of activities in the company, including both business and administrative duties.
- Job satisfaction, responsibility, and flexible work—despite of the uncertainty of business, job satisfaction can be high. Start-ups can stand for creativity and fun, just as much as work. But employees have to be self-motivated. OnePersonalization found that the part-time employee lacked commitment. They decided to employ a full-time administration manager in 2016, who was the sister of a founding director. With stronger commitment and greater responsibility, she worked for an average of fifty hours a week, performing a variety of duties, including payroll and benefits. In addition, flexible working and wide job exposure for personal development were important aspects for working in OnePersonalization. All the directors and the administration manager worked from home or elsewhere at irregular hours. It is more about getting the things done than the place where people work. But it depends a lot on individual personality. Commitment and relationship among the core team members are the most important.
- Transparency and freedom to work—start-ups also place emphasis on their level of transparency. It is not uncommon that start-ups release information to employees that includes the business's performance and financial situation. Leaders are willing to reveal company plans and ask for active feedback from staff when or before implementing changes, as opposed to the top-down decision-making processes in traditional companies. Also, employees are free to do projects on their own (like Google's famous '20 per cent time' initiative). In OnePersonalization the founders made the salaries of their employees transparent to the world. Two reasons might explain this: first, they received funding support from the Innovation and Technology Fund by the HK government for an internship programme, and salary information was posted to the public (www.itf.gov.hk/l-eng/GSP-IP.asp); second, the leaders believed that transparency could give people a sense of purpose, build trust, and retain key talent.

To conclude, the founders of OnePersonalization used four Fs to highlight the critical success factors of a start-up: founder, family, friends, and fool—some angel investors call themselves 'fools' (a joke) because they give money to founders to lose and burn.

Source: Interview information from Howard Lam and T. S. Chan, the co-founders, and Kitty Lam, the administration manager of OnePersonalization.
OnePersonalization company website: https://onepersonalization.com

In sum, Hong Kong remains a highly attractive destination for a variety of companies, including large multinational companies of different countries of origin, small and medium enterprises, and start-up companies. Notably, we have seen a rapid growth of Chinese firms with increased HR sophistication. They are willing to put in resources and efforts to learn and change their management practices. Their high level of pragmatism allows them to progress bolder than their European and North American counterparts. Thus, Hong Kong employees and HR professionals may need to shift their mentality and consider working for Chinese companies with more growth opportunities.

The Technological Environment

Influence of HR technology

Advancement in technology is another important force on managing human resources in organizations. It has transformed the way HR processes are managed, in terms of how organizations collect, store, use, retrieve, and disseminate information about their employees and job applicants. It may cause a 'democratization' of HR data and a rapid expansion of access to data by people inside and outside.[39] Information technology now mediates the relationship between individuals and organizations, as well as those between subordinates and supervisors. It reduces the influence of distance in organizations that employees can work from home or interact with team members with different geographical boundaries, races, and background.[40] Therefore, technology alters the nature of jobs, their relationships, and the method of communication and supervision. Innovations such as telework, virtual teams, and web-based job applications are also becoming popular. Some advantages of HR technology are highlighted in Table 2.5.

Table 2.5: Advantages of using HR technology

Advantages of using HR technology include the following:
- Streamline HR processes and reduce administrative burdens.
- Reduce HR administration and compliance costs.
- Transform HR to play a more strategic role in the business.
- Keep track of information in relation to employee skills, experience, and competencies so that the company can compete more effectively for global talent.
- Improve service and data access for applicants, employees, and managers.
- Provide real-time metrics to allow decision makers to spot trends and manage the workforce more effectively.
- Become an enabler of workflow—enhancing communication and collaboration
- Become an enhancer of work skills through various technological tools.
- Become an adviser by making better decisions through useful technology and analytics.
- Become a disruptor and automator—change the characteristics of jobs, workflow, and relationships, as well as the organizational structures.

Source: Adapted from Johnson, Richard D., and Gueutal, Hal G. (2011). *Transforming HR through technology: The use of E-HR and HRIS in organizations.* Alexandria: SHRM. Retrieved from https://www.shrm.org/hr-today/trends-and-forecasting/special-reports-and-expert-views/Documents/HR-Technology.pdf.
Meister, Jeanne C., and Mulcahy, Kevin J. (2017). *The future workplace experience: 10 rules for mastering disruption in recruiting and engaging employees.* New York: McGraw-Hill Education.

In addition, Table 2.6 describes some of the technologies for HR activities. Often, a human resource management system (HRIS) is the major tool for HR functions. Being a computer system used to integrate hardware, software, and business processes system, it can range from as simple as a small employee database developed internally to a complex fully integrated sophisticated enterprise resource planning (ERP) system mediated by software and technology to provide integrated management of core business processes. Different options are available for implementing HRIS, namely using an integrated solution with a single vendor and one platform with multiple HR functions, or a 'best of breed' solution with multiple vendors for different HR functions. Also, several approaches are possible to deliver the technology: on-premise or purchase and install, hosted or application service provider (ASP), or software as a service (SaaS).[41]

Table 2.6: New technologies in HRM

Technology	Some Features	Examples
Internet portal	A website that brings information and data together from different sources uniformly in a single site. The users may customize data without programming skills. Variants of portals can be mashups and intranet dashboards for managers and employees inside.	HK government portal (www.gov.hk)
Shared services centre (SSC)	An entity responsible for the execution and the handling of specific operational tasks, such as accounting, human resource, purchasing, and sales. Often being a spin-off of the corporate services, it may eliminate redundancy and reduce administrative costs by processing transactions at one time.	Finance, HR, IT SSC in China, HK, Malaysia, Singapore, India, etc.*
Cloud computing	A computing-infrastructure and software model to enable access to shared pools of configurable resources, such as computer networks, servers, storage, applications, and services, often over the Internet. Data may be accessed either in a privately-owned cloud or on a third-party server located in a data centre.	Oracle's Workday & Taleo, SAP's SuccessFactors and HK's local vendors†
Social media	Computer-mediated technologies, with interactive Web 2.0 Internet-based applications, that facilitate the creation and sharing of information, ideas, career interests, and other forms of expression through virtual communities and networks. The rise of social media is used as recruitment and branding tools for both employers and applicants.	LinkedIn, Facebook, Twitter, YouTube, Instagram, WeChat, WhatsApp, Snapchat, Weibo
Artificial intelligence (AI) and robots	A branch of computer science that uses machine learning algorithms to mimic cognitive functions (such as learning and problem solving) and makes machines more human-like. Can perform time-consuming and administrative HR tasks. For HR, AI can be used to shortlist job applications, analyse interviews and facial expressions, answer HR questions, schedule meetings and interviews, track employee growth and development, improve workflow, etc.	IBM's chatbots and Watson, Koru, Fama‡

Table 2.6 *(cont'd)*

Technology	Some Features	Examples
Wearable technology	Smart electronic devices that are easily carried along or worn on the body as implant or accessories (e.g. tablets, fitness trackers, and smartwatches). The designs often incorporate practical functions and features. For HR, they may be used for staff wellness plans, improving workplace safety, communications, onboarding, and learning.	Mobile smartphones and apps, augmented reality (AR), virtual reality (VR), Google Glass, tablets, fitness trackers, smartwatches
Business intelligence (BI)	Technologies for enterprises to get insights and information, trends and patterns in order to make better decisions and implement effective strategies. They may include reporting, online analytical processing, analytics, data mining, process mining, complex event processing, business performance management, benchmarking, and text mining.	Microsoft BI tools using SQL server, IBM Cognos BI
Data mining	Using powerful computer to analyse large amounts of data on employee background traits, pay, and performance. For example, mining data on the relationships among factors such as university attended, previous work experience and employees, a plan can be developed to target certain universities and companies for future hiring. Data mining may also predict employee turnover rate.	IBM, GE, Oracle, Capital One, SAS

* Deloitte and ACCA. (2015). Future challenges facing the shared services centre in China and greater Asia Pacific. Retrieved from https://www2.deloitte.com/content/dam/Deloitte/cn/Documents/process-and-operations/deloitte-op-2015-acca-deloitte-ssc-report-en-151030.PDF

† There are also many HRIS providers using cloud computing, LAN, or mobile versions. Interested readers may study HKIHRM's website on HR service providers. Retrieved from http://www.hkihrm.org/index.php/pe/hr-service-providers-directory/directory

‡ See, for example, Captain, S. (2016, December 9). How AI is changing human resources. Retrieved from https://www.fastcompany.com/3062995/how-ai-is-changing-human-resources

As we know, many HRM activities have now been moved to the Internet, the so-called Internet of things (IoT). Such processing and transmission of digitized HR information is called electronic human resource management (e-HR) that transforms HR service delivery through web-based technology. Employees in different locations can access information or work together. Companies can search for talent without geographical constraints. Recruitment can include online job postings, applications, and candidate screening from company websites, websites specializing in recruitment (such as monster.com.hk, cpjobs.com, and jobsdb.com), or other job information systems like JIJIS (Joint Institutions Job Information System). And while electronic HRM applications allow applicants to apply for jobs online on a 24/7 basis, employees can enrol in learning programmes which fit their time and needs. They may look up answers to HR policies, read company newsletters, or download podcasts. A recent technology trend is cloud computing (see Table 2.6) that has remote server computers to perform computing tasks.

Technology trends shaping Internet use are also shaping e-HRM. Table 2.7 lists some applications that organizations may apply various tools to HRM activities.

Table 2.7: Applications of e-HRM

Application	Purpose	Example
e-Recruiting	• To attract sufficient number of qualified and diverse applicants more efficiently at reduced cost. • To provide convenience to recruiters and applicants.	• Employer branding, online videos, blogs, realistic job previews (e.g. using VR, Second Life Virtual Environment),* etc. • Job postings and online applications • Applicant tracking system (may link with social media or other HR systems)
e-Selection	• To efficiently manage the process of identifying the best job candidates with the right skills, knowledge, and abilities. • To increase flexibility of test administration and improve the utility of selection tests.	• Online assessment tools, such as psychometric tests, and e-tray, assessment centre. • Video/digital interview • Games-based assessment
e-Learning	• To increase flexibility and control over learning.	• Learning management system, learning content system • Computer-based training, web-based training, mobile learning • MOOC, distance learning, blended learning • Webcasts/webinars, podcasts, wikis
e-Performance Management	• To automate the collection of performance data, monitor employee work and support the development and delivery of performance appraisals.	• Web-based PM • PD@GE ('performance development at GE') using mobile devices
e-Compensation	• To manage payroll and benefits more efficiently and effectively. • To help managers design compensation policies by streamlining and automating the compensation planning process, and providing quality information to decision makers.	• Payroll and benefits automation, including outsourcing • Web-based HRIS, mobile devices • Motorola's compensation planning†

Table 2.7 *(cont'd)*

Application	Purpose	Example
Self-Service	• To allow managers and employees inside, and people/applicants outside to have online access to information about HR issues, apply and approve leaves, go online to enroll in programs, etc. • To improve transparency and convenience to managers and employees, and save cost by companies. • To support decision-making.	• Administration of ORSO/MPF (Occupational Retirement Scheme Ordinance/Mandatory Provident Fund Scheme) funds • HR dashboard providing data and analytics • Web-based, mobile devices • Microsoft's self-service portal[‡]
Others	• To conduct online surveys and gather employees' opinions. • To allow online discussions. • To provide networking tools, including teams and online expert communities. • To capture, share and store knowledge.	

[*] Some interactive technologies may enhance the personalization of e-recruiting, for example, for virtual job fair, developing interactive dialogues with staff members and job preview. Sullivan, J. (2014, March). *A walk through the HR department of 2020. Workforce Solutions Review*, 7–9. Second Life Virtual Environment allows multiple users to access simulated worlds, and take the form of avatars that are visible to others. The users are also presented with perceptual stimuli, allowed to manipulate elements in the simulated world and experience a degree of telepresence. Retrieved from http://secondlife.com

[†] Johnson, Richard D., and Gueutal, Hal G. (2011). *Transforming HR through technology: The use of E-HR and HRIS in organizations*. Alexandria: SHRM. Retrieved from https://www.shrm.org/hr-today/trends-and-forecasting/special-reports-and-expert-views/Documents/HR-Technology.pdf

[‡] Microsoft. (n.d.). *Deploying the self-service portal for service managers*. Retrieved from https://docs.microsoft.com/en-us/system-center/scsm/deploy-self-service-portal

Technology is changing the way organizations handle record-keeping and information sharing. In the past, only HR staff worked with personal data. Now there is a rapid expansion of access to data by managers and people inside and outside the organization. Employee self-service (ESS) is an approach in which employees can access and maintain their personal data. ESS websites, often through the HR portal, allow HR questions and transactions handled by employees themselves so that employees can make informed choices and become self-reliant for many HR services. At the same time, managers and supervisors can handle many HR transactions online and receive HR reports in real time. For example, managers may authorize leaves and complete performance appraisal using manager self-service (MSS). A growing number of companies are combining ESS with MSS—for example, to approve expenses and authorize leaves. And more sophisticated systems can extend management applications to decision-making. Data warehouses and data-mining tools provide a repository of selected

HR data and advanced statistical analytical tools respectively to analyse and develop relationships, practices, and policies. A company may also create an HR dashboard, or a display with high-level, real-time data related to critical measures of HR success. Dashboards can be implemented in a visual fashion, similar to the dashboard on a car. By linking the data on the dashboard to organizational metrics, managers can effectively discover the relationships between HR outcomes and corporate goals.

HR analytics

Another emerging trend of computer tools and technology is to develop knowledge that gives organizations an edge over their competitors. Now, employee-related information is not just an administrative responsibility. Using suitable analytics can improve individual and organizational performance. HR analytics is the application of technologies and processes to understand and analyse data for the purpose of improving quality of people-related decisions. It can range from simple reporting of HR metrics using spreadsheets all the way up to predictive modelling.[42] Some HR analytics applications are workforce planning, talent recruiting, and forecasting attrition and turnover rate.

HR analytics adopt an evidence-based approach for making decisions that entails systematic accumulation and analysis of data gathered on the organization, problem-based readings, and discussion of research by members that the making of organizational decisions comes from best available research and organizational information. It demonstrates that HR practices have a positive influence on the company profits and key stakeholders. For instance, studies show that there is a strong link between the extent and level to which the use of analytics and company financial performance.[43] And a famous study of analytics is conducted on Google's Project Oxygen to confirm the value of managers in the organization (Box 2.4). More details on HR analytics will be discussed in Chapter 9.

HRM in Action—Box 2.4

Talent Analytics in Google—Project Oxygen

Google's Project Oxygen is so named because it has found that good managers can keep the company alive. By understanding data from employee surveys, performance management scores, and other sources, its analytics team identified eight key behaviours demonstrated by the company's most effective managers.

A good manager

1. is a good coach;
2. empowers the team and does not micromanage;
3. expresses interest in and concern for team members' success and personal well-being;
4. is productive and results-oriented;
5. is a good communicator—listens and shares information;
6. helps with career development;
7. has a clear vision and strategy for the team; and
8. has key technical skills that help him or her advise the team.

The data reveal that, rather than superior technical knowledge (no. 8 only), periodic one-on-one coaching expressing interest in the employee and frequent personalized feedback ranked as the number-one key to being a successful leader. And there are three reasons to keep managers with the company: the mission, the quality of the people, and the chance to build the skill set of a better leader or entrepreneur.

Source: Garvin, David A. (2013, December). How Google sold its engineers on management. *Harvard Business Review*, 75–82.

The Political-Legal Context for HRM

The political environment

On 1 July 1997 the sovereign authority governing Hong Kong was transferred to the People's Republic of China, ending over one and a half centuries of British rule. It has become a special administrative region (SAR) of China with a high degree of autonomy in all matters except foreign affairs and defence, which belongs to the jurisdiction of the central government in Beijing. According to the Sino-British Joint Declaration and the Basic Law, while implementing the principle of 'one country, two systems', Hong Kong will retain its political, economic and judicial systems and unique way of life and continue to participate in international agreements and organizations as a dependent territory for at least fifty years. The chief executive is the head of the SAR government and the executive branch. That person is elected for five years by a college of 1,200 voters, representing Hong Kong to the authorities of China. The Executive Council assists the chief executive in policy-making and advises on matters relating to the introduction of bills and legislation. The Legislative Council is the law-making body, comprising seventy members, with thirty-five elected directly by geographical constituencies and thirty-five elected by functional constituencies. In principle, the Basic Law has prescribed a stepped process by which the Legislative Council is to undergo a gradual transition towards a more democratic institution.[44] In addition, the Basic Law has specified that Hong Kong can keep its judiciary system basically intact and within the British common law system. The judiciary is independent from the legislative and executive branches of government.[45]

However, the political arena in Hong Kong has been filled with increasing tensions since the changeover. Early in the 2000s the government's requests for judicial interpretations by the National People's Congress in mainland China had prompted heated discussion about the separation of powers and independence of the judiciary in Hong Kong.[46] Since then, political controversies have never stopped. For example, plans for national education, the Occupy Central movement in 2014, and arguments about implementing universal suffrage have been seen as challenges in the territory. Many young people took these matters to the street as a way to voice their grievances. At the same time, the issue of brain drain has re-ignited the attention of people in the society. A record shows that emigrants rose from 6,100 in 2016 to 24,300 in 2017, with a fourfold increase in a year.[47] Another poll revealed that three in ten respondents, mostly from the financial, retail, and manufacturing sectors, wanted to move to a new country in the near future.⁴⁸ We understand that previous waves of emigration were associated with pivotal events, such as the signing of the Sino-British Joint Declaration in 1984, the Tiananmen crackdown in 1989, and the handover of sovereignty of Hong Kong in 1997. But the current outflow is caused by a convergence of factors, like the deteriorating living environment, high property prices, dissatisfaction over education reforms, and the worsening political conflicts, coupled with lower emigration thresholds set by some host countries.⁴⁹ Hong Kong people have become more sensitive to changes in the political landscape than the economic landscape. Many youngsters are worrying about the uncertainty over Hong Kong's political future as the Chinese government tightens its grip in the territory. There is a growing distrust of the central authority and a lack of faith in Hong Kong's leaders to protect the city's interests.

Employment-related laws

With the free market principles, weak bargaining power of trade unions, and Chinese culture of paternalism, it is described as 'institutional permissiveness' in the workplace of Hong Kong.⁵⁰ The term refers to loose and informal regulatory institutions in the labour market that help maintain harmonious industrial relations while the government adopts a non-interventionist framework of legal regulation. There is a preference of both parties to negotiate freely in a market. The employment relationship, implied in the term *market*, is an exchange between wages paid and work done that delineates an array of rights and duties for both parties. The employment law comprises mainly the common law and statute law regulating the relationship between the employer and the employee who carries out work in a subordinate position under a labour contract. The Employment Ordinance, enacted since 1968, is the major piece of legislation governing the employment contract and condition of employment.

Hence, official acts of intervention in the labour arena are not encouraged. For example, although the Employment Ordinance has provided an explicit measure for individual employees to join a trade union and its activities, with an absence of statutory requirements, the recognition of trade unions by employers is entirely voluntary. Employers are not mandated to bargain with their trade unions on work-related matters. Also, collective bargaining is marginalized, even though the trade unions succeeded in soliciting support from the colonial government before 1997. The legislation with collective bargaining rights was, however, repealed by the subsequent Legislative Council at the end of 1997.⁵¹ Now, less than 1 per cent of employees (mostly in public or large organizations) are covered by collective agreements, and their agreements are not legally binding. While there is a strong demand to protect low-income earners, the territory has long lacked a statutory economy-wide minimum wage. It was not until 2010 that the Minimum Wage Ordinance was brought to the statute that came into force a year after. The Minimum Wage Commission was then appointed for fixing and recommending the minimum wage level, subject to review every two years. In general, with a burgeoning economy, such implementation has not caused any significant fall in employment. Instead, a positive wage and employment effect is observed on the vulnerable groups in Hong Kong.⁵²

In addition, in response to the calls for retirement protection since at least the 1980s, the government finally implemented the Hong Kong Mandatory Provident Fund (MPF) in December 2000. Through this, the government has avoided the financial responsibility for providing a central pension system, implicitly signalling that the private market can meet the people's needs. The government plays the role of a regulator only. People are motivated to take part in the private market using their labour force. Employees and their employers are required to each contribute 5 per cent of the salary, subject to an upper limit, to an MPF account monthly. But the MPF scheme is constantly under fire owing to its low return, high management fee, and complexity in selecting funds. It has been reported that two-thirds of the management fees charged by the fund providers are administrative costs. And the return had an annual average of 2.8 per cent from 2000 to 2016, while the Hang Seng index had risen 5 per cent annually.[53] At the time of writing, there are protests and debates on the possibility of introducing a universal pension system for the ageing population. The government, however, favours a means-tested pension system.[54] At the same time, an impasse has been reached between employers and the labour unions on legislating standard working hours for employees, despite the formation of a Standard Working Hours Committee in April 2013 and having rounds of public consultation. The government has proposed implementing 'contract working hours' for low-income employees, instead of a standard working hours system, but that proposal has met with a barrage of criticisms.[55]

In essence, the labour law system has become more protective and interventionist so as to provide a better safety net for employees in a fluid and unstable economy. It has been attested by the introduction of MPF, minimum wage legislation, and an array of anti-discrimination laws (e.g. ordinances against discrimination on the basis of sex, disability, family status, and race).[56] And the Executive Council has mandated employers to pay workers overtime wages at rates no less than their regular salaries for those earning HK$11,000 or less per month.[57] The government has also legislated for paternity leave since 2015 and extended the retirement age of its new hires. A more inclusive society is being developed.

Employment relations

Labour disputes in Hong Kong as a whole have remained at a low level by international standards thanks to a buoyant labour market. Most of the disputes are concerned with individual claims over grievances and violations of the Employment Ordinance or employment contracts. They are settled either at the workplace level or by conciliation provided by the Labour Department. Otherwise, they are determined by the Labour Tribunal or the Minor Employment Claims Adjudication Board of the Labour Department. The statistics of claims in Table 2.8 are indicative of a declining trend in the level of labour conflicts, excepting for the discrepancy in the year of 2009 when Hong Kong was afflicted by the world financial crisis. But occasionally, conflicts arose over wage payment to the workers at construction sites. This type of labour dispute (disputes of rights) involving principal contractor and subcontractor has constituted the major source of disputes handled by the Labour Department in recent years.

Accordingly, the numbers of work stoppage and working days lost from strikes have been low. But there were two landmark disputes that led to prolonged work stoppages. The first was the bar-benders strike in the building and construction industry in 2007. The workers had been on strike for thirty-six days over low pay and in favour of an eight-hour working day. The strike was finally called off after seven rounds of

Table 2.8: Number of claims (disputes of rights and over interests) handled by the Labour Relations Division, 2002–2016

Year	Number of Claims
2002	34,821
2003	33,689
2004	28,396
2005	25,952
2006	24,958
2007	21,698
2008	20,623
2009	24,305
2010	20,434
2011	18,086
2012	18,920
2013	17,515
2014	15,764
2015	14,388
2016	14,672

Source: Labour Department. Retrieved from https://www.labour.gov.hk/eng/public/iprd/2016/figure_en/figure3_3.htm

talks between the employers under the conciliation by the Labour Department. A settlement was made with a lower wage rate increase in favour of a shorter eight-hour working day.[58] Another large-scale labour dispute was the container port workers' strike in 2012 that erupted at the largest terminal owned by Hutchison Whampoa. The cargo handlers and crane drivers working in the terminal went on strike for forty days against two contractors in demand for pay rise and working hour improvement.[59] While these two disputes have shown the ascendancy of the CTU (Confederation of Trade Unions) in protecting workers' rights against the traditional pro-Beijing FTU (Federation of Trade Unions) in Hong Kong, they have also illustrated the controversial nature of the outsourcing and contracting system popularized in the name of labour flexibility.

Although we may argue that the rationale for our employment law system and employment relations could leave a latitude of 'flexibility' in the economy and for free trade and business, the issues of income inequality and labour unrest could undermine our future economic development. We need to pay more serious attention to these matters.

Review Questions

1. What are the major contextual forces affecting HRM development in Hong Kong?
2. What are the changes in different types of Hong Kong workforce?

3. Suggest some ways to motivate the 'millennials' in your workplace.
4. Identify some features of HRM among Hong Kong's start-ups?
5. What are the advantages and disadvantages of working in Chinese companies in Hong Kong?
6. Are HR technologies 'threats' or 'opportunities' to the HR professionals? What are the new competencies required for HR professionals in response to the new HR technologies?
7. Identify major weaknesses of employment laws and employee relations in Hong Kong and suggest ways to improve.

Notes

1. Jackson, Susan E., and Schuler, Randall, S. (1995). Understanding human resource management in the context of organizations and their environments. *Annual Review of Psychology*, *46*(1), 237–264. Wright, P. M., McMahan, G. C., and McWilliams, A. (1994). Human resources and sustained competitive advantage: A resource-based perspective. *International Journal of Human Resource Management*, *5*(2), 299–324.
2. Baker, H. (1991). The English sandwich: Obscenity, punning, and the Hong Kong Cantonese. In R. T. Ames, S. W. Chan and M. S. Ng (Eds.), *Interpreting culture through translation: A festschrift for D. C. Lau*. Hong Kong: The Chinese University Press.
3. Hugh, R. (1976). *Borrowed place, borrowed time: Hong Kong and its many faces* (2nd rev. ed.). Deutsch.
4. England, J. (1989). *Industrial relations and law in Hong Kong*. Hong Kong: Oxford University Press. Wong, W. P. Thomas., and Levin, David A. (2000). The social structure. In S. H. Ng and David G. Lethbridge (Eds.), *The business environment in Hong Kong* (4th ed., pp. 47–73). Hong Kong: Oxford University Press.
5. Public opinion polls measuring Hong Kong residents' identity since 1997 show that the respondents always identify themselves first and foremost as Hong Kong citizens or 'Hong Kongers'. It is followed by 'Asians', then 'members of the Chinese race', 'Chinese', 'global citizens', and finally 'citizens of the People's Republic of China'. University of Hong Kong Public Opinion Poll Programme. (2015). People's ethnic identity. Retrieved from https://hkupop.hku.hk/english/popexpress/ethnic
6. England, J. (1989). *Industrial relations and law in Hong Kong*. Hong Kong: Oxford University Press. Tsui, A., Lai, K. T., and Wong, Isabella H. M. (2009). The development and current state of HRM in Hong Kong, in A. Tsui and K. T. Lai (Eds.), *Professional practices of HRM in Hong Kong: Linking HRM to organizational success* (pp. 11–26). Hong Kong: Hong Kong University Press. Chan, A., and Man, D. (2014). Human resource management in Hong Kong. In Arup Varma and Pawan S. Budhwar (Eds.), *Managing human resource in Asia-Pacific* (pp. 82–96). London: Routledge.
7. Rowley, C., and Benson, J. (2004). *The management of human resources in the Asia Pacific region: Convergence revisited*. London: Taylor & Francis. Cooke, F. L., and Kim, S. H. (Eds.). (2018). *Routledge handbook of human resource management in Asia*. Oxford: Routledge.
8. Ng, S. H., and Wright, R. (2002). Hong Kong. In Michael Zanko (Ed.), *The handbook of human resource management policies and practices in Asia-Pacific Economies* (Vol. 1, pp. 167–259). Cheltenham: Edward Elgar.
9. Chen, S. Y., and Ahlstrom, D. (2018). Human resource management in Hong Kong, Macau, and Taiwan. In Fang Lee Cooke and Sunghoo Kim (Eds.), *Routledge handbook of human resource management in Asia* (pp. 314–332). London: Routledge.
10. OECD. (1996). *The knowledge-based economy*. Paris: OECD. Retrieved from https://www.oecd.org/sti/sci-tech/1913021.pdf

11. Various definitions of knowledge workers are defined; see, for example, OECD's definitions: OECD. (2001). *Competencies for the knowledge economy*. Paris: OECD. Retrieved from http://www.oecd.org/innovation/research/1842070.pdf
12. Census and Statistics Department, HKSAR Government. (2012). *Hong Kong population projections 2017-2066*. Retrieved from https://www.statistics.gov.hk/pub/B1120015052012XXXXB0100.pdf
13. Yip, P. (2014, April 10). Raising the retirement age can work for the whole of Hong Kong. *South China Morning Post*. Retrieved from http://www.scmp.com/comment/article/1471251/raising-retirement-age-can-work-whole-hong-kong
14. PricewaterhouseCoopers. (2011). *Millennials at work: Reshaping the workplace*. Retrieved from https://www.pwc.com/m1/en/services/consulting/documents/millennials-at-work.pdf
15. Census and Statistics Department, HKSAR Government. (2017). *Snapshot of the Hong Kong population*. Retrieved from https://www.bycensus2016.gov.hk/data/snapshotPDF/Snapshot10.pdf
16. Research Office, Legislative Council Secretariat. (2017). *Fact sheet: Poverty of ethnic minorities in Hong Kong*. Retrieved from http://www.legco.gov.hk/research-publications/english/1617fs08-poverty-of-ethnic-minorities-in-hong-kong-20170608-e.pdf
17. Globalization. (n.d.). In *Merriam Webster Online*. Retrieved from https://www.merriam-webster.com/dictionary/globalization
18. Lynch, David. A. (2010). *Trade and globalization: An introduction to regional trade agreements*. Plymouth: Rowman & Littlefield.
19. HKTDC. (2015, May 22). *E-commerce: Recent developments and opportunities for Hong Kong businesses*. Retrieved from http://hkmb.hktdc.com/en/1X0A2EJB/hktdc-research/E-commerce-Recent-Developments-and-Opportunities-for-Hong-Kong-Businesses
20. Luthans, F. (2015). *International management: Culture, strategy and behaviour* (9th ed.). New York: McGrawHill Education. Hill, W. L., and Hult, G. Tomas M. (2017). *International business: Competing in the global marketplace* (11th ed.). New York: McGrawHill Education.
21. Chiang, Flora F. T., Lemanski, Michal K., and Birtch, Thomas A. (2017). The transfer and diffusion of HRM practices within MNCs: Lessons learned and future research directions. *International Journal of Human Resource Management*, 28(1), 234–258.
22. Tsui, A., Lai, K. T., and Wong, Isabella, H. M. (2009). The development and current state of HRM in Hong Kong. In A. Tsui and K. T. Lai (Eds.), *Professional practices of HRM in Hong Kong: Linking HRM to organizational success* (pp. 11–26). Hong Kong: Hong Kong University Press.
23. De Bakker, M. (2017, March 17). *MNCs still employers of choice in Singapore, Hong Kong and Malaysia: Randstad Workmonitor*. Retrieved from https://www.randstad.com.hk/workforce360/articles/media-release-mncs-still-employers-of-choice-in-singapore-hong-kong-and-malaysia-randstad-workmonitor
24. Trade and Industry Department. (2017). *Small and medium enterprises (SMEs)*. Retrieved from https://www.success.tid.gov.hk/english/aboutus/sme/service_detail_6863.html
25. Tsui, A., Lai, K. T., and Wong, Isabella H. M. (2009). The development and current state of HRM in Hong Kong. In A. Tsui and K. T. Lai (Eds.), *Professional practices of HRM in Hong Kong: Linking HRM to organizational success* (pp. 11–26). Hong Kong: Hong Kong University Press.
26. Mayson, S., and Barrett, R. (2006). The 'science' and 'practice' of HRM in small firms. *Human Resource Management Review*, 16(4), 447–455.
27. See, for example, The Hong Kong General Chamber of Small and Medium Business. *Human resource management guidebooks for SMEs*. Retrieved from http://www.hksmehr.org/doc/low/SME%20guidebk_eng.pdf
28. Macfarlane, A. (2017, July 2). Chinese money has changed the face of Hong Kong's skyline. *CNN Money*. Retrieved from http://money.cnn.com/2017/07/02/news/hong-kong-china-handover-real-estate/index.html

29. Wildau, G. (2014, October 2). Hong Kong's value to China goes beyond numbers. *Financial Times.* Retrieved May 1, 2018, from https://www.ft.com/content/acfff900-4a0b-11e4-8de3-00144feab7de
30. Wei, L., and Lau, C. M. (2005). Market orientation, HRM importance and competence: Determinants of strategic HRM in Chinese firms. *International Journal of Human Resource Management, 16*(1), 1901–1918. Wang, X., Bruning, N., and Peng, S. Q. (2007). Western high performance HR practices in China: A comparison among public-owned, private and foreign-invested enterprises. *International Journal of Human Resource Management, 18*(4), 684–701. Rowley, C., and Cooke, F. L. (Eds.). (2010). *The changing face of management in China.* London: Routledge.
31. Ngo, H. Y., Lau, C. M., and Foley, S. (2008). Strategic human resource management, firm performance, and employee relations climate in China. *Human Resource Management, 47*(1), 73–90.
32. Cooke, F. L. (2014). Human resource management in China. In Arup Varma and Pawan S. Budhwar (Eds.), *Managing human resource in Asia-Pacific* (pp. 10–30). London: Routledge. Zhao, S. M., and Du, J. (2012). Thirty-two years of development of human resource management in China: Review and prospects. *Human Resource Management Review, 22*(3), 179–188.
33. Jayaram, S. V. (2016, Dec. 29). Chinese companies in Hong Kong will drive hiring growth in 2017. Retrieved from http://www.hrinasia.com/recruitment/chinese-companies-in-hong-kong-will-drive-hiring-growth-in-2017/
34. Nie, W. (2015, June 1). HR Challenges: Why one-size-fits-all doesn't work in China. *Forbes.* Retrieved from https://www.forbes.com/sites/winternie/2015/06/01/hr-challenges-why-one-size-fits-all-doesnt-work-in-china/
35. Whub. (2017). *2017 Hong Kong startup ecosystem toolbox.* Retrieved from http://www.whub.io/toolbox
36. WeLab. https://www.welab.co/zh-cn
37. GoGovan. https://www.gogovan.com.hk
38. Robehmed, Natalie. (2013, December 16). What is a startup? *Forbes.* Retrieved from https://www.forbes.com/sites/natalierobehmed/2013/12/16/what-is-a-startup/#34b04d334044. Katila, R., Chen, Eric L., and Piezunka, H. (2012). All the right moves: How entrepreneurial firms compete effectively. *Strategic Entrepreneurship Journal, 6,* 116–132.
39. Johnson, Richard D., and Gueutal, Hal G. (2011). *Transforming HR through technology: The use of E-HR and HRIS in organizations.* Alexandria: SHRM. Retrieved from https://www.shrm.org/hr-today/trends-and-forecasting/special-reports-and-expert-views/Documents/HR-Technology.pdf
40. Stone, Diana L., Deadrick, Diana L., Lukaszewski, Kimberly M., and Johnson, R. (2015). The influence of technology on the future of human resource management. *Human Resource Management Review, 25,* 216–231.
41. Johnson, Richard D., and Gueutal, Hal G. (2011). *Transforming HR through technology: The use of E-HR and HRIS in organizations.* Alexandria: SHRM. Retrieved from https://www.shrm.org/hr-today/trends-and-forecasting/special-reports-and-expert-views/Documents/HR-Technology.pdf
42. Bassi, L. (2011). Raging debates in HR analytics. *People and Strategy, 34*(2), 14.
43. Kiron, D., and Shockley, R. (2011). Creating business value with analytics. *MIT Sloan Management Review, 53*(1), 57–63.
44. Ng, S. H., and Wright, R. (2002). Hong Kong. In Michael Zanko (Ed.), *The handbook of human resource management policies and practices in Asia-Pacific economies* (Vol. 1, pp. 167–259). Cheltenham: Edward Elgar.
45. Wesley-Smith, P. (2000). The legal system. In S. H. Ng and David G. Lethbridge (Eds.), *The business environment in Hong Kong* (4th ed., pp. 110–125). Hong Kong: Oxford University Press.

46. Huang, Z. P., and Huang, E. (2016, Nov. 7). *A brief history: Beijing's interpretations of Hong Kong's Basic Law, from 1999 to the present day*. Retrieved from https://qz.com/828713/a-brief-history-beijings-interpretations-of-hong-kongs-basic-law-from-1999-to-the-present-day/
47. Hong Kong brain drain: Why are so many HK'ers abandoning their home city. (2018, October 6). *GAFENCU*. Retrieved from https://www.igafencu.com/r/hong-kong-brain-drain
48. Lam, A. (2013, December 2). Brain drain fears as 3 in 10 want to quit Hong Kong. *South China Morning Post*. Retrieved from https://www.scmp.com/business/china-business/article/1377126/brain-drain-fears-3-10-want-quit-hong-kong
49. Yau, E. (2013, September 2). As more residents leave Hong Kong, experts worry about a brain drain. *South China Morning Post*. Retrieved from https://www.scmp.com/lifestyle/family-education/article/1300687/more-residents-leave-hong-kong-experts-worry-about-brain
50. Ng, Sek Hong. (2015). *Labour law in Hong Kong* (2nd ed.). Alphen aan den Rijn: Kluwer Law International.
51. Ng, Sek Hong. (2015). *Labour law in Hong Kong* (2nd ed.). Alphen aan den Rijn: Kluwer Law International.
52. Wong, H., and Ye, S. Q. (2015). Impact of enforcing a statutory minimum wage on work and quality of life of vulnerable groups in Hong Kong. *International Journal of Social Welfare, 24*, 223–235.
53. Liu, Y. J. (2017, Sep. 20). MPF needs to centralize and digitalize, PwC says. *South China Morning Post*. Retrieved May 1, 2018, from http://www.scmp.com/business/money/markets-investing/article/2111912/mpf-needs-centralise-and-digitalise-pwc-says
54. Lau, J. (2016, June 25). Hong Kong retirement protection debate prompts protests and criticisms. *South China Morning Post*. Retrieved April 1, 2018, from http://www.scmp.com/news/hong-kong/education-community/article/1980777/hong-kong-retirement-protection-debate-prompts
55. Singh, H. (2017, June 21). Hong Kong government working hours plan slammed in legislative council. *South China Morning Post*. Retrieved September 1, 2017, from http://www.scmp.com/news/hong-kong/politics/article/2099240/hong-kong-government-working-hours-plan-slammed-legislative
56. Papadopolous, A. (2009). Equal opportunities laws in Hong Kong. In A. Tsui and K. T. Lai (Eds.), *Professional practices of HRM in Hong Kong: Linking HRM to organizational success* (pp. 163–202). Hong Kong: Hong Kong University Press.
57. Singh, H. (2017, June 21). Hong Kong government working hours plan slammed in legislative council. *South China Morning Post*. Retrieved September 1, 2017, from http://www.scmp.com/news/hong-kong/politics/article/2099240/hong-kong-government-working-hours-plan-slammed-legislative
58. Lam, A. (2007, September 13). Bar benders end strike after deal on pay, hours. *South China Morning Post*. Retrieved August 1, 2017, from http://www.scmp.com/article/607704/bar-benders-end-strike-after-deal-pay-hours
59. Zhou, Yi. (2013). *A concise history of the Hong Kong labour movement* (香港工運史：簡篇). Hong Kong: Nice News Publishing Co.

3
Talent Acquisition Strategies in the New HR Era

Jenny W. Lam

> **LEARNING OUTCOMES**
>
> By the end of this chapter, readers should be able to
> - explain the trends and factors affecting current talent acquisition strategies;
> - understand the impact of artificial intelligence, social media and various HR technologies on talent acquisition;
> - understand the trend of new generations and manage to integrate them in the workforce;
> - identify changes of the recruitment process in the new era; and
> - apply suitable strategies for building employer brands in organizations

Introduction

It is evident that finding and nurturing good talent is crucial to the success of a company, from the too-big-to-fail giants to three-people start-ups. However, these are the years that finding great talent is much harder than before, as technology comes into play that completely reshapes the job market's landscape. Companies are now innovating with technologies such as artificial intelligence (AI) and big data analytics, thus skill sets such as software dexterity and ability to learn become more essential criteria for recruitment. Moreover, new job titles such as social media manager and search engine optimization (SEO) specialist have emerged in the last ten years. On the other hand, a proportion of talent in the job market may not be comfortable to such change, especially for the generation that was not born and raised by smartphones and social media, and many job seekers, in fact, are ill-equipped to make productive use of these newly emerging technologies. The result is an imbalance between the surging demand for digital savvy and the availability of talent. And the demand for these new jobs is expected to rise in the foreseeable future. A survey done by IBM reveals that the job openings of new roles like data scientists and data engineers in the US will increase to more than 20 per cent in 2020.[1] While existing employees may lack the skill sets required to operate the AI engineered tools, to 'fill the skill gaps', International Data Corporation (IDC) anticipates that by 2025, 75% of organizations have to retrain their employees.[2]

The imbalance between job demand and supply inevitably leads to a 'war for talent'. In a book titled *The War for Talent*, Les Wexner, a merchant based in suburban Columbus, was able to turn his listed company from the brink of collapse in the 1990s into a million-dollar business with sustainable income streams. What Wexner did during his company's hard times was to visit other corporate executives in search of a new methodology. He talked with CEO Jack Welch of General Electric who told Wexner that 'having the most talented people in each of our businesses is the most important thing. If we don't, we lose.' The takeaway of the book is that new mindsets are necessary for the survival and growth of the company, and what Wexner learned from the successful CEOs are that talents are the most critical asset to the success of a company; managers should also take the role in nurturing talent, instead of human resource departments alone.[3]

The war for talent today has become even more pitched in the digital age. However, one thing that always prevails is the need for reviewing current human resource management strategies and having an open mindset which allows us to keep abreast with the times. As seen with the dramatic change in the human resource management arena, new strategies are essential to recruit the best candidates, and in fact, many companies in Hong Kong have been innovating their recruitment process to cope with this massive change. In the next section, we discuss the adaptation of new methodologies and also new mindsets needed in response to the new HR era.

Recruiting Strategies Utilizing Big Data

The term *big data* refers to the large volume of data that is both structured and unstructured and can be converted into useful information that facilitates fact-based decisions. Big data has three major measurements—namely, volume, variety, and velocity.[4] In human resource acquisition, volume can be interpreted as the amount of applicant information entering the HR system; variety means the diversity of information, such as candidates' educational background, age, gender, and work experience; velocity is the rate of candidates entering the recruitment funnel within a given period. In contrary to big data's quantitative features, HRM has traditionally been perceived as people-centered, where recruiters screen unsuitable candidates with criteria such as academic performance, related job performance, and career achievements according to the recruiters' own experiences. These qualitative traits seem to be unmeasurable, since they rely on intuitional judgement rather than statistical deduction. However, some candidate data are measurable and can be converted into useful information. For example, the number of times a candidate switches between jobs and the time between promotions. Once these rules are formally set up in the big data analytical tool, it can increase the efficiency and effectiveness of HR's work.

Using big data to analyse candidates can also free up the time for HR professionals to perform other tasks, such as onboard training and employee evaluation. Therefore, big data may serve as a tool that helps HR specialists in talent acquisition. The merits of big data are evident for large corporations, which frequently receive thousands of applicants each month. Big data analysis can help filter out those that are not qualified for the job using rules determined either by HR team or by machine learning, which provides a sustainable and scalable solution for talent acquisition. Big data may also increase accuracy when hiring talent. After all, we HR specialists are humans that will make mistakes, and it is often that we have hired the wrong candidate for the job. The result of wrong hires is costly. According to Cake.hr, 41 per cent of hiring managers who have made a lousy hire estimated the financial costs of that hire in thousands of dollars.[5] Big data can provide analytical results for HR recruiters to make better hiring decisions, which theoretically increases the accuracy of hiring suitable candidates (see also Chapter 9).

Despite the advantages of utilizing big data, only a few companies are picking up the tool for their HR management. The research of Deloitte shows that 4 per cent of organizations think that they have predictive talent analytics capabilities, while only 14 per cent of companies have talent analytics programmes in use.[6] The number makes sense as big data is still a new topic in business, and it currently has only limited application. Yet it is believed the trend of big data is going up, as the research of Deloitte also points out that 60 per cent of the interviewed enterprises are trying to incorporate big data in their HR departments.[7]

Nevertheless, there are critics regarding the application of big data in HRM who believe it has limited application in today's corporate world. One reason is that most companies in the world and especially in Hong Kong are SMEs, and it will be hard for the small HR team to analyse big data which is huge in volume. One article mentions that there is no big data software in the market that is tailor-made for HRM at the moment.[8] The big data software in the market are now mainly focusing on data storage and data management, for instance, IBM Db2 Big SQL. For now, big data seems to be a luxury for big companies, and it may take time for big data to gain traction in HRM.

HRM in Action—Box 3.1

Microsoft's Talent Acquisition Uses HR and Data as a Competitive Edge

To win the war for talent and meet increasing challenges in the environment (such as more competitions and hiring volume), Microsoft's HR has implemented an innovative recruitment process that inspires talent through an attractive candidate experience. Instead of going to campus for career talks, HR invites prospective graduates to visit its company to provide a more realistic preview of the work environment. Candidates can take a glimpse into Microsoft, meet and chat with staff, and get excited about the interview process.

With an increasing number of applications, an interview suite has been developed to receive applications in a digital job application process. A welcome video is available to openly and authentically receive the applicants. While candidates can understand the culture and values of Microsoft, they will be shortlisted using video interviews. Feedback at the end of the video interviews reflects the company's open culture.

Through the new global shared service, Microsoft recruiters store their interactions with prospects in a shared service built on Microsoft Dynamics CRM.

Microsoft embraces talent analytics to analyse the volumes of data it generates from the company's recruiting efforts. HR can adjust how they deploy their recruiters, such as increasing or decreasing recruiting at a university, shifting resources where the need is greatest, to get higher returns on their recruiting efforts. To attract and retain top people, HR needs to connect with candidates and employees in richer, more fluid, and interactive ways. It leverages the power of online social networks to source and engage candidates. Recruiters can view a candidate's LinkedIn profile within CRM instead of using an outdated resume from company files. They can tag and enter notes about candidates when they interact.

HR can also transform the candidate experience. Throughout the interview process, prospective hires are encouraged to use the Candidate Experience app, built on Azure and accessible through the devices of their choice. The app is a digital companion for prospects during the interview process and enables them to experience the company's mobile-first, cloud-first strategy. In addition, using the Candidate Experience app, prospective hires can check in for interviews, view the interview schedule, learn more about their interviewers (including biographies pulled from LinkedIn), book a shuttle to an interview, get alerts if someone is running late, and get information about the city they're interviewing in. And when candidates are hired, to help ease them into their job, HR provides new employees with an onboarding dashboard on HR web. The whole process makes a better experience for potential new hires, enables them to experience the company's mobile-first, cloud-first strategy, and provides a competitive advantage for Microsoft in attracting top talent.

Furthermore, HR use data analytics to find where the great employees come from. For example, employees who first worked with Microsoft as interns often turn out to be excellent performers, in terms of work performance, retention rate, and career development. Thus, HR uses internship programmes to attract talent. Rehires are also found to be a reliable source.

Another useful tool to predict the retention of new hires is to track their status in the early stage. Do the employees meet with their managers during the first week? Are they issued with a computer? Do they have access to email and the corporate network? HR can use data analytics to track these matters to make sure the new hires are onboarded effectively. Otherwise, review of onboard programmes will be performed between HR and line departments.

Sources:
Microsoft. (2015, June). *Modernizing HR at Microsoft*. Retrieved from http://wk.ixueshu.com/file/0e59c6a2d1ba0899318947a18e7f9386.html
Klinghoffer, D., Clem, J., and Masek, O. (2017, May 25). Digital workplace for HR: Supercharging HR with data, insight [Web log post]. Retrieved from https://cloudblogs.microsoft.com/industry-blog/uncategorized/2017/05/25/digital-workplace-hr-supercharging-hr-data-insight/

Recruiting Strategies Utilizing Artificial Intelligence

Artificial Intelligence (AI) refers to the intelligence performed by machines—that is, their ability to mimic human behaviour such as learning, problem-solving, and decision-making.[9] AI has been increasingly used in different stages of HRM, with talent acquisition being one of AI's major functions.

In recent years, phone interview has been replaced by digital interview during recruitment. Big corporations in Hong Kong such as Goldman Sachs and Cathay Pacific Airways have started to use digital interview software like HireVue to conduct interview screening (see various examples of recruitment tools in Table 3.1).[10] Instead of human screening, digital interview software utilizes AI to analyse candidates' performance. For example, HireVue gathers candidate data such as dialogue, facial expression, and gesture during the digital interview to evaluate the competitiveness, personality, and ability of the candidate. Also, this kind of software can use machine learning to improve the accuracy of identifying great talent. In other words, interview software will learn and use new methods for assessments by referencing the past data gathered (see also Chapter 4).

Table 3.1: Examples of recruitment tools in the market

Recruitment Tool	Purpose
Glassdoor	Next-gen recruitment platforms
HireVue, Vieple, Talview	Video job interviewing combined with other recruitment screening and evaluation tools
Ajinga (popular in China)	Applicant tracking system, with shortlisting and candidate testing functions; with personality and culture-fit tests
Monkey Tie, Career Profiler	'Affinity matching' in an open human resource ecosystem; personality and culture-fit tests.

There are various merits to using AI for talent screening. First is the fairness of the AI machine. Although recruiters are professionals who can often restrain their personal views from affecting the assessment of candidates, there are times that recruiters may exhibit biased judgements of candidates' abilities. For example, recruiters may share a common background with the candidates, such as studying in the same high school or having the same ethical identity, which increases the odds of the candidates being accepted; by contrast, it is a psychological tendency that human will reject things that do not share in common with them, and this may lead to misjudgement when it comes to recruitment. The results of our personal interference in recruitment decisions may lead to a less diversified pool of accepted candidates, and possibly hiring the wrong talent for the company. However, AI can help us avoid these pitfalls. AI will determine the suitability of the candidate basing on the preset criteria and analytical screening of the candidates. Therefore, it is believed that AI can provide more accurate selection of talent for the company when more data are being collected and analysed (please also refer to Chapter 9).

Furthermore, digital interviewing software such as HireVue can record every single movement and word uttered by candidates. These real-time data can be stored and used at a later time, for instance, to be used in a review of AI's analysis by HR specialists. Also, the data recorded by software will be more thorough than human recruiters, as sometimes recruiters may fail to accurately transcribe a candidate's words when jotting notes, or when recruiters can only come up with a general and vague conclusion on the candidate's performance.

As AI is evolving to become more human and adept at decision-making, there are fears about whether AI will replace HR professionals in the market. Without a doubt, AI is starting to execute traditional tasks in HRM such as screening and interview, and sometimes may even outperform human HR recruiters. However, HR recruiters are still vital in the talent acquisition process; AI should be regarded simply as a tool that can provide more diversified information when assessing a candidate's suitability. For decades human resource has always been a people-centric department, in which HR specialists use intuition and experience to screen candidates and compare candidates' visions to the company's culture. Analysing these traits relies more on gauging one's gut feeling and personal experience. Moreover, AI generally lacks the spontaneity that we humans have. Human recruiters may ask follow-up questions and have personal interactions with candidates, while AI is still restricted to cold and standardized questions programmed in the system. The flexibility and experience that human HR specialists have are what differentiate human from artificial intelligence.

In the coming decades, AI will only become more prominent in HRM. Recruiters should utilize AI's analytical output as a reference when making the hiring judgement while at the same time recognizing our profession and experience. With human recruiters and AI working hand in hand, talent acquisition will only get better and better in the future.

Recruiting Strategies Utilizing Social Media and Online Platforms

Social media has already been a part of everybody's lives, and for sure it is hard to live without these applications. The first thing that many of us do after our morning alarm is to check Facebook and Instagram newsfeeds, and perhaps it is also the last thing we do before we go to bed each day. Social media has radically transformed how we communicate, disseminate, and acquire new information, and this drastic change affects the talent acquisition process in HRM. In fact, social media has already become a commonly used platform for both job seekers and recruiters to connect, as a study conducted by Robert Walters pointed out that half the employers surveyed are willing to research candidates using social media. One thing that is notable regarding social media platforms is that the perception of different social media platforms varies. LinkedIn is generally perceived as a professional networking site that facilitates formal connection and business exposure, while sites such as Facebook and Instagram are more personal where individuals share their personal lives with their close friends. The stark difference in perception is reflected in the result of Robert Walters' survey, as 84.5 per cent of job seekers surveyed and 69 per cent of employers surveyed believed that Facebook is personal and not professional, whereas nearly 80 per cent of interviewers will research potential candidates on LinkedIn.[11] In short, LinkedIn, compared with Facebook, is still regarded as a dominant platform for professional networking (see also Chapter 9). Examining social media in the context of Hong Kong, the situation is similar with LinkedIn gaining popularity over the years. The usage of LinkedIn in Hong Kong is increasing, with the number of LinkedIn users in Hong Kong exceeding 1 million in 2015, and continuous growth is expected.[12]

Since social media is getting more popular in the recruitment process, the next question HR recruiters should ask is how we should use social media in the best way possible. Among different stages of the recruitment journey, it is found that LinkedIn is mostly used in the application and interview stages, which account for 50 per cent of the usage.[13] Interviewers would like to know more about candidates' background such as past employers, education, and working experience on LinkedIn before face-to-face or phone interviews. In addition, employers may get to know more about candidates' personalities by observing candidates' online behaviour, for instance, the pages that candidates are following, posts created by candidates, and candidates' likes and comments to online materials. These observations can reflect the traits and personality of the candidate that may facilitate the hiring process.

However, there may be drawbacks in using social media to spot talent. Some recruiters may go further to search candidate's personal social media accounts, such as Facebook and Instagram, and this practice may not be appropriate. Research found that 63 per cent of professionals surveyed do not agree that their personal social media accounts reflect their professionalism, as these platforms mostly reveal their personal lives and privacy. Nearly 60 per cent of the surveyed professionals claim that they will hide the information on personal social media from recruiters, or amend the information to appeal to the recruiters.[14] The reason is simple: many individuals are reluctant to reveal their personal lives to strangers. The disguising behaviour performed by candidates implies the inaccuracy of using personal social media accounts as a reference. Consequently, reviewing candidates' information on professional social media sites is a more consistently reliable metric of candidate aptitude (see also Box 3.2).

With well-planned strategies, social media can be a great tool in HR's talent acquisition. Not only that, but social media can also serve as an HR branding tool for companies to market themselves. Later in this chapter we will examine in greater detail how Hong Kong companies are utilizing social media to approach potential candidates.

HRM in Focus—Box 3.2
Is LinkedIn the Best Sourcing Tool?

With the extensive reach to candidates' profiles—having over 590 million of members and counting, LinkedIn is now the largest online professional networking website. Apparently, there are a lot of advantages of using LinkedIn for recruitment, including the access to the vast candidate profiles (both active and passive candidates), the ability to benchmark with industry talents, identification of potential candidate via LinkedIn's advanced search tools, and the ease of making connections with candidates, to name but a few. LinkedIn has been very successful on professional networking where it capitalizes on members' existing networks and connects related professionals effortlessly. It is also very helpful in building an employer brand which allows firms to disseminate their company's values on their pages through curated contents. Among all the good edges, most important, LinkedIn allows recruiters to tap into the passive pool of candidates who may be the hidden gem in the market. Even so, whether LinkedIn is the most effective sourcing channel is still up for debate.

It is undeniable that time is an important asset for recruiters. Since 80 per cent of LinkedIn users are passive—that is, people not actively seeking for jobs—recruiters tend to spend a tremendous amount of time messaging candidates and getting no or slow replies. The large proportion of inactive accounts and not up-to-date profiles also waste a considerable amount of the recruiters' time. Second, the ease of application with just a quick click of Apply brings along disingenuous candidate applications and creates extra workload for recruiters in screening. Moreover, the Recruiter plan of LinkedIn is costly; it costs about US$8,500 per year, which is overkill for SMEs.

All the above validate why traditional recruiting methods such as posting job ads, sourcing talents via recruitment agencies, and cold-calling are still popular go-to options as they may somehow be more efficient, cost-effective, and direct. Recruiters can acquire much more straightforward and precise descriptions of candidates' latest jobs, and keep their own candidate databases up-to-date. Meanwhile, Hong Kong HR directors also reflect that social networking profiles are not resumes. They would not reject a candidate because of some content posted on his or her profile. They should understand how well individuals can fit into the organization based on other means, such as relying on traditional tests. Social media can augment, but not replace, traditional one-on-one contact.

Sources:
LinkedIn Newsroom. (2018). LinkedIn pages to include Crunchbase insights. Retrieved from https://news.linkedin.com/2018/11/linkedin-pages-to-include-crunchbase-insights
O'Donnell, J.T. (2019). This new LinkedIn tool could help you find your dream job in 2019. Retrieved from https://www.cnbc.com/2019/01/02/this-1-new-linkedin-feature-can-help-you-find-your-dream-job.html
HRM online. (2014). LinkedIn: pros and cons. Retrieved from http://www.hrmonline.com.au/section/featured/linkedin-pros-cons/
Reddy. M. (2017). What you don't know about the pros and cons of LinkedIn. Retrieved from https://www.hiresphere.net/blog/pros-and-cons-of-linkedin/
Anand, P. (2012, Nov.). Hong Kong HR directors favour traditional recruitment. *Human Resources*, pp. 4–5.

Recruiting Strategies Using Online Platforms

The emergence of online recruitment platforms has changed how job seekers find jobs, and these platforms provide a vast library of job posts in over hundreds of job categories. The famous platforms for job searching in Hong Kong include Indeed.com, Monster.com, and Jobsdb.com etc. Similar to a search engine, visitors on these websites can search for keywords about the jobs they want to find, and the system will filter out results based on criteria such as salary range, location, and contract type and display relevant job posts listed by recruiters. These platforms provide a convenient solution for recruitment and substantially reduce the time for job matching. In recent years, the popularity of online job platforms keeps rising. For instance, Indeed.com hit 200 million unique visitors in 2016 and had 16 million job postings on the platform;[15] while for JobsDB.com, the database of the company already contains 14.6 million job seekers and over 220,000 corporate clients in the Asia-Pacific region.[16]

Apart from job search engine, more innovative job-matching platforms have also been introduced to the market in recent years. For example, a job platform named Wantedly was found in 2011 in Japan that provides a tailor-made job-matching service. Unlike its competitors, Wantedly allows job seekers to visit companies that they are interested in before having a formal interview. This informal interaction between the job seeker and the employees in the companies facilitates better mutual understanding of the individual's career interests and also the company's culture. The platform favors young start-ups and small and medium enterprises (SMEs); as these companies are small in scale, very often applicants can chat with the CEO and founder of the company directly via Wantedly. The founder of Wantedly, Akiko Naka, compared job matching to finding a partner: in a romantic relationship, both parties should know one another in comfortable situations before jumping to a marriage agreement. In the context of work, the casual meetings between candidates and the CEOs are similar to dating, and signing the contract is like signing a marriage certificate. Therefore, Akiko believe that casual meetings will prove a better way to facilitate job matching results than traditional interviews.[17] Akiko also has a different vision of her company, which is to drive job matchings base on intrinsic motivation such as passion and curiosity, rather than monetary terms such as salary.[18] Fostered by the company's popularity in the Asia-Pacific, Wantedly successfully completed an IPO and listed in the Tokyo Stock Exchange in 2017. The triumphant story of Wantedly conveys the message that in this new era the workforce is putting a greater emphasis on the meaning of work versus the monetary pay. It is foreseeable that the job matching industry may move in a direction where employer and candidate are positioned at the same level concerning negotiating power and influence in the hiring decision.

In addition to new job-matching models, the way people go about accessing job-searching services is also changing. There is an increasing number of job searches using mobile devices. According to a survey conducted in 2014 interviewing over 500 Hong Kong job seekers, 56 per cent of respondents say that they search for job openings mainly by mobile.[19] Big job-searching platforms are entering the mobile arena with mobile apps, for instance, LinkedIn Job Search and JobsDB. Regarding the type of job searched on mobile, the occupations with most searches are labour-intensive jobs such as grounds maintenance and construction, since most workers in the industry use mobile devices more frequently than white-collar workers, who have regular access to a desktop. Furthermore, there are more mobile job search apps that focus on part-time jobs, such as Jobpedia and WorkKing. The possible reason for more labour-intensive and part-time job postings on mobile search engines is the limitation of mobile devices. Although smartphone is more convenient in usage, applicants on mobile devices are restricted from performing complex job application tasks such as submitting CV and performing screening tests. Moreover, mobile devices are typically used for more casual purposes, and thus the nature of jobs searched on mobile device will mostly be temporary and short term. That said, there are still a lot of white-collar job finders that use mobile devices to look for jobs, but most of the time the application journey will require the use of a computer later.

Strategies Targeting Millennials and Generation Z

The term *millennials* is the buzzword people use to describe those born between 1981 and 1996,[20] with the experience of key economic, social, and cultural changes such as the emergence of technology and the rapid rate of globalization. The oldest millennials are now in their mid-thirties and the youngest have already graduated from college and are entering the workforce as of 2018. On the other hand, Generation Z is the group after millennials with individuals born from 1996 onwards. The generation has alternative names such as Gen Tech, I Generation, and Digital Natives.[21] Generation Z is also the group that characteristically embraces digital gadgets like smartphones and social media sites. While there are debates about differentiation between millennials and Generation Z, owing to their similar relationships with technology, it can generally be observed that members of Generation Z are more digitally reliant than millennials. The topic of millennials and Generation Z is an important one in HRM, as it is estimated that millennials will make up to 50 per cent of the workforce by 2020.[22] To attract talented millennials and Generation Z during the talent acquisition phase, new strategies targeting the groups are needed. Below are several traits of millennials and Generation Z that HR recruiters should take note of when approaching the groups.

Digital savvy

Without a doubt, millennials have higher expertise in term of software, applications, and social media than the previous generations. Research in the Asia-Pacific region reveals high reliance on technology among millennials: over 70 per cent of millennials in Thailand, Singapore, and Malaysia use Facebook, and nearly 80 per cent of millennials interviewed claimed that they could not live without smartphones.[23] Managers in Hong Kong also notice millennials' ability to bring in new methods and thinking to companies, as Adam Johnston, the managing director of Robert Half Hong Kong, says, 'Having grown up with technology constantly at their fingertips, millennials are well-equipped to help companies transform into more agile and digitally-minded enterprises. With all of today's industries vulnerable to the impact of innovation disruptors, companies need to be able to attract and further develop the necessary tech-savvy talent to tackle today's business challenges.'[24] In this regard, HR recruiters can make use of these traits to target millennials during the recruitment process, such as social media branding and email pitching.

Flexibility

Another trait that millennials have is that they value flexibility more than the previous generation. Instead of working for a company for life, millennials put long-term job security as a lower priority than flexibility to change jobs. In fact, millennials enjoy wearing different hats in their career path. For example, a 22-year-old woman can be a manager by day and a yoga instructor after work, and perhaps a photographer at the weekend. The multifaceted roles are represented by slashes, hence the term *slash generation*. According to a report by Deloitte in 2016, 66 per cent of surveyed millennials expect to leave their current job, and 22 per cent of them expect to leave in 2 to 5 years.[25] The figures in Hong Kong are even higher, as the survey conducted by AIESEC Hong Kong found that only 19 per cent of young people born between 1983 to 2000 expect to stay with the current employer.[26] In Hong Kong society the years of staying in the company are often referred as a criterion to evaluate the jumpiness of a candidate, and usually, employers prefer candidates with a lower level of 'jumpiness'. However, it seems that switching jobs after a few years will soon become mainstream. As seen with the number of job hoppers on the rise, HR recruiters should begin to adjust their mindset when evaluating candidates' mobility between jobs. The possible reason for such a change in dynamics may be attributed to more job options in the market than before. As Mr. Lau Ming-wai, chairman of the city's Commission on Youth pointed out, 'From jobs to relationships, millennials have more options. The more options you have, the more you want to try [different options].' He also said that the jumpiness does not necessarily reflect something wrong with the generation.[27] It is true that compared to decades ago, millennials have more choices as the job market becomes more diversified, thanks to globalization and technological innovations.

Apart from the increase in jumpiness between jobs, millennials are now looking for flexibility at work, for instance, flexible working hours and the ability to work remotely. According to research conducted by Bentley University, 77 per cent of millennials say that their productivity will increase if given flexible working hours.[28] Although there may be doubts regarding the management efficiency during remote working, over half the Hong Kong managers interviewed are confident that efficient management during remote work can be achieved.[29] The key to having flexible arrangement that works is trust between employers and employees, as employees may abuse the arrangement if they regard the flexible working arrangement as a loophole to gain advantage from their employee. As the director of Bauhinia Foundation Research Centre, Mr. Lawrence Lee Kam-hung said, 'Employees and employers are partners, not enemies. To promote flexible employment practices effectively, mutual trust is the key.'[30]

Different expectations

Compared to Generation X, millennials generally have different expectations in the workplace. In a research study conducted by Roffey Park in 2016, around 2,000 professionals based in Hong Kong were surveyed with questions regarding their expectations for work. Among various options, millennials put work-life balance as the highest priority, which accounts for nearly 50 per cent. On the other hand, there are only 28 per cent of Generation X who put this as top priority.[31] In view of the difference between generations, HR professionals are advised to formulate new strategies hand in hand with the top manager, and to devise millennial-friendly contracts for the talent acquisition process.

New Strategies in the Recruitment Process

Multiple steps constitute a recruitment process, and some experts may list up to ten steps or more, while some may shorten the process to only a few. After all, there is no correct answer to how many steps are needed for compiling a perfect recruitment process. The process is more dependent on the company's needs and the industry in question. For newly emerging industries in the region with few suitable candidates in the job market, the process must be shortened for the sake of closing a hiring contract; likewise, it makes sense for established industries in regions where this is a lot of competition to lengthen the process. This part of the book will focus on the major recruitment steps that are considered crucial to the success of good hire, and we will also discuss the application of new methods such as LinkedIn in the process. The five significant steps of the recruitment process are planning, sourcing, identifying, screening, and hiring.

HRM in Action—Box 3.3

General Electric's New Recruiting Efforts

Hiring digital talent has become a key focus for General Electric (GE). In the process, agile software development methods are being leveraged to get the right people at the right time in the right place. GE creates a unique agile recruiting framework and establishes a new role known as recruiting scrum master. This new role applies many of the scrum techniques used in software development to recruiting by breaking down massive hiring needs into incremental and iterative steps, where the highest value hiring challenges are addressed first for the customer. Through conducting daily scrum meetings, recruiters are able to deliver talent needs and business objectives within two to six weeks, versus the average ten to fifteen weeks. The recruiting scrum master also supports and coaches the recruiting scrum team to maximize recruiting results through continuous corrections and implementations of scrum processes, while supporting the headcount (business) owner.

Recruiters engage and connect with passive talent—using technology hackathons (engagement activities where candidates come together to solve a business problem by creating technology solutions. Most of the time, they are given a case and asked to create an app or a tech solution to meet the needs of customers. They are assessed on how they interact within a team or their way of coming to conclusion) to source candidates, connecting with talent via their open-source code contributions on open-source code sites like GitHub or interacting through gamification. When candidates join the GE Digital talent community, recruiters can stay connected with them in the process, and deliver to the business a successful candidate in record time. It reduces the time to hire by 70 per cent for in-demand roles in software engineering and commercial software sales. The scrum recruiting process limits work-in-progress and in turn increases the quality of the candidate and decreases time to hire.

Source: Meister, J. (2016, May 13). The workplace as an experience: Three new HR roles emerge. Retrieved from https://www.forbes.com/sites/jeannemeister/2016/05/13/the-workplace-as-an-experience-three-new-hr-roles-emerge/#15e709b628ca

Planning

Planning is the first step in the recruitment process. It is vital for employers first to understand and identify the company's need for talent. HR recruiters should understand the underlying objective of the hiring request from the company's team thoroughly. In fact, some hiring decisions can be automated through the use of software. Let us consider the following example. A start-up company that sells electronics online is experiencing a higher volume of customer complaints on Facebook Messenger, and the social media team of the company is frustrated with the piling up of complaints. Given this, the manager asked the HR team to hire several customer service officers for the company. Frequently the HR department will begin by listing job postings on JobsDB and proceeding the screening steps. Yet they can do better by first identifying the hiring purpose. In this case, hiring new workers is only one of the alternatives, and other options should be considered. For instance, software automation such as

Facebook Chatbot can help to identify customer complaints and forward them directly to the appropriate teams, hence possibly making the hiring of additional social media people redundant. Also, the reasons for having an abnormal number of customer complaints may be attributed to real issues in the company, such as delaying shipment to customers or the high defect rate of the product. Instead of hiring new workers, it would be better for the company to solve the problem, perhaps finding a new shipper agency or improving product design. In short, HR recruiters need to identify the underlying reason for new hires by communicating with the requesting team or manager, in order to formulate better solutions to the problem. The recruitment process is costly both in terms of time and money, and for SMEs which have weaker company branding, it may take months to hire suitable talent. Hence, HR recruiters should move to the next stage of the hiring process only if the hiring is their best option.

Sourcing

According to the definition from the Society of Human Resource Management in the US, sourcing refers to proactively searching for qualified job candidates for current or planned open positions, and candidates include both active and passive job seekers.[32] There are several factors that need to be considered when sourcing candidates, which are the types of candidates needed, the preferences of the hiring authorities or recruiters, record of using the method, and the resources of the recruiter.

Before the emergence of smartphones and social media, the sourcing phase was limited to methods such as employee referral or a newspaper classified ad. However, for the present days, there are new ways emerging thanks to social media. This change in dynamics is more evident in terms of approaching passive candidates. For instance, HR recruiters on LinkedIn can use LinkedIn Talent Solutions in recruiting, which helps to create a pipeline of leads in the recruitment process. Using LinkedIn Talent Solutions, recruiters can spot the best talent by filtering information such as location, industry, and years of experience. After defining the specific group of leads that recruiters want to target, LinkedIn Talent Solutions enables recruiters to identify leading candidates and reach out to them directly through their LinkedIn inboxes. Recruiters can schedule interviews with the leads and have the recruitment process recorded in the software. In short, LinkedIn created a great funnel of recruitment with filters that align with recruiters' needs.

Facebook has been used for recruitment in recent years too. For example, MetLife Hong Kong produced a Facebook promotional video about their openings in 2018. The promotional video is about a young adult finding his purpose in career—he attended a recruitment talk of MetLife by chance and joined the company at last which successfully enabled him to fulfill his aspiration. In this recruitment campaign, MetLife collaborated with career-related Facebook pages such as Madman Monologue, and these pages shared Metlife's video on their pages.[33] Such collaboration can increase the exposure of the video to passive talents, as the Facebook users who follow these career-related pages are usually in the workforce already. Furthermore, MetLife has launched an advertisement on Facebook which is similar to LinkedIn's solution in that it enables advertisers to specifically target Facebook users with criteria such as age, gender, and educational background. The accurate targeting of specific audience is believed to attract a pool of highly related talents for further screening.

In short, talent sourcing in HRM is more diversified than before, with social media being a significant driver for the change.

Identifying and screening

Identifying and screening are two steps that often work hand in hand in the recruitment process. Identification is the recognition of traits that candidates should have, and screening is to filter the pool of candidates based on desirable traits. There are common characteristics that HR recruiters look for—for instance, attitude, ability, creativity, communication skills, and work ethic. After identifying comes the screening stage: for screening candidates, it is typical for big corporates to use ability/aptitude tests and virtual interview software. The distinct advantage of these screening assessments is that companies can filter large numbers of candidates with the least amount of human labour involved. However, the drawback of screening tests is that they may not be tailor-made for the job nature. Thus, an applicant's performance on the test may not truly reflect his or her suitability for the role. HR recruiters should note that these assessment methods need modification from time to time to remain relevant to the job openings and industry trends.

Besides reaching out to candidates, in-company promotion is standard in a lot of companies. It gives junior staff the opportunity to be recognized for their skill sets and selected for senior roles. To create systematic structure, lots of companies have implemented HiPo (high-potential) programmes for internal promotion. A HiPo programme is an in-company training programme that aims to train HiPo employees to take up leadership positions in the company. In fact, high-potential talent is the jewel of a company; a research conducted by The Corporate Executive Board Company and its affiliates (CEB) states that HiPo employees put in 21 per cent more efforts at work than other employees and bring about 91 per cent extra value to their organization.[34] Moreover, to understand the nature of a HiPo employee, we may refer to the viewpoint of the HR director of BMR Advisors, Mandeep Singh, 'High potentials showcase an innate ability to take initiatives and have the true spirit of entrepreneurship in them. This comes along with strong networking abilities like the ability to spread out the word, getting new references and building knowledge through references leveraging and enhancing them at the best.'[35] It is observed that companies around the globe put colossal focus on HiPo programmes, as the average company spends 27 per cent of its learning and development budget on its high-potential programme.

However, there are questions regarding the effectiveness of using HiPo programmes to train future leaders. According to the report from the University of California, 50 per cent of HR professionals surveyed do not have confidence in the programme, and five in six HR managers are dissatisfied with the programme's result.[36] One reason is that there is a large number of dropouts who cannot make it through the programme. Moreover, subjective information is considered when choosing candidates for HiPo programmes; for instances, employees are asked to join the programme just because they have worked for a certain number of years in the organization. In response to these issues, it has been suggested that new criteria be considered when identifying HiPo workers for the programme—namely, aspiration, ability, and engagement.[37] These are the traits that can truly reflect a worker's potential, and reviewing them can increase the success rate of a HiPo programme.

Hiring

Hiring, the last step of the recruitment process, involves briefing, negotiation, and signing a contract with the candidate. This step is of great importance as it will affect the incoming employee's expectation about the company, and also that employee's morale.

When it comes to negotiation, the traditional model of negotiation involves two parties with opposing views and results in concession from one party to the other. In the context of hiring, an employee will try to maximize salary, while a recruiter will try to minimize it. This approach creates a hostile relationship, and each party is perceived as the enemy in a battle in which one or the other will lose. Against this approach, Roger Fisher, one of the co-authors of the book *Getting to Yes*, suggests a win-win approach where parties work as peers rather than enemies.[38] The two sides should first base their stance on reasons instead of emotions, and to work on the agreement that opens to various alternatives—for example, flexible working hours with different payment terms or commission based on the months that clients use the company's service. By flexibly adjusting the salary and benefit terms, both employees' and employers' desires can be well met, and healthy relationships can be maintained, which is beneficial to future collaboration.

Another issue that recruiters should note is the authenticity in negotiating. Early on in the hiring process, both employees and recruiter may exaggerate facts in their own favor. It is normal for candidates to exaggerate their abilities on their resumes and during interviews to increase the odds of being hired, while recruiters may exaggerate the career prospects of the job to make the job more attractive. The hiring stage is the time for both parties to be honest and manage expectations. Recruiters should describe the job nature in detail and honestly relate what to expect on the job, while employees should also communicate with recruiters about their actual abilities and expectations. It is essential to have both the candidate's and recruiter's expectations managed because otherwise the employees will not stay long in the company and the manager will be dissatisfied in the long run. It is always better to put both sides' true intentions on the table before signing the contract.

Building Employer Brand

Building employer brands is usually seen as belonging to marketing rather than human resources, but in today's competitive job market, having a good brand is vital to bringing in excellent applicants. Therefore, human resources should also invest time and energy into building the company's brand. Next we will discuss various methods incorporated in Hong Kong for brand building.

Campus marketing

Most candidates start to shape their perception towards corporates during their undergraduate years. It is a culture for Hong Kong undergraduates students to look for internships and placement as a side hustle during their studies. Thus, students are a perfect target for corporates to focus on in building their brand. As undergraduates have limited knowledge of industry and corporate life, building an attractive company brand implants great first impressions which may last for years ahead. Recognizing this, many companies have allocated resources towards campus promotion and recruitment. For example, companies like Swire and PCCW collaborate with the Chinese University of Hong Kong during the career fair each year. Career talks are organized on campus during the job-seeking season by companies such as Adidas, Disney and Vita. These channels are great ways to convey the brand image to students, and the more extravagant these events are, the more attractive the brand becomes to prospective applicants. For instance, J.P. Morgan Chase gives out leather books with customized names to visitors in the event!

In addition to campus talks and promotion, companies are observed to collaborate with schools to organize case competitions. For example, Deloitte hosts the Deloitte Tax Championship with business schools in Hong Kong; L'Oreal hosts the L'Oreal Brainstorm in sixty countries with 25,000 students participating, and finalists of the competition are invited to Paris to pitch their ideas to industry experts.[39] These global and regional events create brand awareness and interests for the company to university students, which are beneficial in attracting high-quality applicants for future job openings.

Campus events for students not only can increase brand awareness but can also help to convey the company's vision. For instance, Microsoft Hong Kong organizes GirlSpark Camp for female undergraduates in response to the lack of female workers in the information and communications technology industry. The programme offers coaching and career talks to female students, with the goal of increasing women's influence in the industry. This programme both increases the brand presence of Microsoft on campus and shows the company's vision of valuing gender equality.

Social media marketing

While social media such as LinkedIn is a useful tool to spot talent, it can also be used for branding. Companies use social media to shape brand image via soft marketing, which refers to subtle storytelling to convey brand messages. A great example of using this approach is UBS Hong Kong. The company has been actively marketing itself on social media. On Facebook, UBS promoted a video ad which is an interview with the company's summer interns. In the video the summer interns share the knowledge they acquired during the internship, and the quality time they spent with the co-workers, which convey the message that UBS values employees' personal growth. On Snapchat, UBS created sponsored ads that reveal the opportunities of working in UBS, and the video ad shows up when Snapchat users view their friends' 'story' videos. Different from LinkedIn, which is more career-focused, Facebook and Snapchat are informal channels that companies can utilize to create content in a soft-selling tone.

Aside from using social media to launch ads, creating social media legitimacy is also important when it comes to branding. Social media legitimacy can be thought of as the number of followers of the page and the page's content quantity and quality. A higher number of social followers and engagement can establish legitimacy, and the content posted by the company can also increase transparency and convey the company's mission. It is very important to have a legitimate social media page, as a survey shows that 67 per cent of job seekers surveyed use social media to research potential employers.[40]

Building Good Candidate Experience

Branding should not be considered a one-off campaign wherein companies blast through a huge advertising budget. Instead, brand image is built by bits and pieces during the recruitment process. Starting from posting job listings, every action that recruiters do shapes applicants' perception. By creating excellent candidate experience, companies are building the company brand at the same time. Below are a few tips that HR recruiters can take note of so that a positive company brand image can be created when recruiting.

Timely response

Not responding to job applications in a timely fashion will negatively affect candidates' perceptions of the company. If companies take too long to respond to the candidate, it shows to the applicant that his or her application is of low priority and additionally that the company decision-making process is slow. Even if the company eventually offers jobs to those candidates, they may turn away on account of the poor first impression. Even worse, failing to create good candidate experience in this regard reduces the chance of hiring the right talent at all, as good talents prefer companies that are more responsive. Moreover, that negative image may spread by word of mouth from dissatisfied applicants, which can lead to further loss of good applicants in the future.

Interview coaching

Interview coaching is a method mentioned in the book *The Sales Acceleration Formula* by Mark Roberge, the former Chief Revenue Officer of Hubspot. In the early days of the company, there was an urgent need to hire many salespersons, and Mark had come up with the 'interview coaching' method when recruiting.[41] During the interviews, Mark combined interview with coaching to understand a candidate's ability. For instance, Mark would ask the candidate to perform a sales pitch to him pretending that he is a client, and after the pitch, Mark would give feedback and ask the candidate to pitch once again. This is a useful way to assess the candidate's ability to learn from feedback and can create deeper interactions between the interviewer and interviewee. The interviewer will switch roles from interviewer to a peer who helps the candidate to improve, which consequently improves the candidate's impression to the company. This method is also applicable to evaluate other skill sets of the candidate like communication and managerial skills.

Conclusion

Human resource professionals are facing dramatic changes, with technology, social media, and demographic shift being the major driving forces. We are living in an era in which talent acquisition strategies are so multifaceted that they may sometimes be overwhelming. As said early on in this chapter, the 'war for talent' phenomenon will only be intensified in the foreseeable future, and it is our responsibility as HR professionals to devise new strategies in response to such change.

Review Questions

1. Why is talent acquisition important in Hong Kong? Identify at least three factors affecting current talent acquisition strategies in Hong Kong.
2. What are the advantages and drawbacks of using social networking websites for recruitment?
3. Identify the characteristics of millennials in Hong Kong and develop suitable recruitment strategies in your company.
4. Suppose your company needs to recruit twenty university graduates. Identify ways to build your employer branding and discuss ways to improve their candidate experience.
5. Review the recruitment process in your company and identify opportunities of using various HR technologies (e.g. AI, social media, and video interviewing) in the process.

Notes

1. Columbus, L. (2017). IBM predicts demand for data scientists will soar 28% by 2020. *Forbes*. Retrieved from https://www.forbes.com/sites/louiscolumbus/2017/05/13/ibm-predicts-demand-for-data-scientists-will-soar-28-by-2020/#61ced5c7e3bd
2. Marr, Bernard. (2020). The top 10 artificial intelligence trends everyone should be watching in 2020. *Forbes*. Retrieved from https://www.forbes.com/sites/bernardmarr/2020/01/06/the-top-10-artificial-intelligence-trends-everyone-should-be-watching-in-2020/#-3be277e8390b
3. Michaels, E., Handfield-Jones, H., and Axelrod, B. (2001). *The war for talent* (p. 10). Boston: Harvard Business School Press.
4. De Mauro, A., Greco, M., and Grimaldi, M. (2016). A formal definition of big data based on its essential features. *Library Review*, 65 (3), 122–135.
5. Guest author. (2017, Oct. 8). 9 ways to use HR analytics and big data in the workplace. Retrieved from https://blog.cake.hr/8-ways-use-hr-analytics-big-data-workplace/
6. Houston, J., and Bersin, J. (2014). *Talent analytics in practice*. Retrieved from https://www2.deloitte.com/global/en/pages/human-capital/articles/talent-analytics-in-practice.html
7. Houston, J., and Bersin, J. (2014). *Talent analytics in practice*. Retrieved from https://www2.deloitte.com/global/en/pages/human-capital/articles/talent-analytics-in-practice.html
8. The big lie of big data in recruiting. (2017). Retrieved from https://newtonsoftware.com/blog/2017/03/01/big-data-in-recruiting
9. Russell, Stuart J., and Norvig, Peter. (2009). *Artificial intelligence: A modern approach* (3rd ed.). Upper Saddle River: Prentice Hall.
10. 人工智能當面試官 招聘告別偏見機會平等 [Artificial intelligence as interviewer: Farewell to bias, fair interview]. (2016, November 16). Retrieved from http://hk.on.cc/hk/bkn/cnt/finance/20161112/bkn-20161112200800711-1112_00842_001.html
11. Robert Walters. (2018). *Using social media in the recruitment process* [Whitepaper]. Retrieved March 15, 2018, from https://www.robertwalters.com/content/dam/robert-walters/corporate/news-and-pr/files/whitepapers/using-social-media-in-the-recruitment-process.pdf
12. Perez, B. (2015). LinkedIn hits 1 million Hong Kong users amid growing online job hunting. *South China Morning Post*. Retrieved July 1, 2018, from http://www.scmp.com/business/companies/article/1729363/linkedIn-hits-1-million-hong-kong-users-amid-growing-online-job on
13. Robert Walters. (2018). *Using social media in the recruitment process* [Whitepaper]. Retrieved March 15, 2018, from https://www.robertwalters.com/content/dam/robert-walters/

14. Robert Walters. (2018). *Using social media in the recruitment process* [Whitepaper]. Retrieved March 15, 2018, from Robert Walters: https://www.robertwalters.com/content/dam/robert-walters/corporate/news-and-pr/files/whitepapers/using-social-media-in-the-recruitment-process.pdf
15. Indeed hits record 200 million unique visitors [Blog post]. (2016). *Indeed*. Retrieved from http://blog.indeed.com/2016/02/08/indeed-200-million-unique-visitors
16. JobsDB. (2018). *Corporate profile*. Retrieved from https://hk.jobsdb.com/HK/en/StaticContent/AboutUs/Company-Profile.htm
17. Naka, A. (2016). 日本外国特派員協会会見映像オフィシャルサイトFCCJ channel [Video file]. Video posted to https://www.youtube.com/watch?v=nNAnSmgtRsw&t=498s.
18. Minami, K. (2016). Interview with Akiko Naka: Wantedly & the future of labor. Retrieved from https://news.slush.org/news/qa/interview-akiko-naka-wantedly-future-labor/
19. Hays. (2014). Hong Kong job seekers move to mobile job searching and applications. Retrieved from https://www.hays.com.hk/press-releases/HAYS_236536
20. Dimock, M. (2018). Defining generations: Where millennials end and post-millennials begins. Retrieved from http://www.pewresearch.org/fact-tank/2018/03/01/defining-generations-where-millennials-end-and-post-millennials-begin/
21. Horovitz, Bruce. (2012). After gen X, millennials, what should next generation be? *USA Today*. Retrieved March 15, 2018, from http://usatoday30.usatoday.com/money/advertising/story/2012-05-03/naming-the-next-generation/54737518/1
22. 63% of Hong Kong firms adjusted hiring processes for millennials. (2017). *Hong Kong Business*. Retrieved from https://hongkongbusiness.hk/hr-education/in-focus/63-hong-kong-firms-adjusted-hiring-processes-millennials
23. Ipsos Loyalty. (2017). *Research 2017: The millennials influence*. Retrieved from https://www.ipsos.com/sites/default/files/2017-07/vocalink-the-millennial-influence-asia_0.pdf
24. *63% of Hong Kong firms adjusted hiring processes for millennials*. (2017). *Hong Kong Business*. Retrieved from https://hongkongbusiness.hk/hr-education/in-focus/63-hong-kong-firms-adjusted-hiring-processes-millennials
25. Deloitte. (2016). *The 2016 Deloitte millennial survey: Winning over the next generation of leaders*. Retrieved from https://www2.deloitte.com/content/dam/Deloitte/global/Documents/About-Deloitte/gx-millenial-survey-2016-exec-summary.pdf
26. Su, X.Q. (2018). Only one in five Hong Kong millennials expect to stay with the current employer, survey finds. *South China Morning Post*. Retrieved April 1, 2018, from http://www.scmp.com/news/hong-kong/education/article/2128125/only-one-five-hong-kong-millennials-expect-stay-current
27. Su, X.Q. (2018). Only one in five Hong Kong millennials expect to stay with the current employer, survey finds. *South China Morning Post*. Retrieved April 1, 2018, from http://www.scmp.com/news/hong-kong/education/article/2128125/only-one-five-hong-kong-millennials-expect-stay-current
28. Bentley University. (2014). *Millennials at work*. Retrieved from https://www.bentley.edu/newsroom/latest-headlines/mind-of-millennial
29. Siu, P. (2017). Hong Kong employers open to flexible work arrangements but fear system abuse: study. *South China Morning Post*. Retrieved May 2, 2018, from http://www.scmp.com/news/hong-kong/economy/article/2064990/hong-kong-employers-open-flexible-work-arrangements-concerned
30. Xu, S.Q. (2018). Only one in five Hong Kong millennials expect to stay with the current employer, survey finds. *South China Morning Post*. Retrieved May 30, 2018, from http://www.scmp.com/news/hong-kong/education/article/2128125/only-one-five-hong-kong-millennials-expect-stay-current

31. Gopal, S., and Lucy, Daniel. (2016). *Roffey Park Research Report: Working in Asia: Key HR and leadership priorities for 2016*. Retrieved from http://www.roffeypark.com/wp-content/uploads2/Working-in-Asia-2016.pdf
32. The Society of Human Resource Management. (2016). *Recruiting: Sourcing: What is sourcing?* Retrieved from https://www.shrm.org/resourcesandtools/tools-and-samples/hr-qa/pages/whatissourcing.aspx
33. Madman Monologue on Facebook. (2018, May 9). *Buddha Youngster* [Video file]. Video posted to https://www.facebook.com/MadmanMonologue/videos/2071243852904207/
34. Duque, S. (2018). Why Business Agility Starts with High Potential Employees. Retrieved from https://gocatalant.com/business-agility/agility-imperatives/why-business-agility-starts-with-high-potential-employees/
35. Agrawal, L. (2014). A HiPo program is not just any training program. *People Matters*. Retrieved from https://www.peoplematters.in/article/hipo-week/a-hipo-program-is-not-just-any-training-program-5870
36. University of California, Corporate Executive Board. (2014). *The HR guide to identifying high-potentials*. Retrieved from https://www.ucop.edu/human-resources/management-development-program/2014/Donna%20Handout.pdf
37. CEB. (2017). How to design a HIPO strategy in an era of constant change. Retrieved from https://www.cebglobal.com/blogs/high-potential-employees-how-to-design-a-hipo-strategy-in-an-era-of-constant-change/
38. Fisher, R., Ury, William L., and Patton, B. (2011). *Getting to yes: Negotiating agreement without giving in*. New York: Houghton Mifflin.
39. L'Oreal Brandstorm. (2018). *Play. Experiment. Innovate*. Retrieved from https://brandstorm.loreal.com/en/challenges/landing
40. Robert Walters. (2018). *Using social media in the recruitment process* [Whitepaper]. Retrieved March 15, 2018, from https://www.robertwalters.com/content/dam/robert-walters/corporate/news-and-pr/files/whitepapers/using-social-media-in-the-recruitment-process.pdf
41. Roberg, M. (2015). *The sales acceleration formula: Using data, technology, and inbound selling to go from $0 to $100 million*. Hoboken: John Wiley & Sons.

4
Talent Assessment Strategies in Hong Kong

Neil Cowieson, Kit K. W. Lam, and Gloria W. Y. Chan

> **LEARNING OUTCOMES**
>
> By the end of this chapter, readers should be able to
>
> - identify the types of psychometric tests used in Hong Kong;
> - understand the issues related to the use of different assessment tools in Hong Kong;
> - analyse the differences between assessment tools used for selection and recruitment and assessment tools used for development;
> - apply best practice approaches to the provision of feedback and coaching as part of a talent assessment process; and
> - understand the application of new technologies and recent trends in the talent assessment field, such as gamification.

Introduction

The value and impact of talent assessments in the staff selection and development life cycle has been well established for decades. A well-developed and implemented talent assessment process provides organizations with valuable insights to support the selection of the right candidates for the right jobs. It will also support the identification of the right capabilities to be developed through subsequent leadership development initiatives. In this chapter we will discuss some of the core components underlying effective talent assessment design and implementation. First, we will focus on some of the traditional and well-established assessment tools and approaches and their applications in talent assessment, including how to tackle issues such as cheating, feedback, and coaching. Second, we will look into some of the newer and emerging tools and approaches such as gamification, in particular those which ride on the trend towards digitalization and have flourished in recent years.

Psychometric Tests

In Hong Kong one of the most commonly and frequently used types of tools in talent assessment are psychometric tests.[1] Oftentimes, a combination of psychometric tests are used to provide a more comprehensive insight into the characteristics of the test takers. Here are two of the more accurate descriptions which reveal what a psychometric test is:

- A test is a systematic procedure for observing behaviour and describing it with the aid of numerical scales or fixed categories.[2]
- A psychological test is an objective and standardized measure of a sample of behaviour.[3]

Both these widely recognized definitions highlight that a test is only a *sample* of a test taker's behaviour and psychological characteristics.

Although there are many different types of tests available (including IQ tests and achievement tests), the most common types of psychometric tests used in Hong Kong are these:

- Tests of 'maximum performance', such as aptitude and ability tests, where there are correct and incorrect answers.[4] Most aptitude tests try to establish 'can the person do the job?' (or does this person have the intellectual capacity for the job or for acquiring further skills to master higher-level roles?). They generally contain questions in a multiple-choice format and cover mental or intellectual capacity such as numerical, verbal, or abstract reasoning.
- Tests of 'typical performance or behaviour', such as personality questionnaires and interest/motivation inventories.[5] Most personality questionnaires try to reveal 'how will the person do the job?' (or 'how will this person's style and behaviour fit within the role context or the organizational culture?'). They contain 'self-report' items in which candidates are asked to rate statements according to their personality preferences and typical behaviours.

What psychometric tests are used in Hong Kong?

Psychometric test usage has grown most significantly over the last two decades. An increasing number of organizations have started to focus even more closely on identifying better quality candidates in a tightening labour market, and on retaining stronger candidates to better manage their internal talent pools. Of the psychometric tests used in Hong Kong, the most common are aptitude/ability tests and personality questionnaires.

With the rapid development of technology, the majority of psychometric tests have been developed from paper-and-pencil versions to online versions. In recent years, more and more organizations in Hong Kong have switched to using unsupervised online testing owing to the benefits of time and cost efficiency. However, this practice carries significant risks, and many HR professionals and users are concerned about the security of conducting tests without supervision. Organizations in Hong Kong are therefore either reverting to supervised testing or will ask candidates to complete a brief follow-up on-site assessment with supervision to verify the candidates' earlier completed unsupervised online score. In addition, many recent psychometric tests have been developed based on Computer Adaptive Testing (CAT), which allows for dynamic selection of questions from a large set of items based on how each candidate is responding. Research findings suggest that CAT creates more secure and efficient assessments.[6]

Aptitude and ability tests

Although these terms are used interchangeably, tests of 'aptitude' are usually thought of as those tests which predict skill in a specific job-related area, or predict whether skill for a particular job can be *acquired*. On the other hand, tests of 'ability' are usually less job-specific, though job-related intellectual characteristics (e.g. spatial orientation or diagrammatic reasoning) may be measured.

According to the research, aptitude and ability tests have been found to be some of the most predictive assessment tools and are widely used in Hong Kong for the purposes of recruitment, selection, promotion, and development. Some examples of such tests include the following:

- Reasoning tests (verbal reasoning; numerical reasoning; inductive or abstract reasoning)
- Graduate and Managerial Assessment (GMA)
- Raven's Progressive Matrices

Some test publishers produce different language versions of their tests while other tests have been written and developed specifically in other languages like Chinese. Some tests attempt to avoid any language or cultural issues by presenting diagrammatic test items with no verbal content. For example, one of the most widely used types of tests in this category is the Raven's Progressive Matrices, a so-called culture-fair test which has been used and validated across many different cultures and languages.

It is difficult to find conclusive evidence that language is a significant issue in the use of aptitude and ability tests in Hong Kong. One of the critical considerations is the use of norms. Many organizations use tests written in English on non-native English-speaking candidates and gain results which they have found to be highly predictive of executive success in their organization. Though testing candidates in their native language is generally considered to be fairer and more reliable, it is more critical to compare like with like, and therefore it is essential that HR professionals understand the importance of norms in using psychometric tests and check to make sure that the right norms are being used. This is especially important in a multicultural society and business environment such as Hong Kong.

Personality questionnaires

There is a much higher degree of controversy surrounding the use of personality questionnaires in recruitment, selection, and development contexts. However, they continue to be widely used in Hong Kong. Personality questionnaires, when properly designed according to psychometric principles, have been found to yield relatively strong predictions of job success and future potential. Research has reliably shown that personality questionnaires are able to help predict future performance and 'fit' and that they can therefore be valuable assessment tools. There has been considerable debate over the added gains of assessing such proposed culturally specific traits in Hong Kong and over the relative merits of locally developed versus internationally developed personality assessment tools. Some Hong Kong validation studies have shown that there is significant predictive value (e.g. future job performance) to organizations of using well-constructed and properly applied personality questionnaires in recruitment, selection, and development contexts.[7] However, HR professionals should ensure that they are well informed and independently knowledgeable about the various different theories, models, and tools since, invariably, many of the challenges and debates originate from authors and publishers who are selling their own alternative personality models or assessment tools. Some have been known to oversell the benefits and merits with unsubstantiated claims of their accuracy and predictive validity.

There are many different models of personality and many different types of personality questionnaire. The choice of which particular model or questionnaire to use is largely a question of preference by the user as long as the core psychometric properties of the questionnaire are sound and as long as the model or questionnaire is suited to the organization's culture, values, and competency framework. Below are two examples of some of the most reputable personality questionnaires commonly used:

- Occupational Personality Questionnaire (OPQ)
- Hogan Assessment

As with aptitude tests, some publishers produce different language versions of their personality questionnaires, whereas others have written and developed questionnaires which are specifically Chinese in origin. As has been mentioned, this is an area of some debate among researchers, academics, and practitioners. A sound general principle is that measurement of a psychological construct is best done in the individual's own language to avoid bias and misinterpretation. However, many organizations find value from English versions of personality questionnaires even on candidates whose first language is not English. For example, in one financial services firm in Hong Kong, the English-language version of the OPQ was found to predict future managerial success among both Chinese and non-Chinese managers.

The critical factor in such applications is very often, as with aptitude testing, the norms which are being used. For example, it would be inappropriate and unethical (and in some countries illegal according to employment legislation) to compare Hong Kong applicants with a norm group consisting of candidates from the US or the UK. HR professionals should ensure that they are aware of the issues in relation to the norms used with personality questionnaires, as well as what norms are available for each questionnaire. Many test publishers in recent years have attempted to circumvent the importance of local cultural norms by applying 'global' or 'international' norms which amalgamate test results from across very wide and highly diverse populations.

> **HRM in Action Box 4.1**
>
> **Using a Chinese Personality Questionnaire**
>
> As part of a major performance improvement process for a global insurance company, insurance agents of different performance levels were invited to undergo personality assessment using a Chinese personality questionnaire. The personality profiles of insurance agents at different performance levels (e.g. high vs. mediocre) were compared to identify critical gaps that related to the competencies required in the job. In addition to the Dependability aspect of personality, the Interpersonal Relatedness aspects such as Harmony were also found to be associated with high performance. Based upon the gap analysis, areas for improvement among the insurance agents were formulated, which in turn contributed to measurable improvements in the business performance of the insurance company.

While there are many other types of personality questionnaire available, some are not recommended for use in recruitment and selection. For example, the MBTI (Myers–Briggs Type Indicator) and FIRO-B (Fundamental Interpersonal Relations Orientation Behaviour), whose authors and publishers state that their value and the stated intention of their usage is more for applications such as team building, development, or coaching. Others, such as the CPI (California Personality Inventory) and MMPI (Minnesota Multiphasic Personality Inventory) are highly clinical in nature and are not recommended for use in the world of work for HR applications such as talent acquisition or talent management.

Additional guidelines on the use of psychometric testing

HR professionals and users are advised to seek expert advice or consult professional guidelines for selecting assessment methods, particularly in the matter of psychometric tests. An industry standard set of guidelines on the use and application of psychometric tests is offered by the British Psychological Society (www.bps.org.uk). When considering using psychometric tests, HR professionals in Hong Kong should consider either becoming trained themselves in these recognized accreditation standards or consulting with a psychologist. This would ensure that the standards of test use and test choice are maintained at levels which meet recognized industry benchmarks. Where these standards are not maintained, the results of either using poor assessment tools or of applying assessment tools without following recognized guidelines will have serious and dangerous consequences for individual candidates, for the organization as a whole, and for the HR function.

Coping with candidate cheating

One of the most frequent and commonly raised concerns relating to the use of psychometric tests is whether candidates can 'cheat' at the tests, or in the case of personality questionnaires, whether they can 'fake' their profile so as to present a more positive or favourable impression of themselves. In considering the issue of cheating, it is important to distinguish between tests of maximum performance (e.g. ability tests), which have right answers, and tests of typical performance (e.g. personality questionnaires), which do not.[8]

With tests of maximum performance such as ability or aptitude tests, while cheating can occasionally occur in supervised testing settings, its prevalence is likely to be much higher in an unsupervised testing situation. Without a test administrator acting as an invigilator, candidates are much freer to try to subvert the assessment process. Therefore, one of the ways to overcome the potential issue of candidates cheating is to conduct testing in a supervised environment. This may present logistical, financial, or resourcing challenges for some organizations, and in such circumstances it is recommended that if unsupervised (e.g. online) testing has been conducted, that validation of the results is conducted at a later stage (e.g. through a verification test).

On the other hand, with tests of typical performance, such as personality tests, people may try to 'fake good' with their responses to the questionnaire, which can occur whether the questionnaire is administered under supervision or unsupervised. This issue of potential faking, otherwise known as 'motivational distortion', has therefore been a major consideration for HR professionals to take into account in relation to the use of personality tests. It is clear that candidates in a recruitment or selection situation may try to present a picture of themselves through the responses they give to the questionnaire according to what they perceive will be the most favourable profile for the target job position. In the recruitment and selection context, candidates may be 'faking good' in order to try to show higher scores on the dimensions which they assume to be relevant for the job. Studies have found that between 30 and 50 per cent of candidates fake on personality questionnaires in order to get hired and that, in particular, candidates with lower proficiency scores were more likely to fake.[9]

Some studies have examined the factors which underlie faking and have found that faking is influenced by both individual differences and situational characteristics.[10] In terms of individual differences, faking behaviour depends on individuals' ability to fake (e.g. general mental ability and experience), motivation to fake (e.g. age, gender, and personality) and intention to fake (e.g. attitude towards faking). Social desirability and importance of the outcome also have an impact on faking behaviour.

In terms of the impact of faking in personality questionnaires on selection accuracy, while faking affects selection accuracy more for 'lower-scoring' candidates, recent research findings suggest that the overall impact of faking is relatively small. Selection decisions may consequently not be substantially affected by candidates faking.[11] However, it is still important for HR professionals to exercise care in the choice, application, and interpretation of personality questionnaires, given some of the potential risks. With careful risk management, any potential impacts can be significantly minimized.

Whilst studies have found that the susceptibility of personality questionnaires to faking has led to many organizations deciding not to use such tools for selection,[12] many of the more reputable and well-validated personality questionnaires have incorporated techniques to manage or control the impact of faking into their design. For example, measures of 'consistency' and 'social desirability' have generally been found to work more effectively than so-called lie scales, although, like interviews, no method is perfectly free from the impact of 'positive self-reporting'. As a result, HR professionals and users should be especially careful when selecting personality questionnaires to investigate and understand what methodology has been employed by the publisher of the tool to try to detect or control for 'faking'. For example, HR professionals and users can review 'consistency' measure scores: if the score is very low, they may ask the candidate to redo the personality questionnaire.

Recruitment and selection research has found that there are differences in the degree of faking good among samples of non-applicants, applicants, and incumbents.[13] Individuals who are motivated to fake (e.g. applicants) are more likely to fake good. In light of this, HR professionals and users should be careful to choose the right norms, based on samples of representative applicant candidates, in order to avoid bias against any particular group. HR professionals are also recommended to validate a candidate's responses to the questionnaire through a follow-up interview at a later stage of the selection process. In addition, positioning the assessment in an appropriate context for the candidate can help to deter candidates from distortion and cheating. The mutual benefits of accurate testing (i.e. to both the applicant and the organization) should be explained to the candidate before embarking on the test. An accurate result will help the employer to identify the best candidates but will also help candidates to avoid positions for which they would not be suited.[14]

Assessment Centres/Development Centres

When assessment centres were first introduced early in the twentieth century (for example, to select army officers) there was frequently a physical location where the assessment took place. The term *assessment centre* is now commonly recognized to mean a *process* which is used to identify behaviours for the purposes of recruitment, selection, and promotion. Development centres are a further application with a very different purpose, but with a similar methodology. A development centre is a process which is used primarily on internal staff (predominantly managerial and professional staff) to aid the identification of competency strengths and development areas. It is intended to support development planning, career development, and succession and talent management.

Both assessment centres and development centres could include many different varieties or flexible applications of a number of fundamental core principles. Most assessment centres and development centres which are used by organizations in Hong Kong involve a number of candidates/participants completing a number of exercises, leadership/business simulations, and tests, while being observed by a number of trained assessors/observers. The tests and exercises are chosen or designed to reflect and simulate situations and activities which are likely to be encountered in a target position or a future role.

Assessment centres and development centres provide valuable insights for organizations in relation to talent assessment and development. In terms of the accuracy and value which they bring to an organization's HR processes, meta-analysis research findings have consistently shown that among the wide variety of assessment tools and methodologies available, assessment and development centres have the highest validity (Figure 4.1).

Figure 4.1: Validity of assessment and development centres

ACs / DCs: A Well Proven, Reliable & Valid Methodology

"ACs / DCs have been found to have high validity value in predicting future potential, performance and career advancement"

Correlation / Validity Coefficients (Range from 0.00 to 1.00)

- Random Prediction (0.00)
- Perfect Prediction (1.00)

Low validity:
- Graphology (0.02)
- Education qualifications (0.10)
- Years of job experience (0.18)

Low to medium validity:
- Reference checks (0.26)
- Unstructured interviews (0.38)
- Personality tests (0.39)

Medium to high validity:
- Assessment / Development Centres (0.65)

High validity:
- Structured interviews (0.51)
- Ability tests (0.53)

Source:
- F.L. Schmidt, & J. E. Hunter (1984). Validity and utility of alternative predictors of job performance. *Psychological Bulletin*, 96(1), 72-98.
- M. Smith (1988). Calculating the sterling value of selection. *Guidance and Assessment Review*, 4(1), 6-8.
- F.L. Schmidt, & J. E. Hunter (1998). The validity and utility of selection methods in personnel psychology: practical and theoretical implications of 85 years of research findings. *Psychological Bulletin*, 124(2), 262-274.
- I.T. Robertson (2001). A critique and standardization of meta-analytic validity coefficients in personnel selection. *Journal of Occupational and Organizational Psychology*, 74, 235-277.
- I.T. Robertson, & M. Smith (2001). Personnel selection. *Journal of Occupational and Organizational Psychology*, 74, 441-472.

Source: Meta-analysis studies.

How are assessment centres and development centres used in Hong Kong?

Assessment centres are a relatively common method of selecting candidates in Hong Kong, particularly among larger organizations. The most frequent application is for graduate selection. However, the methodology is becoming increasingly popular and increasingly broad in application, particularly for wider recruitment scenarios such as evaluating mid-career hires. In Hong Kong development centres are also widely used. Model examples of best practice approaches to combining assessment and development centres for the purposes of recruitment, promotion, and development are found in large organizations across many industries.

Given the increasing trend towards the adoption of artificial intelligence (AI) and machine learning both in Hong Kong and globally, an increasing number of organizations in Hong Kong are considering the application of digital technology in conducting assessment and development centres. Utilizing the latest technology is helping organizations to ease the administrative burden, and to save time, costs, and resources in the assessment and reporting of candidates'/participants' behaviour and in the feedback processes. There is also a growing interest in Hong Kong in conducting 'virtual' assessment and development centres which allow candidates/participants to participate from remotely dispersed geographic locations. The benefits of applying AI, and more recently virtual reality (VR), technology when conducting assessment and development centres have also started to be recognized in relation to creating a positive 'candidate/participant experience'. These technology-related benefits have been further enhanced very recently by the adoption of 'gamification'.

Differences between assessment centres and development centres

While assessment and development centres share many similarities such as using multiple assessors/observers and using multiple exercises to evaluate the candidates'/participants' behaviours, there are some critical factors which differentiate assessment centres and development centres and are vital for HR professionals to know and understand:[15]

- **Purpose.** Assessment centres are used principally for selection, recruitment, fast-tracking, and promotion. Development centres, on the other hand, are most often used to support developmental objectives relating to the identification of potential and training and development needs.
- **Outcomes.** In an assessment centre, based on all the evidence gathered from observations of candidates in all the various situations, the assessors confer together to agree on a final rating (and invariably a pass/fail outcome) for each candidate. However, there are no pass/fail outcomes in development centres, and scores or ratings may not even be allocated to participants. Development centres focus more on collecting observations and evaluations to provide feedback to the participants on their comparative strengths and development needs rather than on making 'yes/no' or 'in/out' decisions.
- **Duration and cost.** Development centres are usually longer in duration and therefore have a higher cost, since the process will include feedback to the participants, and subsequent developmental activities.
- **Ownership.** While the ownership of the outcomes from an assessment centre lie more with the organization for selection and placement purposes, in a development centre participants should have the greater ownership of the outcomes, in particular, for acting on the feedback with follow-up development planning and for driving their own developmental journeys (with appropriate support of HR and line management) using the feedback outcomes which they have gained from the development centre.
- **Feedback and development.** Assessment centres may or may not include a feedback session to the candidate, since the objective is mostly to help with organizational decision-making and hence arranging individual feedbacks for external candidates can be time-consuming, resource intensive, and expensive. However, best-practice organizations do offer to provide feedback to candidates (e.g. a brief written summary or an offer of a brief verbal feedback call), given the importance of generating a positive candidate experience to upholding and maintaining a market-leading reputation and strong employer branding. On the contrary, for a 'true' development centre, feedback is a 'must-have' element without which the process would not be able to be referred to as a 'development' centre. Best-practice organizations will also provide follow-up developmental activities after the development centre, such as coaching and other leadership development initiatives (see the section on Feedback and Coaching on p. 76).

Though both assessment and development centres can have significant pay-offs—not only to individual candidates and participants but also to the organization—it is important that the objectives are clarified and the use of the outcomes and access to the results carefully planned and thought through before use; this will ultimately be determined by the stated objectives for the process and the desired outcomes. HR professionals must ensure that the distinction between an assessment centre and a development centre is made clearly and that the right process and methodology are applied for the appropriate objective and desired outcome. Otherwise, the outcome will risk being of questionable value either to the individual or to the organization; in the worst-case scenario, if the right process and design approach is not applied for the right application, the outcome could even be damaging to both parties. Given some of the differences outlined above, language and terminology become important in relation to reinforcing the objectives and intended outcomes. In an assessment centre the terms 'candidates' and 'assessors' are most often used, while in a development centre the most appropriate terms are 'participants' and 'observers/coaches'.

Assessment and development centres: Best practices

Some pointers are presented below to outline some of the best practices for designing and implementing assessment and development centres. These follow established best practice guidelines (e.g. *Guidelines and Ethical Considerations for Assessment Centre Operations* by the International Congress on Assessment Centre Methods and *Design, Implementation and Evaluation of Assessment and Development Centres* by the British Psychological Society).[16] HR professionals are encouraged to refer to established best-practice guidelines such as these for further details. It is also recommended that HR professionals seek further advice and guidance from assessment and development professionals, such as chartered organizational psychologists who specialize in this field. Assessment and development centres which are not designed in accordance with the above principles are unlikely to be valid and may not bring value to the organization.

- **Use multiple criteria.** Assessment and development centres should be designed on the basis of a carefully selected range of job-related criteria or competencies. Most organizations in Hong Kong use a defined set of behavioural or leadership competencies. The general principle is that between six to eight competencies is the ideal number which can be assessed reliably in an assessment or development centre.
- **Use multiple assessors/observers.** The value of assessment and development centres comes from the use of a group of assessors/observers rather than relying on the more subjective views of just one individual. Ideally, each assessor/observer should be able to observe each participant in at least one of the various situations in which they are asked to perform, to aid objectivity. Research suggests that the best combination of assessors/observers is internal line managers coupled with HR professionals or psychologists.[17] This tends to produce the most accurate results and the most valuable predictions of the candidates'/participants' future performance. The assessors/observers must be sufficiently trained in the methodology and in the specific exercises which they will assess to ensure that their judgements and evaluations of the candidates'/participants' behaviour is benchmarked to the appropriate levels and standards and that this is as consistent as possible from one assessor/observer to the next.
- **Use behavioural assessment guides and structured rating scales.** Instead of simply relying on the assessors'/observers' qualitative observations and

'feelings' about the candidates/participants, the assessors/observers should always be trained thoroughly in behavioural assessment skills and techniques (e.g. the observe, record, classify, and evaluate (ORCE) process) and in the evaluation of assessment exercises with the use of structured rating scales in order to objectively assess each candidate/participant.

- **Ensure an appropriately qualified centre manager is appointed.** There should be an 'independent' party who is able to provide consistent benchmarking and comparisons relative to the competency standards as well as a reference to past candidates/participants to ensure consistency and fairness of observations and evaluations made by the assessors/observers.
- **Conduct a thorough 'integration session'.** At the end of the assessment/development centre, assessors/observers should gather together and review their evaluations and judgements in order to establish a shared consensus on the performance of each candidate/participant. This ensures that the judgements are as fair as possible and are reached through an objective and balanced discussion and review.
- **Decide on a group versus individual process.** Most assessment/development centres are conducted on a group basis, especially for more junior candidates/participants such as graduates. For more senior candidates/participants, organizations will sometimes assess on an individual basis (typically referred to as an 'executive assessment' process) which may also bring some cost advantages (see the section on Leadership Assessment on p. 73).
- **Use the right combination of assessment exercises.** The selection of exercises, business cases, leadership simulations, and testing is critical to the effectiveness of the assessment/development centre. The general guiding principle is that there should be a minimum of at least two assessment exercises per competency to be assessed.
- **Balance the timetable.** Designers should ensure that the 'loading' of the exercises is balanced sufficiently across the timetable for both the candidates/participants and assessors/observers. For example, it would be desirable to allow sufficient time between exercises for the assessors/observers to complete their evaluations, judgements, and ratings before moving on to the next exercise.
- **Decide on feedback processes.** Ideally, feedback sessions would be organized during or after the assessment/development centres to share with the candidates/participants on their performance. As described earlier, in the case of a development centre, feedback is a critical and essential element in the process and is often combined with follow-up development planning support and coaching for the participants. Feedback should be provided promptly after the centre and should cover the key themes which emerged from the assessment/development centre (ideally structured around competencies or leadership framework) as well as the overall outcomes from the process and recommended next steps for the candidate/participant (see the section on Feedback and Coaching on p. 76). In a development centre, feedback and coaching is often provided during the process (i.e. through immediate post-exercise feedback and coaching from an observer).

The choice of exercises which are typical of assessment and development centres in Hong Kong cover behavioural simulation exercises, leadership business cases, role-plays, aptitude tests, personality questionnaires, and interviews of the following main types:

- **Business case exercises (sometimes referred to as in-box exercises).** Candidates/participants are presented with written information and are required to analyse this information and to identify recommendations within a set time (the information is increasingly delivered online using e-enabled 'in-tray' software). This information may cover letters, memos, emails, financial information, market or customer information, product data, competitor data, papers and reports, etc.
- **Analysis presentation exercises.** Candidates/participants are presented with information and given a set time to analyse it before being required to deliver a verbal presentation to the assessors/observers based on their analysis of the information.
- **Group discussions.** Candidates/participants are given a topic to discuss as a group while being watched by the assessors/observers.
- **Role-plays.** Candidates/participants are asked to play a role in an interactive meeting with other 'colleagues' or 'stakeholders' (played by the assessors/observers or role players). The typical interactive meeting scenarios which are used include a peer meeting where the candidate/participant is required to resolve a conflict or to facilitate collaboration during the meeting to reach consensus; a subordinate meeting where the candidate/participant is required to 'coach' the subordinate or deal with a performance issue; and a customer interaction where the candidate/participant is required to deal with a customer issue such as a customer complaint; an incident situation where the candidate/participant is required to manage the incident or to come up with an incident handling plan, and present a corporate statement before addressing questions from the media or the public.

In the majority of assessment and development centres, the cases, exercises, and simulations are designed to provide challenge and stretch to the candidates/participants. In an assessment centre the exercises are typically set within the context of the target role, job, or level. In a development centre, the exercises are typically designed to reflect the requirements and expectations of at least one level higher than the participants' current level.

HRM in Action—Box 4.2

Selection Process of a Global Manufacturing Company

A global manufacturing organization used an assessment centre to recruit MBA qualified candidates. Junior graduates were being recruited at entry level for the organization's talent pipeline, and internal development, supplemented with mid-career hires, was used to further support the talent flow and development at more senior levels. As part of an enhanced talent strategy it was identified that MBA graduates with between two and three years of working experience would be recruited to further fuel business growth and expansion in Hong Kong,

Asia-Pacific, and globally. Following approaches and talks at selected business schools, applicants were first screened using a formal online application form and self-assessment. Shortlisted candidates were then asked to submit a video presentation of themselves which was reviewed by an internal panel. Further to this shortlisting, candidates completed online verbal and numerical aptitude tests and a personality questionnaire before being invited to an assessment centre. At the assessment centre, candidates completed custom-designed assessment exercises set in a global organizational context. These included a written analysis exercise, a presentation, a group discussion, a peer meeting, and a leadership role play. The one-day assessment centre culminated in a competency-based interview before the assessor integration session during which four of the sixteen candidates attending the assessment centre were selected for job offers. This combination of screening tools to shortlist suitable candidates, followed by a more in-depth face-to-face assessment, led to a lower rejection rate at final interview stage and to a higher success rate among selected candidates.

Leadership Assessment

In the context of talent assessment, leadership assessment can be defined as a process to identify individual strengths and development needs as they pertain to leadership success and how such characteristics fit into a given leadership position's requirements. In Hong Kong some of the commonly used methods and tools for leadership assessment include the following:

- Structured interviews—such as competency-based interviews, behavioural interviews, and career dialogue interviews.
- Psychometric tests and profiling instruments—such as personality tests, ability tests (as described earlier), and other profiling tools such as motivation and values inventories and EQ profiling.
- Behavioural simulation exercises (as described earlier)
- Multisource feedback—such as 360-degree feedback instruments and structured interviews with line managers and key stakeholders.

To increase the comprehensiveness of the leadership assessment and the overall validity of the leadership assessment process, a combination of the above tools is often used. For example, in a global utility company with a major presence in Hong Kong, an Individual Executive Leadership Assessment Process has been developed to assess senior-level talent in the company, as well as external senior executive candidates for targeted 'strategic hires'. The process includes a combination of a competency-based interview, a career interview, a personality test, a motivation profiling tool, ability tests, behavioural simulation exercises, and an EQ-based 360. The process yields key insights into individual strengths and development needs in order to support succession planning and individual leadership development for senior-level talent. The process helps to prepare them for succession into strategic leadership roles in the company. Individual-based feedback and coaching are provided to support the participants' development. In another example, a global automotive parts manufacturer has implemented a leadership assessment process which consists of a competency-based interview and personality and ability tests to support hiring decisions for senior-level leadership. The same benchmarked process is applied globally, including for the recruitment of senior-level leaders in China.

How to select the right method for leadership assessment?

Much of this chapter concentrates on how HR professionals can differentiate between the different types of assessment methods and between good and bad assessment tools. HR users of assessment tools should also consider how and when to use these types of methods in order to gain the most value for the organization as well as for the participants/candidates. Some of the key considerations and a brief outline of the guiding principles to consider are provided here.

Job criteria

It is critical that a thorough understanding of the key job criteria to be assessed is gained prior to the use of any assessment method. The best approach is to identify clear *competencies* (captured in a 'success profile') for the role/job level on the basis of a clear *job analysis*. Success profiles and competency definitions should incorporate clear descriptions of the behaviours which are specific to the role or job level in question. This will not only help in choosing and designing the assessment methods but also in evaluating candidates'/participants' results by providing a benchmarking or scoring framework against which to compare candidates'/participants' performance.

Evaluation of assessment methods

After ensuring a clear understanding of the key job criteria to be assessed for the purpose of recruitment, selection, or development, HR professionals can evaluate each assessment method based on these criteria:[18]

- Validity—HR professionals should consider whether the assessment method is accurate and valid for predicting job performance in relation to the role, level, job nature, or behaviours and competencies identified in the success profile or competency definitions.
- Adverse impact—HR professionals should consider if the members of specific groups (e.g. minorities, women, and employees in certain age categories) are found to systematically score lower than others. It is recommended that HR professionals in Hong Kong consult Equal Opportunities Commission (EOC) requirements to ensure adverse impact is not encountered, in particular for members of any protected groups (i.e. those who are protected under Hong Kong's anti-discrimination ordinances).
- Cost—HR professionals may need to consider whether the assessment method is cost effective by considering the expense of developing, administering, and maintaining the assessment. For example, assessment and development centres have much higher costs than other methods such as interviews. Therefore, most organizations adopting assessment centres in Hong Kong use them at a later stage in the selection process for entry-level positions such as graduate trainees

(i.e. after screening out unfavourable candidates). Similarly, for senior leadership positions, executive assessments are often conducted with the final one or two candidates to support the final-stage decision-making. Since the costs of wrong hiring or placement (or investment in developing senior-level potential) at senior levels are far more significant, this often justifies using a more elaborate comprehensive approach to leadership assessment—for example, with the incorporation of multiple tools—despite the higher costs.
- Candidate/participant reactions—HR professionals should also consider the candidate/participant reactions to the assessment. Steps should be taken to ensure a positive 'candidate/participant experience' (through briefings, prior information, preparation, clear communication over the purpose and outcomes, etc.) since this can determine whether candidates/participants react positively or negatively to the assessment. Such steps are also critical in determining the candidates'/participants' acceptance towards the outcomes as well as their perceptions of the process and the organization.

Getting buy-in for leadership assessment

In order to help their organizations to realize the benefits of using a more structured and scientific approach towards leadership assessment, HR professionals in Hong Kong are advised to invest effort in the following areas:

- Advise senior management on the benefits to be gained from using more structured and scientific approaches to leadership assessment. For example, some organizations use case studies to showcase successful implementation (e.g. making reference to well-known companies with strong employer branding, or companies from the same industry, can be a convincing way to sell the benefits).
- Quantify and evaluate the impact of 'good' assessment tools, and the greater returns which could be expected from investing in better assessment tools in the leadership assessment process such as cost savings, productivity gains, motivation and retention, and senior leadership succession planning.
- Recognize the differences between the 'good and the bad' of the different assessment methods available and advise senior management accordingly and share the perils and dangers of getting it wrong.
- In addition to getting senior management's buy-in to the leadership assessment process, it is equally important to get the participants'/candidates' buy-in in order to yield the best benefits that the process will bring to the organization, and to enhance employer branding. For example, 'leadership assessment' can be used as a diagnostic tool to support targeted, effective leadership development, to help identify leadership potential, and to support succession planning. In all cases, it is important to share the objectives of the leadership assessment process openly and transparently with participants in advance, as well as what sort of activities they will be participating in, and how the results would be used to support their development. Similarly, when leadership assessment is used for recruitment and selection, the briefing provided to candidates should outline the stages and tools to be used and the intended usage of the results.

Feedback and Coaching

'Feedback' is an integral part of the success of using leadership assessment to drive effective leadership development activities. After participants have undergone the leadership assessment process, insights into their individual strengths and development needs are typically captured in the form of a written assessment/development report. In addition to providing the participant with this report, it is recommended to arrange a feedback discussion with the participant. The aim of this feedback session is to provide further guidance to support the participant in accurately interpreting the assessment outcomes, facilitating their reflections on their key learning from the process, and enhancing their self-awareness of their own strengths and development needs. The ideal goal is that based on the feedback, the participant will be equipped with 'what to do about the results'. The feedback has been found to be essential in enhancing participants' commitment to taking action to leverage their strengths and to further improve on their development needs. The feedback session should therefore be followed by concerted and structured development planning involving regular reviews of the participants' progress on their development plan, in conjunction with their line managers and facilitated by HR.

Recent research has shown that more than 50 per cent of leaders do not regularly reflect on what is going well for them at work.[19] Feedback sessions therefore provide the opportunity for participants to actively reflect on their own performance through structured observations from the assessment outcomes. Feedback should therefore not only focus on participants' areas for improvement but also recognize their strengths or what they did well in the assessment. Since acknowledging success reinforces further success, this enhances the participant's confidence and motivation and inspires participants to continue working towards their goals. Feedback sessions should therefore ensure a well-balanced discussion of both the participant's strengths and development needs since this can promote loyalty, commitment, and retention. Handled well, an in-depth, constructive feedback discussion sends a strong message to participants that the organization supports their development and invests in their career progression.

Feedback can be arranged in different formats, the most common (and most desirable) approach in Hong Kong being through a face-to-face meeting. On the other hand, when the feedback involves parties who are not in the same physical location, other formats such as phone, WebEx, or video conferencing can be arranged. Typically, it is recommended that the first feedback meeting is arranged on a one-to-one basis between the feedback provider and the participant. This provides a private and confidential environment in which the participants feel safe and comfortable to share their own reflections, comments, and questions about the results with the feedback provider. The feedback provider should be a professional who is knowledgeable about the leadership assessment process and who has expertise in the assessment methods used, as well as extensive experience of handling feedback discussions. For example, in a typical individual leadership assessment, the assessor is an internal leadership development specialist, a consultant, or a psychologist who has conducted all the activities with the participant. The same assessor should also be an accredited user of any psychometric tools which are used as part of the leadership assessment. If leadership assessment activities are conducted in the form of an assessment or development centre, it is recommended that one of the centre assessors/observers be the feedback provider.

The feedback provider should share the consensus observations and recommendations from the whole assessor/observer team, using insights generated from the integration discussion meeting held at the end of the centre and before the feedback session.

Immediate feedback and coaching

In most cases, feedback is arranged at the same time as sharing the assessment report with the candidate/participant. During the feedback discussion, significant value for the candidate/participant comes from providing guidance on interpreting the assessment report and generating developmental insights from the report. On the other hand, significant developmental value for participants also comes from providing feedback on an immediate 'real-time' basis right after the leadership assessment activities. Where the objective of the process is developmental, this is a highly recommended feature to be incorporated in the design of the leadership assessment process, in particular for a development centre. For example, in a global insurance company with a major presence in Hong Kong, the element of 'immediate feedback and coaching' was built in as one of the key features of a 'development centre' which was designed to support leadership development of middle- to senior-level talents. Through careful design of the development centre timetable, specific time slots were allocated immediately after each of the simulation exercises for the observers to provide immediate feedback of 'what the talent did well' and 'what the talent could have done differently'. This was accompanied by coaching and guidance to help the participants to self-reflect on their strengths and development areas. In addition, a further dedicated time slot was arranged so that participants could provide 'peer feedback' to each other, immediately after a simulation activity which was conducted on a 'group' basis. Further coaching and guidance was also provided to participants on giving and receiving feedback. This provided significant reinforcement to participants of the developmental objectives and outcomes of the centre, and helped to overcome any potential perceptions of the process being seen as a 'pass or fail' experience in their careers. Based on the evaluation conducted on the development centre outcomes and the participants' reactions, their feelings of engagement and motivation were significantly positively affected by the design of the process, specifically the nature of the feedback and coaching which they received.

Later in this chapter, we will describe how other emerging assessment approaches are being applied to enable the provision of immediate feedback.

Coaching: Developmental support after leadership assessment

Sharing assessment results and feedback with participants helps them gain a clearer idea of what they need to focus on for their development and what their strengths are. In many cases, participants may benefit from receiving continuous further guidance and support to achieve leadership success. Coaching is often arranged as one of the development initiatives after a leadership assessment has been conducted in order to support leaders in their ongoing development journey. Coaching can also support developmental performance enhancement and serve as a motivation-enhancing management practice. The coach can help to keep track of the participant's development progress and can provide support and advice to the participant, while the participant is accountable for achieving the goals.[20] Some organizations in Hong Kong now provide coaching in conjunction with leadership assessment in order to provide continuous development support to their leadership talents.

While the traditional approach to coaching is face-to-face, the dynamic work nature in Hong Kong (e.g. 'fly-in, fly-out' work schedules) may sometimes make this difficult for leaders, especially for senior managers. So leaders are increasingly employing alternative formats for coaching, such as telephone, video conferencing, Skype, and email—sometimes collectively referred to as 'e-coaching'. Although there may be some concerns over the lack of visual cues in e-coaching, research has found that the experience of using e-coaching has been positive for both coaches and those being coached. The research has also revealed that supplementing telephone coaching with text-based tools can enhance the coaching process.[21] Combining e-coaching with one or more face-to-face coaching sessions has found to be the most beneficial in relation to the coaching outcomes.

Coaching arrangement: Practical considerations

The pointers below may help HR professionals and organizations to consider what and how to arrange coaching, as one of the ways of providing developmental support to participants after conducting a leadership assessment:[22]

- Timing of coaching—HR professionals should consider when to start the coaching sessions, depending on the coachee's identified development needs and engagement in other developmental activities. In most cases, in order to effectively support the coachee's development plan after the leadership assessment, coaching is best arranged as soon as possible.
- Duration of coaching—depending on the participants' needs, generally speaking, HR professionals should arrange the coaching for a period of at least six months. More frequently scheduled coaching sessions may be beneficial immediately after the leadership assessment. This may 'taper' to relatively less frequently towards the end of the overall coaching period, in order to follow up on the participant's development progress and to provide continuous support for his or her development journey.
- Selection of coaches—HR professionals should select coaches with the specific skillsets which match the coachee's needs (e.g. the identified strengths and development needs emerging from the leadership assessment). Besides the coach's skill sets, the personal connection between the coach and coachee is important in determining the effectiveness of the coaching. In many organizations in Hong Kong the coachee is given two to three options of coaches with whom the coachee can have a 'chemistry session'. In most cases, external coaches are used in order to maintain complete confidentiality. While an internal coach may bring knowledge of the organization, some coachees express concerns over the confidentiality of the discussion which may undermine the impact and benefits of the coaching.
- Contracting—the organization, coach, and coachee should reach an agreement on the confidentiality, desired outcomes and progress measurements. During this stage, it is best to outline the key duties and responsibilities of all

parties involved in the coaching process. HR professionals should share the organization's expectations from the coaching programme and highlight the key strengths and development needs of the coachee, as indicated from the leadership assessment results. HR professionals should also clearly state the confidentiality principles to the coach and coachee and ensure that all parties are clear and comfortable with the arrangements.

- Involvement of the organization—after the contracting stage, it is recommended that the ownership for driving the coaching activities should be left in the hands of the coach and the coachee. Some suggest that the less involved the organization is in the coaching process, the more freely the coachee is able to share personal work issues with the coach, which makes the coaching more effective. Nonetheless, HR professionals may play a support role with a regular 'check-in' to ensure the programme is progressing as planned. On rare occasions HR professionals may need to intervene, for example if the coaching outcomes are not evident or if the programme has stalled or derailed). In many Hong Kong companies who have used coaching as one source of developmental support after a leadership assessment, the coach is asked to provide regular updates of the coaching progress; these are high-level only and do not divulge confidential topics and information discussed in each coaching session.

Gamification

Earlier in this chapter, we focused on 'tried-and-tested' approaches to talent assessment and discussed their applications in recruitment and leadership assessment. On the other hand, increasing competition to recruit top-tier talent continues to present challenges to organizations who are looking for new and innovative ways to attract, engage, and assess potential candidates. As a result, many organizations are integrating the latest technologies into their recruitment processes in order to hire the right talent.[23] Some organizations have turned to the use of *gamification* in the assessment of talents. This phenomenon derives from the popularity of online/mobile games which have shown to drive problem-solving and enhanced learning.[24]

Gamified assessment

Gamification in assessments allows organizations to test candidates' soft and technical skills as well as behavioural traits via interactively engaging scenarios related to particular job roles.[25] It is important to note that a gamified assessment is not just a game; it is the modification of a pre-existing form of assessment with the addition of game-like elements.[26] Moreover, there is a difference between a gamified assessment and a game-based assessment. The distinction lies in the initial intent of the test. A gamified assessment is created mainly for recruitment purposes, but also appeals to candidates. In contrast, a game-based assessment is a 'game' that is designed for the candidate's enjoyment rather than to assist recruiters in assessing a candidate's skills, competencies, and personality traits.[27] Although both gamified assessments and game-based assessments incorporate game-like elements into a process which is not otherwise a 'game', the information that they provide organizations with on prospective talents is very different.

Potential benefits of gamified assessment

According to service providers in the field, besides the use of gamified assessments being a rising trend, organizations are seeing tangible benefits in relation to enhancement of their recruitment processes. Some of the benefits are listed below:

- Better assessment of skills—organizations often assess potential talent through the use of tests to determine the role and cultural fit of the candidate. This can sometimes become a tedious task as it involves the application of several different tests. However, a gamified assessment can be designed to incorporate a real-life representation of the job role and work environment. Through a gamified assessment, an employer can view a candidate's abilities (e.g. working memory, problem-solving, and decision-making) and behavioural traits in 'live-action' situations.[28] In addition, given some of the concerns with regard to the use of conventional assessment tools (such as perceived risks concerning 'faking' and vulnerability to cheating) some argue that the chance for gamified assessment tools to elicit genuine answers and responses is higher, since the context is set to replicate a real-life scenario and the apparent perception is that 'faking' is less easy.[29]
- Appeal to candidates—the use of gamified assessments may make the recruitment process more engaging. Some therefore suggest that this can potentially lead to the attraction of a wider range of interested candidates, particularly from the pool of 'millennials' and 'Generation Z' talent, given the constant interaction with technology among these age groups, who view technology to be an essential element to life.[30] An organization that embraces the use of technology may appear to external candidates to be more modern and may therefore appeal to the priorities of these age groups. Additionally, since one of the challenges often faced in the recruitment process is having to filter through a high volume of candidates, the use of gamification is also seen as a way of automatically 'pipelining' candidates based on the assessment data collected.[31]
- Enhance the 'candidate experience'—in a typical job search situation, candidates often speak of having to endure the experience of completing countless standardized assessments which can become 'dull and tiresome'. Gamified assessments can offer interactive and dynamic content that is potentially more enjoyable for candidates, encouraging them to become more immersed in the assessment process and more engaged with the organization.[32] In addition, some argue that when candidates are more engaged, they will be motivated to be more truthful in their replies allowing the recruiter and the organization to gain a more accurate view of the candidate.[33]
- Branding—the use of gamified assessments is an opportunity for an organization to build on its brand and value proposition, especially towards younger 'millennials' and 'Generation Z' talents.[34] Since gamification is still relatively new in the field of talent assessment, organizations who choose to use this approach often quickly gain public attention. In one leading technology company, for example, a gamified coding challenge was created in order to scout new talent. This challenge proved to be extremely popular among the technology community, making the company a highly sought-after employer and increasing its

attractiveness to candidates.[35] Designing a gamified assessment can therefore help organizations to create a bigger name for themselves and to appeal to a larger talent pool.

> **HRM in Action Box 4.3**
>
> **Using a Game in the Recruitment Process**
>
> A global professional services firm set a recruitment goal in one of its European operations: to more fully engage its pool of candidates during the search process. Traditionally, candidates would spend less than fifteen minutes on the firm's career website, so the objective was to attract more suitable, qualified candidates. This resulted in the development and launch of a game which allows candidates to virtually test their readiness and suitability for working at the firm by working in teams to solve real-world business scenarios. The game presents users with tasks based on competencies such as building business acumen, increasing digital skills, and embracing relational skills. The results showed that candidates who played the game were better prepared for the 'live' face-to-face interviews. New hires with experience of playing the game also found the onboarding process easier, as they had already experienced the company culture through the game. Overall, the game increased the number of applicants by 190 per cent, with 78 per cent of those completing the game subsequently interested in joining the firm.

How can gamification enhance the assessment experience?

As described earlier in this chapter, the use of gamified assessments can help organizations to enhance the experience for candidates going through an assessment process. Studies show that a candidate's reaction to assessments is associated with perceptions of the organization's image such as perceived attractiveness and fairness.[36] When perceptions are explored further, the following elements of gamified assessments have been found to foster some of the most positive reactions from candidates:

- Interactive challenges
- Unlocking of different levels
- Immediate feedback
- The feeling of being taken seriously

The last point mentioned is an interesting one. Although a partial reason for using gamified assessments is to enhance candidates' enjoyment, it appears that the experience still needs to convey a certain level of seriousness. Therefore, if a gamified assessment is perceived as being 'too fun' or 'overly game-like', a candidate may feel as though it is inappropriate, and as a result may misinterpret whether the organization is taking his or her application seriously.[37] Other elements that have been shown to instigate negative reactions from candidates include the use of inappropriate sounds/music, overelaborate transitions, and irrelevant information.[38] As such, organizations need to be careful in the way they design gamified assessments so that they do not appear unprofessional.

As advancements continue to be made with regard to technology and use of the Internet, besides expecting that the assessment experience will be more interesting and engaging, candidates will also grow to expect that the experience will provide instant feedback. Organizations should consider expectations such as these when reviewing the use of gamified assessments, since these types of factors can increase test-taking motivation.[39] For example, one of the suggestions of how immediate feedback can be provided to candidates is through the attainment of a 'badge' which signifies that the candidate has successfully accomplished certain 'stages' in the gamified assessment. According to goal-setting theory, this is likely to encourage a candidate's motivation and commitment to achieving a particular goal, especially if the task or performance level required to receive such a 'badge' is 'challenging yet attainable' and if this is perceived as 'being valued and relevant to the candidate'. Furthermore, a recent study suggests that if the attainment of such a 'badge' can be displayed to a candidate's peers (e.g. through social media) as a form of status, then this can further motivate the candidate to remain engaged and committed to the assessment.[40] However, before deciding to adopt this approach, it is recommended that HR professionals and organizations should further evaluate potential implications for other aspects of the assessment or recruitment process, for example, any legal and privacy implications associated with publicizing candidate's results through social media (see also Chapter 9).

Using gamified assessments: Key considerations

Although there are potential benefits to be gained from the use of gamified assessments, it is recommended that HR professionals and organizations should also consider the following issues before including gamification in their assessment process:

- Measurable and objective criteria—as is the case when developing any valid and reliable assessment tool, to gamify an assessment it is first important to clearly define the attributes that are required for a particular role for which the assessment will be used. In other words, the gamified assessment needs to involve skills that are relevant for the job and also needs to be able to measure the skills in an efficient and timely fashion.[41] Some interactive games might involve content that is irrelevant to the context,[42] and may also take more time than desired before any measurable results can be seen. Not all skills can be measured quickly, and many are not directly measurable or quantifiable. As such, a gamified assessment may be more suitable for measuring objective criteria (e.g. logical reasoning). Upon the identification of the relevant skills, a form of measurement needs to be established and translated into a set of requirements for the candidate to participate in the gamified assessment.
- Interaction issues—as described earlier, some interactive games may include content that is irrelevant to the context of the gamified assessment. The interactive nature of gamified assessments may sometimes contradict the way candidates are expected to behave during assessments. The situation may foster illogical or unexpected behaviour. However, if a gamified assessment limits its measurement to only relevant behaviours, there may be a risk of designing an assessment that is dull and repetitive, thus causing candidates to become disengaged.[43] Therefore, the challenge is to find an appropriate balance of

behaviours to measure so that relevant data is collected, and so that the assessment remains enjoyable. Another concern involves overinteraction with the gamified assessment, including replaying and making multiple attempts and revisions.[44] Assessments are used to measure a candidate's ability, and if he or she is given the opportunity to take the assessment repeatedly, then his or her performance will inevitably improve. In such a case, a candidate may achieve a high score on a particular task, but the recruiter would not know whether the score is the result of the candidate's natural ability or of a significant and false 'practice effect' gained through repeated experience.[45]

- Cost, content, and context—measuring the return on investment from gamification can be difficult, and sometimes impossible. This is significant because the cost of recruitment-focused games can accumulate. There are important fixed costs that are not always obvious, such as compliance/legal costs, community management and policing, and ongoing creative costs (e.g. to develop avatars and challenges).[46] Evidence has suggested that top-tier candidates expect personalized assessments. However, most gamified assessments do not provide tailored tests to candidates, which means top-tier candidates may experience less engagement during the assessment process, unless it is complemented by special events or face-to-face communication.[47] For organizations that choose to use bespoke gamified assessments, they may face another type of challenge—with technological developments moving at such a fast pace, customized games can appear to be outdated quickly after launch, resulting in further costs and ongoing investment which will further detract from the ROI and which not all organizations would be able to afford.[48]

There is also the risk that some candidates simply do not enjoy games; hence, their level of engagement with the organization and the assessment process may not be as high. In such cases, there is the risk that the candidate will decide to drop out of the assessment process, which then presents the significant risk to the organization that otherwise highly qualified or suitable candidates may be lost on the basis not of their skills, knowledge, or capabilities but purely because of their 'enjoyment' of the process and its perceived relevance to them. Unfortunately, this would cause the organization to lose potentially suitable candidates without knowing the real reasons why.[49] Thus, it is recommended that organization which choose to gamify their assessments provide clear explanations or guidelines for the assessment process.

Key questions to be asked before applying gamification in talent assessment

The aspects of gamification which have been covered in this chapter have highlighted the relevant areas which HR professionals and organizations need to consider before implementing gamification elements in their recruitment processes. To further assist organizations in their decision-making process, the following questions should be asked:[50]

- What specific benefits could gamification offer?
- Are there examples of successful gamification in your sector or context?
- Which platforms do your target audience currently use?
- Is gamification mandatory or optional for applicants?

- For which vacancies could gamification be considered appropriate?
- Could gamification aid or detract from your diversity initiatives?
- How will gamification be measured and assessed? Can ROI be accurately calculated?

Video/Digital Interviewing

Apart from using assessment tests and tools, interviews are still the most commonly applied tool as one of the selection stages in talent assessment or recruitment. At times, arranging interviews with prospective candidates can be seen as a long and tedious process, since this may involve a lot of filtering, communication, and time coordination for scheduling. In many situations, when there is a large pool of applicants, HR professionals may have a difficult time keeping track of everyone. This has led to the creation of step-by-step guides on the management and coordination of the interviewing process, now adopted by many organizations in Hong Kong. A market need has also emerged in recent years for technology-enabled enhancements to be made to the interviewing process. Service providers now offer video/digital interviewing services, positioning this as an alternative to conducting face-to-face interviews.

In recent years, many organizations in Europe, the US, and China have turned to the use of technology for interviews. Some Hong Kong companies have started to adopt video interviewing as part of their talent selection process—for example, for mass recruitment exercises such as graduate management trainee assessment. Nonetheless, according to one service provider based in Hong Kong, it may take longer for this to become a prevalent trend in Hong Kong, given that Hong Kong is a comparatively small city where conventional face-to-face interviewing processes could typically be arranged in a somewhat feasible and convenient manner for both organizations and the applicants.[51]

HRM in Action Box 4.4

Benefits of Using Video Interviewing

A Hong Kong start-up company has developed and launched a product which aims to help organizations objectively analyse short videos from applicants where they answer a set of predetermined interview questions.* The software is designed to determine the suitability of the applicant through facial expressions and answers to the preset questions. Based on the job requirements, the software will help screen applicants' profiles (e.g. education and working experience) and also screen the video interview by using artificial intelligence. The service provider claims that HR can then make use of the analysis to decide whether the applicant should progress to the next stage of selection. While services like this are not aimed at replacing HR professionals who may have previously conducted interviews with applicants face-to-face or by phone, they do provide a chance for organizations to reduce the time and costs spent on first-round interviews. In addition, such services may help eliminate some of the discrepancies in interviewers' subjective judgements which are often found in traditional interview processes.

* What is ViHire. (n.d.). Retrieved April 1, 2019, from http://www.vihire.com/

Other technology developments have led to some organizations radically changing their hiring and recruitment processes (particularly for 'tech hires') to move away from more traditional forms of assessment and to incorporate newer assessment methods such as 'hackathons' (group programming marathons).[52]

Despite the convenience that technology-based services can provide, not all HR professionals are optimistic about the dependability of such services. Some concerns include

- the accuracy of 'scoring' facial expression and language detection;
- the difficulty in detecting whether the applicant is cheating;
- the difficulty in detecting and differentiating applicants on 'soft factors' such as the sincerity level of the applicants and their genuine interest in applying for the job;
- the potential for discrimination; and
- the validity, relevance, and accuracy.[53]

While these concerns may not be unique to video interviewing, one way to address the concerns could be to arrange HR professionals to review the video clips in order to form a more accurate, informed decision. In a similar way to gamified assessments, some companies may find that the benefits of properly using video interviewing as part of their talent assessment strategies would outweigh the potential concerns, while other companies may take the opposite view. To further assist organizations in making a better decision in this regard, some of the questions suggested earlier in relation to gamified assessments will also be applicable here. For example, before deciding to switch from using 'human-based' interviews to 'video-based' interviews, it is recommended that HR professionals help their organization to ask questions like these: What will be the specific, unique benefits that the use of video-interviewing techniques will bring to the overall recruitment process? How can the cost-benefit of using video interviewing be measured? (See also Chapters 3 and 9.)

Conclusion

In conclusion, HR professionals should exercise careful judgement in the selection and application of assessment methods, including the use of new technologies such as gamification within talent assessment processes. Clear criteria and guidelines should be established before using any assessment tool to ensure that organizations gain the benefits which such tools bring when chosen well and applied professionally. HR professionals should seek additional professional advice from assessment experts where needed.

Review Questions

1. What are psychometric tests, and what are some of the commonly used types in Hong Kong?
2. What are some of the potential considerations to take into account in relation to candidates cheating when psychometric tests are used? What could be some useful strategies in addressing this?

3. What are the similarities and differences between assessment centres and development centres?
4. What are some of the best practices for designing and implementing assessment and development centres?
5. What are some of the typical objectives behind the use of leadership assessment?
6. A professional-services firm is looking to use leadership assessment to address its senior leader's succession-planning needs. How would you advise this firm in relation to designing suitable leadership assessment activities and gaining buy-in from stakeholders?
7. How would leadership assessment activities provide valuable information for feedback and coaching? What would be some of the best practice approaches in sharing these insights through feedback and coaching?
8. What are some of the potential benefits and drawbacks associated with gamified assessments?
9. Why would some companies choose to include video interviewing as part of their talent selection and recruitment process? What are some of the likely benefits and drawbacks?
10. A listed company with quite a traditional management-style culture is looking to improve its graduate recruitment process by making greater use of technology. What recommendations would you make to this company, with a consideration of both the 'traditional' (e.g. psychometric tests) and 'emerging' (e.g. gamified assessment and video interviewing) assessment tools and approaches?

Notes

1. Cowieson, N. (2009). Selecting the Right People: Using psychometric testing and assessment centres in Hong Kong. In A. Tsui and K. T. Lai (Eds.), *Professional practices of HRM in Hong Kong: Linking HRM to organizational success* (pp. 43–68). Hong Kong: Hong Kong University Press.
2. Cronbach, Lee J. (1990). *Essentials of psychological and educational testing* (5th ed.). New York: Harper Collins.
3. Anastasi, A., and Urbina, S. (1997). *Psychological testing* (7th ed.). Upper Saddle River: Prentice Hall.
4. Definitions of 'maximum performance' and 'typical performance' are made by Cronbach, Lee J. (1990). *Essentials of psychological and educational testing* (5th ed.). New York: Harper Collins.
5. Although personality questionnaires are frequently referred to as 'psychometric tests', strictly speaking, they are not 'tests' since they do not comprise correct and incorrect answers. In HR and the world of work, while some personalities may be better suited to certain jobs and roles than others, it is generally considered that there is no 'right' or 'wrong' personality. You can't answer questions wrong which ask you about your preferences or your typical behaviour!
6. Pulakos, E., and Kantrowitz, T. (2016). *Choosing effective talent assessment to strengthen your organization*. Alexandria, VA: Society for Human Resource Management (SHRM) Foundation.
7. See e.g. Tyler, Graham P., Newcombe, Peter A., and Barrett, P. (2005). The Chinese challenge to the Big 5. *Selection and Development Review, 21*(6), 10–14.
8. Baron, H., & Bartram, D. (2006). *Using online assessment tools for recruitment*. British Psychological Society. Retrieved from https://ptc.bps.org.uk/sites/ptc.bps.org.uk/files/guidance_documents/using_online_assessment_tools_for_recruitment.pdf

9. See e.g. Griffith, R. L., Chmielowski, T., & Yoshita, Y. (2007). Do applicants fake? An examination of the frequency of applicant faking behaviour. *Personnel Review, 36*, 341–355.
10. McFarland, L. A., & Ryan, A. M. (2000). Variance of faking across noncognitive measures. *Journal of Applied Psychology, 85*, 812–821.
11. Lee, H. S., Smith, W. Z., & Geisinger, K. F. (2017). Faking under a nonlinear relationship between personality assessment scores and job performance. *International Journal of Selection and Assessment, 25*, 284–298.
12. Tyler, Graham P., Newcombe, Peter A., and Barrett, P. (2005). The Chinese challenge to the Big 5. *Selection and Development Review, 21*(6), 10–14.
13. Salgado, J. F. (2016). A theoretical model of psychometric effects of faking on assessment procedures: Empirical findings and implications for personality at work. *International Journal of Selection and Assessment, 24*, 209–228.
14. Baron, H., & Bartram, D. (2006). *Using online assessment tools for recruitment.* British Psychological Society. Retrieved from https://ptc.bps.org.uk/sites/ptc.bps.org.uk/files/guidance_documents/using_online_assessment_tools_for_recruitment.pdf
15. Boyle, S., Brooks, A., Bywater, J., Edenborough, R., Parker, A., Povah, N., Stear, S., & Wilson, P. (2012). *Design, implementation and evaluation of assessment and development centres best practice guidelines.* British Psychological Society. Retrieved from https://ptc.bps.org.uk/sites/ptc.bps.org.uk/files/guidance_documents/assessment_and_development_centres1.pdf
16. British Psychological Society. (1992). *Psychological testing: A guide.* Leicester: BPS Publications.
17. Coyne, I., and Bartram, D. (2006). Design and development of the ITC guidelines on computer-based and internet-delivered testing. *International Journal of Testing, 6*(2), 133–142.
18. Pulakos, E., and Kantrowitz, T. (2016). Choosing effective talent assessment to strengthen your organization. *SHRM.* Retrieved from https://www.shrm.org/hr-today/trends-and-forecasting/special-reports-and-expert-views/documents/effective-talent-assessments.pdf
19. Gillespie, K. (2018, July 26). Celebrating success. It's good for you and your team. *Linkedin.* Retrieved from https://www.linkedin.com/pulse/celebrating-success-its-good-you-your-team-karen-gillespie
20. Jiang, K., Lepak, D. P., Hu, J., & Baer, J. C. (2012). How does human resource management influence organizational outcomes? A meta-analytic investigation of mediating mechanisms. *Academy of Management Journal, 55*(6), 1264–1294.
21. Geissler, H., Hasenbein, M., Kanatouri, S., and Wegener, R. (2014). E-coaching: Conceptual and empirical findings of a virtual coaching programme. *International Journal of Evidence Based Coaching and Mentoring, 12*(2), 165–187.
22. Terblanche, N. H. D., Albertyn, R. M., & Van Coller-Peter, S. (2017). Designing a coaching intervention to support leaders promoted into senior positions. *Journal of Human Resources Management, 15*, 1–10.
23. Resource Solutions (n.d.). *Gamification in recruitment.* Retrieved from https://www.robert-walters.com/content/dam/robert-walters/corporate/news-and-pr/files/whitepapers/gamification-in-recruitment.pdf
24. Menezes, C. C. N., & De Bortolli, R. (2016). Potential of gamification as assessment tool. *Creative Education, 7*(4), 561.
25. Schulz, K. (2017, March 17). Gamification is changing assessments for the better. Talent Management and HR. Retrieved from https://www.tlnt.com/gamification-is-changing-assessments-for-the-better/
26. Armstrong, M. B., Ferrell, J. Z., Collmus, A. B., & Landers, R. N. (2016). Correcting misconceptions about gamification of assessment: More than SJTs and badges. *Industrial and Organizational Psychology, 9*(3), 671–677.

27. Justenhoven, R. (2018, May 9). What distinguishes good gamification from bad? *HRZone*. Retrieved from https://www.hrzone.com/talent/acquisition/what-distinguishes-good-gamification-from-bad
28. Biswas, S. (2017, July 18). Gamifying the recruitment process. *HR Technologist*. Retrieved from https://www.hrtechnologist.com/articles/recruitment-onboarding/gamifying-the-recruitment-process/
29. Schulz, K. (2017, March 17). Gamification is changing assessments for the better. *Talent Management and HR*. Retrieved from https://www.tlnt.com/gamification-is-changing-assessments-for-the-better/
30. Resource Solutions (n.d.). *Gamification in recruitment*. Retrieved from https://www.robert-walters.com/content/dam/robert-walters/corporate/news-and-pr/files/whitepapers/gamification-in-recruitment.pdf
31. Schulz, K. (2017, March 17). Gamification is changing assessments for the better. *Talent Management and HR*. Retrieved from https://www.tlnt.com/gamification-is-changing-assessments-for-the-better/
32. Justenhoven, R. (2018, June 6). Can there be 'too much fun' when we include games in the assessment process? *Aon*. Retrieved from https://insights.humancapital.aon.com/talent-assessment-blog/can-there-be-too-much-fun-when-we-include-games-in-the-assessment-process
33. Schulz, K. (2017, March 17). Gamification is changing assessments for the better. *Talent Management and HR*. Retrieved from https://www.tlnt.com/gamification-is-changing-assessments-for-the-better/
34. Schulz, K. (2017, March 17). Gamification is changing assessments for the better. *Talent Management and HR*. Retrieved from https://www.tlnt.com/gamification-is-changing-assessments-for-the-better/
35. Biswas, S. (2017, July 18). Gamifying the recruitment process. *HR Technologist*. Retrieved from https://www.hrtechnologist.com/articles/recruitment-onboarding/gamifying-the-recruitment-process/
36. Justenhoven, R. (2018, June 6). Can there be 'too much fun' when we include games in the assessment process? *Aon*. Retrieved from https://insights.humancapital.aon.com/talent-assessment-blog/can-there-be-too-much-fun-when-we-include-games-in-the-assessment-process
37. Justenhoven, R. (2018, June 6). Can there be 'too much fun' when we include games in the assessment process? *Aon*. Retrieved from https://insights.humancapital.aon.com/talent-assessment-blog/can-there-be-too-much-fun-when-we-include-games-in-the-assessment-process
38. Justenhoven, R. (2018, May 9). What distinguishes good gamification from bad? *HRZone*. Retrieved from https://www.hrzone.com/talent/acquisition/what-distinguishes-good-gamification-from-bad
39. Armstrong, M. B., Ferrell, J. Z., Collmus, A. B., & Landers, R. N. (2016). Correcting misconceptions about gamification of assessment: More than SJTs and badges. *Industrial and Organizational Psychology*, 9(3), 671–677.
40. Armstrong, M. B., Ferrell, J. Z., Collmus, A. B., & Landers, R. N. (2016). Correcting misconceptions about gamification of assessment: More than SJTs and badges. *Industrial and Organizational Psychology*, 9(3), 671–677.
41. Aon. (n.d.). Gamified assessment by Aon: Engaging. Innovative. Proven. *Aon*. Retrieved from https://assessment.aon.com/en-us/assessment-solutions/gamified-assessment
42. Menezes, C. C. N., & De Bortolli, R. (2016). Potential of gamification as assessment tool. *Creative Education*, 7(4), 561.
43. Menezes, C. C. N., & De Bortolli, R. (2016). Potential of gamification as assessment tool. *Creative Education*, 7(4), 561.
44. Menezes, C. C. N., & De Bortolli, R. (2016). Potential of gamification as assessment tool. *Creative Education*, 7(4), 561.

45. Aon. (n.d.). *Gamified assessment by Aon: Engaging. Innovative. Proven. Aon.* Retrieved from https://assessment.aon.com/en-us/assessment-solutions/gamified-assessment
46. Resource Solutions (n.d.). *Gamification in recruitment.* Retrieved from https://www.robert-walters.com/content/dam/robert-walters/corporate/news-and-pr/files/whitepapers/gamification-in-recruitment.pdf
47. Resource Solutions (n.d.). *Gamification in recruitment.* Retrieved from https://www.robert-walters.com/content/dam/robert-walters/corporate/news-and-pr/files/whitepapers/gamification-in-recruitment.pdf
48. Aon. (n.d.). *Gamified assessment by Aon: Engaging. Innovative. Proven. Aon.* Retrieved from https://assessment.aon.com/en-us/assessment-solutions/gamified-assessment
49. Aon. (n.d.). *Gamified assessment by Aon: Engaging. Innovative. Proven. Aon.* Retrieved from https://assessment.aon.com/en-us/assessment-solutions/gamified-assessment
50. Resource Solutions (n.d.). *Gamification in recruitment.* Retrieved from https://www.robert-walters.com/content/dam/robert-walters/corporate/news-and-pr/files/whitepapers/gamification-in-recruitment.pdf
51. Zeng, K. Y. (2018, July 16). [AI面試] 拍片自我介紹——即可分析能力? 初創:非要取代HR. *HK01.* Retrieved from https://www.hk01.com/%E8%81%B7%E5%A0%B4/207720/ai-%E9%9D%A2%E8%A9%A6-%E6%8B%8D%E7%89%87%E8%87%AA%E6%88%91%E4%BB%8B%E7%B4%B9-%E5%8D%B3%E5%8F%AF%E5%88%86%E6%9E%90%E8%83%BD%E5%8A%9B-%E5%88%9D%E5%89%B5-%E9%9D%9E%E8%A6%81%E5%8F%96%E4%BB%A3hr
52. Consultancy.asia. (2018, Oct. 26). *Deloitte adopts hackathon approach for talent recruitment in China.* Retrieved from https://www.consultancy.asia/news/1558/deloitte-adopts-hackathon-approach-for-talent-recruitment-in-china.
53. Zeng, K. Y. (2018, July 16). [AI面試] 拍片自我介紹-即可分析能力? 初創：非要取代HR. *HK01.* Retrieved from https://www.hk01.com/%E8%81%B7%E5%A0%B4/207720/ai%E9%9D%A2%E8%A9%A6-%E6%8B%8D%E7%89%87%E8%87%AA%E6%88%91%E4%BB%8B%E7%B4%B9-%E5%8D%B3%E5%8F%AF%E5%E5%88%86%E6%9E%90%E8%83%BD%E5%8A%9B-%E5%88%9D%E5%8-9%B5-%E9%9D%9E%E8%A6%81%E5%8F%96%E4%BB%A3hr

5
Learning and Development Strategies in Hong Kong

Eliza C. P. Chan

> **LEARNING OUTCOMES**
>
> By the end of this chapter, readers should be able to
>
> - identify the value of changing the concept from 'training and development' (T&D) to 'learning and development' (L&D);
> - understand the mission of L&D in various organizational structures, and the transformation of 'training' and 'development' roles in organizations;
> - understand the dynamics of L&D management; and
> - evaluate the redefined roles and competencies for L&D professionals.

Introduction

This chapter is about learning and development strategies in Hong Kong. A couple of decades ago we were used to describing this area of human resource as 'training and development'. When delivering training programmes in classroom, trainers need to be familiar with the subject and facilitate class discussion effectively. They may also lead role plays, interact with the audience, and conduct debriefings to drive home key learning points. Sometimes trainers may design training programmes. A professional trainer needs to possess competencies in the areas of content knowledge, instructional design, and fundamental knowledge of development theories, as well as classroom management. A competent trainer should also have strong communication and presentation skills in order to deliver messages clearly, ask questions that inspire responses, listen well for messages behind words, and capable of thinking conceptually to consolidate findings and make improvement recommendations. The Association for Talent Development (ATD, formerly known as American Society for Training and Development [ASTD]), created a competency model with three tiers some years ago.[1] But often they are relevant to face-to-face classroom training programmes. With the advancement of technologies and learning methodologies, the field has changed. Training and development is now more appropriately called learning and development. The drivers of change are certainly not just technologies. 'Learning' is better terminology than 'training' to illustrate growth and changes of organizations, employees, and, indeed, every individual.

This chapter shares the experiences and observations of a practitioner through the development and changes of learning and development. Discussion covers subjects from evolution of training and development to learning and development, organization dynamics of learning and development, transformation of learning and development function, and implications to management of curriculum, programmes, and contents. We also discuss the relationships of big data and digitization to learning and development management, changes of employee demographics, and their impact on the roles of in-house learning and development staff and that of external training partners. The chapter concludes with the author's view on being a professional in the career of learning and development.

From Training and Development to Learning and Development

A fundamental understanding of the concepts of training, development, and learning can be based on their definitions. The online edition of the *Cambridge Dictionary* defines the terms thus:

> Training—'the process of learning the skills you need to do a particular job or activity';
> Development—'the process of growing or changing and becoming more advanced'; and
> Learning—'the activity of obtaining knowledge'; 'the process of getting an understanding of something by studying it or by experience'.

Training can thus be defined as the systematic acquisition of the knowledge, skills, and attitudes required by an individual to perform adequately at a given task or job. *Development* refers to the process by which individuals improve their capabilities and learn to perform more effectively in their roles. Development is often associated with one's career progress. While training implies uplifting one's skills and capabilities in the existing job, development relates to a planned process focusing on long-term growth for progression. In the context of an organization, training and development (T&D) is referred to as a function supporting employees to acquire the skills and fundamental knowledge to do a job and in a continuous approach in order to do it better and better.[2] *Learning* and development (L&D), on the other hand, has a wider scope than just jobs or individuals but actually entails a continuous process of gaining knowledge and growth of the work force as a whole.[3]

However, doing a job well with continuous improvement is no longer sufficient to meet work requirements in today's competitive market. By the same token, organizations with a staff force that just does a job well are unsustainable. Employers need talents rather than just position fillers or job doers. Thus, the function of T&D must also transform. The word *learning*, as opposed to *training*, indeed reflects more accurately the contemporary needs on staff development. L&D as a function in an organization needs to be accountable with full ownership on staff training to meet business requirements. The function must also facilitate learning of the entire organization to advance continuously.

In this chapter L&D is taken to mean an organization function, whereas *training* refers to general training and training-related activities.

Learning and Development: Structure and Mission

Learning and development can be centralized as a corporate function itself (Figure 5.1) or decentralized to be within business units (Figure 5.2). Whether centralized or decentralized, it usually depends on team size, structure, and relevant resources devoted by the organization. In fact, where this function sits in the organization can reflect the reason for its existence and also indicates contribution of the function as a whole. HR and L&D professionals can be someone in the value chain who can influence and make a difference. While some organizations structure learning and development as an independent function with dedicated resources, others keep it as one of the HR roles and include it as part of the responsibilities of assigned HR officers.

Figure 5.1: Centralized L&D function

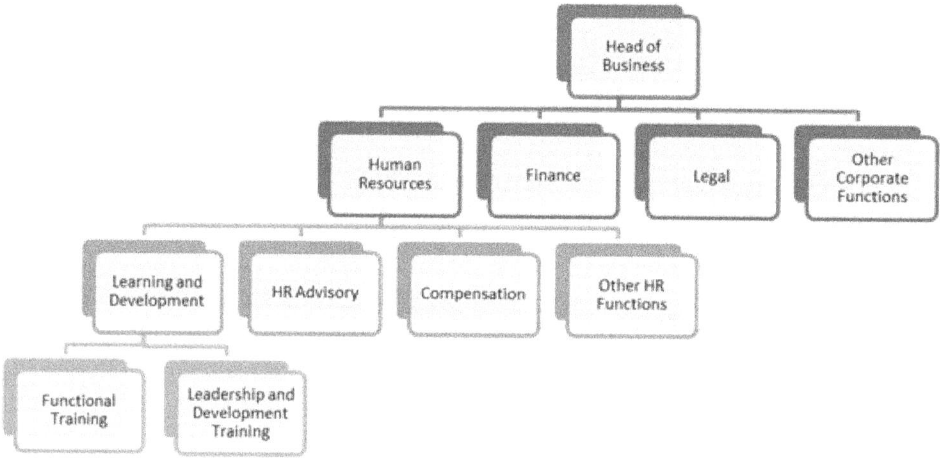

Figure 5.2: Decentralized training function

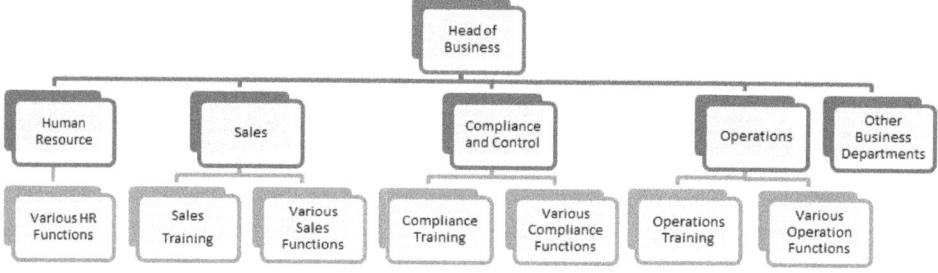

Decentralized L&D functions can sit in any departments within business units. However, it is usually the 'training' part of the function that is decentralized. For example, a sales training team under sales function provides training in product knowledge and selling skills. These programmes can be delivered by dedicated sales trainers or experienced line managers who integrate their sales experience to skills-training programme contents. More popular lately is compliance training—independent from L&D, but directly under compliance or control functions. Programmes offered, either in classroom or online, provide core and latest compliance contents relevant to the business. A training team structured under a compliance unit utilizes knowledge expertise of compliance professionals of the department, facilitates timely content update, and conveniently owns completion tracking to meet business and regulatory requirements.

A training function within business units is mostly to support business results or to meet practical, functional, and operation needs. The financial industry, for example, has the mandatory requirement for all front-line business-generating staff to be licensed by their relevant regulatory bodies. One of the roles of in-business training function is to support all new employees to meet the basic licence requirements and for all existing staff to meet continuous development rules for licence renewal. In the transport industry, mass-transport companies have their operations-training function separated from L&D to provide training for drivers and technicians. These functional-training activities are mostly structured with mandatory tests and assessments to ensure quality standards that meet the requirements of the organization, industry, and regulations. The in-business training function also sets the standard required to achieve accreditation, creates systems to allow employees to meet accreditation standards, and tracks completion of standards.[4]

Some organizations have L&D functions in human resource department as well as training teams in business units (Figure 5.3). Others put L&D as a function independent from human resources (Figure 5.4).

Figure 5.3: L&D in both HR and business functions

Figure 5.4: L&D as an independent function

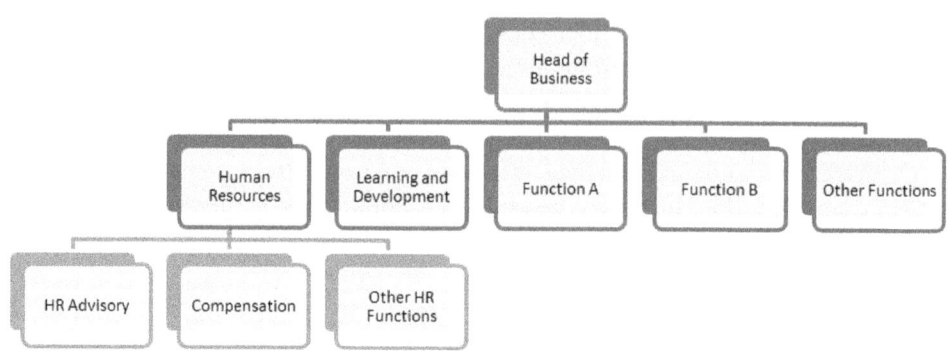

Learning and development is a function with two areas of accountability: the training or learning piece and the development piece. While the training aspect of L&D is more flexible in the organization's structure, as illustrated above, the development aspect of L&D has experienced relatively more challenging transformation in the last couple of decades. Functional training, as stated, is fundamental for business operation; developmental type of training could sometimes be viewed as a 'variable'. At challenging times of business, resources in all senses have to be prioritized. Developmental training is not the prescription for immediate result but is rather a choice, albeit a critical choice, for business longevity. Because it is a variable, development piece of function, it can exist in various forms in an organization. Whether this piece of function is perceived as one of the factors in business success or just message transmitter, or a lighthouse to guide learning, it will be a mission for HRM and L&D professionals to drive. Its shape of existence rests on the level of influence that the HR and L&D leads can have on senior management. Corporate university, leadership academy, organizational development, talent development, L&D are some examples of their forms of presence. They are different, each with a specific mission and yet all have the element of development at the core.

Where the development part of L&D sits in the organizational structure could in a way reflect the learning culture of the organization, both in its current and aspirational instantiations.[5] When an organization is in the process of significant change, L&D is usually charged with the mission of driving this change management process. The L&D professionals would partner with senior management to lead communications of changes. L&D is also one of the key partners to strategize and communicate corporate mission and value, developing and implementing strategic plans for the whole organization. When L&D is structured as part of the human resource department (Figure 5.3), the entire department as one unit will take responsibility to incorporate the organizational values via all people relevant policies including recruitment, performance management, and certainly including leadership training. In some cases, L&D is charged with a specific mission and is placed independent from the HR department, reporting directly to the head of business. This is the situation when L&D sits independently in structure as illustrated in Figure 5.4.

Times of challenge very often coincide with restructuring. This also applies to L&D. Changes of reporting line, team mix, and resource allocation reflect priorities of organizations. These could be attributable to various reasons, including the organization's business operations, dynamics of the macroeconomic environment, evolution of the industry, regulations and control of local and global environments, demographic change of population, and the customers or general population as a whole. One example is the financial industry. With enhanced control environment, financial organizations have put more resources or redirected resources to meet the increasing requirements for employees' professional standards, and operational compliance and control. Training teams of some retail banks are realigned with more people resources to functional training in order to support front-line staff's licence to business. Where viable, some developmental types of training are tuned to technology-supported channels which can accommodate a greater number of participants and are more flexible in logistic arrangement. These could be self-driven online programmes, instructor-led virtual training, mobile learning, or other forms. In such situations, in-house people resources for soft-skills training or a development type of training could decrease.

In the face of a changing environment and rapidly growing technological capability and accessibility, all resources are realigned. L&D is no exception, but there are unique patterns to how realignment is executed in L&D. In some situations, teams simply shrink. In other instances, team size does not change, but the team mix could change and the responsibilities of members be redefined. For example dedicated headcount and resources for leadership and development training are reduced, but new or more resources are added to better utilize technology-based training methodology. Some L&D functions may take on the new role as training programme specialists to develop online programmes by various methodologies. Certain organizations, like some conglomerates and international financial institutions, have completely revamped L&D to maintain only functional training and are decentralized to business units (Figure 5.2). In other words, the training budget might appear the same in dollar terms but allocation is different, and in above example a much smaller share is set for development training. In extreme cases, there could be no dedicated training resource at all and no in-house full-time trainer for L&D.

From the perspective of L&D as a career, core competencies and responsibilities of trainers have certainly been transformed. This will be discussed further in a later section of the chapter.

Transformation of L&D Functions

Today's world of digitization has significant implications to L&D. At a programme level, digitization has highly enhanced the quality and effectiveness of training programmes. Digitized record of training material, including training slides, exercises, workbooks, and videos are kept at consistent clarity no matter how many times they need to be duplicated for use. Through virtual reality (VR) and augmented reality (AR) technology, remote training programmes can come remarkably close in effectiveness to traditional on-site training.[6] Digitization has also enhanced the quality of videos used in virtual and classroom training. Employees can now communicate with senior management real time via digital audio visual platforms. These contents can conveniently be recorded and stored for retrieval and be used as 'training materials' whenever needed. Learning opportunities are now more widely available and more easily accessible. Many interviews and speeches of world leaders are available online.

Thus, in-person talks and forums, if to be organized in-house, have become more selective, if they are considered at all.

L&D management can be described paradoxically as somehow easier and yet more challenging. Technological advancement allows information to be more widely accessible. As such, employees are more demanding and have higher expectations on development activities offered by the in-house L&D function. On the other hand, from the perspective of L&D planning, development activities selected have to be different from and of added-value to what employees can access by themselves online. They have to be more specific and able to be tailor-made for unique development objectives. Senior management wants in-house programmes to be more cost effective, deliver higher ROI, be able to address specific staff development needs, and be more closely aligned with the organization's values. Managers demand shorter training courses that focus only on the necessary content. L&D departments may be expected to reduce the numbers of courses or offer only programmes that directly address business issues or performance problems.[7] L&D professionals must manage the function at a standard in line with benchmarks set by the internet world. With online platforms opening the door to greater accessibility of information and knowledge, the bar is raised, and specialization becomes paramount. This change of expectation also impacted on the employment of external training supports. The reasons and objectives of engaging external partners are different now.

Before the digital world, training functions of many sizeable organizations had a team of in-house management programme trainers, and their roles spanned from programme development to classroom delivery. Management trainers researched on various subjects and developed programmes for in-house offers. They delivered programmes on subjects including people management, personal effectiveness, and customer service. Popular programmes on the shelves were supervisory skills, delegation, presentation skills, problem-solving, influencing skills, communications, interpersonal relationships, customer service, and handling complaints, and more. Sources of information were mostly books and articles. Reasonable amount of budget would allow purchase of packaged programmes with trainer manuals and facilitation guides. Alternatively, there would be train-the-trainer programmes to bring renowned programmes for in-house offers. Corporate trainers then were multitasked and multiskilled. External partners were engaged when special subjects demanded their skill sets. These partners could be subject matter experts on some thinking skills, presentation skills, or quality management that was popular a couple of decades ago. The subjects that needed external training support varied depending on experience and skills of the organization's training team. And sometimes external vendors were brought in when in-house training resources were unable to support the training demands. An example is a special project to deliver some fifty or more training classes on a customer service initiative. External individual freelance training professionals and many external training vendors were usually capable of supporting a wide range of training activities.[8]

Today there is a demand for specialized L&D professionals. Consequently, there is a heightened need for partnership with external vendors with a mastery of specific subjects. As stated above, the fundamentals of practically any subject is now freely accessible through a variety of sources, and there are many resources online for self-learning. As such, L&D professionals rarely engage with external free-lance trainers simply as extra resources but rather as training partners or vendors specialized in particular subjects who can provide developmental activities or services unavailable through virtual platforms. Thus, for example, public-speaking programmes are facilitated not just by any trainer but by professionals with specialization in the subject. NLP (neural linguistic programming) courses by 'master trainers' have higher participation than general communication. Programmes on mindfulness by the masters are organized rather than stress management delivered by trainers. A good portion of the L&D budget is sometimes set aside for development activities for high-potential talent on a selective basis.

In the *2018 Workplace Learning Report* of LinkedIn Learning Solutions, one of the findings is that 69 percent of L&D professionals comment that talent is the number-one priority in their organizations. And over one-quarter of them are expecting a budget increase for L&D programmes.[9] Other times, L&D investment is on projects for specific development objectives, like digitization forums, re-engineering, big data management programmes and others. Specialization also explains for smaller team of training resources on general personal effectiveness and management training. In sum, L&D function has been transformed. It is no longer a function providing in-house programmes on a wide range of topics. It is now an L&D project management team or an in-house consultancy team that works as a closer partner of business to provide specific and specialized development support—not just by classroom training, but by all approaches deemed most optimal.

Changes in Training Curriculum and Programme Contents

The macro world of L&D has followed in the footsteps of technology disruption and digitization by various dimensions. In-house L&D as a corporate function must also progress at the same pace, if not faster. The term *learning and development* implies 'in advance' or 'ahead' of what is currently required. At working level, trainers are the ones who need to learn ahead of others in order to deliver training. At a corporate level, L&D is the function of an organization that needs to learn first. L&D leaders need to be strategists to prepare the workforce with the competencies for upcoming needs and to drive the learning culture of the organization for continuous growth. They should therefore have the sensitivity, curiosity, and mindset to go after continuous learning. A learning organization has the drive and the culture to be at the forefront of evolution.

The corporate training curriculum is one of the indicators that reveal part of such footprints of L&D evolution.[10] Once-popular topics like time management, problem-solving and decision-making, and general communications skills are probably be off the list for classroom training now. That's not because these subjects are no longer important. Rather, they are likely to be offered by an alternative training methodology, most likely through virtual channels. Besides, technological advancement has practically overhauled the contents of some classical personal development programmes. One example is time management. Manual time planners are replaced by Outlook and mobile phone calendars, which do not just support planning but can also set up reminders, repeated occurrences, for both individuals and groups. Time management principles like 'urgency' and 'importance' have been redefined. Another example is presentation skills training. 'Visual aids' that used to be discussed in popular training programmes in the past were transparencies, flip charts, cue cards, and the like. They are now PowerPoint slides, tablets, and mobile phones.

In some industries, presentations take place in a totally different format, and content of training courses on this subject also changed accordingly. Illustrative examples are product launch presentations and media conferences of mobile phones, online shopping platforms, mobile apps, and electronic products. These 'presentations' are made on real stages or stage-like settings where there are no tables and podiums. Speakers stand on stage and 'present', holding their mobile phones, which replace notes and cue cards. They usually use just a couple of simple PowerPoint slides, and sometimes none at all. Towards this new trend of communication, traditional training programmes on 'presentation' for 'speakers' would eventually be replaced by those on 'public speaking' for 'hosts'. Programmes on people skills are another case in point. Supervisory programmes are almost obsolete, replaced by those of people management skills. The contents of these programmes now have fewer topics on delegation and appraisal and more on coaching and empowerment, for example.

This reflects not simply a superficial change in terminology from 'supervisory' to 'people management' but a deep revamp stemming from changes in the workplace and the world in essence. But these previously popular programmes have not disappeared totally; they are still around, but in new approaches. Today they are offered in content of contemporary workplace context and in up-to-date formats such as real-time online instructor-led virtual programmes, on mobile platforms, or through mixed-mode or blended training approaches. Theories and contents of relevant key principles are offered virtually. The classroom format is devoted to skill practice workshops. A two-day presentation skills programme in the past can now be a half-day public-speaking workshop, plus a five-hour online pre-course before the workshop. And a five-day supervisory programme in the past has turned to a one- or two-day people management course, plus a five-hour online pre-course preparation. These changes are commonly seen in the training curricula of most organizations, reflecting the progression of the L&D world.

Impact of Big Data and Digitization

STEM (science, technology, engineering, and mathematics) is a terminology in the academic world relevant to direction of education. This direction of STEM is also relevant in the learning and development context. In association with big data and digitization, STEM is relevant to strategic L&D management, training curricula, and training programme contents. While big data is still in the process for more general mastery in usage, it does support to enhance efficiency and effectiveness of L&D management.[11] Training needs analysis (TNA) which relies on just a questionnaire approach is doomed to go astray. Fundamental corporate training needs can be conveniently comprehended from major HR data or linked learning management system data. Data analysis can indicate the specific number of people or managers needed for core leadership training, completion percentage, number of those outstanding to complete, number of those new in role added to the population for participation, and more (Figure 5.5). Such data can also be the basis to organize and manage necessary communications of corporate messages like mission and values, important programmes on new processes and procedures, and critical training to meet legal and regulatory requirements (Figure 5.6). All data relating to attendance can be properly recorded in the system for further analysis as it is needed.[12]

Figure 5.5: Sample report on employee work information and training record

Employee Name	Function / Department	Grade	Date of Hire	Date of Last Promotion	Date in Current Role	Name of Manager	People Manager (Y/N)	Layers of Staff Managed	Number of Direct Staff	Total Number of Staff Managed	Completion Date of (core prog X)	Completion Date of (core prog Y)

Figure 5.6: Sample employee data analysis for L&D plan

	Number of Employees ('000)
New hire in Year X	
By grade	
Newly promoted to Grade X in Year Y	
With 3 or more direct staff	
With 3 or more direct staff at Grade X and above	
In team head role	
In department head role	
In function head role	
Outstanding for Program X	
Outstanding for Program Y	

Analysis is even more convenient in cases of programmes offered virtually. By using virtual channels, the platform should automatically capture registration, completion, and access duration for example. Such data are available for review by various dimensions as needed. For example, to review participation number by programme, cancellation rate, incompletion rate, programmes of high access numbers, of high demand and others. Further analysis can be performed by criteria required and relevant to L&D and business.

Popular human resource information systems (see Chapters 2 and 9) and learning management systems are capable of capturing and reporting such data.[13] With further technological advancement, easy-to-use, lower-cost systems that can provide more comprehensive data analysis will likely become more prevalent.

It is envisaged that paper-based training evaluation will soon be history. Free and simple apps are widely available for use. For virtual programmes, Kirkpatrick's Four-Level Training Evaluation (Reaction/Learning/Behavior/Results) may need to be comprehended differently, especially for level I, Reaction. The definition of *reaction* for virtual programmes will be interpreted differently from that of classroom training. Participants give high ratings for satisfied classroom programmes when they enjoy sessions that are led by trainers who delivered clear key messages with a sense of humour, have inspirational exercises and discussions that facilitate participants' experience sharing and networking, and the like. High rating for a 'satisfied' virtual programme, on the other hand, is likely to be regarded as one with less audio talking by the trainer, short and simple contents, and easy-to-read on-screen visuals. An online programme with a couple of questions inviting participants to type in responses is interactive. Interaction may also be polling-type exercises in real-time instructor-led online programmes which invite participants to click on a given choice and receive a response summary on-screen immediately. Networking as criteria for Level I evaluation becomes irrelevant and in addition when the on-line audience group is unknown to each participant owing to privacy considerations.

Big data is not just supportive for L&D in logistics and training management. It is a subject for learning by itself. As one of the corporate change agents, professional L&D team should have the mission to help the workforce on the learning path of digital revolution that makes STEM relevant. It is not just IT employees who are 'technical', and not just finance staff who work on numbers. Everybody, including L&D professionals, needs to understand the technology. HR should be able to communicate and utilize digital technology. In a certain respect, they need to be analysts with the ability to 'read' and 'use' data. This is neither a training programme nor a special project but a journey, and a professional L&D function is one of the important leads and partners with business departments along the way. Organizations progress in this journey at different rates. Some sizeable companies and conglomerates may be in a better position to stand at the forefront. With bigger employee populations, it may be easier for these organizations to achieve the critical mass needed to justify the higher initial budget to adopt new technology platforms for cost effectiveness. L&D curricula of some of these organizations already have programmes on subjects of big data management and digitization, and are supported by digital methodology. On the flip side of the coin, small and medium companies are sometimes more innovative and more willing to take challenges. The L&D function itself needs to embrace this inside out—to transform from needs analysis to programme contents, methodology, evaluation, trainers' competencies, logistics, management, and everything else.[14]

Implications of Changing Employee Demographics to L&D Plans

The millennials are the new blood in the workforce. This generation typically refers to those born in the 1980s to 2000—hence they are in their twenties or thirties. The younger members of this group are just beginning their career lives; whereas those in their mid to late thirties who have had smooth career development should now be at the middle management level. There have been many studies and findings about the very different aspirations and expectations on career and work-life balance of this generation. For organizations with longer histories, there are also baby boomers and Generation X employees in the workforce. Some organizations are extending the retirement age. In other words, the current workforce is multigenerational. For organizations with diverse employee population, L&D plans need to cater for learners with potential age differences of forty or more years. Learning needs, habits, preferences, and suitable training approaches are likely to vary among these groups of employees. While some employees prefer flexibility from virtual programmes, other groups like networking opportunities in classroom training and be totally away from work while in training.[15]

Big data can lend a strong helping hand to L&D planning for such a diverse employment population. For example, such data can facilitate analysis of employee demographics, giving the number and proportion of employees in each category as it is relevantly defined. Findings of the analysis are a valuable basis for planning of organizational development, talent development, and L&D curriculum. Findings can give good direction to development focus, subject matter, and delivery channels in L&D strategic plan. For instance, a workforce with a higher proportion of millennials may need leadership programmes with more emphasis on career coaching for managers who supervise this younger staff group. Programmes for employee populations of such a mix need to be offered in dual versions, where millennials can attend by virtual channels and others can opt for classroom offers.

There are, however, further considerations in actual L&D planning. Some other things to keep in mind are the preferences of employees and specific organizational requirements. Training needs surveys gather input on training preference, on what employees would like to have. A demographically diverse employee group is likely to result in a broad spectrum of unique interests. In addition, many sizeable organizations in various industries have systematic leadership competency frameworks outlining specific standards of leadership and expectations in competency terms by level. Such structured frameworks outline specific leadership skills and practices for development. Integration of all these elements and in the context of business objectives and priorities will point to a good principle framework of a strategic L&D plan. The framework will need to be thoughtfully dissected further to address the needs of a very diverse staff force.[16]

Added to the complexity is a workforce with offshore employees, contractors, temporary workers and sometimes also consultants. More organizations now have official policies for flexible work arrangements. For example, companies provide policies for employees to work from home for one or more days a week, supported by technology that gives access, with controlled security, to work systems from home.

The challenge to L&D is the translation of all the above considerations to practical implementation that cares for the varied development needs, learning preferences, and learning habits of a diverse employee population. L&D leaders need to cater for all these elements in development plan from strategic objectives, curriculum consideration, to programme contents, delivery approach, and even logistics arrangement. Development strategy needs to address employees of different ages, educational backgrounds, and experiences. People management and coaching programmes, for example, must be free from value judgements and stereotypes of any age group and yet be sensitive to recognize generational difference.[17]

Learning and Development as a Career: Redefined Competencies

L&D is one of the career paths of HR professionals. As discussed in earlier paragraphs, a few decades ago in a T&D environment the fundamental requirements as a 'training officer' were strong communication and presentation skills and comfort speaking in front of a group of participants. T&D professionals also needed to be able to present themselves in an exceptionally clear, skilful, and tactful manner even when relaying the most complex messages and ideas. With the transformation of T&D to L&D, in today's digital world the career of trainer has developed in a few new directions. Core competencies have evolved from classroom facilitation skills to web facilitation skills, from using classroom visual aids to web training tools, from programme design with classroom exercises of role playing, group discussions, and icebreakers to design digital programmes and assessment by web tools.[18]

When the classroom was the major mode of training, the primary role of a training officer was as a trainer, a programme manager, a programme designer, and sometimes a procurement officer of packaged training programmes or a training vendor. A competent trainer prepared his or her own set of visual aids for the programme to deliver, thus needed to comprehend the programme to such level as to be able to illustrate major learning points, no matter their complexity. Such visual aids should not be just texts but also diagrams and pictures that were easy to read. In addition, a professional trainer always had a 'session plan' for every programme, detailing the time assigned for each activity, whether it be lecture, discussion, role playing, and even warm-up and icebreakers. This plan served as a record for trainers to repeat training and pass along to other trainers. In the classroom, a competent trainer displayed strong listening and comprehension skills in order to immediately select key and exact wordings of participants to note on flip charts. A caring trainer also prepared with several ice-breaking activities so that participants sitting an entire day in the classroom could stay engaged and enjoy the training programme in the classroom.

Now, the digital platform is an alternative core channel of training delivery. The responsibilities among various roles of an L&D officer have shifted. The classroom is employed only when face-to-face contact is critical to transmit the message or when extensive interactive skill practice is critical and there is a need for immediate feedback. As discussed in earlier sections, some fundamental skills programmes are now offered online via mobile phone and are often broken into modules offered in a blended training mode. Digitization and the transformed L&D structure and function have changed the roles of L&D officers. The current L&D world brings forward a shifted set of competencies which lead to a newly defined career path of L&D officers.

Leadership programmes can be delivered by HR officers or full-time trainers. Some programmes where classroom is still selected as the mode of delivery may not, however, be delivered by a trainer. Examples are programmes of corporate values and mission at times of changes or on compliance-related subjects where 'trainers' could be senior management, business leaders, or subject-matter experts. These programmes could have been designed by another group of programme design specialists using various learning models filled with interactive exercises. The role of L&D officer in these cases becomes programme manager or project manager. They are responsible for an entire programme or project launch logistics and arrangement. Core competencies for this role become those of training event management, including management and arrangement of class schedule, enrolments, arrangement of participant attendance by grade, job function, department, years of service in the organization, or other dimensions depending on training objectives. Classroom set-up, training materials, and all other logistics must also be taken into consideration by the L&D project manager, who must collaborate with the actual trainer or speaker of the programme to provide full training support. These scenarios are not uncommon in today's environment. L&D officers may not need to deliver programmes at all. Major responsibilities are training projects or training events management. As a result, core competencies and career paths of L&D professionals are redefined.[19]

Another dimension to review the transformed role of L&D officers is to consider programmes offered as instructor-led online programmes. L&D officers of these programmes need to manage participants virtually. The facilitation skill of a trainer is mostly expressed through the keyboard. There is no need for ice-breaking exercise and energy booster but constant status updates of programme progress, letting participants know where they are in the programme flow. L&D officers needs to be skilful with all virtual programme applications, which can be as simple as recording a programme for replay, or muting an audio channel to invite participants' input.[20] Technology allows real time on-line programmes to have virtual breakout discussion by groups, and programme leaders can provide coaching in similar ways as in a real classroom setting. But L&D officers of the programmes employing this technology must be able to master the software well. At times, some of them may still need to design in-house programmes for repeated use. Required skills are not the same as those for classroom types, as mentioned in previous paragraphs. In addition to the learning theories and programme design principles, L&D officers must learn to use the most common design software applications for content. For self-driven online programmes with exercises and assessments, programme contents are not structured linearly. They need to be designed to cater for different choices of answers selected by participants in these exercises along the course. An example is the need to design for four scenarios corresponding to a question with four answer choices. Depending on the choice selected by the participants, the course will flow to the appropriate response page. The course then continues by looping back to the main flow (Figure 5.7). L&D officers responsible for designing such programmes must work their mind as training programmers. For technically specialized situations—for example, virtual reality programmes—there may be a dedicated role of digital programme managers to work with external programme producers for programme production and continuous maintenance. In situations that engage external training vendors, the L&D officers are the procurement representatives (Table 5.1).

Figure 5.7: Flow of virtual programme with multiple-choice questions

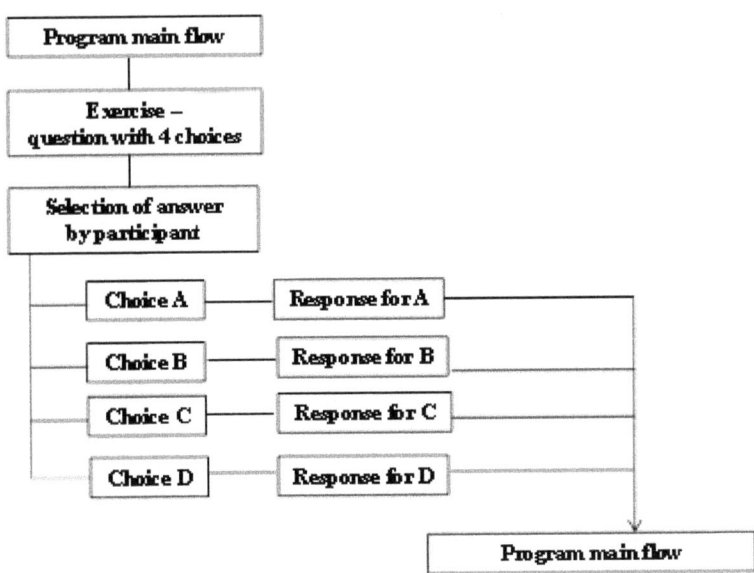

Table 5.1: Job profile and requirements of a learning and development professional

Responsibility	Requirement
• Identify and analyse staff training needs • Identify, design, and develop various training activities • Design and prepare appropriate training materials • Deliver various training programs • Evaluate the training performance, provide recommendations and action plan for enhancement • Liaise with managers and meet employees to identify and assess L&D needs • Liaise with other departments, partners and external parties on L&D needs • Recommend training solutions • Liaise and communicate with external consultant • Ensure employees receive statutory required training	• Strong communication and presentation skills • Training and facilitation skills • Capability to design training programs and develop curriculum • Able to build cross-functional and cross-business relationships • Able to work effectively across different cultures and seniority • Proficient in key software applications • Good understanding of e-learning techniques • Participate in creation and/or delivery of e-learning packages • Research new techniques and methodologies in workplace learning • Analytical skills • Able to manage / assist to manage L&D budgets

As seen, L&D is a career path that requires constant learning to meet contemporary needs. To be able to talk about a subject in front of a group, an L&D professional has the privilege to learn ahead of others. For example, he or she can study new leadership models and management concepts to strengthen the self-understanding needed to deliver leadership training. And they sometimes attend personal effectiveness programmes before bringing the programmes to the organization. Therefore, the drive for self-learning should continue to be the real core competency of an L&D professional. Whether it is facilitation skills in the classroom or to control the keyboard in virtual programmes, the L&D career will continue to be a critical HR function as long as L&D professionals allow themselves to positively transform along with the rest of the HR world and be agile training leaders.

Conclusion

There is no doubt that L&D will continue to ride the current wave of technology disruption. In the 2017 *Training Needs and Development Survey* published by the Hong Kong Institute of Human Resource Management, one finding was the upward trend of companies adopting online learning, at a level of 65 per cent for companies that participated in the survey.[21]

No matter whether it is 'training and development' or 'learning and development', the future trend in this function is well summarized in Noe's book:

- Need to contribute to sustainability
- Use of new technologies for training delivery at instruction

- Breakthroughs in neuroscience about learning
- Greater emphasis on seed in design, focus on content
- Increased emphasis on capturing and sharing intellectual capital and social learning
- Increased use of just-in-time learning and performance support
- Increased emphasis on performance analysis, big data, and learning for business enhancement
- Increased use of stakeholder-focused learning, training partnerships, and outsourcing training[22]

As an L&D professional in the industry, it should be exciting to see and face the challenges since 'the L&D industry is complicated, with varying structures, shifting priorities, disruptive technologies and multiple audiences to appease. It's a lot to keep tabs on, and it's becoming increasingly more complex as new skills and new ways of learning emerge.'[23]

Review Questions

1. Define *training*, *development*, and *learning*. Explain why the *training and development* function has been transformed to *learning and development*.
2. Distinguish and identify different structures of L&D functions in organizations.
3. What are the implications of the change of employee demographics to L&D plans?
4. What are the impacts of big data and digitalization to L&D function?
5. What are the changes in L&D careers nowadays? What are the new roles and competencies of L&D professionals?

Notes

1. Based on findings in 2004, the model was developed with three tiers, in terms of foundational competencies, areas of expertise and roles for career growth and professional development of training professionals. ASTD. (n.d.). *ASTD competency model*. Retrieved from https://astdbigsky.wildapricot.org/Resources/Documents/091132.Competency_Model.pdf; see also Association for Talent Development. (2019). *ATD competency model*. Retrieved from https://www.td.org/certification/atd-competency-model
2. Blanchard, P. Nick, and Thacker, James W. (2013). *Effective training: systems, strategies, and practices* (5th ed). Boston: Pearson Education. Lynton, Rolf P. (2011). *Training for development*. Los Angeles: Sage.
3. Page-Tickell, Rebecca. (2014). *Learning and development*. London: Kogan Page.
4. Ashton, David. N. (2004). The impact of organizational structure and practices on learning in the workplace. *International Journal of Training and Development, 8*(1), 43–53.
5. Smerek, Ryan. (2018). *Organizational learning and performance: The science and practice of building a learning culture*. New York: Oxford University Press.
6. See for example, Veronica S. Pantelidis. (2009). Reasons to use virtual reality in education and training courses and a model to determine when to use virtual reality [Special issue]. *Themes in Science and Technology Education*, 59–70.
7. Noe, A. Raymond. (2017). *Employee training & development* (7th ed.). New York: McGraw Hill Education.

8. Gainey, Thomas W., and Klaas, Brian S. (2003). The outsourcing of training and development: Factors impacting client satisfaction. *Journal of Management, 29*(2), 207–229.
9. LinkedIn. (2018). *2018 Workplace learning report: The rise and responsibility of talent development in the new labor market*. Retrieved from https://learning.linkedin.com/elearning-solutions-guides/workplace-learning-report-2018
10. Billet, S. (2006). Constituting the workplace curriculum. *Journal of Curriculum Studies, 38*, 31–48.
11. Cook, B., and Kalantzis, M. (2016). Big data comes to school: implications for learning, assessment, and research. *AERA Open, 2*(2), 1–19.
12. Garner, R. (2017, October 4). Getting started with learning analytics. *Training Journal*. Retrieved from https://www.trainingjournal.com/blog/getting-started-learning-analytics
13. Shawar, A. (2010). Learning management systems: Are they knowledge management tools? *International Journal of Emerging Technologies in Learning, 5*(1), 4–10.
14. See also, Cabrera, B., Fraize, J., and Runkle, M. (2010). *The use of technology for teaching and learning in Hong Kong* (Unpublished Bachelor's thesis). Worchester Polytechnic University, supported by Lingnan University of Hong Kong, Hong Kong. Retrieved from https://web.wpi.edu/Pubs/E-project/Available/E-project-030410-230553/unrestricted/The_Use_of_Technology_for_Teaching_and_Learning_in_Hong_Kong.pdf
15. Langer, Arthur M. (2018). *Information technology and organizational learning: Managing behavioral change in the digital age*. Boca Raton, FL: CRC Press.
16. Marquardt, Michael J. (2011). *Building the learning organization: Achieving strategic advantage through a commitment to learning*. Boston: Nicholas Brealey Pub.
17. Paine, Nigel. (2014). *The learning challenge: Dealing with technology, innovation and change in learning and development*. Philadelphia: Kogan Page. Quinn, Clark N. (2014). *Revolutionize learning & development: Performance and innovation strategy for the information age*. San Francisco, CA: Wiley.
18. ASTD. (n.d.). *ASTD competency model*. Retrieved from https://astdbigsky.wildapricot.org/Resources/Documents/091132.Competency_Model.pdf. Association for Talent Development. (2019). *ATD competency model*. Retrieved from https://www.td.org/certification/atd-competency-model
19. Sarder, Russel. (2016). *Building an innovative learning organization: A framework to build a smarter workforce, adapt to change, and drive growth*. New Jersey: Wiley.
20. Purewal, Semmy. (2014). *Learning web app development*. Sebastopol, CA: O'Reilly Media.
21. HKIHRM. (2018). *2017 Training and development needs survey*. Hong Kong: Hong Kong Institute of Human Resource Management. See also, Hung, H., and Cho, V. (2008). Continued usage of e-learning communication tools: A study from the learners' perspective in Hong Kong. *International Journal of Training and Development, 12*(3), 171–187.
22. Noe, A. Raymond. (2017). *Employee training & development* (7th ed., p. 493). New York: McGraw Hill Education.
23. LinkedIn. (2018). *2018 Workplace learning report: The rise and responsibility of talent development in the new labor market*. Retrieved from https://learning.linkedin.com/elearning-solutions-guides/workplace-learning-report-2018

6
Development of the Performance Management System

Evolution or Revolution?

Wilfred K. P. Wong

> **LEARNING OUTCOMES**
>
> By the end of this chapter, readers should be able to
> - understand the concepts of performance management system and performance appraisal;
> - identify the benefits and concerns of performance management system and performance appraisal in organizations;
> - understand and evaluate the trends of performance management practices in organizations; and
> - identify the roles of HR professionals in performance management.

Introduction

Performance management is not something new to people. It has existed and been debated in the human resource management arena for years. While some applaud the benefits of using it as the foundation of performance excellence to motivate employees to work harder and achieve better results, others argue that it could demotivate employees, costing valuable time and money and becoming nuisance to both the managers and employees. It may also fail to deliver value originally aimed at.[1] Often, it is a major HR controversy. But despite the challenges with performance management, we envisage that organizations would not do away with it in the near future. Instead, companies have to revamp the system to fit into the current business needs and environment.

This chapter begins with the fundamentals of the performance management cycle and the performance appraisal process. Examples are presented to illustrate them in practice. In particular, we examine the issues, problems, and common errors associated with them. We then discuss how the performance management system has changed and where it is at today. The latest trends of development and examples will be highlighted.

Development of the Performance Management System

We offer opinions and insights for HR professionals, managers, academicians, and students and anticipate the future of performance management: Should the trend be evolutionary or revolutionary? Could we delink rewards from performance management? How can performance management be implemented smoothly in organizations? Readers should be able to review and implement their own performance management system more effectively in the workplace. We conclude the chapter with a summary of the factors affecting performance management system success in Hong Kong.

Some Fundamentals of the Performance Management System

In general, the term *performance management system* (PMS) refers to managing the entire performance cycle in the organization. It is a broad collection of activities designed to maximize individuals, which will be eventually extended to improve organizational performance. It includes setting expectations, measuring employee behaviours and results, providing coaching and feedback, and evaluating performance over time to use in decision-making. Its purpose is to align individual efforts to achieve organizational goals. For performance appraisal, it is part of the PMS process that involves the assessment of past performance within a given time frame. The purpose is to judge how well employees have performed with respect to the expectations set. Information will be used to make a variety of HR and organizational decisions.[2]

Figure 6.1: A typical performance management cycle

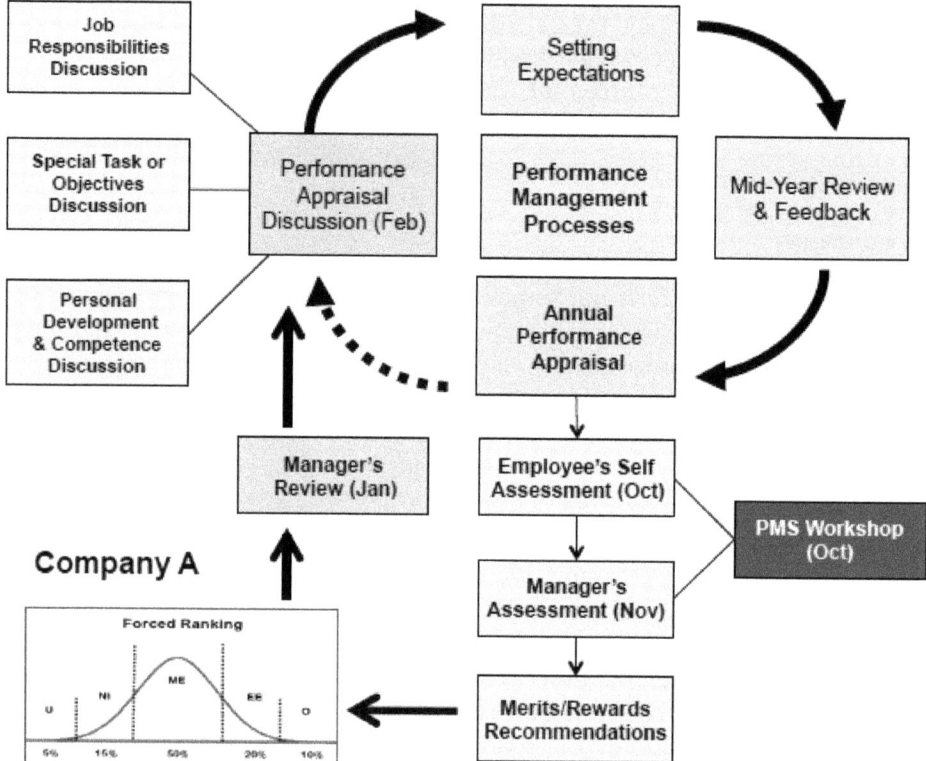

The performance management cycle

Figure 6.1 is a typical performance management cycle, starting with 'Setting Expectations'. It defines the standards and objectives of the forthcoming performance appraisal exercise that involves discussion between the supervisor/manager and his or her subordinate based on the organizational goals cascaded down to each functional, departmental, or individual level. The contents and extent of the dialogue/discussion should also make reference to the subordinate's own job responsibilities. At times, it may go beyond to stretch someone's potential. It would also be advantageous to understand a subordinate's personal development needs, and to utilize his or her skills and competencies. Some or all of the agreed expectations can become the special tasks or objectives, as shown on the left, which the subordinate will have to deliver within the agreed time frame.

After setting and agreeing on the expectations, the performance management cycle moves on to regular reviews and feedback. Most companies have an interim review and a feedback process. Some companies require a formal documentation of the discussion, whereas some merely arrange a sit-down conversation. It could facilitate a review of the agreed expectation, the changing courses of action, revision of the deliverables or timeline, where necessary. It encourages communication and understanding between supervisor/manager and his/her subordinates besides day-to-day business transactions.

The aforementioned PMS process is implemented based on the corporate directives or objectives set up by the top management. For HR professionals, they should encourage managers and subordinates to fully utilize the PMS to set agreeable key performance indicators and deliverables, foster regular dialogue, and manage their performance accordingly.

Problems of PMS

In a typical PMS, there can be multiple purposes of performance management (Table 6.1) that require different measures, assessments, and systems. But in reality organizations have often attempted to make use of PMS to achieve too many objectives using a single approach. They relate performance results to salary increase, rewards management, development, and training needs and thus distract from its prime focus on managing performance. For example, if the performance management system is used for personnel decision-making (like promotion or salary increase) and employee development, these two opposing objectives are rarely supported equally well by a single system or process. When a performance management system is used for development purposes, managers' ratings would tend to be more accurate. The ratings could somewhat reflect the truth, showing the employee's strengths and development needs. However, when a performance management system is used for personnel decisions, the ratings would tend to be more inflated. Unsurprisingly, top management or HR department may believe that managers could play favouritism in performance appraisal and therefore warrant a cumbersome written documentation system for close monitoring and control. It can result in mistrust between different parties (see Box 6.1).

Table 6.1: Typical purposes of performance management system

Administrative Purpose	Developmental Purpose
Help make compensation decisions (e.g. pay increases and bonuses)	Identify training and development needs
Identify individuals ready for new opportunities (e.g. promotions and assignments)	Provide career guidance and developmental opportunities
Provide documentation to defend against legal challenges	Enhance communication and relationships between managers and employees
Hold poor performers accountable for improving	Ensure employees receive effective feedback
Provide data for adverse impact analyses	Increase employee engagement and empower employees to take ownership of performance goals

Source: Society for Human Resource Management (SHRM). (2017). *Performance management that makes a difference: An evidence-based approach.* Alexandria: SHRM.

HRM in Action – Box 6.1

An Enhanced Performance Management System Cycle or Otherwise

Company A is a multinational company headquartered in Hong Kong. It had adopted a typical performance management system for years. Over the last decade, the company had introduced a forced-ranking system in the performance appraisal to put employee performance into different categories in order to grant their merit pay, incentive or bonus payout, as well as to decide on career advancement of the employees. The typical process was similar to the one illustrated in Figure 6.1.

At the beginning of the year, the organizational business goals and targets were cascaded down with details to each function or department. They became the basis for setting the expectations or KPIs of the individual employees each year. By fall of each year, formal notice was sent out by the HR department to all employees requiring them to take the formal annual performance appraisal. For new employees, supervisors, managers or general staff, or someone who would like to take refresher training, performance appraisal workshops were conducted prior to the appraisal process.

Employees were given opportunity to complete a self-assessment to gauge their own performance and accomplishments. It was an opportunity for them to review development needs and career aspirations with their supervisor.

After the manager's assessment of the subordinates' performance, the appraisal results were gathered by the HR department. The appraisal dialogue was arranged between the managers and subordinates to seek out clarification and feedback. However, in Company A, this kind of dialogue was put on hold because the company wanted to find out whether the appraisal results had fallen within the forced-ranking distribution requirements. If not, the HR department would advise the supervisor/manager to adjust the subordinates' assessments to fit the forced-ranking distribution.

The relevant supervisors/managers were unhappy especially when they were asked to downgrade their subordinates' ratings. They blamed the HR department and did not take accountability. Only on very rare occasions were subordinates' ratings adjusted upward. Usually employees were not aware of such downward adjustment unless their supervisors/managers told them. In this case, the employees would complain that their supervisors/managers could not do anything. As a consequence, all parties were unhappy and denied the ownership of the performance results.

Furthermore, Company A took the adjusted appraisal results and made reference to the compa-ratio* of each employee to determine the final merit pay. Since most employees did not understand the compa-ratio system, the performance appraisal and merit pay adjustment outcomes could be a total illusion to the employees. Eventually, most people took the entire performance management and appraisal as a ritual rather than a strategic tool in managing the organization and people performance. The worst is that most people lost trust in the performance management system.

* Compa-ratio is calculated as the employee's current salary divided by the current market rate as defined by the company's pay policy. It is position specific, with a salary range including a minimum, a midpoint, and a maximum. A compa-ratio of 1.00 or 100 per cent means that the employee is paid the industry average and is at the midpoint for the salary range. A ratio of 0.75 means that the employee is paid 25 per cent below the industry average and is at the risk of seeking employment with competitors at a higher pay that is perceived equitable.

As observed in most organizations, PMS is often accompanied with a sophisticated system of procedures and rules to follow, forms to complete, and criteria and ratings to comply with. These factors, which have little impact on actual performance, can be adopted at the expense of investing in good communications, feedback, and relationships among employees, managers, and even HR people. As a consequence, they result in a lack of buy-in from managers and employees that PMS is implemented poorly.

Additionally, the problems of PMS can be exacerbated by the faulty assumptions that candid performance ratings can motivate employees to achieve higher performance. However, we have to admit that most employees believe that they are above-average performers. They have no desire to hear the opposite. Even superior performers find their PMS demotivating.[3]

Problems of performance appraisal

Performance appraisal can be traced back to the US military merit rating system created during World War I to identify poor performers for discharge or transfer. The system continued after the World War II until the 1960s when 90 per cent of the US companies were using the performance appraisal system. Hitherto, strong merit results represented good advancement opportunities and rewards for people, and improving performance was only an afterthought. Until recently, managers allocated rewards and determined employee career progression according to the results of the performance appraisal. But again, performance appraisal ratings have long been controversial owing to their negative effects on employee morale and potential for bias and discrimination.

For example, when Jack Welch became the CEO of General Electric in the 1980s, he introduced a famous forced-ranking (or 'stack-ranking' system with a 'vitality curve'). While the top 20 per cent of the workforce was the most productive, the other 70 per cent (the 'vital 70') performed adequately. But the bottom 10 per cent people were classified as non-productive and had to be dismissed. This stack ranking was later copied by most large organizations in the world. Managers were compelled to use forced ranking in appraising their employees—usually assuming a normal distribution curve with most people being classified as 'average' performers. It has drawn many criticisms, such as compelling managers to sacrifice otherwise good employees, causing unhealthy competitions between employees, and assuming extrinsic motivation only.[4]

Another major drawback of the appraisal process is the lack of consistency of assessment results by different assessors. There could be inconsistent observations, personal bias, prejudice, or unfairly harsh ratings. Interestingly, the *Journal of Applied Psychology* has revealed that 62 per cent of the variance in ratings could be accounted for by the individual raters' peculiarities of perception. Actual performance only accounted for 21 per cent of the variance![5] Other studies echo that ratings often reflect rater goals, organizational norms, and political realities.[6] An interesting example showing rater and ratee dynamics is illustrated in Box 6.2.

HRM in Action—Box 6.2
Is It a Justifiable Performance Appraisal Decision for Mark?

Allan, a senior manager of ABC Advertising Agency heading a production team based in Hong Kong, reported to Charles, the regional head of advertising and production in Singapore. Over the years, the company adopted a typical PMS system—for instance, setting the annual KPIs at the beginning of the year, conducting a mid-year review and year-end appraisal. The overall performance rating system was a five-point scale, a score of three being a satisfactory level of meeting the KPIs and five being the exceptional performance. Attainment of a two would result in no merit increase and bonus payout; a rating of one would lead to PIP (performance improvement plan) or a subsequent dismissal.

Allan's subordinate Mark, who had been with the company for about ten years, had consistently achieved outstanding performance. Mark was promoted to the team head with a team of five people two years ago. Allan had been very pleased with Mark's performance and was prepared to promote him to be an assistant manager in the coming year. However, in November, Mark seemed to be losing his edge. He had missed deadlines and upset an important client. Subsequently, Allan talked to Mark and found out that his wife had been ill and hospitalized; at that time Mark had to take care of his wife and find someone to look after his young son. At the year-end appraisal in December, despite Mark's drop in performance, Allan gave a rating of three to Mark—meeting the standard (in the previous two years, Mark received a four and a five).

Despite Allan's intervention, the client had escalated his complaint to Charles. At the performance review meeting, Charles disagreed with Allan's rating on Mark, and insisted on adjusting it downward to two. Allan reckoned that a rating of two would hurt Mark's merit increase and bonus. He understood that Mark was in need of the bonus money to settle for the heavy medical expenses incurred from his wife's illness; and furthermore, it would jeopardize his promotion in the coming year.

We discussed PMS in Hong Kong in a previous book by highlighting a number of potential errors in the areas of setting desirable performance standards, informing employees on the performance standards, and appraising employees' performance, as well as feedback on performance. Factors stemming from Chinese culture, values, and rater biases are explained.[7] We reckon that Hong Kong society depicted in Hofstede's cross-cultural studies has high scores on 'power distance'. The superior must always be accorded face while the subordinate tends to accommodate to the wishes of the superior. And many Chinese managers culturally tend to be moderate and are taught not to make extreme decisions, either on the positive or negative sides, but to be in a state of equilibrium. In addition, the maintenance of harmony governs a great deal of the manager-subordinate relationship in Chinese business settings. In the organization, these managers tend to avoid giving extreme or harsh ratings (i.e. with central tendency).[8] On the other hand, some other managers would inflate the performance ratings for some political reasons as they want to protect a worker whose performance is temporarily suffering because of personal problems (see Box 6.2). Otherwise, some managers may deflate the performance ratings to jolt a worker to rise to his or her performance level. Also, Chinese managers who have a personality trait view of performance would not see there is a need to give performance feedback to the employees. Since being a good worker comes from having a 'good personality', then, being a bad worker comes from having a 'bad personality'.[9] As a result, appraisal results are not useful. Interested readers can understand more about various rating errors and psychological factors (such as central tendency, leniency/strictness, halo/horn effect, recency effect, bias, and favouritism) from available textbooks or reference works, including the previous chapter on performance management in Hong Kong.[10]

We now highlight one of the appraisal errors here. The following exercise was tried in several performance appraisal workshops conducted by the author with managers. The results were all similar. The exercise: a short movie clip extracted from the British comedy movie *Notting Hill* was shown to the participants. In the movie three different ladies were separately invited by Hugh Grant's family members to have dinner with Hugh Grant at his home. Each lady presented different personality traits and characteristics.

In each performance appraisal training workshop, individual participants were first asked to evaluate the three ladies' characteristics according to the participant's own perceptions. Participants were asked to mark their assessments on an enlarged chart posted on the wall. The collective ratings shown were interesting.

A sample of the collective assessments was shown in Figure 6.2. Despite the distinctive differences among the three ladies, the collective ratings showed some convergence. The participants of the performance appraisal workshop collectively considered the third lady the best among the three.

Figure 6.2: Assessment results after watching *Notting Hill* video

(Rating Scale: 1 = Poor, 5 = Excellent)

Lady: First	1	2	3	4	5
Attire	✓	✓✓✓	✓✓		
Tone of Voice		✓✓✓	✓✓✓		
Manner		✓✓✓✓	✓✓		
Overall Impression		✓✓✓✓	✓✓		

Lady: Second	1	2	3	4	5
Attire	✓✓	✓✓✓	✓		
Tone of Voice	✓✓	✓✓✓	✓		
Manner		✓✓✓✓	✓✓		
Overall Impression	✓	✓✓✓✓	✓		

Lady: Third	1	2	3	4	5
Attire			✓✓✓	✓✓	✓
Tone of Voice			✓✓	✓✓✓	✓
Manner			✓	✓✓	✓✓✓
Overall Impression			✓	✓✓✓	✓

Is the third lady the best dating target for Hugh Grant? When the participants were asked the rationale behind their assessments, they reflected that they were only based on their own personal judgement, background, and perception. But who should be the best and ideal girlfriend for Hugh Grant, and what were the factors to base that determination on? Of course, we could not have asked the actor. . . . It was only an exercise.

We may ask why there was a convergence (or divergence) of the views? Based on the author's judgement, as the exercise was mainly carried out among the companies in Hong Kong, the participants were mostly brought up and influenced by the local Chinese culture. Many people are modest, avoiding extreme answers. In addition, this statement 'beauty always wins', is always true since the third person is the most beautiful. In other words, 'halo effect' was important among the assessors.[11] And as HR professionals, we must be aware of human errors in the performance appraisal. Regular training to line managers and employees by HR regarding different types of assessment errors using rehearsal exercises, role playing, and feedback would be useful.

HRM in Action—Box 6.3
A Forced Ranking Model in Practice

Company A presented in Box 6.1 had adopted a typical performance management process and introduced the forced-ranking system of the performance appraisal by putting employees into different bands in order to manage their merit pay, incentive, or bonus payout. Unlike General Electric's 20-70-10 model, Company A subdivided the ranking into five zones as follows according to its employees' performance appraisal results:

- 10 per cent 'Exceptional & Outstanding'
- 20 per cent 'Exceeding Expectation'
- 50 per cent 'Meeting Expectation'
- 15 per cent 'Improvement Needed'
- 5 per cent 'Unsatisfactory Result'

The company had introduced a grid table such that the merit salary increment would be determined by the forced-ranking distribution and the compa-ratio of the employee (see Chapter 7 for more details). There would be no salary increment to employees classified as 'Improvement Needed' and 'Unsatisfactory Result'.

Evolutionary or Revolutionary Changes of PMS?

Improving existing PMS

In view of the above criticisms, the performance management system is generally viewed by stakeholders as ineffective and unable to meet the purpose of performance improvement. Many organizations perceive that the PMS process has become a ritual and an administrative burden. Indeed, Deloitte's survey in 2015 found that 58 per cent of the executives believed that their performance management system drives neither employee engagement nor high performance.[12] They want something new to 'fuel performance' in the future, rather than focus on individual performances in the past (see Box 6.4).

HRM in Action—Box 6.4
New Thoughts on Performance Management

Deloitte's new radical design is built on the following objectives. The first is to *Recognize Performance*, particularly through variable compensation. The second enables the people to *See it Clearly*. They ask what their supervisors/managers would 'do' with their subordinate, rather than what they would 'think' of the individuals. The third is to *Fuel Performance*, meaning what should be done to strengthen the performance.

On the other hand, we note that many organizations are still reluctant to change their current PMS. They may fear that the disruption could lead to poor employee morale and cost a great deal of money, among other potential costs. The problems are especially acute for small and medium firms without sufficient resources and expertise.

And we judge that failures of PMS often arise from the implementation and sustainment efforts, rather than from the design of a PMS. Therefore, we hereby make some suggestions to companies to address the above problems in their PMS:

- Clear purpose of PMS—organizations may look for changes of their PMS by questioning whether they should retain the performance reviews and ratings. Here is a better question: What business outcomes is the organization trying to achieve, and how can PMS support these outcomes? As we argued, a PMS with too many purposes will serve none of them well. Instead, an important first step of designing a PMS is to define what purpose it should achieve, and how it should align with the organizational goals or strategies. It may also state the rationale of the design and the problems it helps solve (for example, changing work behaviours for business improvement).[13]
- Defining performance standards/measurements—organizations should decide what 'high performance' means in their context. Take fast-food restaurants as an example: they typically seek to deliver good-tasting food efficiently. Their competitive advantage is probably speed, low cost, and predictable service and quality. Workers who serve efficiently and follow established procedures are effective performers. But in the same organization, different job roles and work activities will have different levels of complexity and needs for autonomy, and therefore different performance standards. There are both objective standards/measurements (such as number of hours worked) and subjective/behavioural standards/measurements (e.g. communication skills and courtesy with customers). They can be gauged from multiple sources (e.g. managers, customers, or peers) and methods. In addition, effective goal setting can lead to better performance if they fulfil certain criteria (remember SMART goals—specific, measurable, achievable, realistic, and time-bound?) that are personally meaningful, flexible (in timelines and formats) and within the individuals' control to achieve in order to encourage greater ownership. Characteristics of effective performance goals can be easily found in available references.[14]
- Feedback and coaching—providing effective feedback is one of the most useful ways to boost employee performance. However, most feedback is ineffective. Sometimes, feedback does not lead to performance improvement.[15] The difference between feedback that improves performance and feedback that does not depend on the content, the manner of delivery and the way of receiving it. Effective feedback should be fair and accurate, specific, and oriented towards an employee's strengths and behaviour. And employees would be receptive to criticisms if they believe the process is fair. It should be based on objective results rather than subjective judgements. And it has to be timely and a two-way dialogue between the employee and a credible source who knows the employee well and could provide insights for improvement. Therefore, improving feedback and coaching should start with training the managers. The role of communication is important as well. Managers should always communicate to their employees how performance management can contribute to the success of business.
- Issues on performance ratings—performance appraisal typically entails rating on one or more dimensions, using a 3-, 5-, or 7-point scale (some organizations

choose 4-, 6-, or 8-point scales for other reasons). Others have adopted competency-based approaches with behaviourally anchored rating scales. Despite decades of research to improve the reliability and accuracy of these rating systems, results have been disappointing. Regardless of how scales are constructed, who is providing the ratings and how raters are trained, ratings are substantially unrelated to external measures of performance. And different raters can hardly agree on performance ratings, even when they observe the same behaviours.[16] These considerations have thus led to a fierce debate about whether to abandon performance ratings. Proponents of keeping ratings argue that performance is always evaluated, whether explicitly or implicitly. Without ratings, it is difficult to differentiate rewards. Though ratings may not positively affect performance, they can serve to ensure employees receive periodic feedback and provide some level of consistency in giving rewards.[17] And there are good suggestions to improve performance evaluations.[18] In Hong Kong some ways to tackle the performance-rating issues are proposed as well (see Box 6.5).

HRM in Focus—Box 6.5
Ways to Tackle Performance-Rating Issues in Hong Kong

The author notes that a few companies in Hong Kong have adopted computerized systems for tackling performance-rating issues. It keeps track of the rating behaviours of assessors in order to normalize the differences. After being input into the computer system using predefined algorithms, the raw performance ratings are adjusted according to past evaluation behaviours of the assessors. Though the adjusted performance ratings are more reliable and made known to the assessors, the ownership and accountability of the process and results, however, is diminished.

To maintain consistency of appraisal results, an alternative can be achieved through pre-appraisal discussion among all functional/department heads. In the meeting, a typical employee (say, John) known to most (or all) function/department heads was identified and his past performance and achievement was discussed and evaluated. Consensus of opinions (different from the 360-degree feedback) is to be achieved in order to arrive at an agreed performance rating, which shall become the yardstick to measure the other employees' performance in the company. For anyone whose performance is above John's shall be assessed with a higher rating, or vice versa. But this method would only work on a small scale as it is difficult to find someone known by all functional/department heads in a large company or across regions or countries.

Revolutionary changes of PMS?

Yet still, many executives are questioning whether their current performance management approach drives neither employee engagement nor high performance. Companies are dedicating much time and effort to setting objectives at the beginning of the year, rating and commenting on employees' objectives, and factoring evaluations into a single year-end rating after lengthy consensus meetings and discussion sessions among managers, counsellors, and employees. Debates on eliminating ratings continue. As a result, consulting firms such as PricewaterhouseCoopers (PwC) has conducted research on swapping the performance management paradigm with a performance management scheme. They suggest a need for radical change of the PMS. It should be something nimbler, real-time, and more individualized, which can fuel performance in the future rather than assessing the past (see Box 6.6). At the same time, performance management technology tools facilitating goal setting and instant feedback are available in the market (Table 6.2; see also Chapter 9 about HR technologies). They may cause disruptive change of PMS in organizations.

HRM in Focus—Box 6.6
New Paradigm of Performance Management

PricewaterhouseCoopers (PwC) has embarked on a new performance management scheme with new definitions of behaviour, simplification of rating scale, introduction of performance reviews after milestones or projects and integration into a new HR information system. The scheme put forward the following innovative practices:

1. Abandoning the annual PMS cycle—shorten or delink the appraisal process from the standard PMS cycle and move to a continuous feedback dialogue.
2. Changing the focus of performance appraisal—putting less emphasis on backward-looking appraisal; aiming for a forward-looking approach with dynamic goal setting and regular conversations.
3. Simplifying the PMS process by tools and technology—the traditional PMS process is replaced by an online real-time system offering immediate feedback to employees.
4. Removing the individual performance ratings—it allows meaningful and honest discussion on personal development, career progression, and performance improvement.
5. Changing the link between pay and performance—change the rigid timeline to reward the employees in a timely and appropriate fashion (see Chapter 7 on total rewards management).
6. Getting insight from data—'big data' can provide meaningful and reliable information on talent management to make better decisions.
7. Integrating people challenges to drive business performances—HR activities should be aligned with performance management to improve business needs and performance.

Source: PricewaterhouseCoopers. (2015, October). The changing performance management paradigm: Evolution or revolution? Is there a future for performance management? Retrieved from https://www.pwc.nl/nl/assets/documents/pwc-performance-survey-2015.pdf

Indeed, a number of Fortune 500 organizations have revamped their PMS in a similar vein. Some examples are given in Boxes 6.7 and 6.8.

HRM in Action—Box 6.7

General Electric's New Performance Management System

More companies are abandoning their traditional performance management system as leaders find more timely and efficient systems to drive employee engagement and high performance. The former process of long appraisals in a static annual cycle is now considered out of place in a new world which is constantly changing and highly dynamic. The need to change is also driven by a younger workforce that want faster and more frequent feedback on work efforts to move forward, rather than look backwards. General Electric (GE) is one of the forward-thinking companies which eliminated ratings and rankings and has implemented frequent performance conversations to enable future employee growth.

GE, an American multinational conglomerate founded in 1892, is now operating in several industries ranging from energy and transportation to healthcare and has 300,000 employees globally. Hong Kong is its global headquarters for the Global Growth Organization, a unit focused on accelerating growth outside the US.

GE recognized that to succeed in the twenty-first century it needed to shift gears and align to the new business environment by incorporating more contemporary elements of performance development with strengths of the previous employee management system process. 'Command and control is what Jack was famous for. Now it's about connection and inspiration,' noted a GE executive at the Crotonville leadership centre.

The change also reflects the rise of mobile technology and fast information sharing, which better caters to millennials and a more globalized workforce. The new performance development system, fully implemented across the company at the end of 2016, includes a mobile app to enable frequent and easy connection and dialogue. Called PD@GE (performance development at GE), the app provides a platform to define near-term goals (or 'priorities') for employees. Leaders are expected to have frequent conversations, called 'touchpoints', with their employees on their progress, outcomes, and considerations to close the gap on reaching their priorities. The app can provide summaries through typed notes, photographs of a notepad, or even voice recordings of these touchpoints when desired. With higher flexibility, the app supports managers to provide forward-looking development and unlock constant improvement with an emphasis on coaching. Employees can also give or request insights at any point through a feature in the system not limited to their immediate manager, teams, or their division.

Leaders still have an annual touchpoint with their employees at the end of the year as a summary of what has been discussed throughout the year, the progress against these ongoing conversations, and the contribution against the priorities that had been defined. It is short, to the point, less formal, and less time consuming compared to the former process. The annual salary decisions are still linked to employee performance under the new system, with leaders deciding (with the support of HR) how to distribute the salary increase budget, according to each employee's contribution to the company's success. The only difference is that leaders are not depending on any rating framework anymore. It is clear to leaders that in the world where they had the ratings, almost 80 per cent of their employees were falling into the middle zone anyways. If they can differentiate 80 per cent of the employees who had the same rating, do they really need ratings to differentiate 100 per cent of the employees? It is really related to contribution of the employee, the insights that leaders received about the employee, and how much the leader knows his or her team.

Throughout the journey, GE asked employees and leaders across regions and businesses to answer a few simple questions to help them truly understand where their employees are in this transformational journey. They found that 81 per cent of people leaders felt the reward planning was the same or easier than the previous year. They also felt the new system gives the opportunity to focus on people's talent with a forward-looking view about their development and future state, supported by ongoing discussions. Since this is a massive change for a company with over 300,000 employees, the calibre of leadership is becoming even more important. GE is investing a lot on leadership development with different programmes to design the leaders of tomorrow.

Sources:
Interview information from Ms. Belgin Ertam, Senior Human Resources Director, Global Organization and Talent Development Director, and Global Growth Organization of GE. She was based in Hong Kong in summer 2017.
Nisen, M. (2015, August 13). Why GE has to kills its annual performance reviews after more than three decades. Retrieved from https://qz.com/428813/ge-performance-review-strategy-shift

HRM in Action—Box 6.8
Microsoft's New Approach to Performance Management

Microsoft believes that a new approach to performance management needs to support a culture that helps facilitate changes and achieves the greatest results. Three areas are prioritized: delivering results differently through teamwork; giving feedback that helps people learn and delivers results; and reinforcing through the rewards employees receive. Performance is now redefined as 'impact', which evaluates an employee's performance in a team or business and with the customers.

For speedy and true collaboration, Microsoft also looks into three individual accomplishments: the contributions made to others' success, the leveraging of each other's ideas, and work to deliver better and faster results.

The company focuses on ongoing discussion between managers and employees, centering on their learning and growth, the impact on business, and the opportunities to create greater impact. While no year-end assessment exists, ratings of performance are not used. Conversations on performance are called 'connects' and are designed to encourage faster, more iterative points of reflection, learning, and application of that learning to move forward.

The new approach was introduced in November 2013. Each function, department, or team works out their own pattern based on their business nature. This move by Microsoft mitigates the threat, distraction, and internal competition that may be associated with performance ratings.

As such, the Microsoft managers would need to embrace new ways of thinking about what performance should look like, and seek out guidance on how to think about impact on business, and the relevant questions to ask. However, the said guidance is not rigidly defined or described. Rather, it is somewhat directional to help managers understand the higher or lower impact of performance on business results.

Source: Armstrong, M. (2017). *Armstrong's handbook of performance management: An evidence-based guide to delivering high performance* (6th ed.). New York: Kogan Page.

Table 6.2: Performance management technology tools in the market

Performance Management Tool	Purpose
BetterWorks	Goal and performance management platform
High Ground	Goal, feedback, recognition and engagement platform
Impraise	Performance and goal management
Reflektive	Feedback & performance management platform
Small Improvements	Agile performance & goal management platform

Nevertheless, the biggest challenge when moving to a 'ratingless' PMS is making the reward decisions. The traditional approach of pay-for-performance system (see Chapter 7 for details) is relatively straightforward when personnel decisions are tied to performance ratings or rankings. It works best when organizations can isolate, measure, and clearly link employee effort to outcome. It motivates job roles in sales or production well. But in many instances, pay for performance does not work as well as intended.[19] Now, removing the linkage between performance and reward decision could lead people to be more receptive to PMS (Box 6.9). However, a legitimate question immediately arises: How can organizations reward employees in an unbiased or objective manner without ratings?

Readers may take note of how large organizations such as General Electric and Microsoft reward their employees in the new PMS. Impact on business is rewarded and managers are given the discretion of granting the rewards. Here, insights from a study may also be useful. A recent investigation has found that performance is often not normally distributed—that is, it is skewed, with most employees clustered tightly together at the low end, with about 20 per cent of the population outperforming their peers by several orders of magnitude.[20] The finding is instructive in the way that we may only need fewer distinctions of ratings, if not ratingless (for example, a 3-point rating scale). A simple system to classify employee performance into three groups is good enough: top performers receiving greatest rewards; underperformed employees requiring improvement; and a vast majority of employees with adequate performance deserving rewards.

And at the same time, interestingly, CEB has revealed in its 2016 large-scale *Pay for Performance Employee Survey* that when organizations have eliminated their performance ratings, positive feedbacks were received initially. However, the initial positive reactions tended to fade out gradually when key performance outcomes were eventually affected. Both managers and employees found difficulties with the change. For example, employees' perceived manager conversation quality decreased without ratings. Additionally, top performers were less satisfied with the pay differentials.

Employee engagement also declined. In fact, CEB identified that half of the surveyed companies, among 296 organizations, did not plan to remove their rating system. Hence, it is argued that rather than focusing on the ratings debate, organizations should improve their performance management and reward practices. Performance feedback should be ongoing and forward-looking. Peer feedback on employee performance, apart from managers', would also be useful.[21]

To sum up our discussion and to decide whether organizations should have ratings, we suggest the following questions and recommendations:

- What assumptions do organizations use about ratings (for example, to help poor performers to improve)? Are these assumptions supported by evidence—for instance, do poor performers receive lower ratings?
- How have ratings been used historically in the organization? What would be gained or lost if ratings are eliminated?
- What is the cost of the current rating system? How much time has been spent? And how much value has been added?
- What is the link between performance and rewards? Do we have the means to provide differential rewards? Do ratings help the organization make the decisions?
- Do we have other means to evaluate performance or make various effective talent decisions without ratings?
- Are the managers and employees receptive to change, including eliminating performance ratings without affecting performance reviews?
- For organizations without performance ratings, managers should provide continuous performance feedback. Managers should be trained to send quality messages about performance and development by providing concrete evidence of employee performance.
- Performance reviews should be forward-looking, discussing future performance with clear understanding of employee abilities to meet future business needs.

HRM in Action—Box 6.9

Delinking Pay from Performance Appraisal Results

Company D started its business in Hong Kong in the 1980s, and now it has grown to a size of more than 1,000 employees, with branch offices in Taiwan, Singapore, and Indonesia. It had implemented a formal PMS in the 1990s, with a mid-year dialogue and year-end appraisal. Documentation of the activities had been supported by a computerized system. Forced-ranking distribution was applied and performance results were tied to pay decisions. But unfortunately, the annual performance appraisal exercise had become a ritual as managers were burdened with documentation via computer system input. And people were skeptical about the forced-ranking distribution.

Two years ago, putting increased emphasis on managing performance, the chairman and CEO wanted to focus on the development and growth discussion of the employee and the company. He decided to separate the annual performance appraisal from the pay decision. He instructed the HR director to propose the required processes and logistics.

After some careful study, the HR director proposed a new annual performance management cycle. KPIs were agreed in January and managers would conduct monthly review dialogues with their subordinates, with one year-end formal review in December of each year. The salary adjustment date would be changed to April (instead of the previous month, January) so that the formal review discussion in December would not link with the pay decisions. The enhanced performance review would mainly focus on discussing the performance impact on business, the competency gaps, and growth opportunities of the individuals. Regular monthly dialogues could also enhance the relationship between managers and subordinates.

It was determined that the salary adjustment decision should be left to the responsibility of the department heads, based on the approved budget. And the salary discussion between the manager and subordinates was conducted in March, one month before the adjustment date.

To aid the implementation of the enhanced process, the HR director had initiated a series of communication sessions with training workshops and printed materials in the following performance cycle year.

Conclusion

In this chapter we have discussed the PMS cycle and the performance appraisal. Organizations have attempted to use PMS to achieve purposes such as rewarding performance, development and training of employees, and improving employee performance. But controversies are found in the PMS and the appraisal process, with different perceptions, rating errors, and problems of implementation. Famous multinational organizations such as Deloitte, PwC, Microsoft, General Electric, just to name a few, have put forward a revolutionary, if not evolutionary, approach to revamp their PMS, including elimination of the annual performance reviews and the ratings. A more dynamic and engaging process of ongoing feedback and coaching is now emphasized. Stories of their transformation are inspiring. Critics, however, have commented that changing the traditional PMS could 'kill' the performance reviews.[22] Other concerns involve pay for performance and associated talent management decisions. In addition, managers may be intrigued by the idea of replacing performance appraisal with more frequent dialogues. While more time would be spent in the conversations, they wonder how the goal of PMS can be achieved while still rewarding their employees fairly.

Despite the above, research has supported the value of PMS practices to achieve various organizational goals.[23] Here, we provide some insights that would affect PMS success in Hong Kong. Given the fact that the mental models of the local managers may be different from those used by Western managers, it is necessary to examine how these differences might influence HR managers in the design and conduct of performance management in Chinese societies. We understand that culture is extremely difficult to change in the short term. It might be wise to choose only those practices that have a good chance of success, and then transplant those into Hong Kong with appropriate adaptations.[24]

- Understanding an organization's performance culture and employee characteristics—a performance-oriented culture can enhance standards of excellence and ensure results and accountability in the organization. Some building blocks of such culture include openness and trust, communication, managed differences, and relying on people's strengths.[25] Interestingly, an earlier study found that appraisal was more widespread in Hong Kong than in Britain. The latter type of appraisal tended to be more participative with greater emphasis on discussing objectives, development, and career plans. Hong Kong's performance appraisals, however, appeared to be more directive. While Hong Kong employees perceived a higher level of 'negative' appraiser behaviour (i.e. with more autocratic management style), they showed stronger support for using appraisal for reward and punishment and less support for objectives setting and training and development. And the negative supervisor behaviour did not result in less confidence in appraisal. They were more likely to favour involving a more senior manager in appraisal, and less likely to have more frequent appraisals.[26]

    The findings might suggest to us that Hong Kong employees do not show more resistance to performance appraisal than their counterparts (in Britain). They are more receptive to a directive top-down approach, given the higher power distance and stronger respect for authority culture. To them, PMS is a matter of employee acceptance, rather than an issue of 'selling'. It gives us a clear example that implementation of HR practices, such as performance appraisal, has to take into account of cultural compatibility. And Hong Kong's HR professionals need to understand their organizational culture and employee characteristics and make adaptations to nurture a culture for PMS success. At the same time, active senior leadership support is required. Without top management commitment and leadership acceptance, employees would have the tendency to give lower priority to the system.[27]

- Setting a clear purpose of PMS—we note in this chapter that the general dissatisfaction of PMS is a lack of agreement on its purpose. Managers would evaluate the employees differently according to different objectives. For salary determination, managers may have to consider the budget constraint from the organization directives. This may lead to deflating the performance rating. Alternatively, if the objective is for training and performance improvement, managers may be more honest with their evaluation. Thus, managers and employees should understand the clear purpose of PMS.

- Setting desirable performance standards—standards of performance desirable in Chinese societies often relate to Confucian values such as honouring the hierarchy and maintaining harmonious relationships and seriousness about tasks.[28] These moral standards as performance standards seem logical to Chinese employees. And many managers see no reason to use objective performance standards. While objective performance standards can reduce the impact of personal bias in assessment, they also have limitations to their efficacy, as the changing external environment or other uncontrollable factors can affect them. Using objective performance standards therefore may ignore the adaptability requirements of employers in order to deal with the changing environment.

    While personality traits like integrity, initiative, and hard-working are highly subjective, they are traits important to business, and managers may make personnel decisions based on them. These personality traits should be evaluated, but putting controls on the level of subjectivity in the appraisal system. In some instances, a person's personality may be a significant factor in his or her poor performance, for example, not everyone's temperament is suited to customer service. In these cases, the organization may consider moving the individual to another position more in keeping with his or her personality.[29]

- Choice of appraisal methods and rating system—though many appraisal methods (e.g. narrative description, rankings, graphic rating, critical incident, behaviourally anchored rating scale, and management by objectives) have been widely used together with the recent discussion of a ratingless system, research has shown that the difference between the use of rating scales and evaluation formats is ultimately trivial as the particular format used does not generally make a significant difference to the results produced. A ratingless system has also got its drawbacks. Our advice to managers is that they should aim to use the method most appropriate for the jobs being evaluated.[30]

- Provide training to managers—a global study found that managers are often unskilled in communicating and delivering various steps of PMS while they do not hold accountability of the system.[31] Therefore, organizations should not just focus on trying to improve the appraisal method or rating system. They should train the managers to understand the purpose of PMS, set desirable performance standards, evaluate performance by gathering and recording supporting evidence in order to discriminate performance, clarify expectations with their employees, provide feedback, and help improve employee performance.[32] Good training can also improve the skill of managers in handling dynamics with their employees, such as fear, anger, and a gamut of other emotions.

    We should note that local employees may respond poorly to negative feedback. There is a growing need for performance appraisal being an ongoing process. If a performance appraisal is a formal process conducted at scheduled times of the year, all employees, including those in Hong Kong, tend to feel uncomfortable and perceive feedback as criticisms. But if performance appraisal is structured in the form of regular coaching and review between managers and employees throughout the year, or after an incident, employees would be more receptive to advice and suggestions. Managers need to learn how to provide feedback in a timely and effective fashion.

- Linking pay/rewards to performance—managers should understand the links between performance results and both the extrinsic and intrinsic rewards. It is known that reward is conducive when the employees show readiness to contribute to the profitability of the organization through additional efforts. And employees should see a visible link between the day-to-day tasks and the expected rewards through enhanced motivation and improved performance.[33] Studies have also shown that employee satisfaction is caused by a properly implemented reward system, which has a direct effect on their performance.[34] Thus, the prospective reward system should be well communicated to employees at all levels and receive top management support and commitment while being driven by the managers. (See Box 6.9. We will discuss this issue further in Chapter 7.)

We should note that PMS / performance appraisal is not only an evaluation process of a person's performance with reward, development or improvement. Its purpose is to align and improve the performance of an individual in order to meet the overall organizational objective. We believe that with better understanding and collaborative effort from various stakeholders, we can develop an effective system that improves the performance of employees and the organization itself.

Review Questions

1. Describe a typical performance management cycle.
2. There are benefits and concerns about the performance management system. Describe a benefit and a concern—and suggest way to improve it.
3. Why does the performance management system require a formal annual review process? Can mid-year or regular performance appraisal dialogues improve the effectiveness and receptiveness of the performance management?
4. If you were going to replace your company's performance appraisal by a 'ratingless' system, as advocated by Microsoft, what are the hurdles that you might encounter?
5. What are the potential issues if your company introduces regular performance appraisal dialogues throughout the year?
6. In your workplace what would be the potential issues and bottlenecks if the rewards decisions delink from the performance appraisal results?

Notes

1. Aguinis, H. (2014). *Performance management* (3rd ed.). Boston: Pearson. Adler, S., et al. (2016). Getting rid of performance ratings: Genius or folly? A debate. *Industrial and Organizational Psychology, 9*, 219–252.
2. Society for Human Resource Management (SHRM). (2017). *Performance management system that makes a difference: An evidence-based approach*. Alexandria: SHRM. Retrieved from https://www.shrm.org/hr-today/trends-and-forecasting/special-reports-and-expert-views/Documents/Performance%20Management.pdf
3. Aguinis, H., Joo, H., and Gottfredson, R. K. (2011). Why we hate performance management—and why we should love it. *Business Horizons, 54*, 503–507.
4. Cappelli, P. and Tavis, A. (2016). The performance management revolution. *Harvard Business Review, 10*, 58–67. Retrieved from https://hbr.org/2016/10/the-performance-management-revolution
5. Scullen, S. E., Mount, M. K., and Goff, M. (2000). Understanding the latent structure of job performance ratings. *The Journal of Applied Psychology, 85*(6), 956–970.
6. Murphy, K. R., and Cleveland, J. N. (1995). *Understanding performance appraisal: Social, organizational, and goal oriented perspectives*. Newbury Park: Sage. Culbertson, S. S., and Henning, J. B., and Payne, S. C. (2013). Performance appraisal satisfaction: The role of feedback and goal orientation. *Journal of Personnel Psychology, 12*, 189–195.
7. Lee, Jenny S. Y. (2009). Performance management: Concept and practice. In A. Tsui and K. T. Lai (Eds.), *Professional practices of human resource management in Hong Kong, Linking HRM to organizational success* (pp. 87–98). Hong Kong: Hong Kong University Press.
8. Hofstede, G. H. (1980). *Culture's consequences: International differences in work-related values*. Beverly Hills: Sage. Bond, M. H. (1991). *Beyond the Chinese face*. Hong Kong: Oxford University Press.

9. Hempel, Paul. S. (2001). Differences between Chinese and Western managerial views of performance. *Personnel Review*, *30*(2), 203–226.
10. Lee, Jenny S. Y. (2009). Performance management: Concept and practice. In A. Tsui and K. T. Lai (Eds.), *Professional practices of human resource management in Hong Kong, Linking HRM to organizational success* (pp. 87–98). Hong Kong: Hong Kong University Press. Armstrong, M. (2017). *Armstrong's handbook of performance management: An evidence-based guide to delivering high performance* (6th ed.). New York: Kogan Page. Noe, Raymond A. et al. *Human resource management: Gaining a competitive advantage* (10th ed.). New York: McGraw Hill. Dessler, G. (2017). *Human resource management* (15th ed.). Upper Saddle River: Prentice Hall.
11. Halo effect is a cognitive bias where a person making an initial assessment of another person, place, or issue will assume ambiguous information based upon concrete information. For example, when a person is attractive, well groomed, and properly attired, an individual will assume, using a mental heuristic, that the person is a good one based upon the rules of that individual's social concept. Nisbett, Richard E., and Wilson, Timothy D. (1977). The halo effect: Evidence for unconscious alteration of judgments. *Journal of Personality and Social Psychology*, *35*(4): 250–256.
12. Buckingham, M., and Goodall, A. (2015, April). Reinventing performance management. *Harvard Business Review*, 40–51. Retrieved from https://hbr.org/2015/04/reinventing-performance-management
13. Mueller-Hanson, R. A., and Pulakos, E. D. (2015). *Putting the 'performance' back into the performance management*. Retrieved from https://www.shrm.org/hr-today/trends-and-forecasting/special-reports-and-expert-views/Documents/SHRM-SIOP%20Performance%20Management.pdf
14. Dorsey, D., and Mueller-Hanson, R. (2017). *Performance management that makes a difference: An evidence-based approach*. Alexandria: SHRM. Retrieved from https://www.shrm.org/hr-today/trends-and-forecasting/special-reports-and-expert-views/documents/performance%20management.pdf
15. Kluger, A. N., and DeNisi, A. S. (1996). The effects of feedback interventions on performance: A historic review, metanalysis and a preliminary feedback intervention theory. *Psychological Bulletin*, *119*, 254–284. Gregory, J. B., and Levy, P. E. (2015). *Using feedback in organizational consulting*. Washington, DC: American Psychological Association.
16. DeNisi, A. S., and Murphy, K. R. (2017). Performance appraisal and performance management: 100 years of progress? *Journal of Applied Psychology*, *3*, 421–433.
17. Adler, S. et al. (2016). Getting rid of performance ratings: Genius or folly? A debate. *Industrial and Organizational Psychology*, *9*, 219–252.
18. Dorsey, D., and Mueller-Hanson, R. (2017). *Performance management that makes a difference: An evidence-based approach*. Alexandria: SHRM. Retrieved from https://www.shrm.org/hr-today/trends-and-forecasting/special-reports-and-expert-views/documents/performance%20management.pdf
19. London, M., and Smither, J. W. (2002). Feedback orientation, feedback culture, and the longitudinal performance management process. *Human Resource Management Review*, *12*, 81–100.
20. O'Boyle, E. Jr., and Aguinis, H. (2012). The best and the rest: Revisiting the norm of normality of individual performance. *Personnel Psychology*, *65*, 79–119.
21. Brown, B. (2017, Fourth quarter). What does performance management change mean for you? *HRBP Quarterly*, 16–19.
22. Culbert, S. A., and Rout, L. (2010). *Get rid of the performance review!: How companies can stop intimidating, start managing—and focus on what really matters*. New York: Business Plus. Rock, D., Davis, J., and Jones, B. (2014, August). Kill your performance ratings. *Strategy + Business*. Retrieved from https://www.strategy-business.com/article/00275?gko=c442b

23. Aguinis, H. (2014). *Performance management* (3rd ed.). Boston: Pearson. Adler, S., et al. (2016). Getting rid of performance ratings: Genius or folly? A debate. *Industrial and Organizational Psychology*, *9*, 219–252.
24. See also, Aguinis, H., Joo, H., and Gottfredson, Ryan K. (2012). Performance management universals: Think globally and act locally. *Business Horizons*, *55*, 385–392.
25. Reid, J., and Hubbell, V. (2005, March/April). Creating a performance culture. *Ivey Business Journal*. Retrieved from https://iveybusinessjournal.com/publication/creating-a-performance-culture
26. Snape, Ed., Thompson, D., Yan, K. C. Fanny., and Redman, T. (1998). Performance appraisal and culture: Practice and attitudes in Hong Kong and Britain. *International Journal of Human Resource Management*, *9*(5), 841–861.
27. Law, R., and Tam, P. (2008). Employees' perception of performance appraisal. *Journal of Human Resources in Hospitality and Tourism*, *7*(1), 25–43.
28. Shenka, O., and Ronen, S. (1990). Culture, ideology, or economy: A comparative exploration of work goal importance among managers of Chinese societies. *Advances in International Comparative Management*, *5*, 117–134. Redding, G., and Wong, G. Y. Y. (1986). The psychology of Chinese organizational behaviour. In M. H. Bond (Ed.), *The psychology of the Chinese people* (pp. 267–295). Hong Kong: Oxford University Press.
29. Lee, Jenny S. Y. (2009). Performance management: Concept and practice. In A. Tsui and K. T. Lai (Eds.), *Professional practices of human resource management in Hong Kong, Linking HRM to organizational success* (pp. 87–98). Hong Kong: Hong Kong University Press.
30. Lee, Jenny S. Y. (2009). Performance management: Concept and practice. In A. Tsui and K. T. Lai (Eds.), *Professional practices of human resource management in Hong Kong, Linking HRM to organizational success* (pp. 87–98). Hong Kong: Hong Kong University Press.
31. Mercer. (2013). 2013 Global performance management survey report executive summary. *Mercer*. Retrieved from file:///S:/Assess-BrochurePerfMgmt.pdf
32. Baird, K., Schoch, H., and Chen, Q. (2012). Performance management system effectiveness in Australian local government. *Pacific Accounting Review*, *24*(2), 161–185.
33. Bajorek, Z. M., and Bevan, S. M. (2015). Performance-related-pay in the UK public sector. A review of the recent evidence on effectiveness and value for money. *Journal of Organizational Effectiveness: People and Performance*, *2*(2), 94–109.
34. Armstrong, M., Brown, D., and Reilly, P. (2011). Increasing the effectiveness of reward management: An evidence-based approach. *Employee Relations*, *33*(2), 106–120. Pritchard, Robert D., and Diazgranados, D. (2008). Motivation and performance management. In A. Varma, Pawan S. Budhwar and Angelo DeNisi (Eds.), *Performance management systems: A global perspective* (pp. 40–54). London: Routledge.

7
Managing Total Rewards Strategies in Hong Kong

Norris Y. W. Wong and Wilfred K. P. Wong

> **LEARNING OUTCOMES**
>
> By the end of this chapter, readers should be able to
> - describe the concepts and strategies of total rewards;
> - understand recent development of total rewards in Hong Kong;
> - evaluate the advantages and disadvantages of different rewards strategies; and
> - apply total rewards strategies in different types of Hong Kong organizations.

Introduction

The concept of total rewards has been discussed for more than two decades. It is not an entirely new concept. Employers increasingly view the employment of their employees in a holistic manner—beyond just compensation that includes both extrinsic and intrinsic rewards. They want to ensure that good employees are retained and highly engaged, who will in turn perform at their best to achieve desirable business results. It will be a win-win situation to employers and employees if total rewards programmes work effectively in their intended way. This chapter shall discuss various aspects of total rewards management, including the definitions and strategies of total rewards, recent development of total rewards in Hong Kong, and total rewards strategies and their applications in various types of organizations.

The Concept of Total Rewards

If we ask employees what they receive as part of their remuneration package, they probably say base salary, cash allowances (for employees in certain job roles), bonus, annual leave days, and a few benefits items that they are entitled to. Other intangible items, albeit provided by organizations, are not immediately recalled or included in their minds. Obviously, some employees may start to look beyond their base salary; however, it still lacks a complete view.

In fact, total rewards can be defined as 'the monetary and non-monetary return employers provide employees in exchange for their time, talents, efforts and results'.[1] It includes everything the employee perceives to be of value resulting from the employment relationship. Total rewards involve the integration of five key elements in a customized package to attract, retain, and motivate employees. The five key elements are (1) compensation (or cash reward), (2) benefits, (3) work-life balance, (4) performance and recognition, and (5) development and career opportunities.

Willis Towers Watson, a global consulting firm, defines total rewards framework as possessing three components: foundational rewards, performance-based rewards, and career and development rewards.[2] Foundational rewards include base salary and benefits. Performance-based rewards consist of short- and long-term incentives, as well as recognition programme offered to drive a high-performance culture in the organization. Career and environment rewards enrich the employee value proposition. They include career development opportunities, coaching, and mentoring programmes, flexible work arrangements, and wellness programmes. The objectives of all types of reward programmes are to optimize, drive, and align employees' effort to deliver business results for the organizations.

Total rewards can also be divided into extrinsic and intrinsic rewards.[3] If we apply the distinction of Willis's rewards framework, extrinsic rewards cover foundational and performance rewards whereas intrinsic rewards relate to items that generate internal satisfaction or fulfilment to individuals (i.e. career and environment rewards).

Importance of understanding total rewards

It is very important for managers to understand the concept of total rewards thoroughly. First, managers are accountable for managing team budgets in which people-related cost is a major item on the profit-and-loss account. Top executives are tightening business budgets. HR budget is no exception. It becomes crucial to understand what alternatives are available for managers to retain and motivate their employees. Employees may feel under-rewarded when they do not understand the full value of their package, especially when they focus exclusively on salary and bonus. When employees understand their total rewards package, it helps create a happier and more engaged workforce. By laying out a total rewards package, it attracts the right group of talent to join the organization.

Total Rewards Philosophy

Organizations provide a range of compensation, incentive, and benefits programmes to employees. However, the programmes are sometimes fragmented and do not necessarily align with organization objectives as business evolves. Therefore, there is a need to translate an organization's vision, strategy, and values into a total rewards philosophy to guide the design of various compensation and benefits programmes and practices.

Total rewards philosophy of organizations contains broad statements of the value and beliefs of what and how an organization rewards its employees. They are aspirational statements or guiding principles of an organization's direction of managing total rewards.

Philosophy statements (or 'principles') are developed in relation to organization objectives and culture, corporate values, shareholder interests, equity, business affordability, and performance.

HRM in Action—Box 7.1

Total Rewards Philosophy in the Port of Seattle

The Port of Seattle, a special purpose municipal company providing port services to support trade and commerce in King County, US, shares a clear total rewards philosophy with the employees:

> Total Rewards—a Bright and Sustainable Future for the Port and You
>
> Mission, Values and Strategy—Total Rewards must reflect and support the port's mission, values and long-term business strategy, nurture our unique culture, and grow our business.
>
> Employees—Total Rewards must support employees performing their best, as well as their growth and well-being.
>
> Sustainability—Total Rewards must be managed in a fiscally responsible way that is sustainable over time, and Total Rewards decisions must recognize the financial impact on our organization, customers and community.
>
> Inclusiveness—Total Rewards must be applied fairly and consistently among all employees to support one organization working to accomplish overall port goals.

The above overarching principles are further broken down into five areas of core principles—namely, pay, benefits, learning and development, recognition, and port experience to make it a complete total rewards philosophy. It sets a clear expectation with employees internally. It also serves as a powerful recruitment tool to attract potential candidates who would like to understand the Port's business as well as the way the management commits to treating their employees.

Source: Port of Seattle Organization. (2018). *Total rewards philosophy*. Retrieved from https://www.portseattle.org/sites/default/files/2017-12/Total_Rewards_Philosophy_1.pdf

We also find an example of total rewards principles of a Hong Kong listed company in its annual report.

HRM in Action—Box 7.2

Principles of Remuneration of Senior Management in CLP Holdings

CLP Holdings (CLP), a public utility company listed on the Stock Exchange of Hong Kong, outlines its remuneration principles in its 2017 annual report:

> Our policy is based on the following principles that guide our remuneration programmes and decisions:
> - Appropriateness and fairness of remuneration in relation to the assigned job responsibilities and capabilities demonstrated;
> - Alignment with Company strategy and shareholder interests;
> - Competitiveness with respect to pay levels in the relevant reference market;

- Performance based in terms of sustained results, behaviours and values; and governed by and compliant with the relevant regulatory frameworks.

In CLP the remuneration principles are 'part of the Group's strategy and expression of [the Company's] culture' aligned with the business strategy and shareholder interests. The company emphasizes the long-term careers of its employees. While the reward programmes are externally competitive, they have to be balanced by internal equity.

Source: CLP Holdings. (2017). Human resources and remuneration committee report. *CLP Holdings 2017 Annual report* (pp. 153–154). Hong Kong: CLP Holdings.

The practice of sharing total rewards philosophy and principles publicly in the annual report varies among Hong Kong companies. It ranges from being silent to a more comprehensive description. When we try to understand the total rewards philosophy disclosure of Hong Kong companies, a few questions warrant human resource and total rewards professionals' consideration:

- To what extent do the companies in Hong Kong (listed or private) have a clear total rewards philosophy and strategy in place within the organization?
- If philosophy statements do exist, how well do human resource and total rewards professionals communicate them to their managers and employees?
- How well is the total rewards philosophy (or principles) being understood by the managers and employees?
- What competitive advantages are human resource professionals creating for companies that take a proactive approach of sharing the principles with the shareholders and general public?
- Total rewards aim to attract and retain talent. How do human resource and total rewards professionals make the philosophy (or principles) more transparent to the employees and outsiders, including potential candidates?

HRM in Action—Box 7.3
Management Support and Total Rewards Principles in Reality

In a Hong Kong–based real estate development company, its human resource team set up a compensation and benefits structure for different employee grades. There was also an annual performance review process to assess employee performance. A major compensation item in this company was the bonus reward, reflecting individual impact on business financial performance. Paul, an employee, successfully concluded several mega property sale cases, met his financial targets, and expected a good bonus at the end of the year. But Paul's manager expected Paul to follow his method of handling some of the deals. In spite of a good performance review session with his manager, Paul's contribution was not formally recorded in his performance appraisal. There was no particular reason or explanation for the omission. The manager subsequently marked Paul's bonus down. Paul was given an explanation that senior executives had the sole discretion to make adjustments to the bonus. Paul was so frustrated with the inconsistent behaviour of his manager that he filed a complaint with the human resource team.

The HR business partner stepped in to understand the issues and liaised with Paul's manager. In the end, the senior executive, Paul's manager, insisted on his decision regarding Paul's bonus reward.

As illustrated in this case, even if total rewards principles are written and compensation structures are in place, they can be sabotaged easily by the lack of management support and inappropriate leadership behaviours that are contradictory to the stated principles. This leads to poor morale and unnecessary attrition, with loss in knowledge and experience as well as business performance.

In order to make total rewards principles work, HR professionals have to go back to the core—that is, getting the commitment of top executives. And top executives need to apply these principles consistently.

Total Rewards Strategy in Practice

Total rewards strategies are developed to address two fundamental questions: (1) What can we do to make total rewards principles real and relevant to the business and organization culture? (2) How should we implement them?

Total rewards strategies concern how we apply the philosophy in the context of the business strategy. A well-articulated strategy supports employees to perceive the employer and reward practices as transparent and fair. It encourages a culture of trust and openness between employers and employees.

Total rewards strategies typically cover the following areas:

- Linkage with corporate culture and values—using, for example, pay for performance.
- Comparator set—organizations have their target industry and business competitors in different geographies to compete for hiring the right talents.
- Target market position—organizations set a target aggregate pay level in the market to enable them to hire talent. Target pay level is an anchor that total rewards professionals use to benchmark the base salary of all employees (in aggregate) against the market salaries. Very often, total rewards professionals advise targeting base salary at market median position in a mature market. They may set a higher market position for total cash (base salary plus variable pay), for example, at upper quartile level. Benefits, all items in aggregate, may be set at a similar level to base salary for many organizations.
- Pay mix—it means the proportion of fixed pay (base salary and cash allowances) versus variable pay (bonus and incentive). For instance, junior positions tend to have a high proportion of fixed pay (can be up to 90 per cent of the total package) when employees do not have much direct impact on the organizational results. Remuneration of senior positions may be set with a significant portion of variable pay (pay at risk) as senior executives can influence the business results. Putting more variable pay at senior-level roles is to link their pay with the business results and be in line with shareholder interests.
- External competitiveness and internal equity—organizations want to pay employees competitively in the market. Nonetheless, such a practice has to be balanced with an appropriate view of internal relativity with existing employees in the organization.

- Business affordability—total rewards decisions shall be financially sustainable over time.
- Role of recognition, work-life balance and talent development—organizations describe how these elements complement the overall employees' work experience.

Aligning business strategy and total rewards strategy

Total rewards strategy cannot stand alone. It is effective only when total rewards are aligned with business strategy. McCormick quoted a survey done by HR analyst firm Accelir that total rewards strategies are not updated frequently in most organizations. Accelir found that only 15 per cent of the organizations had revised their total rewards programmes over the last two years.[4] Indeed, rewards strategies should be dynamically aligned with the organization and business needs. They shall be reviewed periodically with business strategy and kept current with changes in the external environment, both business and talent markets.

Box 7.4 below is an example of how merit budget is adjusted in response to the external environment and future direction of business growth.

HRM in Action—Box 7.4

Business Growth, Talent Retention, and Merit Increase Budget

Top executives of a global company faced with unfavourable business results in 2015 and foresaw a challenging business environment in the coming year. They decided to set the 2016 merit increase budget for all countries at a nominal percentage of total payroll, which was below market rate of salary increase. In its communication note to line managers, the merit increase budget was put into two tiers:

Tier 1: Developed countries with solid business performance
Tier 2: China and India were given a market-level merit increase budget.

There were several considerations in giving a bigger merit increase budget to tier 2 countries:

- The plan was to achieve massive growth in business scale in these countries in the coming three years.
- The projected 2016 salary increase in China and India was high, based on market survey results.*
- Other international and local competitors were operating and/or expanding in these countries, which led to fierce competition in recruiting the talent required to support business growth.
- It was pivotal to retain talent who had already been trained by the company. The loss of these employees was costly, and the time required to recruit a replacement candidate typically took longer (two to three months).
- Supply of talent with good English communication and technology-related skills was limited in these countries.

In order to ensure additional funds were used for the right employee groups, local human resource professionals worked with line managers to identify key contributors. They reviewed the contributions and assessed the retention risk of these contributors before adjusting individual salaries to the target market pay level.

* Willis Towers Watson. (2016, October 4). *2016 Salary budget planning report—Asia Pacific* (Q3). Retrieved from https://www.willistowerswatson.com/en/press/2016/10/asia-pacific-2017-salary-rises-projected-at-5-point-9-percent

Rewards Strategy: Pay for Performance

Pay for performance is a core reward strategy for executives to create a performance culture in organizations. It means that reward is tied to the achievement of performance goals—organization, team, and/or individual goals as set by the organization. Under this notion, managers are accountable for differentiating pay for employees in accordance with business and individual performance through differentiating pay components such as base salary and variable pay (discretionary bonuses will be discussed later in this chapter) for individual employees.[5] The most common way of reflecting this strategy is to link individual performance ratings with base salary adjustment and variable pay.

Base salary

Base salary is a fundamental component in an individual reward package. There are two aspects to look at with respect to base salary: its size and what proportion should be included in the overall reward package. Base salary (how much) is determined by a view of similar jobs internally and in the external market. It is also affected by the skills possessed by individuals. If a niche skill or knowledge is in high demand, the base salary will be set higher to reflect the talent market situation. For instance, if there is a high demand for candidates with risk and compliance knowledge, banks and financial institutions have to increase base salary to attract candidates. It also urges HR professionals to manage salaries of existing employees closely for retention purposes. In addition, the proportion of base salary in the overall package varies by job level. Executives at a higher job level tend to receive a higher proportion of variable pay in which their pay is linked to business results and long-term shareholders' interest.

Pay differentiation through merit increase

The annual salary increase budget for many Asian countries has remained at a low level for many years. The 2016 actual salary increase for Hong Kong was 4.1 per cent.[6] The 2017 increment remained at a similar rate of 4 per cent.[7] While cost of living is a factor being considered in setting annual salary increase budgets, private organizations, in general, do not provide cost-of-living salary budget as a guarantee unless it is mandatorily required in a country. If we take out the inflation rate of 1.9 per cent from 2017's overall salary increase for Hong Kong, salary increase in real terms was merely 2.1 per cent. It further compresses the budget available for pay differentiation through individual performance. In fact, many organizations would make use of the overall salary increase budget for performance pay differentiation.

Merit increase has been and continues to be the most prevalent approach of connecting individual performance to base salary. The 2016 WorldatWork *Compensation Programmes and Practices Survey* showed that 70 per cent of the respondent companies' individual base salary increases were determined by individual performance against job standards;[8] 59 per cent of the respondents used position in (salary) range; and 52 per cent of the respondents considered market value of the positions in making salary increase decisions.

Figure 7.1: Salary increase matrix guide with a 3 per cent average budget increase

Performance Rating	Compa-ratio (Salary against Range Midpoint)			
	< 90%	90%–100%	101%–110%	>110%
1 – Exceptional	5%–6%		~ 3.5%	—
2				
3 – Meet expectation		~ 2.5%		—
4				—
5 – Does not meet expectation	—	—	—	—

Total rewards professionals usually provide a 'salary increase matrix guide' (Figure 7.1) to help managers award salary increase to employees. The matrix is referenced to the individual performance rating and position in salary range (compa-ratio is often used as a compensation metric). Compa-ratio measures the relationship between an employee's base salary and the salary range midpoint. For example, an employee's annual base salary is $250,000 and salary range midpoint is $275,000. The compa-ratio for this employee's salary is 91 per cent ($250,000 divided by $275,000). Some companies may alternatively use market index when the comparison is matched directly against market reference salary. The principles behind a salary increase matrix guide are twofold: (1) exceptional performers should get more than low performers; and (2) exceptional performers paid low in salary range or below market level significantly should receive the biggest increase. However, by using a matrix guide based on percentage increase as shown in Figure 7.1, it is questionable whether a 2.5 per cent to 3.5 per cent merit increase is sufficient to excite exceptional performers. The impact of pay differentiation would diminish when the same percentage increase applies to different base salary levels.

Many managers, in reality, find this guide useful as they can look for an exact answer in the matrix. Yet the pay differentiation is not as wide as they would like to see. Salary review decision somewhat becomes a 'human resource function' decision instead of managers' decisions. The guide is perceived as a product of the human resource function. Managers may shy away from communicating their decisions to employees despite the fact that people management decisions, including rewards decisions, are part of a manager's accountability. It sometimes results in employees' disappointment when they receive their salary increase letters from their managers. On the one hand, employees are disappointed with the salary increase in comparison to what they think they have contributed to the company. On the other hand, they are frustrated with managers who are unwilling to explain their decisions.

HRM in Action—Box 7.5

What Salary Increase Percentage Should Managers Give to an Average Performer?

A few years ago, a company set an annual salary increase budget at 3 per cent of total salary. A manager insisted on giving a 3 per cent salary increase to the average performers. He believed that it was fair for an employee who met performance expectations to receive a budgeted salary increase. In the annual performance appraisal, he rated many of his employees as average performers and gave a few employees the top performance ratings. When the manager did the annual salary review exercise for his team, his budget quickly ran out. He wanted to give a significant percentage increase (i.e. an increase higher than 3 per cent) to the exceptional performers. As the manager had spent a lot of his budget on average performers' salary increment already, he went to the HR business partner (HRBP) to complain and ask for more budget for his exceptional performers for differentiation purposes. The manager did not get extra funding for this reason.

While the manager had the good intention of rewarding his team, the total rewards professional and HRBP helped him understand the company's pay principles:

- All managers received the same salary increase budget in terms of a fixed percentage of total salary in the annual salary review exercise. The 3 per cent budget should not be deemed as a minimum or an expected increase for employees.
- The total rewards professional presented cost of living (COL) information to top executives for reference before they approved the annual salary increase budget. The company's pay philosophy was based on performance (of company and individuals) and external competitiveness in the context of business affordability. The salary increase budget was not built on top of COL.
- Individual salary differentiation could be done if line managers took a more progressive approach in rewarding top versus average performers. They needed to be selective in making their salary decisions.
- Among the average employees, the manager needed to consider whether an employee's base salary was competitive against the market.

Some organizations adopt a salary increase matrix guide with multiples (Figure 7.2) to improve the view of formulated salary increase under the matrix in Figure 7.1. It focuses more on the pay differentials between exceptional and average performers whatever the percentage increase may be. The extent of multiples between exceptional and average performers depends on how rigorous the executives want to be, which is agreed at the top or corporate level. As a general principle, we see a multiple of three or more between average and exceptional performers in order to have a positive impact on the latter. Managers need to put more thought into identifying the exceptional performers and starting with a higher increase percentage for them. Managers are accountable for their decisions and the reasons for award increments under this kind of matrix guide (Figure 7.2).

Figure 7.2: Salary increase matrix guide with multiples

Performance rating	Compa-ratio (Salary against range midpoint)			
	< 90%	90%–100%	101%–110%	>110%
1 – Exceptional	3X			–
2				
3 – Meet expectation		X		–
4				–
5 – Does not meet expectation	–	–	–	–

To avoid the misconception that approved budget increase is equal to a minimum or an average salary-increase percentage, total rewards professionals may first communicate the annual salary review budget as a percentage of total payroll to managers in a briefing session before the annual review exercise commences. Second, the budget available for managers' distribution is better expressed in absolute dollar value in the tool provided (be it in the form of spreadsheets or electronic platform). The purpose is to discourage conceiving of the salary increase budget percentage as a minimum percentage increase for employees. If the approved salary increase budget is X per cent, for example, then Y dollars will be presented as the amount for a manager to distribute.

While many organizations are still operating annual performance review process, factors affecting a salary decision are now beyond an individual performance rating. We see a recent example in a US headquartered company. Total rewards professionals provide supplementary information to managers in addition to a similar matrix like Figure 7.2. The additional information includes

- market position of individual salary to the company's target market reference salary (pre- and post-salary increment);
- notes on potential position level an employee can reach in the company in a defined period based on talent review discussions; and
- records of unfavourable or non-compliant work behaviours (if any) of an employee in carrying out his or her work.

In other words, managers make salary decisions with a broader set of information than merely based on individual performance rating.

Reinforcing pay for performance by reallocating fund or holding reserves

During stagnant salary growth periods, top executives may reallocate a portion of the merit increase budget to businesses, locations, or employee groups that are most needed. Human resource and total rewards professionals may advise top executives in the context of business performance, strategic initiatives in the coming year, talent acquisition and retention challenges. Another common method is to withhold part of the budget and subsequently apply it to top performers after managers' recommendations. Normally the reserve fund is held at the most senior level in the organization, such as head of department or group chief executive to ensure the fund is used appropriately.

Discretionary Bonus

The allocation of discretionary bonuses is done simultaneously with annual salary review in most organizations. Individual performance rating is a predominant driver of determining the bonus reward for individual employees.

A bonus plan is one of the reward vehicles to drive organizations' quantitative results, strategic initiatives, and desirable employee behaviours. The design of discretionary bonus plans connects bonus reward with organization, business, team, and/or individual performance with different weightings. The Hong Kong Stock Exchange Limited (HKEX) stated in its 2017 annual report that the group employee performance cash bonus was based on the achievement of four corporate performance measures with different weighting: financial measures (40 per cent), strategic measures (25 per cent), market and regulatory development (20 per cent), and organization development (15 per cent).[9]

In terms of individual performance, HKEX management assessed employees with a performance rating (on a five-point scale) based on pre-agreed work objectives for the year. An additional multirater appraisal process was applied to employees at management level to ensure the assessment was multidimensional. The bonus distribution was guided by employee grade, performance of multiple years, overall total compensation position (i.e. base salary plus the performance bonus and share reward), internal equity, and external benchmark level.

HKEX is only one example of how organizations implement a pay-for-performance programme through discretionary bonuses. When we look closely at the linkage of bonus reward with individual performance, there are variations in corporate practices, ranging from giving managers total discretion of bonus allocation to semi-formulaic payout.

HRM in Action—Box 7.6

Individual Performance and Discretionary Bonus Allocation

Company A

Managers were given a bonus pot for distribution to the team at their discretion. Managers could give bonus to employees in any amount as long as the total bonus amount did not exceed the allocated pot. The guidance provided to managers was the same as in the annual salary review—in other words, individual performance ratings. Managers were fully responsible for making their decisions within reason.

Company B

Managers could adjust individual bonus rewards by applying a multiplier to the bonus amount initially generated by business performance achievement. A multiplier was associated with each individual performance rating. The multipliers were X_1 per cent (negative, or '-ve'), X_2 per cent (-ve), X_3 per cent (positive, or '+ve'), X_4 per cent (+ve) and X_5 per cent (+ve). X_1 could be 50 per cent (-ve), whereas X_5 could be 150 per cent (+ve), depending on how much differentiation top executives agreed to set.

For instance, the business achievement generated an initial bonus of $300,000 for the top performer. The manager applied X_5 (+150 per cent) to the bonus amount and the employee received a final bonus of $450,000 (which was $300,000 × 150 per cent). The same logic applied if the manager applied X_1 (-50 percent) to the initial bonus, the final bonus amount would be reduced to $150,000.

The bonuses of both Companies A and B were based on the organization and individual performance. Company B's plan seemed to provide more guidance to managers with information of individual performance ratings and corresponding multipliers. Nonetheless, new questions arose under Company B's plan:

- Were managers allowed to use a multiplier not under the default options?
- If managers were empowered to use salary increase and bonus rewards appropriately, was the bonus multiplier guideline useful to managers in giving bonuses to employees?
- Were managers given the latitude to manoeuvre the salary increase and bonus reward, considering individual performance, external market competitiveness, and budget limit?

The bonus plan structure was transparent and fully communicated to eligible employees at the beginning of the plan year. Company B ultimately allowed managers to have slight variation of using multipliers at their discretion so long as managers were able to explain their decisions. By allowing such variation, it created communication challenges to managers when some employees found that their bonuses were not tied with the multipliers corresponding to their performance ratings.

In Company A, provided that managers were adequately trained, they had more flexibility in making bonus awards based on individual contributions and other factors beyond a performance rating.

Using bonus to drive the right behaviours

A good bonus plan shall drive the desired employee behaviours with positive impact on business results. In return, managers will reward employees for their contribution. When designing a bonus plan, the choice and number of performance measures should reinforce the linkage of employee behaviours with performance. The plan design would directly influence how satisfied employees are with the bonus plan and their level of motivation to perform.

HRM in Action—Box 7.7
Setting Bonus Plan Measures

A Hong Kong–based manufacturer set up a discretionary bonus plan with six performance measures of different weightings:

- Three production-related measures—volume, production schedule timeliness, and machine downtime
- Financial measure
- Strategic initiative
- Individual objective

The strategic initiative and individual objective were eventually broken down into multiple items under which the smallest performance measure was given a weight of 2.5 per cent. The bonus plan ended up with fifteen measures in total.

How excited would the employees be when they looked at a list of fifteen performance measures? When the employees were asked which areas they should focus their efforts on in order to get a bonus, it was not surprising that they felt perplexed.

Top executives should send clear messages to managers where the organization is heading through the bonus plan measures—with focus, clarity, and priority. Managers may direct their efforts to goals that can easily be achieved in order to earn a bonus. However, these goals may not be the top priority of organizations. In terms of the weight of performance measures, it is unlikely to get managers' attention on any measure with a weight of less than 5 per cent. As shown in Box 7.7, the effectiveness of a bonus plan as a vehicle to reward organization and individual performance is undermined if there are too many trivial measures.

Performance measures of a bonus plan are critical in reinforcing the pay-for-performance concept. Total rewards and HR professionals should work with top executives closely in setting clear focus and challenging performance measures in designing a bonus plan.

HRM in Action—Box 7.8

Frequency of Bonus Payment

Most organizations adopt annual bonus plans based on the achievement of the full year's business results. However, Alan Yip, CEO and Chairman of Guru Online, said that he had launched a new incentive scheme with a quarterly payout.*

His approach aimed to engage the younger generation of employees who valued reward and recognition more instantly. He recognized that his young employees, impatient with the annual bonus cycle, expected to receive the reward on a more frequent basis. This conforms to the principle of instant reward to acknowledge desirable performance and induce stronger motivation.

Organizations in conventional industry sectors also deploy short-term incentives other than annual bonuses to specific groups of employees, typically to sales roles. It is no doubt that the expectation of the new generation of employees has begun to put pressure on total rewards professionals who need to review the appropriateness and effectiveness of bonus systems more frequently.

* Guru Online (Holdings) Limited is a leading internet company, listed on the Hong Kong Stock Exchange, stock code 8121.

Recognition

Besides base salary and variable pay, recognition is another powerful lever to reward exceptional performance. Recognition programmes take many forms, for both tangible and intangible recognition. And the reward may range from a thank-you note to cash payments, gifts, plaques, and the like.

Some organizations put in place formal and structured recognition programmes. Employee achievement can be identified through internal nomination directly by managers. Peer-to-peer or cross-departmental nominations are also commonly found in the workplace. The achievement can be recognized publicly in staff or department meetings, or informally conveyed to the employees. Individuals or teams are recognized for their dedication and efforts in achieving special goals, generating new ideas, creating processes for improvement, and more. The key purpose is to show how much leaders value employees' dedication and commitments. Richard Branson wrote on his Virgin website, 'As all good leaders know, letting their teams know they appreciate their work can make all the difference to an employee's confidence, morale and wellbeing.'[10]

The Virgin Stars of the Year Awards, a group-wide recognition programme, encourages employees to 'shout out about the amazing work their colleagues have been doing.'[11] The winning nominee from each company around the world is invited to London for the party of the year. Branson definitely sees business value in recognition. His belief in recognition programmes is simple: 'Happy employees equal happy customers.'

In the financial services industry in Hong Kong recognition programmes take the form of top sales award, glamourous dinners, and incentive trips. An annual award presentation dinner becomes an important event for insurance sales professionals. The award recipients dress up and get ready to be called onstage to celebrate their sales achievements, both as individuals and teams. Furthermore, it is an honour for insurance sales professionals to achieve the Million Dollar Round Table (MDRT) status, a global industry benchmark for sales achievement. MDRT achievers participate in the annual global conference, partly for learning and partly for celebration purposes. The MDRT status is an aspiration for new insurance sales professionals.

Making recognition personalized, memorable, and culturally sensitive is another key to success. For instance, a global energy company runs a global Spot Award programme to reward extraordinary individual achievement. A few years ago, the rewards specialist in Vietnam, for example, received a return air ticket to her home town in the country after completing the reward integration project ahead of the planned schedule with positive feedback from business leaders. The award item was chosen after knowing her desire to visit her parents whom she had not visited for almost a year.

HRM in Focus—Box 7.9

Performance Management and Rewards

As discussed in the performance management chapter, some organizations are moving away from annual or focal performance appraisal process to an ongoing dialogue with frequent and more comprehensive feedback on individual performance. In that case, how can a pay-for-performance strategy be supported effectively?

Martin and Hongell suggest that managers should focus on identifying differences in employee contributions to the business rather than making small decisions on whether an employee delivers what is expected to determine a performance rating.*

They list three open questions to shift the focus of performance and pay decisions:

- Who are your top contributors?
- How much should we pay top contributors relative to our core contributors?
- What contributions could lead to those decisions?

It is about managers embracing a broader concept of individual performance instead of relying on an annual performance rating to determine rewards. Other factors, such as employee potential, possession of critical skills, market competitiveness, internal relativity, retention or flight risk, business environment, and budget spent form part of the consideration. Thinking about individual contributions to the team and business in formulating reward decisions would certainly make conversation with employees more relevant and real.

It opens up opportunities for total rewards professionals to rethink the linkage between performance and pay. This is the place to start with, as there may be opportunities for increased clarity or to overhaul the whole pay review process here.

* Martin, J., and Hongell, C. (2017, April). The new pay for performance: From many small decisions to a few big ones. *Workspan*, 22–27.

Communicating Total Rewards Programmes

As seen above, the design of a total rewards programme requires considerable expertise and efforts from the total rewards professionals and managers. Although organizations provide attractive total rewards to employees, effective communication of the programmes is equally important. Some questions may arise from other stakeholders when rolling out the programmes. Do the managers convey the message of total rewards programmes to the employees effectively? Do the employees perceive the value of their rewards as fair vis-a-vis their efforts or contributions? Unfortunately, communication materials are often developed shortly before conducting employee briefing sessions. Some of the information can be inadequate or unduly complicated. Sometimes, we may just 'tell' the employees what we want to say about the programmes instead of giving details useful to them. When employees appreciate what they receive from their employers, they feel engaged and will hopefully bring their best selves and performance to the company.

Some organizations provide employees 'total rewards statements' with a comprehensive description of what they are receiving from the company. It is a personalized statement that shows monetary items with a total value and intangible items that an employee is eligible for. Setting up total rewards statements, however, involves collecting volumes of employee data from the internal human resource information system and service vendors. Thus, providing total rewards statements is still controversial and as such is a practice primarily found in some sizeable multinational companies.

But effective communication of rewards should go beyond a statement of items with associated values. Below are a few tips for communicating total rewards:

- Know your employee groups—today's workforce is diverse; find out what catches employees' attention and how they learn about rewards.
- Segment your audience—provide customized materials for different employee groups; one set of materials does not fit all.

- Address employees' concerns—employees care about what value they receive from their rewards. Their concerns will be intensified when changes in rewards packages or structure are introduced. Total rewards professionals must be aware of potential emotions inherent in new changes in rewards programmes when they develop communication strategies and programmes.
- Present information in simple and visual ways—some compensation programme details are technical and difficult to understand. Convert information into layman's terms and use visuals to help employees understand.
- Identify internal ambassadors—train a number of managers and employees who show deep interest in rewards topics. Let them reach out to their connected groups. Peer influence can be an influential communication channel when used properly.
- Continuous communication—communication has to be continuous. Communication does not stop at the introductory session. Especially when a reward programme involves changes, it takes time for employees to understand what it is about.

Current Trends of Total Rewards

Mercer's Senior Partner Steve Gross shared his view of the future of total rewards at the 2015 WorldatWork Total Rewards Conference.[12] He foresaw several things happening in the next five years. First, pay information would become more transparent. A lot of pay information can now be found on social media websites, despite the doubtful quality of much of the information. Second, performance ratings would not disappear (see Chapter 6). Even though some organizations do without performance ratings and are moving towards frequent feedback with employees, implicit ratings behind the scene are used for making rewards decisions. Another prediction concerned the emergence and existence of contingent or multigenerational workforce in organizations.[13] Benefits would be offered with choices to suit employees with different needs.

Total rewards professionals in Hong Kong should not inwardly focus on the Asia-Pacific region. It is important to know what is happening worldwide and the potential implications to the region. Globalization implies that practices in other parts of the world are extended to different regions. Instead of being reactive to implement new global practices and standards, total rewards professionals should be more proactive in participating in the thought process of developing total rewards strategies and implementation plan.

We see some of the predicted practices in Hong Kong. For example, job search consultants publish salary information on websites (for example, Michael Page and Robert Half) and even invite people to download the information. While we do not know how rigorous the process of collecting and processing the data is, information is easily available to employees. As a golden principle, individual salary information is always treated as personal and confidential information within organizations. However, increasing transparency of salary information in the market urges HR and total rewards professionals to think proactively about what salary-related information should be shared with internal employees. HR professionals need to help employees understand the philosophy and competitiveness of their rewards in the talent market. If HR decides to share information e.g. internal salary ranges, it will be best for HR to explain how salaries are benchmarked against the market. It may pose challenges to both HR and line managers if employees start to have high expectations of remuneration because of freely available information.

Furthermore, there is a trend of enhancing benefits in the past few years. Global companies have been taking the lead in making benefits changes. Very often, global practices are extended to multinational companies in Hong Kong. The most obvious development is found in leave benefits, flexible work arrangement, and employee wellness programmes.

Family centred and other leave benefits

Parental leave

Traditionally, benefits are provided to employees and spouse of married employees (provided organizations extend the benefits to cover dependents). Various organizations have been making leave benefits enhancement to address the increasing family need of employees at different stages of life. We see enhancement in two main areas of family-centred benefits: maternity and paternity leave benefits. HSBC[14] and Hang Seng Bank[15] have increased their maternity leave for female employees to fourteen weeks. Other global companies like Shell Hong Kong[16] and DLA Piper[17] (a global law firm with an office in Hong Kong) have also announced sixteen weeks and eighteen weeks of paid maternity leave respectively. Standard Chartered Bank[18] is ahead of the competition by extending its maternity leave to twenty weeks with full pay. Paid paternity leave for male employees in these companies has been increased to two weeks.

Schneider Electric used a different family definition when the management announced its new global family leave policy in September 2017.[19] Schneider offers a minimum of twelve weeks of paid leave to the primary parent for both natural and adoptive birth. It does not specify such leave to be applied to female employees only. Olivier Blum, Chief Human Resources Officer and Executive Vice President, said, 'The new policy will reinforce our diversity and inclusion ambition of providing equal opportunities to everyone, everywhere and ensuring that all employees feel uniquely valued and safe to contribute their best.'

The trend of benefits enhancement is also seen in neighbouring countries in Asia. A few companies took the initiative even earlier than the blue-chip companies in Hong Kong. For example, Singtel has been giving new fathers a total of two weeks' paternity leave each year since January 2015.[20] DBS Bank has already raised paternity leave to two weeks. Malaysia's Maybank offers eligible female employees to extend their maternity leave up to 365 days with variable pay levels. The first ninety days are with full pay; the next three months are half pay; and the remaining six months is at no pay.[21]

Annual leave

Annual leave is another area of enhancement. For example, Hang Seng Bank employees enjoy annual leave between eighteen to thirty days depending on eligibility. It is the same level as HSBC, its parent company. As reported in the *South China Morning Post*, such accommodations will enable employees to have a better work-life balance and increase the bank's competitiveness.[22]

Implications to HR and total rewards professionals

In Hong Kong global organizations are bringing international standards and practices of benefits to the local companies. And as seen, the benefit levels of the above examples are well above what the HKSAR government is proposing. For instance, paid paternity leave under the Hong Kong Employment Ordinance has been increased from three days to five days since 18 January 2019.[23] However, the pace of improving statutory benefits is not as quick as in commercial organizations. If HR professionals need to be pro-active in attracting and retaining employees, should total rewards professionals move faster to align their practices with the international norm? In the first instance, we think total rewards professionals shall put benefits review and assessment as priorities in the people agenda.

Organizations should be aware of the importance of retaining employees from a long-term career perspective. And important life events such as creating a family or accompanying family members during serious sickness should not be seen as detrimental disruption to employees' careers. When Shell enhanced its maternity leave benefits, the management wanted to 'ensure that female colleagues at all levels are encouraged to remain with us and to continue to develop their careers if/when they have children, and in particular that our policies and practices relating to maternity leave are aligned and support their further career development.'[24] As a result, HR professionals should help managers and employees change their mindsets about taking family leave as part of their life journey. Employees will then not feel guilty about taking parental leave or otherwise be forced to make a tough choice between career and family.

In addition, when family (or dependents) benefits are reviewed, it calls for a review of the definition of 'family'. Traditionally, benefits for married employees, if offered, are extended to the employee's spouse and children. From a perspective of inclusivity, HR needs to review the definitions of dependents and whether they transcend gender orientation. It requires rewards professionals to think vertically (benefits level) and laterally (definition of coverage) in redesigning the benefits in today's world.

Flexible work arrangement

Nowadays, many organizations are having several generations in the workforce. Generation Z is joining the career world, too. With the emergence of new industries and job roles, work can be done with greater flexibility with the support of technology. Millennial and Generation Z employees look for more flexibility and good balance in their work life.[25] Employees of other generations are joining the new generations as they are going through different life stages such as getting married, having children, or preparing for retirement. Hence, the request for greater work flexibility and choices to suit employee needs is increasingly heard. Common flexi-work arrangements include flexible scheduling of workweek, flexible start and finish times, working part-time, compressed workweek (for example, instead of having a five-day week, employees work the same number of hours in four days to enjoy an extra day off), extended lunch break, job sharing between employees, or work from home. Employees with young children welcome simple arrangements like flexible time off to attend kids' school activities.

Some of these arrangements are not new to managers. They may be offered informally or on a case-by-case basis rather than through a formal company policy.

Whether flexible work arrangement shall be made a formal policy is a choice made by executives. Surely, they can create a culture of making these arrangements 'legitimate' and empowering employees to feel comfortable to take up the offer.

Flexible work arrangement has a positive impact on employees and benefits organizations. Employees feel more engaged and satisfied when their needs are fulfilled. They feel motivated to contribute with enthusiasm. In order to achieve the desired results, it may be important to consider some questions: What types of work are suitable for remote or home-based working or even working in different hours of the day? Are employees ready to work remotely? How do they interact effectively as a virtual team? What level of commitment are employees ready to make? As an organization, are our work systems and structure ready to support the flexible work arrangement? Are employees' mindsets and behaviours aligned with the divergent work pattern?

These questions are not meant to be hurdles towards putting flexible work arrangements in place. Managers addressing these questions upfront is far more effective than dealing with employees' disappointment as a result of abruptly changing or dropping the policy after being rolled out.

Employee wellness

Employee wellness has recently become a hot topic on human resource management agenda. The key is for executives to make employees' health and well-being a genuine concern. Large multinational companies have been offering wellness programmes on a piecemeal basis, such as annual health check-ups, health benefits, insurance plans, employee assistance programmes (EAP). EAP includes counselling service to employees to discuss work or personal matters on a confidential basis. The focus of employees' well-being has been considered at a new level that wellness is taken with a holistic view. People easily relate wellness to physical wellness. Some companies in Hong Kong subsidize employee gym memberships, grant cash allowances for buying fitness wearables, or organizing body stretching classes. But beyond physical health, emotional health and financial wellness are also part of a wellness programme. Some human resource teams organize stress management workshops and meditation classes as precautionary measures. The starting point is to create employee awareness of their mental health conditions. Similarly, financial wellness programmes are organized to help employees learn about financial planning concepts and plan for individual financial needs at different stages in life.

But wellness programmes differ among companies. They should be responsive to employee needs and aligned with corporate cultures.

HRM in Action—Box 7.10

Organizational Support and Employee Wellness Programmes

There are few companies in Hong Kong that are able to provide on-site gym facilities to employees.

Some state-of-the-art gym facilities are found at the Wanchai office building of AIA Group, the pan Asia leading insurance company. Employees can sign up with personal trainers to develop an individualized fitness plan. A variety of fitness and yoga classes are available for employees to join during lunchtime or after work.

The company also organizes health seminars such as weight-loss strategies and stress management.

Sources:
(2011, December 20). Nice workout—if you can get it. *South China Morning Post*. Retrieved July 1, 2018, from http://www.scmp.com/article/988210/nice-workout-if-you-can-get-it
http://www.yoga-privates.com/yoga-privates/file/files/SCMP201211.pdf

Employee wellness is not a topic designed solely for large organizations. Wellness programmes can be as simple as employees taking a thirty-minute walk together during lunchtime. Ideas for wellness programmes can start from changing employees' habits. To encourage healthy eating habits, colleagues can suggest frequent-travelling co-workers stop sharing souvenir food when returning from business trips.

HR professionals can invite employees to participate in the programme design of company-sponsored wellness programmes. While executives are keen to know the ROI for launching wellness programmes, it is a difficult metric to measure. Many programmes are customized to address different employee needs and are difficult to get a like-for-like comparison. Kohll suggests understanding the value of these programmes brought to employees may be an alternative of measuring the success of employee wellness programmes. Employee feedback can be used as a guide for further improving the programmes. Executives should view wellness programmes as a long-term investment in employees and create a culture of wellness in organizations.[26]

HRM in Action—Box 7.11
Launch of Employee Wellness Programme

Eastman Chemical, a Fortune 500 company, launched a worldwide Wellness Programme in 2015. One of the values of the company is quoted as follows:

Safety & Wellness We believe all work-related injuries are preventable. We watch out for each other and practise injury-free habits at home and at work. We make personal choices to promote a healthy lifestyle that includes appropriate work/life balance.

Eastman conducted a wellness workshop for its employees in the Shanghai area. The workshop aimed to enhance employee awareness of individual health and diet. It covered topics on healthy diet, taking regular exercises or activities and stress management, and how various aspects of life programmes supported employees to enjoy and live a happier and better life so as to reduce risks and enhance safety at the workplace.

Source: Eastman. (n.d.). Values. Retrieved from https://www.eastman.com/Company/About_Eastman/Pages/Values.aspx

Conclusion

It is a challenging time for HR and total rewards professionals. The future of total rewards will no longer be confined to cash compensation and tangible benefits items.

The future of total rewards will become more complicated as employees start to count everything in their calculations of compensation, including career advancement, personal development opportunities, work purpose, and personal growth. To make total rewards a powerful people strategy, it requires a collaboration of various human resource teams, from talent management to total rewards teams, to present a meaningful package to employees.

HR and total rewards professionals have to stay alert to the changing expectations of employees and review and make appropriate adjustment to total rewards strategies accordingly. Effective rewards communication is as important as the technical design of the rewards programmes. We hear feedback from managers that rewards programmes are often too complex for employees to understand the real value. Managers and employees urge for simple and engaging communication. Total rewards professionals should therefore prepare an effective strategy using different channels to communicate complex programmes to the employees.

A final word—developing an effective total rewards package is both a science and an art. While it requires effort to craft a clearly defined total rewards philosophy and principles, it also demands extensive knowledge and skills in understanding business strategies, getting market intelligence and data, and doing research and statistical analyses. In its capacity as an art, it demands us to think about total rewards from a 'human' perspective. Effective communication and implementation of total rewards strategies balancing the interests of the company and the employees is important. It needs collaborative efforts from executives, department heads, and total rewards professionals.

Review Questions

1. A US fast-moving consumer goods company plans to set up its first overseas company in Hong Kong. What do you need to know to develop a total rewards strategy for the company?
2. In your organization, what gaps and opportunities do you observe in making total rewards a better tool to support the organization's strategies?
3. What would you advise management if they enquire about abolishing performance ratings? What are the implications to total rewards?
4. What would you do to enhance employees' understanding of their total rewards package?
5. Discuss the expectations of multigenerational employees on organizations and their implications when it comes to total rewards offers?

Notes

1. Christofferson, J., and King, B. (2006, April). The new total rewards model leads the way. *Workspan*, 19–27.
2. Willis Towers Watson. (2012). *Total rewards: The right time is right now*. Retrieved from https://www.towerswatson.com/en/Insights/IC-Types/Ad-hoc-Point-of-View/2012/Total-Rewards-The-Right-Time-Is-Right-Now
3. Reif, William E. (1975). Intrinsic versus extrinsic rewards: Resolving the controversy. *Human Resource Management*, 14(2), 2–9.
4. White, S. (2013). Rewards and recognition: 2014 trends report. *Accelir*. Retrieved from ttps://www.slideshare.net/imsosarah/2014-trends-report-rewards-and-recognition. UNC

Executive Development. (2015, April 30). *Does your organization have a total rewards strategy?* Retrieved from http://execdev.kenan-flagler.unc.edu/blog/rethinking-total-rewards

5. Types of variable pay plan can be found in for example, Armstrong, M. (2015). *Armstrong's handbook of reward management practice* (5th ed.). London: Kogan Page.
6. Willis Towers Watson. (2016, October 4). *2016 Salary budget planning report—Asia Pacific* (Q3). Retrieved from https://www.willistowerswatson.com/en/press/2016/10/asia-pacific-2017-salary-rises-projected-at-5-point-9-percent
7. Willis Towers Watson. (2017, December 14). Salary budget planning survey—Asia Pacific (2017 Q1 and Q3 Edition). Retrieved from https://www.willistowerswatson.com/en/press/2017/12/India-China-Vietnam-2018-salary-increases-to-lead-way-in-Asia-Pacific-Willis-Towers-Watson-Study
8. Aon Hewitt. (2016, August). *Compensation programmes and practices survey*. Scottsdale: WorldatWork. Retrieved from https://www.worldatwork.org/docs/research-and-surveys/survey-brief-survey-on-compensation-programmes-and-practices-2016.pdf
9. Percentage (X per cent) in brackets represent the weight of each performance measure of the company's performance cash bonus. Hong Kong Stock Exchange. (2017). *2017 Annual report* (pp. 85–86). Hong Kong: Hong Kong Stock Exchange.
10. Branson, R. (2017, August 4). *Thank you* [Blog post]. Retrieved from https://www.virgin.com/richard-branson/thank-you
11. Raymundo, O. (2014, October 28). *Richard Branson: Companies should put employees first*. Retrieved from https://www.inc.com/oscar-raymundo/richard-branson-companies-should-put-employees-first.html
12. Miller, S. CEBS. (2015, May 26). *Total rewards trends for the next five years*. Retrieved from https://www.shrm.org/resourcesandtools/hr-topics/compensation/pages/total-rewards-trends.aspx
13. Mercer. (2015). *HR 2020: What the future holds*. Retrieved from https://www.mercer.com/content/dam/mercer/attachments/north-america/us/the-future-of-hr-mercer.pdf
14. Wong, A. (2016, March 30). HSBC to offer two weeks of paternity leave for local staff. *Human Resource*. Retrieved from http://www.humanresourcesonline.net/hsbc-offer-two-weeks-paternity-leave-local-staff/
15. Siu, P. (2017, August 10). Hang Seng Bank employees given more annual leave after strong company performance. *South China Morning Post*. Retrieved May 1, 2018, from http://www.scmp.com/news/hong-kong/economy/article/2106156/hang-seng-bank-employees-given-more-annual-leave-after-strong
16. Shell Hong Kong announces new paid maternity leave policy. (2017, June 27). Retrieved from https://www.shell.com.hk/en_hk/media-center/news-and-media-releases/2017-press-releases/shell-hong-kong-announces-new-paid-maternity-leave-policy.html
17. DLA Piper overhauls parental leave in Hong Kong. (2017, August 1). Retrieved from https://www.dlapiper.com/en/hongkong/news/2017/08/dla-piper-overhauls-parental-leave-in-hong-kong/
18. Standard Chartered Bank (Hong Kong) Limited. (2017, March 20). *Standard Chartered to substantially extend maternity leave to 20 calendar weeks*. Retrieved from https://www.sc.com/global/av/hk-extends-maternity-leave-eng.pdf
19. Schneider Electric. (2017, September 26). *Schneider Electric launches global family leave policy*. Retrieved from https://www.schneider-electric.com/ww/en/documents/Press/2017/09/26-release-global-family-leave-policy-tcm50-336261.pdf
20. Bolza, M. (2015, September 1). *Double paternity leave for Singtel fathers*. Retrieved from https://www.hrdmag.com.sg/news/double-paternity-leave-for-singtel-fathers-204983.aspx
21. Human Resource Director. (2017, March 14). Malaysia bank offers year-long maternity leave. *Human Resource Director Asia*. Retrieved from https://www.hrdmag.com.sg/news/malaysian-bank-offers-yearlong-maternity-leave-234007.aspx
22. Siu, P. (2017, August 10). Hang Seng Bank employees given more annual leave after strong company performance. *South China Morning Post*. Retrieved May 15, 2018, from

http://www.scmp.com/news/hong-kong/economy/article/2106156/hang-seng-bank-employees-given-more-annual-leave-after-strong
23. Paternity leave press release. (2019, January 11). Retrieved from https://www.info.gov.hk/gia/general/201901/11/P2019011100352.htm
24. Shell Hong Kong announces new paid maternity leave policy. (2017, June 27). Retrieved from https://www.shell.com.hk/en_hk/media-center/news-and-media-releases/2017-press-releases/shell-hong-kong-announces-new-paid-maternity-leave-policy.html
25. Nhlapo, Z. (2018, February 20). Millennials in the workplace—not entitled, just different. *Huffpost*. Retrieved August 1, 2018, from https://www.huffingtonpost.co.za/2018/02/20/millennials-in-the-workplace-not-entitled-just-different_a_23366149/
26. Kohll, A. (2018, February 27). Are you measuring the real impact of your employee wellness programme? *Forbes*. Retrieved from https://www.forbes.com/sites/alankohll/2018/02/27/are-you-measuring-the-real-impact-of-your-employee-wellness-program/#1f03098123b5

8
Employment-Related Laws and Employee Relations in Hong Kong

Francis Hon

> **LEARNING OUTCOMES**
>
> By the end of this chapter, readers should be able to
>
> - understand the key concepts of employment-related laws in Hong Kong;
> - identify the objectives and major developments in Hong Kong's employment-related laws;
> - understand the major process and channels of labour dispute resolution;
> - evaluate the social, economic and political factors behind proposed labour legislation;
> - identify key drivers of effective employee engagement; and
> - describe major elements of employee communications and surveys.

Introduction

As long as an organization needs employees to work for it, employee engagement will remain as one of the key success factors for any organization, and therefore would be a primary objective for managers and HR professionals. And in order to keep employees engaged, one of the 'hygiene factors' is compliance of employment-related laws. Hence, we need to study employment laws. But it is impossible for this chapter to cover all the details of the laws. A few key concepts and sections that are fundamental to the understanding of the legislation will instead be introduced.

At the same time, we note that labour disputes are often the result of a lack of employee engagement. Disengaged employees have poor work performance and low job dissatisfaction, causing grievances and disputes in the workplace. The way these disputes are handled is crucial to employees' perception of their employers. Effective resolution of grievances and disputes can lead to harmonious employment relationship between employer and employees and thus high employee engagement. It is therefore another objective of this chapter to address the labour dispute resolution mechanisms in Hong Kong. Discussion on employee engagement will follow, including an introduction of the concept and process.

Key Concepts of Employment-Related Laws

Continuous contract of employment

The Hong Kong Employment Ordinance (Cap. 57) has a concept of 'continuous contract of employment' which eligibility for a majority of benefits under the Employment Ordinance depends on. An employee who has been employed continuously by the same employer for four weeks or more, with at least eighteen hours worked in each week is regarded as being employed under a continuous contract (the so-called 418 rule).[1] But the status of being under a continuous contract of employment is fluid—employees gain or lose that status dependent on their work patterns in the previous four weeks. By law, an employee would be entitled to rest day and statutory benefits with pay like maternity or paternity leave, statutory holidays, sick leave, annual leave, severance and long-service payments (all subject to further conditions specific to the benefit item) only if he or she is in continuous employment. It should also be noted that this concept does not apply to protection and benefits under other employment-related laws like the Employees' Compensation Ordinance (Cap. 282) and the Mandatory Provident Fund Schemes Ordinance (Cap. 485).

In the past two decades, the ratio of 'non-418' employees in private sector has been stable at around 5 per cent, within which about one-third are job changers who expect that they could be qualified as 418 employees after working for four weeks. Those non-418 employees are mostly part-timers or casual workers without statutory employment benefits. From time to time, there are public concerns over the 418 threshold for continuous contracts. But 'given the complexity of the subject and the considerable practical operational problems involved', the government is unlikely to relax the 418 threshold in the near future.[2]

HRM in Action—Box 8.1

Definition of Continuous Employment

In the case of *Lui Lin Kam & Others v. Nice Creation Development Ltd t/a Fu On Seafood Restaurant*, the employee was employed by the restaurant for 4.5 years under three contracts. None of the contracts lasted for more than twenty-four months, and each of them was separated by a break of two weeks. The Employment Ordinance offers various benefits to employees who are employed under a continuous contract for not less than twenty-four months, including the right to claim for unfair dismissal, which was the claim for this case. The Court of First Instance found that there had been continuous employment for not less than twenty-four months because there was effectively a 'global contract', which was an overriding arrangement governing the whole relationship between employer and employee, regardless of the number of separate written contracts. On appeal, the Court of Appeal disagreed with the finding that there was a global contract.

It said that the breaks were 'designed to break the continuity of employment. An employer is entitled to arrange its affairs to take advantage of the provisions of Schedule 1 [on continuous contract of employment].'

Sources:
Hong Kong Case Law Admin. (2016, November 25). *Lui Lin Kam & Others v. Nice Creation Development Ltd t/a Fu On Seafood Restaurant*. Retrieved from https://www.hongkong-caselaw.com/lui-lin-kam-and-other-v-nice-creation-development-ltd/
Hong Tran, Johnson Stokes & Master. (2006, September 22). No continuity of employment with successive fixed term contracts. *CThr*. Retrieved July 15, 2018, from https://cthr.ctgoodjobs.hk/article/show_article.aspx/1043-10468-no-continuity-of-employment-with-successive-fixed-term-contracts

Contract of service versus contract for service

The definition of continuous employment also leads to a related question—Who is an employee? The question is important because not only is a non-employee not entitled to benefits covered by the Employment Ordinance, a non-employee would also be unprotected by the Employees' Compensation Ordinance, which in some cases can involve an eight-figure monetary amount of damages. However, neither the Employment Ordinance nor the Employees' Compensation Ordinance provide a definition of employee. In accordance with the common law system, discussion and judgement related to one's employment status are referred to precedent cases. Generally, the court would consider a basket of indicators before deciding, on balance, whether someone works under a 'contract of service' (as an employee) in contrast to working under a 'contract for service' (as a contractor or an independent service provider). Some indicators of 'contract of service' include a company's provision of equipment, the requirement of an individual to perform a task personally, and the fact that the person would not have to bear financial risk regardless of whether the task would result in a profit or a loss. On the other hand, some indicators of 'contract for service' include the requirement to bring one's own equipment to work, the ability to delegate tasks to someone else, and the possibility (and risk) of financial gain or loss. One Court of Final Appeal case would illustrate the point.

In *Poon Chau Nam v. Yim Siu Cheung t/a Yat Cheung Airconditioning & Electric Co.* (FACV 14/2006), the claimant was a welder who was welding a part in an air conditioner when the welding rod suddenly shattered and a fragment struck his left eye. The facts of the case were that the company had no obligation to supply the claimant with work, and he had no obligation to turn up for work. He was free to take up jobs for others. He was paid a daily wage plus overtime salary, and whenever items had to be purchased by the claimant for work purposes, he was reimbursed by the company. The court found that the claimant bore no financial risks and reaped no financial rewards beyond his daily-rated remuneration. He also personally did the work assigned to him and did not hire anyone to help. The court decided that the claimant was a casual 'employee', and the fact that neither party was under an obligation to employ or to be employed is irrelevant, as this is the nature of casual employment. The company was therefore liable to pay employees' compensation as a result of the injury.

Unlawful dismissal and unfair dismissal

> **HRM in Focus—Box 8.2**
>
> **Employment Status under 'Gig' Economy**
>
> Some people are using the concept of the 'gig' economy to describe an emerging employment pattern. It is explained by Investopedia that 'in a gig economy, temporary, flexible jobs are commonplace and companies tend toward hiring independent contractors and freelancers instead of full-time employees. A gig economy undermines the traditional economy of full-time workers who rarely change positions and instead focus on a lifetime career.' This has obvious implications towards the application of the Employment Ordinance, which mainly provides protection for employees in the 'traditional' economy.
>
> Some flagship companies in the gig economy include Uber and Deliveroo. According to an article in *Forbes*, Uber is arguing that the drivers are not their employees, although that is now being challenged in courts, with a variety of outcomes. In any case, it is indisputable that the company, and also most of its drivers, are seeking a working relationship that is different from the full-time employee model. And even if the drivers are employees, it is not clear how many of them would fulfill the 418 rule of continuous contract of employment.
>
> As the gig economy and the workforce engagement pattern becomes more prominent, it would challenge the effectiveness and relevance of Employment Ordinance (as well as a number of other pieces of labour legislation) as a tool to protect the workforce. The Industry Schemes of the Mandatory Provident Fund Schemes Ordinance (provided to people working in the catering and construction industries) is one of the early attempts to incorporate the protection of casual workers. It may set an example for the future, probably inevitable, amendment of the Employment Ordinance.
>
> Sources:
> Gig economy. (n.d.). Retrieved from https://www.investopedia.com/terms/g/gig-economy.asp
> Ben-Shahar, O. (2017, Nov. 15). Are Uber drivers employees? The answer will shape the sharing economy. *Forbes*. Retrieved from https://www.forbes.com/sites/omribenshahar/2017/11/15/are-uber-drivers-employees-the-answer-will-shape-the-sharing-economy/#13b8b79d5e55

A common question among employers and top management is, 'Can a certain employee be fired'? Unlike some other jurisdictions, for the most case, employment-related laws in Hong Kong do not prohibit employers from terminating an employee's contract, provided that the statutory minimum compensation is being offered. The Employment Ordinance stipulates that it is unlawful to terminate an employee under certain situations, including when the employee is under maternity protection, on paid sick leave, because of him or her giving evidence or information to the authorities, because of trade union activities, and because of his or her injury at work. Terminations in these circumstances are liable to prosecution, subject to fine upon conviction. In some other circumstances, the termination can be unfair. If an employee has been under continuous contract of employment for more than two years but fewer than five years, and he or she is not terminated because of one of the following reasons, the employee is being unfairly dismissed:

- The conduct of the employee
- The capability or qualifications of the employee for performing work
- Redundancy or other genuine operational requirements of the business
- Statutory requirements
- Other substantial reasons

In this case, the employee will be entitled to termination payment with the same formula as long-service payment.[3]

Statutory holidays

The distinction between statutory holidays and public holidays is also an interesting feature in Hong Kong's employment. The Employment Ordinance only requires the granting of statutory holidays (twelve days per year) for employees. But there is a separate set of public holidays (seventeen days per year) that are observed by a considerable number of employees in Hong Kong. It used to be common for statutory holidays to be called 'factory holidays', presumably because those were holidays offered to blue-collar workers. Hong Kong now has far fewer factories than it had a few decades ago, but it is still a common practice for construction workers and foreign domestic helpers, to name but a couple of job types, to be offered only statutory holidays. There have been sporadic voices over the years to scrap the distinction between statutory and public holidays, and to let all employees enjoy public holidays.[4]

Contracting out

The Employment Ordinance would not prohibit offering of benefits which are better than what are required in the ordinance. In other words, the ordinance only provides a minimum standard. For example, it is required by law to offer ten weeks of maternity leave to a pregnant employee, with four-fifths of the normal pay (subject to other conditions). It is not against the law to, say, offer employees full pay for a maternity leave period of fourteen weeks.

Employment-Related Laws in Development

At this juncture, it would be appropriate to turn to certain aspects of the employment-related laws that are under debate and some possible new pieces of legislation. We have to reckon that Hong Kong is no longer a developing economy as it was in the mid- or late twentieth century when jobs and wages grew quickly. It is now regarded as an affluent city with countless luxury motorcars and designer boutiques. There are, however, many others who live in another world. It is one of the most unequal cities in the world. The Gini coefficient has been over 0.53.[5] With a workforce of around 3,500,000 in 2010, some 410,000 employees (more than 10 per cent of the workforce) were paid less than HK$4,000 a month. Hong Kong is also famous for having long working hours and a hard work culture that has often been perceived as exploitative. Therefore, employees in Hong Kong have urged for an environment that can uplift their livelihood and protect their employment rights. Regulatory and protective employment laws with respect to minimum wage, retirement protection, and working hours, common in developed countries, would be important. In addition, in line with the global trend of growing consciousness on human rights and justice, protective laws such as anti-discrimination ordinances for an increasingly diverse workforce in the society would be necessary.

Minimum wage

The Minimum Wage Ordinance (Cap. 608) was enforced in Hong Kong on May 1, 2011, and is one of the major pieces of new employment-related legislation. The law stipulates that wages payable to an employee for any wage period, when averaged over the total number of hours worked in the wage period, should be no less than the statutory minimum wage rate.[6] The minimum wage level is reviewed every two years by the Minimum Wage Commission. With effect from May 1, 2017, it is $34.5 per hour.

Before the law enactment in 2010, the government's proposal of stipulating minimum wage had drawn a huge debate among employers' associations, trade unions, and members of the public. One of the arguments against the legislation was that, by artificially setting a minimum wage, the government would take away jobs from people who can only attract a lower salary, thus depriving them of employment opportunities.[7] There were also arguments around the affordability of employers, especially the small- and medium-sized ones. On the other hand, the government was of the view that 'safeguarding the interests of the vulnerable and enhancing social harmony are equally important social policy objectives. Experience elsewhere suggests that the possible economic downside of an SMW [statutory minimum wage] can be mitigated by careful design.'[8] Since the law's enactment, the Minimum Wage Commission has published a report every two years to analyse the impact of minimum wage. In the report in 2018, the commission concludes that 'positive impact of the implementation of SMW has outweighed the negative impact'.[9]

Nevertheless, outside the government, there are also continuing discussions about the effectiveness and desirability of minimum wage. A study conducted in 2014 found that 'enforcing minimum wage induced a positive impact on quality of life, job and pay satisfaction, and a monthly income of vulnerable groups'.[10] The study also concludes that the statutory minimum wage brought benefits without sacrificing employment rate. Research conducted by the Confederation of Trade Unions, however, finds that the minimum wage level of $34.5 only benefits less than 2 per cent of the employee population, and that the rise of minimum wage level over the years is not catching up with inflation. The confederation therefore advocates a minimum wage level that is linked to the cost of living.[11]

Anti-discrimination ordinances

Anti-discrimination ordinances are other major considerations when it comes to compliance in employment practices. While the Sex Discrimination Ordinance and Disability Discrimination Ordinance were enacted in 1995, the Family Status Discrimination Ordinance was enacted in 1997, followed by the Race Discrimination Ordinance in 2008. These ordinances cover a wide range of aspects including education and provision of services, as well as employment (including recruitment). It is unlawful to make a recruitment decision—that is, to decide for or against recruiting a certain candidate—on the grounds of sex, family status, race, or disability. The same set of rules applies to employment practices, such as wage level, benefits, and HR policies. Details can be found in a previous book.[12]

But it should be noted that there are certain elaborations to the rule. First, an employer may make a seemingly discriminating decision based on genuine occupation qualifications. For example, it would not be discriminatory to hire a female caretaker to serve elderly female residents in an elderly home, in which the duties would include bringing the female residents to the shower and bathroom. Second, positive action is also allowable by law, which ensures certain groups of people have equal opportunities, or to provide them with services and facilities to meet their special needs in relation to employment.[13]

There are voices for additional pieces of anti-discrimination legislation, especially on enacting against discrimination on the basis of sexual orientation. Indeed, the Equal Opportunities Commission has commissioned a study on legislation against discrimination on the grounds of sexual orientation, gender identity, and intersex status.[14] The study finds that there is a 'clear majority public support for legislation against discrimination on the grounds of sexual orientation, gender identity and particularly intersex status'. It also recommends 'forums, workshops and training sessions be developed to increase dialogue and better understanding between different groups in society' on related issues. In employment-related aspects, some of the controversies are around whether religious institutions would then be forced to employ homosexual candidates, or whether employers are to offer insurance benefits to an employee's same-sex partner, in the same manner as it is offered to other employees' opposite-sex common-law partners. However, a number of religious organizations and politicians are strongly opposed to the legislation, arguing that the move would signal the government's approval of same-sex partnerships, which, it is claimed, undermine traditional family values. And at the same time, there is no strong political push for the legislation. As a result, there is no official indication as to whether the government will go ahead with the legislation at the time of writing. It is possible that the government has put it at a lower priority, or even shelved the legislation.

Standard working hours

Standard working hours is another issue that has entered the government agenda. There are various versions as to how standard working hours can be legislated. One version is to set a figure as to the standard number of hours that an employee would work in a week. Hours worked beyond the standard would attract additional wages with a statutory multiplier.[15] Some commentators see this as a logical consequence of minimum wage legislation because it has been argued that 'longer working hours is a key factor for the increase of a monthly income among the vulnerable groups'.[16]

Henceforth, following the *Report of the Policy Study on Standard Working Hours*, a Standard Working Hours Committee was set up by the government in April 2013. Studies were conducted on work patterns of Hong Kong employees, and issues such as extra expenditure by employers should the law be enacted, among other things. With a heated debate, the committee eventually suggested in 2017 that 'as a first and foremost step in taking forward working hours policy, . . . the approach of legislating for mandatory written employment contracts could provide an important working hours management framework'.[17] Under the proposal, a written employment contract, including specified working hours terms, would be mandatory. In other words, it would be up to the mutual agreement of employers and employees to decide what the 'contractual working hours' are, and the amount of wages that the overtime work would attract. The proposal has resulted in strong pushback from employees' associations and trade unions. Again, at the time of writing, there is no official indication as to what the next steps are. For the time being the government is spending a lot of its efforts on sorting out the Mandatory Provident Fund 'offsetting' arrangement (see next section), and it is unlikely that it will choose to fight two major battles at one time. It is envisaged that legislating for standard working hours would be a major move against the relatively flexible labour policy and production schedules that Hong Kong employers are used to (Box 8.3). Policing against a breach of standard working hour can also be tricky, which could be one of the reasons why the government shies away from the legislation.

HRM in Focus—Box 8.3
Media Discussion on Standard Working Hours

There are polarized views as to whether standard working hours should be legislated. For example, the *Hong Kong Free Press* published an impassioned article about the vices of long working hours, including many social and family problems. In particular, the poor working conditions of the service workers, such as a cook, could wear employees down both physically and mentally. Chronic exposure to the heat and emissions can lead to occupational hazards and health problems such as kidney dysfunction, high blood pressure, and respiratory disease. Thus, there are calls for standard working hours in order to promote work-life balance, employee morale, occupational safety and health, and reduce uncompensated overtime work while offering more employment opportunities.

On the other hand, there are opposing arguments that the legislation would be a blow to Hong Kong's labour market flexibility, resulting in an increase of business expense. It can bring serious employment distortion and reduce economic efficiency. The extra work hours created would have to be contributed by the female labour force, making them work longer hours, and delaying retirement. There would thus be severe consequences in terms of fertility patterns, mothers' time spent with young children, mobility prospects for younger workers, and intergenerational income inequality.

Nevertheless, there looks to be no consensus, however sketchy, as to how the discussion should proceed. Even a seemingly middle-of-the-road recommendation of 'contractual working hours' is being strongly opposed. Ultimately, the future of the legislation depends on the government's political will to take it forward—which seems to be lacking at the time of writing.

Sources:
Leung, J., Yu, B., and Fan, R. (2017, December 27). Chronically overlooked: Long hours and poor working conditions in Hong Kong's service industries. Retrieved from https://www.hongkongfp.com/2017/12/26/chronically-overlooked-long-hours-poor-working-conditions-hong-kongs-service-industries/
Wong, R. (2015, February 24). Are standard working hours a good thing for Hong Kong? *South China Morning Post.* Retrieved July 15, 2018, from http://www.scmp.com/comment/insight-opinion/article/1722330/are-standard-working-hours-good-thing-hong-kong

Mandatory Provident Fund

Mandatory Provident Fund (MPF) offsetting is another hot topic in Hong Kong. The Employment Ordinance stipulates that, for an employee who has worked for not less than two years and is dismissed because of redundancy, or for one who has worked for not less than five years and is being dismissed (rather than resigning), the employer is to give them severance payment (in the former case) or long-service payment (in the latter case). The two payments have the same formula, and even if an employee is entitled to both, he or she will only be paid one. With the Mandatory Provident Fund Schemes Ordinance (Cap. 485), the employer is allowed to use the accrued benefits of an employer's contribution portion of the MPF (contributions with investment gain or loss and fund management fees taken into account) to offset severance payment or long-service payment payable to the employee. In other words, an employer would be paying less, or would even not have to pay, because part or all of the payment would be covered by the MPF. It is estimated that in the past fifteen years, a total of over HK$30 billion of the MPF contributions have been used to offset severance and long-service payments, causing significant loss in the MPF accounts of individual workers.[18]

Trade unions have long been complaining that the arrangement is depriving employees from part of their legal entitlements. The government's proposal is that a fund will be set up by the government with government contribution ($15 billion, in a proposal made in March 2018) to it. At a certain point after the abolition of the offset arrangement, employers would be subsidized from that pool, and after a certain number of years, this interim arrangement will come to an end. Employers will then have to pay by themselves the full amount of severance and long-service payments. The proposal continues to attract intensive discussions and controversies at the time of writing.[19] In any case, trade unions expect that the arrangement is giving employees nothing less than the full severance payment and long-service payment and the entire Mandatory Provident Fund that they are currently entitled to. Employers disagree among themselves as to how the arrangement is to be funded, and negotiations are ongoing with the government. Some compromise between the government and employers seems to be unavoidable. The government would need to guarantee a large sum of money to unwind the policy. On the other hand, it is a long-standing policy that the government will not permanently pay for employees' benefits (for example, current legislation determine that employees' compensations are taken out from insurance policy, Mandatory Provident Fund are from employers and employees' contributions, and even the Protection of Wages on Insolvency Fund is paid for by business registration levy), so the government is likely to ask employers to make some additional commitments.

Collective bargaining

Collective bargaining could be defined as 'a right by which workers are able to negotiate on equal footing with their employer on issues of wages, working conditions, and all other issues that affect the terms and conditions of work'.[20] The last two decades have been a terrible time for workers and low-income groups, who have suffered from stagnant wages, government cutbacks and outsourcing with short-term contracts providing little perks or labour protection. On the other hand, it has been a most generous period to those with capitals and properties. There are thus intermittent calls for legislating for the rights of collective bargaining.[21] And it has been in the media again after an early 2018 labour dispute within Kowloon Motor Bus.[22] As a matter of historical fact, collective bargaining used to be required by law for a very brief period in 1997 before it was abolished by the Provisional Legislative Council in the same year.

We have to admit that the impoverishment of labour and the obscene enrichment of capital in recent decades have been a universal phenomenon among developed economies. But different economies may exhibit different responses to the same phenomenon. Hong Kong is used to running an 'open-door' policy for the business elite. The business sector often argues that collective bargaining may worsen the tensions between workers and bosses, and a free economy does not need heavy labour regulations. For a long time, both the local and Beijing governments have believed that our local tycoons' support is crucial to the prosperity of the economy and a successful transition to Chinese rule. Therefore, support for collective bargaining by the government is also weak. At the same time, our trade unions are fragmented with low union participation rate, and employees in the same company are often represented by different trade unions. Except in some large public organizations and airline companies, it would be difficult for employees to have the same bargaining power against the employer. As a result, there is probably no sign that the government is considering re-enacting the legislation.

Retirement age

Finally, there are recent discussions about retirement age, with one of the objectives of encouraging the so-called young old in contributing to the economy in the light of an ageing population and labour shortage in the society. Although there are provisions under the Employment Ordinance which stipulate that an employee is entitled to long-service payment when he or she becomes sixty-five and that the Mandatory Provident Fund Schemes Ordinance allow an employee to get his or her full accrued benefits at sixty-five, there is no statutory requirement as to the retirement age. In other words, there is no legal requirement for an employee to leave employment when he or she reaches a certain age. In fact, in usual practice and in common company policy, when a company says that an employee is to retire by say, sixty, it often means that it is by mutual agreement that the employee will resign when he or she turns sixty, with all the entitlement that he or she is promised, not that the employer seeks to dismiss the employee at that point. The government has extended the retirement ages for its new civil servants after June 1, 2015, in general and disciplined services to sixty-five and sixty, respectively.[23] Some large corporations have followed in a similar vein. And in February 2018 the government launched a consultation over whether civil servants who joined the government between June 2000 and May 2015 should be allowed a choice to extend their retirement date.[24] At the moment, there is no indication that the government would extend the policy citywide. Again, this would be a major change to the relatively flexible labour policy, and there is for the time being no strong advocacy and political pressure for such legislation.

Labour Disputes and Resolution

Labour disputes take different forms and shapes. It can be about the legality of a certain action by employer—for example, whether a certain dismissal is discriminatory. It can also be about the interpretation of a certain contract terms—for example, on whether an employee is entitled to a year-end payment. In addition, it can be about an employer's fairness—for example, dissatisfaction about working conditions or long working hours. It can even be about a claim by the employer towards the employee, for example, for payment in lieu of notice when an employee leaves employment without notice.

There is a dispute resolution channel that the government strongly encourages people to follow:

1. Labour Department—the Labour Department has ten labour relations district offices under its Offices of Labour Relations Division, which offers conciliation services on a voluntary basis.[25] An individual or a company who wishes to engage the Labour Department in the services can request the department to conduct a conciliation meeting. The Labour Department will then invite the other party in the dispute for a meeting, where an officer will try to help the parties to reach a mutually acceptable solution, except in the event when there is a possible breach of law; in such a circumstance the case would be referred to the Employment Claims Investigation Division. Participation of the conciliation meeting is voluntary. Agreement reached in the meeting is, however, not enforceable by court. Conciliation is usually more effective in cases with grey areas, such as unfair dismissal. For many other cases, like those regarding non-payment of wages or holidays being denied, employees often see the incidents as miscarriages of justice, which is not for conciliation. Those cases usually end up in courts.
2. Labour Tribunal and Minor Employment Claims Adjudication Board—if conciliation is not successful, a claimant can file a case in either the Labour Tribunal[26] or the Minor Employment Claims Adjudication Board (MECAB).[27] Claims in the amount of under $8,000 and involving ten people or fewer would go to MECAB. Otherwise, all cases go to the Labour Tribunal. They are both part of the judiciary system. But their approach is to first encourage settlement, and for cases that could not reach settlement, a judgment will be handed down. No lawyers are allowed in the courts, and the adjudicator/tribunal officer takes an active role in understanding and facilitating the hearing and settlement. Despite criticisms about the courts' strong inclination towards settlement, the system indeed provides a cheap and relatively quick channel to settle labour disputes. Interested readers can also get more details in the previous book.[28]
3. High Court and above—judgements made in the Labour Tribunal and MECAB are subject to appeal. In the High Court, Court of Appeal, and Court of Final Appeal, normal rules apply to employment-related cases, such as the admission of lawyers and the adoption of the adversarial approach in case proceedings. In the common law system, lower courts are to follow the precedents established by the higher courts, so certain important judgements made in the higher courts, such as the Court of Final Appeal case mentioned under the

discussion above on 'contract of service' versus 'contract for service', would become important references as to how the statutes are to be interpreted.

Many of the claims under the Employment Ordinance are civil in nature. The government will not be involved in investigation and will not be a party of the case. However, breaching of certain employment ordinance stipulations would be a criminal offence, for example, non-payment of wages and unlawful dismissal. In those circumstances, the Labour Department will step in to investigate the cases with a view towards prosecution. The convicted party could also be subject to jail and fine, instead of (or in many cases, in addition to) compensation and damages. Some other common offences subject to prosecution include the failure of taking out an employee compensation policy and failure to keep appropriate employment records.

Offences under anti-discrimination ordinances take another route. In the context of employment-related situations, anti-discrimination cases often proceed in parallel with the Employment Ordinance claims and investigations. For example, if an employer is suspected of dismissing a pregnant employee, the employee in question will often be advised to file a case both at the Labour Department and the Equal Opportunities Commission. There could then be a civil law claim of termination payment against the employer via the Labour Department and the Labour Tribunal, an investigation carried out by the Labour Department for unlawful dismissal, and another investigation undertaken by the Equal Opportunities Commission for the breach of the discrimination ordinance.

There is no law or regulation that prohibits people from engaging parties other than the Labour Department's labour relations offices to resolve their disputes. Arbitration, which the Hong Kong International Arbitration Centre describes as a 'flexible, efficient and confidential method of dispute resolution resulting in a final, legally binding and enforceable award', are being supported by the legislative regime.[29] But there is little sign that the practice is being taken up en masse in labour disputes, and the Labour Department conciliation services remain a very popular channel as the first step towards labour dispute resolution.

That being said, the Labour Department does not necessarily play an active, or at least publicly visible role, in some of the more high-profile labour disputes. For example, in the labour dispute between Kowloon Motor Bus and the drivers in April 2018, where the discussions were around salary, working hours, and safety, the main parties seemed to be the employer and multiple trade unions. The tragic accident on Tai Po Road was just a catalyst to the dispute, while the government was focusing on the handling of the aftermath of the accident. In this and similar cases, the disputes are usually not about breaching of certain legal requirements, but about dissatisfaction or different expectations as to benefits and working conditions. The dispute resolution process is hence less on the legal side than on negotiations between employers, employees, and possibly other stakeholders. As noted above in the discussion around collective bargaining, one observation about employer-employee negotiations in Hong Kong is that there is usually more than one trade union representing the employees, each of them being backed by a different trade union association which is affiliated with a political party. This is especially the case with large or public utilities companies. Dispute resolutions then call for understanding of different parties' needs, and comprehension of the political scene if necessary. In order to minimize labour disputes, employee engagement is also essential, which will be discussed below.

Employee Engagement through Communications and Surveys

Employee engagement can be a tool for minimizing labour disputes. More positively viewed, it is also a process to maximize employees' job satisfaction, among other things, by which a lowered risk of labour disputes is a desirable result. There are various definitions of employee engagement.[30] For example, Dell, a computer technology company, has the view on engagement that 'to compete today, companies need to win over the MINDS (rational commitment) and the HEARTS (emotional commitment) of employees in ways that lead to extraordinary effort'.[31] Hewitt Associates, a consultancy company, describes that 'engagement is the state of emotional and intellectual commitment to an organization or group producing behaviour that will help fulfill an organization's promises to customers—and, in so doing, improve business results.'[32] Engaged employees are 'happy productive workers'.[33] In general, employee engagement can be defined as a set of positive attitudes and behaviours enabling high job performance of a kind which is in tune with the organization's mission. It is a process that seeks to ensure employees' willingness to contribute to the organization, for the benefit of their employers, and also for their own satisfaction. It is also worth noting that the two quotes above, plus many other definitions available, carry both the elements of heart and mind. Employees have to be rationally convinced, and emotionally attached.

Furthermore, 'communication is a critical aspect of employee engagement', according to the Chartered Institute of Personnel and Development (CIPD) in the UK. It comments that communication 'in turn promotes better performance, employee retention and well-being. Employees are more engaged when information flows freely and they're aware of organizational activities and management decisions that affect their jobs'.[34] That is especially so during the time of organizational change, for employees new to the position or the organization, and for organizations with a large geographical span.

A research report named *Harnessing the Power of Employee Communication*,[35] published by the CIPD, argues that successful communication

- is built on a shared sense of purpose and aligned to business strategy;
- receives attention and support from senior leadership;
- is driven by genuine dialogue;
- is part of the expectation of good people management;
- draws on a range of digital channels and tools; and
- is reviewed and assessed for effectiveness.

CIPD also suggests a few principles of an effective employee communications strategy:

- **Role of senior leaders and people managers.** Senior leaders are the embodiment of the organization. When resources permit, communications professionals should partner with leaders to help them be authentic, clear, and inclusive in their communications. A separate survey also reveals that managing difficult conversations is considered by HR professionals as one of the main leadership skills needed.
- **Use of social technology.** Some organizations are seeing benefits from internal social media, in quickly resolving operational issues and enabling employee

interaction. Social media is being used in place, or alongside, static intranets, which are increasingly seen as outdated repositories of information.
- **Two-way and multidirectional dialogue.** With the advent of enterprise social networks, communication is increasingly becoming not only two-way but multidirectional. Good two-way communication supports employee engagement, as employees feel listened to and valued.

Communication effectiveness has to be assessed to determine whether it has successfully engaged employees. Employee surveying is a tool that serves this purpose. Surveys, in turn, are also part of the communication process that shows an organization's emphasis on employee feedback, and that reflects its priorities in business directions and employment practices.

As observed by the Society for Human Resource Management, 'Today's employee surveys are often shorter, more narrowly focused and more frequently administered than traditional instruments. . . . Survey questions or statements now explicitly link employee attitudes to business objectives.'[36] One example is that, in an annual employee survey that the US Office of Personnel Management (OPM) requires for federal agencies, there are assessment requirements of the law, which reflects areas required in the survey:[37]

- Leadership and management practices that contribute to agency performance
- Employee satisfaction with
    - leadership policies and practices;
    - work environment;
    - rewards and recognition for professional accomplishment and personal contributions to achieving organizational mission;
    - opportunity for professional development and growth; and
    - opportunity to contribute to achieving organizational mission.

It should be noted that employee communication and survey should not be considered the sole, or even predominant tools for employee engagement. As seen from some of the high-profile labour dispute cases earlier in the chapter, dissatisfaction and disengagement arise from the perception of poor working conditions, long working hours, and unfair employment practices, which cannot simply be 'communicated away'. Communication and survey should play the role of collecting feedback and discussing plans as to how to win over minds and hearts of employees, which are items that the OPM has accurately captured.

HRM in Focus—Box 8.4

Employee Engagement in Hong Kong

In a 2014 report on Employee Engagement by Aon Hewitt, a consultancy, 29 per cent of the responding employees rated themselves as passively engaged, compared with the Asia-Pacific average of 24 per cent, and only 49 per cent plan to stay with their current company for the foreseeable future. A 2016 report by IDC, a market intelligence firm, also mentioned that only 28 per cent of Hong Kong workers said they found their work engaging and satisfactory, compared with 59 per cent in the Philippines and India, and 42 per cent in Australia.

Aon Hewitt suggests that career opportunities and managing performance is at the top of the wish list of employees, and IDC is of the view that HR strategies must be aligned to corporate business goals. At the same time, both these reports emphasized the importance of communication. IDC commented that exposing individual employees to a better understanding of how they can contribute to the success of their companies will help improve their engagement. Aon Hewitt also opines that, even though a company may already have good career opportunities and performance management processes, many employees are still looking for enhanced understanding and communication of these factors. In this sense, it is not enough for good HR work to be done. It also has to be seen to be done, and communication is how the good work is brought to employees' attention and appreciation.

Sources:
Aon Hewitt report highlights key employee engagement trends in Asia-Pacific. (2014, November 15). Retrieved from https://www.cpjobs.com/hk/article/aon-hewitt-report-highlights-key-employee-engagement-trends-asia-pacific
Chow, C. (2016, June 28). Hong Kong firms must do more to keep employees happy: Survey. Retrieved from http://www.ejinsight.com/20160628-hong-kong-firms-must-do-more-to-keep-employees-happy-says-survey

Conclusion

In this chapter we have looked at the key concepts in employment-related laws, and the various controversies and development around them. We have also discussed the labour dispute resolution mechanisms and the concept and process of employee engagement. These are some of the core areas of an HR professional, aspects which HR practitioners are key contributors to the success of an organization and well-being of its employees. Employment-related laws is also one area which requires a keen sense of political environment and social trend. HR professionals, therefore, have to be employee champions, a term used by the HRM guru Dave Ulrich for some time. They have to understand what motivates and demotivates people—not just on a micro level such as individual compensation and benefits, but also on a macro level, in terms of the push-and-pull factors behind the legislation and socio-economic developments, and how they influence society, organizations, and the employees. HR professionals have to be open-minded, curious, and stay abreast of the latest developments in order to be a real business partner of the organization.

As an optimistic person, the author agrees with the trend of the new employment laws. Despite the details that are to be thoughtfully sorted out, the developments represent a move towards a better protection of employees' rights and benefits. As Hong Kong grows into a developed economy and job creation and career advancement opportunities possibly become less rosy than in the past, it is even more important for employees to enjoy a more stable environment, with protection against discrimination, unfair dismissal, and the like. Minimum Wage Ordinance and a lot of the existing labour (and welfare) legislation are also contributing to a better 'safety net' for employees in a more competitive environment.

Even the keenest advocate of new employment laws would not deny that the economics behind the proposed developments are to be carefully considered. No one wants to see minimum wage and standard working hours bring unemployment and hardship. Theoretically, communication and understanding between employers' and employees' groups should also be valued. However, a lack of effective mechanisms where government and politicians seek compromise and agreement is probably one of the biggest constraints for new and valuable pieces of labour legislation to move ahead. Despite the existence of a tripartite consultative body, the Labour Advisory Board,[38] most legislation agendas are driven by the government. Unless it is convinced that there is a real and urgent need, or that there is an enormous pressure from society, the government has an inclination to be reactive and conservative (see standard working hours and discrimination against sexual orientation as examples). In those cases, the government does not look to be keen in actively bringing different opinions together to drive labour legislation forward. There are no obvious channels and mechanisms for concerned groups to discuss and reach consent among themselves. Hong Kong society also lacks a consensus as to where the society is headed in terms of its people's well-being. It is unlikely to see a major update of labour legislation in the foreseeable future.

Review Questions

1. What is meant by 'continuous contract of employment'? Please evaluate the pros and cons of it.
2. Compare between 'contract of service' and 'contract for service'. What are the criteria for each concept?
3. Specify some conditions of unlawful and unfair dismissal.
4. Identify two areas of employment law under development. Discuss their prospects of development in Hong Kong.
5. Name the anti-discrimination laws in Hong Kong. What areas of improvement can you recommend in this area?
6. Comment on the labour relations and dispute resolution system in Hong Kong. Discuss and explain the prospect of trade unions in Hong Kong.
7. Define employee engagement and explain why it is important to organizations.
8. How would you describe the level of engagement of Hong Kong employees?

Notes

1. Labour Department. (2018, February). *A Concise Guide to Employment Ordinance*. Retrieved from https://www.labour.gov.hk/eng/public/ConciseGuide.htm
   Interested readers can also get employment law information from the following website: Community Legal Information Centre, Law and Technology Centre, University of Hong Kong:
   http://www.clic.org.hk/en/
2. Yu, C. H., Research Office, Legislative Council Secretariat. (2017). *Review of employment benefits under continuous contract in Hong Kong*. Retrieved from https://www.legco.gov.hk/research-publications/english/1617in13-review-of-employment-benefits-under-continuous-contract-in-hong-kong-20170525-e.pdf
3. For a monthly paid employee, the formula is last month wages × 2/3 × reckonable years of service, when last month wages is subject to a cap of $22,500.

4. Labour unions want paid holidays increased to 17 days a year (2016, March 21). Retrieved from http://www.ejinsight.com/2016034-labor-unions-want-paid-holidays-increased-to-17-days-a-year/
5. Yau, C., and Zhou, V. (2017, June 9). What hope for the poorest? Hong Kong wealth gap hits record high. *South China Morning Post.* Retrieved April 1, 2018, from http://www.scmp.com/news/hong-kong/economy/article/2097715/what-hope-poorest-hong-kong-wealth-gap-hits-record-high
6. Labour Department. (2017, April). *Concise Guide to Statutory Minimum Wage, Labour Department.* Retrieved from https://www.labour.gov.hk/eng/public/smw/Concise_Guide_to_SMW_2015.pdf
7. Lion Rock Institute was one of the advocates. Retrieved from www.lionrockinstitute.org/2008/05/2010-02-23-09-21-25
8. Legislative Council. (2009, June). *Legislative Council brief on Minimum Wage Bill*, LD SMW 1-55/1/4(C).
Retrieved from http://www.legco.gov.hk/yr08-09/english/bills/brief/b24_brf.pdf
9. Minimum Wage Commission. (2018). *2016 Report of the Minimum Wage Commission*, p.75. Retrieved from https://www.mwc.org.hk/en/downloadable_materials/2018_MWC Report_Eng.pdf
10. Wong, H., and Ye, S. (2014). Impact of enforcing a statutory minimum wage on work and quality of life of vulnerable groups in Hong Kong. *International Journal of Social Welfare 2015, 24,* 223–235.
11. Hong Kong Confederation of Trade Unions. (2017, September 14). HKCTU and member unions' proposal to Minimum Wage Commission (職工盟及屬會會見最低工資委員會之意見書). Retrieved from www.hkctu.org.hk/cms/article.jsp?article_id=1782&cat_id=8
12. Papadopolous, A. (2009). Equal opportunities laws in Hong Kong. In A. Tsui and K. T. Lai (Eds.), *Professional practices of HRM in Hong Kong: Linking HRM to organizational success* (pp. 183–202). Hong Kong: Hong Kong University Press.
13. See various codes of practice on employment published by Equal Opportunities Commission from: www.eoc.org.hk
14. Equal Opportunities Commission and Gender Research Centre, CUHK. (2016). *Report on study on legislation against discrimination on the grounds of sexual orientation, gender identity and intersex status.* Hong Kong: EOC.
Retrieved from http://www.legco.gov.hk/yr15-16/english/panels/ca/papers/ca20160215-rpt201601-e.pdf
15. This was advocated by employee members of the Labour Advisory Board in the Standard Working Hours Committee, as reported in the *Report of the Standard Working Hours Committee*, January 2017
16. Wong, H., and Ye, S. (2014). Impact of enforcing a statutory minimum wage on work and quality of life of vulnerable groups in Hong Kong. *International Journal of Social Welfare 2015, 24,* 223–235.
17. Report of the Standard Working Hours Committee, January 2017, Par. 11.8
18. 30 billion dollars were set off in 15 years (15年沖走打工仔300億). (2016, December 21). *Apple Daily.* Retrieved April 1, 2018, from https://hk.news.appledaily.com/local/daily/article/20161221/19872383
19. Viewpoints on cancelling MPF hedging mechanism proposal and opinions from stakeholders [In Chinese]. Retrieved from http://www.liberalstudies.hk/pdf/20170626181537_170626_Daily%20Topc_Table_Hedging%20Mechanism.pdf. Siu, P. (2017, June 20). Scrap MPF offset mechanism now or expect no change in Hong Kong status quo. *South China Morning Post.* Retrieved May 1, 2018, from http://www.scmp.com/news/hong-kong/economy/article/2099046/scrap-mpf-offset-mechanism-now-or-expect-no-change-hong-kong
20. Yoon, Y. M. (n.d.). *The view of the ILO on the legislative situation of collective bargaining in Hong Kong.* Retrieved from http://www.hkctu.org.hk/cms/images/userfile/file/The%20view%20

of%20the%20ILO%20on%20the%20legislative%20situation%20of%20collective%20bargaining%20in%20Hong%20Kong.pdf

21. Lee, A., and Man, J. (2013, June 14). Labour unions hindered by lack of collective bargaining law. *South China Morning Post*. Retrieved May 1, 2018, from http://www.scmp.com/news/hong-kong/article/1216889/labour-unions-hindered-lack-collective-bargaining-law
22. Yeung, R., and Su, X. Q. (2018, Feb. 24). Road strike by KMB bus drivers' union over pay dispute ends before it takes off. *South China Morning Post*. Retrieved June 1, 2018, from http://www.scmp.com/news/hong-kong/community/article/2134576/kmb-bus-driver-union-plans-8pm-strike-stopping-buses-hong
23. Ng, K. C. (2015, March 24). Hong Kong's new civil servants' retirement age increased by five years. South China Morning Post. Retrieved May 1, 2018, from http://www.scmp.com/news/hong-kong/article/1745582/hong-kongs-new-civil-servants-retirement-age-increased-five-years
24. Cheng, C. (2018, Feb. 21). Gov't begins consultation on extending retirement age of civil servants—scheme could cost up to HK$5.8 bn. *South China Morning Post*. Retrieved April 1, 2018, from https://www.hongkongfp.com/2018/02/21/govt-begins-consultation-extending-retirement-age-civil-servants-scheme-cost-hk5-8-bn/
25. Labour Department. (n.d.). *Offices of Labour Relations Division*. Retrieved from https://www.labour.gov.hk/eng/tele/lr1.htm
26. HKSAR Government. (n.d.). *Labour Tribunal*. Retrieved from https://www.judiciary.hk/en/crt_services/pphlt/pdf/labour.pdf
27. Labour Department. (2016). *A simple guide to the Minor Employment Claims Adjudication Board*. Retrieved from https://www.labour.gov.hk/eng/public/mecab/SGMECAB.pdf
28. Van Langenberg, B., and Loughrey, F. (2009). Employment laws in Hong Kong. In A. Tsui and K. T. Lai (Eds.), *Professional practices of HRM in Hong Kong: Linking HRM to organizational success* (pp. 163–182). Hong Kong: Hong Kong University Press.
29. Hong Kong International Arbitration Centre: http://www.hkiac.org
30. Interested readers may also look at some definitions of employee engagement from the following sources: Vance, Robert J. (2006). *Employee engagement and commitment*. Alexandria: SHRM. Retrieved from https://www.shrm.org/hr-today/trends-and-forecasting/special-reports-and-expert-views/Documents/Employee-Engagement-Commitment.pdf
31. Vance, Robert J. (2006). *Employee engagement and commitment*. Alexandria: SHRM.
32. Vance, Robert J. (2006). *Employee engagement and commitment*. Alexandria: SHRM.
33. Bakker, A. B., and Demerouti, E. (2008) Towards a model of work engagement. *Career Development International*, *13*(3), pp. 209–223.
34. CIPD. (n.d.). *Employee communication*. Retrieved from https://www.cipd.asia/knowledge/factsheets/employee-communication
35. CIPD. (2010). *Harnessing the power of employee communication*. London: CIPD. Retrieved from http://www.synergycreative.co.uk/images/Download_documents/CIPD_Effective_Employee_Communication.pdf
36. Vance, Robert J. (2006). *Employee engagement and commitment*. Alexandria: SHRM.
37. US Office of Personnel Management. (2008). *Annual employee survey guidance*. Retrieved from https://www.opm.gov/policy-data-oversight/data-analysis-documentation/employee-surveys/surveyguidance.pdf
38. Labour Department. (n.d.). *Labour Advisory Board*. Retrieved from https://www.labour.gov.hk/eng/rbo/LAB.htm

9
Digital Transformation of Human Resource Management in the Era of Disruptive Technology

Josh Bersin[1] and Anna P. Y. Tsui

LEARNING OUTCOMES

By the end of this chapter, readers should be able to

- describe HR trends that encourage adoption of HR technologies;
- identify features of HR technologies and their applications in different HR functions;
- explain how the HR functions can be transformed when using these technologies;
- understand the skills required from HR professionals in the new digital era;
- understand the actual status and extent of adopting HR technologies in Hong Kong; and
- analyse the motivations and barriers of implementing HR technologies in Hong Kong.

Introduction

In this chapter we discuss digital transformation of HRM in the era of disruptive technology. We begin by explaining some terms. Disruptive technologies are those that significantly alter the way businesses operate. Examples of disruptive technologies are smartphones and e-commerce. An associated term, disruptive innovation, defined by Professor Clayton Christensen, is one in which a new market value proposition disrupts the existing market and displaces traditional firms, products, or services that used to dominate that market.[2] When he talked about disruptive innovation, he referred to external markets instead of internal corporate functions. But the concept can be applied to HR. Disruptive innovation of HR could be one that delivers a new value proposition in the internal corporate functions in which HR operates and disrupts the way it provides services to the people inside.[3] For digital transformation, it means 'the investment in and development of new technologies, mindsets, and business and operational models to improve work and competitiveness and deliver new and relevant value for customers and employees in an ever-evolving digital economy'.[4] In the context of HR, it carries the potential of a new discourse about HR operations and provides new ways for streamlining various HR activities leading to better employee engagement, innovation, motivation, and company performance. This calls for a new way of thinking as new skills and competencies are required.[5]

Over the years, we have seen an explosion of new technologies and innovations disrupting our business systems and operations. We now live in a world flooded with apps, mobile and cloud-based technology, various data communication devices, artificial intelligence (AI), virtual reality (VR) and augmented reality (AR), web content analysis, and organizational network analysis technologies, blockchain platforms,[6] cognitive bots, and analytics software. These changes have also brought new functionalities to the world of HR. There is an explosion of tools for recruitment, learning, feedback and surveys, well-being, analytics, organizational network analysis, and engagement. As a consequence, traditional HR functions such as talent acquisition and recruitment, performance management and compensation, and training and development are being transformed. Our tasks are streamlined and companies can become more efficient and productive. While there are improvements of candidate, employee, and recruiter experiences, HR activities can also be more forward-looking and strategic, helping organizations make better decisions based on data and more information.

Indeed, the HR technology market is undergoing one of the most disruptive years in this millennium so far. A report estimated that companies in the world had plunged more than US$14 billion into HR technologies in 2015.[7] HR and workforce-related products are found in business, well-being and education markets, and many start-ups are formed to build new tools and innovations. In Hong Kong companies' investment in HR technology also exhibit a general upward trend. In a HKIHRM survey, 57 per cent of the 139 respondents reported a rise in HR technology spending in 2017 compared with 2016. Further growth had been expected in 2018, with two-thirds of the companies anticipating significant or moderate increases in their expenditure.[8]

In this chapter, we first seek to understand the evolution of HR technologies and the way they affect HR management. Next, we study the potential impact of disruptive technology to transform HR in terms of several functions: talent acquisitions, performance management, providing feedback and survey, corporate learning, and HR analytics. We also highlight the new skills and competencies for HR to survive in the new era. Finally, to be in line with the theme of this book, we examine the status and extent of adopting HR technology in Hong Kong companies. On the basis of a survey done by HKIHRM, we look at how companies utilize different technologies, their motivations and readiness, and the barriers they face when implementing the technologies. A case study on using data analytics in Hong Kong is also given.

Evolution of HR Technology: From Talent Management to People Management to Team Management

Evolution of HR technology has mirrored the evolution of management and HR philosophies. During the 1970s and 1980s organizations focused on traditional HR approaches—creating standards for HR records and administration, compensation and benefits, hiring and staffing according to law. HR software vendors emphasized building systems of compliance, records, and calculating payrolls and benefits. HR technology used for these purposes was mainly mainframe-based. In the 1990s and early 2000s vendors shifted to PC technology and built client/server HR software, leading companies to replace their mainframe systems with new ERP (enterprise resource planning) systems such as PeopleSoft, Oracle, SAP, and Baan. They could deliver core HR applications including hiring, payroll, and some training management.

Following the recession in the early 2000s, competition for talent became fierce, creating a new term, 'war for talent'. This new business focus enabled a market for talent management software which quickly exploded with innovation. Companies such as Taleo, BrassRing (recruiting), Saba and SumTotal (learning), SuccessFactors and Softscape (performance management), and others began to automate and integrate talent management. A new technology architecture, software as a service (SaaS), or on-demand software, was developed. As vendors convinced companies to use their hosted solutions, organizations began to shift their HR technology away from on-premise systems. The period between the mid-2000s and early 2010s was a time of consolidations and acquisitions of companies and products, such as SAP's acquisition of SuccessFactors (which itself had previously acquired Plateau Systems), Oracle's owning of PeopleSoft and Taleo (which acquired Learn.com), IBM's acquisition of Kenexa (which acquired BrassRing), and ADP's acquisition of Workscape. All the while, the computing world was moving to the cloud developed by vendors, which is deployed remotely and accessed through a web browser.[9] Companies like Google, Facebook, and LinkedIn have proved to HR departments that they no longer need to run software on their own systems—connecting cloud-based HR systems to social networks is the future. 'Built from the cloud' solutions such as Workday look appealing.

Since the early 2010s many major multinational corporations have made plans to replace their legacy systems with one of the major vendors (Oracle, SAP, and Workday being the top three). But many of the talent management vendors have grown and survived. For example, among others, Cornerstone OnDemand continues to grow rapidly. Altogether, these four systems have attracted more than 150 million users to their cloud systems. And companies have shifted from purchasing to leasing these products. At the same time, a new breed of built-for-the-cloud mid-market vendors has emerged, including companies such as Ultimate Software, BambooHR, and Zenefits. But some large global companies separate their payroll by using services from payroll-centric vendors (such as ADP, Ceridian, Paychex, SAP, or some Indian companies) around the world or local providers.[10] Today, we believe we are in a fourth phase, one that demands technology designed around teams, individuals, and networks—tools that implement agile talent practices and help people be more productive. Tools that facilitate collaboration, video conferencing and other forms of communication are popular—namely, Microsoft Teams, Workplace by Facebook, Slack, Skype, HipChat, BlueJeans Network, and other offerings. Meanwhile, several other technology shifts have also occurred.

- People analytics—as was argued in Chapter 2, HR departments should realize that their prospects are dependent on their ability to harness people data and build analytics models. This has led to a huge investment in analytics by HR vendors (Workday has acquired Platfora, Cornerstone OnDemand acquired Evolv, IBM introduced Talent Insights powered by Watson, and Ultimate Software owns Vestrics).

- Mobile platforms—HR software of the future would be built on mobile architecture, with cloud technology being invisible behind the scenes. Mobile apps allow users to access data anywhere, anytime, either for information dissemination or manager/employee self-services. They enhance speedy communication within and outside companies. But a mobile app is not just a 'rehosting' of a cloud app. It would be an entirely different experience designed in a different way. We swipe, pinch, and expect to be able to use sensors for location, proximity, acceleration, and even temperature. Mobile apps can listen to voices, understand speech, and sense our moods.
- Platform as a service (PaaS)—PaaS technologies let vendors create an array of partner applications that leverage and extend their core offerings—a family of exciting, intimate apps connected to the platform. Vendors such as ADP (ADP Marketplace), SAP (HANA Marketplace), IBM (IBM Cloud), and Cornerstone OnDemand (Cornerstone Edge) have created app stores to enable software developers to build applications that take advantage of their services. An example is the Salesforce AppExchange programme that offers tools for Salesforce customers.

In sum, there has been a major shift in HR focus. Companies today may not concentrate on automating and integrating their talent practices. Instead, they are worried about employee engagement, teamwork, innovation, and collaboration. They want HR technologies and solutions to be engaging, useful and productivity-oriented. Integrated talent management, though still important, has become a 'hygiene' issue. The focus should be reinventing how people work, creating team-based tools for goal alignment and coaching, putting in place systems to provide timely feedback and measure engagement, rethink the way we measure performance, acquire talent, as well as learning and development. Also, tools should enable and empower teams, drive team-centric engagement and performance, and support agile, network-focused HR practices. Significant shifts from integrated talent management practices to people management then to team management have been observed.[11]

HR Transformation Due to Disruptive Technology

With the above disruptive innovations, companies and their HR professionals should stay aware of these changes that shape their strategies and activities in the years ahead. We now discuss the impact of some HR technologies have had on transforming some major HR functions.

A new landscape for talent acquisition

Hiring people is by far the most important activity companies do. And the recruitment and talent acquisition market is enormous. This massive market focuses tools to build an employment brand; post and distribute job postings (job advertisements and networks); manage and interact with job boards; source and recruit candidates into network with candidate marketing and communication; assess/shortlist candidates; and perform psychometric testing, interviewing (interview management and video interviewing), and finally, onboarding and orientation. They involve management of the entire complex process end to end (using applicant tracking and recruitment management systems).

This market is driving a large number of new and disruptive changes. First is the growth of LinkedIn. It had grown to more than US$26 billion by end of 2016 with a talent database of over 500 million profiles in 200 countries, becoming a standard toolset for large and midsize companies. It has expanded into learning and a variety of other markets (sales, marketing, publishing). Second, the applicant tracking system (ATS) market (or recruitment platform) is ripe for change. Incumbent vendor products include Taleo/Oracle, IBM/Kenexa, Jovite, and ADP. They are efficient at sourcing, capturing resumes, posting advertisements, workflow management, assessment, interview scheduling, video or data-driven interviewing, and other forms of assessment. These platforms may also include chatbots that can interact with candidates. Examples of chatbots are Mya and JobBot.

ERP systems and platform providers can integrate recruitment systems, but most are not fully fleshed out. Big companies still have Oracle's Taleo, IBM/Kenexa's BrassRing, or other legacy platforms in place. These older systems have been configured to deal with multiple business units, different global regulatory requirements and integration with tools such as reference checking and candidate referral systems. At the same time, a new breed of platforms, including vendors such as SmartRecruiters, Lever, and Greenhouse have started from scratch, building end-to-end recruitment management systems. They can directly connect to LinkedIn and other job boards and can store candidate information to be revisited later. They will mature and move upstream to sell to larger clients. There are also other disruptive players such as HireVue, Google Talent Solution, Textio, SuccessFactors, Entelo, Amberjack, HackerRank, and Switch Recruitment.

Among the talent assessment tools, video-based assessment tools for 'predictive hiring' (such as HireVue and Talview) have grown from a niche to a mainstream part of recruitment. They offer sophisticated I/O psychology assessment and analytics to screen, assess, and provide onboarding formalities to candidates using mobile-video hiring as well as video-proctored written and code tests. They can even literally read candidates' faces, detect their tone of voice and eye movement, and assess their honesty and quality of answers (see also Chapters 3 and 4). In addition, there are game-based assessment tools for talent assessment and learning using the application of game design principles to measure human performance when people are striving to perform at their best. This approach can motivate the candidates while saving time of the recruiters. Assessing the soft skills and personality traits of the candidates, they are powerful, objective, and unbiased. For example, Pymetrics' twelve games apply neuroscience and AI to measure fifty cognitive and emotional traits of the candidates using sophisticated data science algorithms. Other examples of game-based assessment include Knack and Arctic Shores (see also Chapter 4).

Finally, there is the impact of Google and big data on recruiting. The launch of Google Cloud Job Discovery has put the world's largest Internet search company into the talent acquisition market. Google has developed a job family architecture, technology to categorize jobs in a meaningful way, and a set of search tools that leverage location. Google Maps and other Google data sources can give candidates an accurate listing of local relevant jobs in the area. Google has also introduced a low-end ATS called Google Hire for small and midsize recruitment markets.

Continuous performance management

As discussed in the chapter about performance management systems (Chapter 6), leading companies are now reinventing the way they manage and measure performance. They are creating a more agile approach with periodic check-ins, shared goals from the bottom up that are transparent to the entire team, frequent and regular developmental conversations and feedback that go from employee to employee, employee to manager, and manager to employee. These changes have spurred the growth of a set of innovative new performance management vendors that build systems to manage and automate the process. These tools can have the following features:

- Manage performance by team
- Goals are transparent, easy to change, and simple to track and measure progress
- Feedback mechanisms are built in via simple pulse surveys, end-of-period surveys and ad hoc feedback presented via tags and word clouds
- Development plans are prepopulated and easy to build, and are often data-driven based on the experiences of other people in the role
- Online assessments, help, and tools for managers are built in (e.g. tools to help with difficult conversations, personality assessments, and leadership tips)
- Systems as simple mobile apps—they have activity streams and other gamification features that make them engaging and easy to browse
- Applications are integrated with employee directories and other HR tools to make them as daily routine—rather than something to do at the end of the year

ERP vendors are in various stages of building these functionalities. While SuccessFactors' Continuous Performance Management is coming along, Workday and Oracle have added these features. Others, such as ADP's StandOut, Cornerstone OnDemand, PageUp People, PeopleFluent, Saba + Halogen, and Ultimate Software are doing similar things.

In Chapters 6 and 7 we discuss how the companies are rethinking the ways they give ratings and make compensation decisions as well as how they perform periodic reviews. A study found that over 60 per cent of the variance of employee ratings were attributable to managers' bias, implying that the rating systems rarely provide a reliable and fair accounting of performance. More companies realize that evaluating people with a number can be perceived as demeaning, demotivating and unfair. Companies are now using some kinds of annual evaluation process, often a set of qualitative criteria or other measures that go beyond 'numbers'. It may evaluate people based on performance (achievement of goals), capabilities (how they built their skills), career (how well they are progressing), and connections (how well they are connected within the company). People are placed in one of three categories: 'well-aligned and performing', 'adequate', or 'inadequate'.

When it comes to compensation reviews and other talent decisions, the new breed of apps will give decision makers more detailed data, helping these decisions become more open and data-driven. Compensation decisions would then be driven by factors beyond individual performance, including contributions to the team, relative contribution as compared to their peers, financial and operational achievements, and external market changes.

Explosion of feedback and pulse survey

When companies implement continuous performance management, feedback and engagement survey systems should be connected to the process. In other words, companies are gauging feedback with their employees. Over 100 vendors now provide pulse survey tools, employee mood-monitoring systems, culture and engagement assessments, and other tools that enable employees to provide anonymous or confidential feedback to others.[12] They may use open text fields that allow employees to simply type things on their minds. The system then categorizes those comments so that managers and HR departments can see the trends.

Historically, the employee engagement market has been a stand-alone space, with consultants taking responsibility for a once-a-year 'climate' survey. More companies now realize the limited use of annual surveys and recognize that the real action takes place on a real-time local level. Some organizations perform weekly, monthly, or quarterly surveys or event-based feedback when an organizational change takes place.[13] As these tools begin to grow in popularity, employees will feel more comfortable sharing their feelings and observations. In turn, companies will become better at gathering and using the feedback. The feedback products are unlike traditional surveys—not only can they support mobile pulse surveys, but as 'smart systems', they can algorithmically decide who to survey and when. They can also have analytics capabilities built in that can instantly identify trends and outliers worthy of further exploration. Moreover, the new 'always-on' engagement market is starting to converge with parts of the HR landscape. Most performance management systems are now built around regular team assessments and surveys. Team management tools often have surveys built in. Events such as hackathons and product innovations sessions are built around always-on feedback as well.

In the talent recruitment market, there is also a small but fascinating market for anonymous feedback tools. Glassdoor, one of the top job search sites in the US, has emerged as a leading provider of unbiased data about companies. It offers data for their HR about true employment brand, candidate recruitment experience, and competitive salary. Glassdoor, LinkedIn, PayScale, Salary, and others can now crowdsource salary data—meaning that both candidates and existing employees can find typical pay for certain roles. Salary transparency has been an important trend, causing employers to be more competitive with salaries and even encouraging some companies to offer raises and bonuses more frequently than once per year.

We also anticipate an integration between feedback tools and performance management in the years ahead. Employee engagement data, manager feedback, coaching, and social recognition are all different forms of feedback, so ultimately they belong in one place. Employees tend to want a single 'team management' platform to use.

Reinvention of corporate learning

In Chapter 5 we discussed the change of concept from 'training' to 'learning' in organizations. In parallel, the corporate learning market has experienced a great deal of transformation. Most employees experienced in-classroom training before the 1990s. Starting in the late 1990s, companies were experimenting with e-learning. Since then, we have seen the rise of blended learning, social learning, mobile learning, and

70-20-10 learning.[14] Today, people learn in a more dynamic and self-directed way than before. Since 2009, companies have shifted from 77 per cent instructor-led training (ILT) to only 32 per cent in 2015. The use of collaborative learning, virtual learning, apprenticeships, and on-the-job learning have exploded. Companies may not have enough facilities, budget, time or patience to allow their employees to sit in classes the way they did some years ago.

We do not mean that traditional face-to-face learning is useless. Rather, L&D professionals should realize that they have to focus their time on high-value face-to-face experiences and radically redesign their content systems to accommodate the huge demand for high-quality and high-fidelity learning online. As they do so, they should also push the organization and its management to focus on coaching, apprenticeship, and expert support.

Mirroring these changes, we now have a marketplace of next-generation learning management systems, learning experience platforms, microlearning platforms, massive open online courses (MOOCs), and programme management systems, as well as an amazing set of virtual reality and assessment tools.[15] Though some companies may be slow or still hesitating to adopt these new technologies, businesses around the world have already spent about $140 billion on learning and development annually. Of this expenditure, around $4 to $5 billion is used on core learning platforms. The rest is spent on tools, content, instructors, classrooms, and facilities. Learning and career platforms are now the fastest growing segment in the industry, as virtually every company is worried about reskilling and the future of work.[16]

A decade ago, when e-learning was new, almost every company focused on buying a learning management system (LMS). Vendors such as Saba, SumTotal, Cornerstone Ondemand, Plateau Systems, GeoLearning, and Learn.com were popular. Most major HR platform vendors acquired LMS platforms. As these vendors grew, however, the market started to shift. Companies saw the LMS as part of an integrated talent management platform. Vendors reallocated their resources toward performance management, assessments and recruiting. For example, SuccessFactors acquired Plateau while Learn.com was acquired by Taleo (and then Oracle). Many other LMS players built talent features which put them in competitions with SAP, Oracle, Workday, and other ERP vendors.

Meanwhile, the learning industry was exploding. Driven by mobile phones and low-cost video production, MOOCs, YouTube, and video-learning platforms took off. Companies such as Coursera, EdX, Udacity, Udemy, Skillsoft, CrossKnowledge (owned by Wiley), and Lynda (owned by LinkedIn) all have high-fidelity learning programmes. Suddenly, many LMS vendors were falling short when corporate buyers and employees asked for video-learning solutions. This led to the emergence of a market for what we now call learning experience platforms that integrate and enable video and other forms of content to be produced, managed, and delivered in a TV-like user interface. With these new useful products, the LMS has generally been relegated to the role of a back-office training management application.

Leaders of the learning experience segment include Degreed, Pathgather, EdCast, Fuse, Skillsoft's Percipio and Cornerstone OnDemand. Oracle, Workday, and SAP SuccessFactors also invested in video-based learning. These systems are designed to operate like YouTube rather than as a course catalogue. Their solutions can be categorized as embedded experience platforms as their L&D functionality can be tied to the core systems. In addition, many vendors are expanding their functionalities. For instance, Degreed is developing skills assessment; Pathgather is performing career management and development; and EdCast has embedded performance support. They are mobile-enabled, simple to use, and scalable.

Another innovation is called a microlearning platform, which manages the proliferation of video, assessment, and other small content objects with tools for curation, tracking, recommendations, and AI-based prescriptive learning. Vendors such as Axonify, Grovo, Qstream, Blackboard, and Fuse are building delivery systems that can take contents away, reorganize them, and deliver exactly what people want. LinkedIn is also looking at ways to deconstruct and expose all the video learning available on Lynda.com.

With video-learning, mobile-learning, and microlearning content now available, it is important to build an entire designed experience that uses and embeds these contents into work. In other words, we may have embedded learning into business processes through design thinking. An example of this is onboarding. Instead of having an ineffective one-day cultural introduction, with a series of design thinking efforts, companies may revamp their onboarding into comprehensive three- to six-month new-hire orientation solutions that include embedded learning, collaboration, formal training, and other on-the-job assignments.

The content market is growing healthily. We understand that there is a huge market for high-fidelity video-based content authored by experts and accredited institutions. The content can take the form of MOOCs, online libraries (like LinkedIn Learning), those offered by Skillsoft (using a library called Percipio), CrossKnowledge, Cornerstone OnDemand (with TED talks and niche topics), and other small vendors. LinkedIn may become a total learning solution for small businesses that can link all its content to employees' career history and aspirations. Companies such as Udemy, NovoEd, Udacity, Skillshare, and Grovo offer thousands of expert-authored courses at a very modest price. Even Harvard Business Publishing and McKinsey & Company are getting into the content market.

Our discussion would not be complete without mentioning the hot trend of using virtual reality and augmented reality. VR is a kind of computer-generated three-dimensional image or environment that simulates a realistic experience. It is near to our everyday human reality. In contrast to VR, AR projects simulations on to the real-world environment. A recent AR storm hitting the world is *Pokémon GO*, a game which allows user to capture Pokémon hidden in the map of the real world. These are powerful tools for learning and performance support. For example, VR and AR can be used for training drivers. They allow us to transport learners into simulations and help teach them what to do in real time. In safety training, they enable companies to simulate emergency situations. They can also be used for employee onboarding. Google Glass, BlackBerry, Lenovo, and other hardware manufacturers are now getting into AR.

We should also note that learning can become a large market for artificial intelligence (AI). With hundreds of courses, books, articles, videos, and other artefacts of learning, both employees and L&D department are trying to assess the relevance of these materials. And employees have different learning experience. Some learn best by reading, others through conversation, and others by listening to instructions or immersing themselves into experiences. AI can begin to address these issues by tagging content and creating taxonomies while also recommending content to learners according to their prior positive experiences. IBM, Skillsoft, LinkedIn, Workday, EdCast, and some others have this vision. These capabilities may become available very soon.

Growth in HR analytics

We cannot talk about HR disruptive technology without discussing the enormous growth of HR analytics. As the data from Global Human Capital Trends shows, analytics expertise and maturity has grown in every aspect (Table 9.1).[17] Most organizations are now finding analytics people in finance, marketing, operations, and HR. Online and classroom-based education in analytics has expanded rapidly for people who want to build a career in this field.

Table 9.1: HR analytics is taking off

		2015	2016	% Change
Plan	Organizations performing multiyear workforce planning	38%	48%	+26%
Correlate	Organizations correlating people data to business performance	24%	39%	+63%
	Organizations correlating people data to business performance (% self-rated as 'excellent')	5%	11%	+120%
Predict	Organizations using people data to predict business performance	28%	36%	+29%
	Organizations using people data to predict business performance (% self-rated as 'excellent')	4%	9%	+125%

Source: Bersin, J. (2016). *HR technology disruptions for 2107: Nine trends reinventing the HR software market*. Oakland: Deloitte. Retrieved from https://www2.deloitte.com/content/dam/Deloitte/us/Documents/human-capital/us-hc-disruptions.pdf

There are quite a few disruptive changes in this marketplace. First, as seen in Table 9.1, the percentage of companies that have moved to advanced reporting is on the rise. Second, the idea of creating predictive models is becoming more widespread in HR. The percentage of companies having predictive modelling has almost doubled over the past few years. It is now common for companies to build predictive models for retention by using data to understand precisely why some high-performing people leave. We perceive that while the problem of retention is not always the most important issue to study via data analysis, performing these analyses can remind HR and managers a lot about the company culture or politics.

Facebook has recently announced that it would offer employees $10,000 or more if they moved closer to the company's headquarters office.[18] This decision came after a detailed analysis of turnover and performance that clearly showed commute time was a major factor in the productivity and retention of their people. Some other companies are using tools like HiQ Analytics to look at the 'pull' drivers that encourage key people to leave to work for competitors. This kind of data helps organizations decide where to locate new facilities, whose salary should be revised, when people should change jobs to create career growth, and other HR issues. Other companies have made use of analytics in the following areas:

- Reduced planned absences—companies may identify the drivers of unplanned absences among workers, resulting in radical changes in shift schedules, managerial activities, vacation times, and other transformations.
- Increased innovation—an automobile company analysed what drives innovation and discovered that innovative and successful project teams are more connected and meet more often than others. This led to a redesign of the company's entire innovation strategy.
- Increased retention—after analysing employee retention in different countries in the world, one company identified the need to change its compensation models in Asia and the employee career paths in Europe.
- Reduced fraud and compliance violations—an organization revealed certain 'trusted agents' who were more likely to commit fraud. A similar analysis at the same company found that 'toxic employees' (who are more liable to tell lies or cheat) are contagious to others. These people can be identified during interview via the use of certain specially worded questions.
- Increased collaboration and performance—based on data analysis, one company looked at employee engagement and feedback data at a detailed day-to-day level, leading to a redesign of office space and meeting rooms in order to improve collaboration and performance.

Companies are now taking this domain seriously and putting in place data quality programmes, analytics fluency learning, dashboards, and data-driven decision-making processes for HR and business. We see a mature and robust vendor market. While tools such as Excel, SPSS, Power BI by Microsoft, RStudio, and Python are being used, Oracle, SAP SuccessFactors, Workday, ADP, Visier, and Ultimate Software all have built-in retention predictors (among many other modelling features) embedded in their software. Workday can recommend employee job changes that are more likely to result in high-performance outcomes. Oracle and SuccessFactors can tell what training employees should use on their roles and activities at work. Cornerstone can also predict who is likely to become noncompliant or lapse in their mandatory training and certification. Visier's end-to-end solution has workforce optimization, recruitment analytics, and dozens of integrated analyses to uncover bias, drivers of turnover and notably includes all systems integrations and maintenance in the standard subscription fees. And IBM's Watson Analytics provides a drag-and-drop set of analytics that helps understand almost any pattern.

As new ways of using feedback and innovative models of performance management emerge, new types of data and vendors enter the scene. One vendor, Starling Trust can analyse patterns of emails and other communications to build 'trust networks',[19] and can predict where a security leak or fraud is likely to occur. Another, Humanyze, sells smart employee badges that monitor location and voice tenor to understand when and where stress occurs. The data can help companies reorganize facilities, change meeting times and formats, and learn how to drive engagement in new ways. A third vendor, recently acquired by Microsoft, can analyse email communications to understand how people's communications and time management practices differ. It reveals that high-performing sales people spend more time with certain groups and customers than their peers. These data can be used to coach and nudge others to change their behaviour. In addition, a new wave of vendors is providing various benchmarking offerings. Bersin offers an interactive benchmarking, analytics, and reporting platform that lets organizations compare themselves against their peers in terms of L&D spending, recruitment metrics, organizational design, and other talent measures. Cornerstone OnDemand, Saba, and ADP also have their own benchmarking products.

Moreover, we must mention the market for artificial intelligence (AI), which is a close cousin to analytics. In fact, the journey from operational reporting to predictive reporting is now being enhanced with AI, which is essentially real-time analytics using large data sets and more advanced algorithms. IBM (using Watson) and new vendors like Crunchr are now delivering smart analytics with AI out of the box.

IBM promotes its Watson Career Coach. It has an advanced analytics solution that examines patterns of successful career mobility in a company and asks a series of conversational questions to help individuals fit into one of the paths.[20] Workday offers a similar solution packaged into analytics. IBM's Watson Recruitment looks at the patterns and costs of different sourcing channels and success criteria to give organizations smarter recommendations for sourcing and assessment.[21] Visier's recruitment analytics do this as well. Over the coming years, AI will redefine the marketplace for analytics solutions. Vendors will become intelligence providers, not just analytics providers. Many major HR application providers are now hiring AI experts to analyse and deliver pattern recognition, algorithm refinement, machine learning, and natural language processing solutions embedded in their platforms.

More disruptive technologies

Many other HR-related disruptive technologies are growing in different types of markets. For example, there are new apps, management tools, and systems to support communications, employee experience, team management, contingent workforce management with 'gig' work and part-time jobs, and wellness and fitness.[22] For instance, in the well-being market, the focus has shifted from reducing health and insurance costs to helping employees perform better, engage with their colleagues, and contribute to a positive company culture. And the new generation of workers (like the millennials and Generation Z) are excited about the idea of the 'quantified self'[23] and using wearables such as Fitbit, tools like Strava, and others to help monitor their exercise, jogging, heart rate and time spent at the gym. In addition, there is a fast-growing trend of AI, natural language processing, and robotic process automation and self-service. The huge area of the latter can cover products that can listen to voices (such as Amazon Echo, Siri voice recognition software, and Viv), products that augment and automate call centre work (software that can record keystrokes into an ERP system and then immediately automate it for repetitive transactions), and software that brings transactions together from many systems and makes it easy to implement new workflow on a screen or device (such as ConnectMe from Deloitte). And AI-based conversations can handle many traditional HR processes. Every employee transaction can be performed via a chatbot.

Is Our HR Department Transformed in the Era of Disruptive Technology?

We can note from the above that every HR function and activity is now facing an opportunity for transformation. Growth in apps, software, social media, mobile and cloud computing, videos, platforms, AI and robotics, and the like is taking place with a new outlook on almost every aspect of HR activity. In the past, people have written articles about bureaucratic and unhelpful HR teams. HR professionals often conjure up images of bureaucracy, conservatism, and paper-pushing, always claiming confidentiality of their operations and data. Now, with the technology enhancement and web-based capabilities, employees should be able to enjoy high-quality, transparent, and timely information and data.[24] With manager and employee self-service as well as various feedback tools (like Glassdoor), HR data, policies, and salary information are more accessible. We also discuss major advantages of having HR technologies in Chapter 2. Apart from automating and streamlining the HR processes to reduce administrative burdens, they should help transform HR. And instead of passing the work to the IT teams, HR departments are facing pressures to be experimental, innovative, and technology-savvy in their digital transformation journey. HR professionals have to try new recruiting and assessment tools, experiment with new performance management and compensation practices and feedback and learning technologies. They should redesign their workflow using AI, robotic process automation, or self-service transaction integration. In other words, HR departments should increasingly focus on design thinking to redevelop what they perform as not a series of transactions or processes. Rather, their performance is a series of 'journey maps' and a total new automation experience to help companies and HR be more strategic, make better decisions, and improve the value of HR itself.

As a consequence, HR professionals have to develop new skills and capabilities. They demand a massive reskilling of HR professionals that requires knowledge of various functional areas and technology applications. While sometimes acting as consultants, researchers, psychologists, analysts, or statisticians, HR professionals also need to have a team pursuit in partnership with IT department, functional managers, and various internal and external stakeholders in order to achieve future business success with more informed decisions.[25]

In view of the new HR technologies and people analytics, HR needs new skills and capabilities, which are more exciting but demanding for HR professionals. Six major ones including business acumen, consulting, work psychology, data sciences, human resource and communications are suggested.[26]

HR Technology Adoption in Hong Kong

Despite the power of disruptive technology discussed above, many HR departments are yet to embrace this trend of transformation. An international survey in 2016 revealed that only 38 per cent of companies were thinking about HR technology adoption, and only 9 per cent were fully ready for HR digital transformation, although three-quarters of them understood its importance.[27] Regarding HR analytics, various reports find that HR people may lack skills and techniques to interpret complex statistical analysis or provide insightful predictive analytics. Many just offer generic and basic operational and transactional measurements using spreadsheets or manual reporting functions. Otherwise, they focus on reporting rather than advanced analytics or predictive analytics. In essence, HR lacks skills and credibility in talent metrics and analytics.[28] Corroborative evidence shows that only 30 per cent of business leaders believe that HR has a reputation for sound business decisions, while most of them feel that HR does not have the right capabilities to meet the current business needs.[29]

Similarly, in Hong Kong, HKIHRM's study on adopting HR technology found that among 138 respondent companies, only 23 per cent of them believed that they were ahead of their competitors while 47 per cent felt that they lagged behind. Opinions were divided on the preparedness of the HR professionals in driving technology adoption. At least half of them thought that they had not prepared well. Large multinational companies with more than 500 employees were more likely to report that they were well prepared to drive technology-related initiatives or stake a position ahead of competition in HR technology implementation. On the other hand, local and small companies tended to believe that their organizations or HR staff were not ready to handle the change.[30] Although most HR professionals (77 per cent) believed that technology facilitated HR decision-making, the prime motivation to leverage technology was to improve efficiency. A total of 87 per cent cited this as a reason. The second and third drivers were to improve availability of HR data for better workforce management (50 per cent) and standardization of HR data (46 per cent) (Figure 9.1).

Figure 9.1: Motivations to deploy HR technology

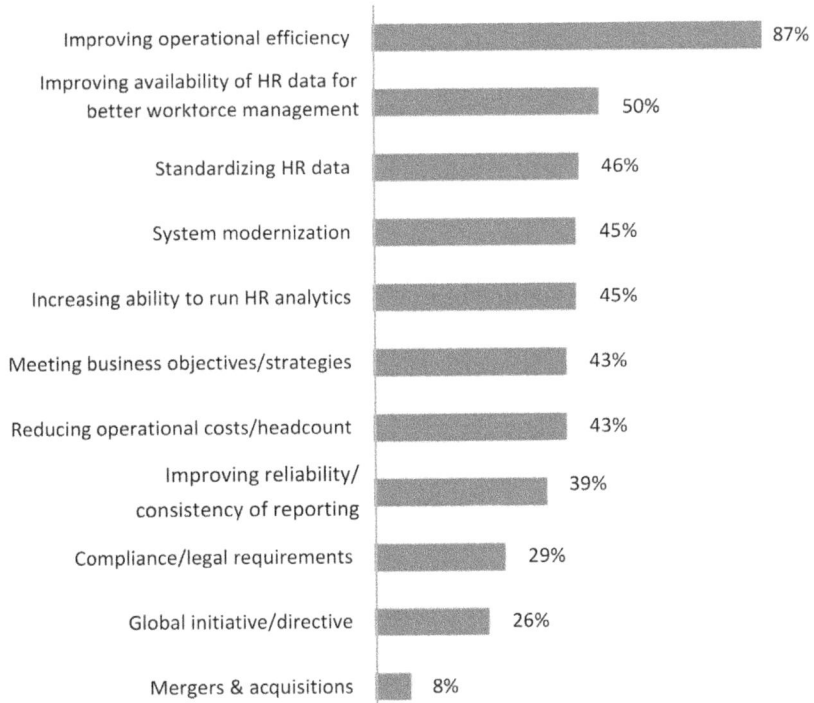

Base: All responding to the question N = 137

Source: HKIHRM. (2017, November). *2017 HKIHRM topical study: Survey on adoption of technology in HR management*. Hong Kong: HKIHRM.

Figure 9.2: Benefits of adopting HR technology

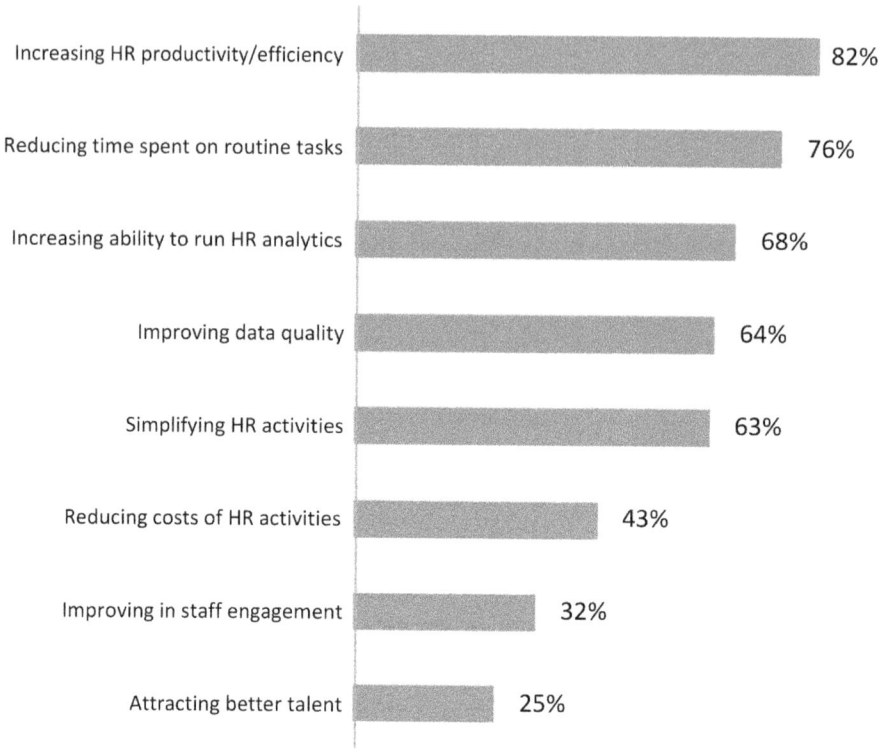

Base: All responding to the question N = 136

Source: HKIHRM. (2017, November). *2017 HKIHRM topical study: Survey on adoption of technology in HR management*. Hong Kong: HKIHRM.

Most organizations aimed to achieve higher HR productivity/efficiency (82 per cent) and reduce time spent on routine tasks (76 per cent) as major benefits of using HR technology (Figure 9.2).

Of all the functional areas to adopt HR technology, payroll as well as compensation and benefits were the two major ones; 83 per cent of the companies used for payroll calculation, and 65 per cent had the technology for compensation and benefits. Spending priorities between 2016 and 2018 were also mainly on payroll and compensation and benefits. There was much room for improvement in talent acquisition, talent management, and succession planning. Over two-thirds of the organizations were still operating on paper-based systems in these areas. And around 39 per cent of the companies used analytics and workforce planning (Figure 9.3). Among the ten types of HR applications, learning experience platforms and applicant tracking systems were the most commonly known tools by the respondents. The awareness level was 65 per cent and 64 per cent, respectively (Figure 9.4). However, the degree of implementation was still low. Only around one-fifth of the companies reported that they had already deployed a learning experience platform (21 per cent) or applicant tracking system (19 per cent). Fewer than a tenth (9 per cent) of the respondents had

Figure 9.3: Adoption of HR technology by functional areas

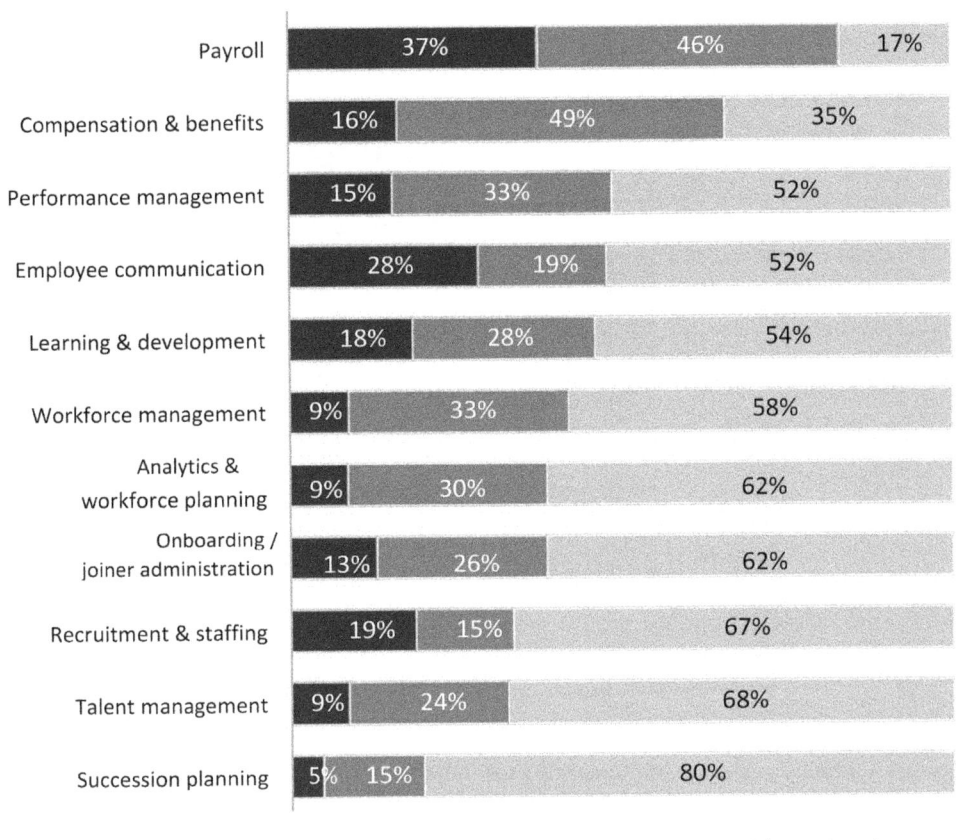

Source: HKIHRM. (2017, November). *2017 HKIHRM topical study: Survey on adoption of technology in HR management.* Hong Kong: HKIHRM.

deployed predictive people analytics, while very few companies were using games for learning, AI/chatbot, VR/AR MOOC, or wearables (all 5 per cent or below).

When using HR technology, the key challenges included integration with current HR and business systems (51 per cent), HR processes redesign (49 per cent), and change management (44 per cent) (Figure 9.5).

In particular, companies had concerns of adopting mobile technology and cloud computing. Although these technologies are growing fast, there were potential risks of moving business applications to these platforms. For example, regarding mobile technology in Hong Kong, 80 per cent of companies indicated major problems with data security, and 72 per cent indicated misgivings about employee privacy. Cost considerations was the third factor (53 per cent). Similarly, for adopting cloud-based technology, data security (91 per cent) and privacy (80 per cent) issues were the two top concerns of most organizations. The Society for Human Resource Management has also highlighted the potential risks to the HR community when it comes to data

Figure 9.4: Awareness of different types of HR technology

Technology	Aware	Unaware
Learning experience platform	65%	35%
Applicant tracking system	64%	36%
Real time/continuous talent management	44%	56%
Predictive people analytics	39%	61%
Gamification/badges for learning	31%	69%
Robotics/artificial intelligence	28%	72%
Voice interface/Chatbot	23%	77%
Augmented reality / virtual reality	19%	81%
MOOCs	14%	86%
Wearables	12%	88%

Source: HKIHRM (2017, November). *2017 HKIHRM topical study: Survey on adoption of technology in HR management*. Hong Kong: HKIHRM.

Figure 9.5: Challenges when implementing technology

Challenge	%
Integrations	51%
HR processes redesign	49%
Change management	44%
Vendor selection	35%
Configurations	31%
Stakeholders of other business units	30%
HR organizational redesign	24%
Project management	22%
No challenges during implementation	4%

Base: All responding to the question N = 135

Source: HKIHRM (2017, November). *2017 HKIHRM topical study: Survey on adoption of technology in HR management*. Hong Kong: HKIHRM.

security on the cloud. People may question whether sensitive data should be posted on the Internet at all. Risks of compromised or hacked data may exist. And no one is really clear about the exact location of the data.[31]

HRM in Action—Box 9.1
A Case Study on Adopting HR Analytics in Hong Kong

A business conglomerate in Hong Kong invited consultants to evaluate their HR activities so as to review their effectiveness and make improvements. The following questions were addressed by the consultants in the beginning:

1. Where did the company have significant talent excess or shortage?
2. How should the company forecast its hiring needs for next year?
3. How could HR create a high-performance work culture?
4. What factors would drive employee retention?
5. How inclusive were the HR programmes?
6. What were the key characteristics of an ideal leader?
7. What were the returns on investment on the HR programmes (for example, relationship of psychometric test during recruitment and subsequent employee work performance)?

The following process of performing data analytics was then undergone:

1. Identifying business problem statements
2. Developing the hypotheses
3. Obtaining the data
4. Exploring the data
5. Analysing the data
6. Creating insights
7. Presenting findings

As a result, several benefits were found. It helped improve HR's credibility and visibility based on more rational and thorough decision-making supported by data. Also, more focused development programmes were designed. But the company noticed that new technology required the right type of people. The consultants advised that expertise in the areas of analyses, statistics, consulting, and research was necessary. This posed a challenge to the company as it noticed that most existing HR people had not equipped themselves with these skills, including the necessary mindsets to perform these tasks.

Conclusion

We have noted that growth of various technologies has created exciting opportunities to transform HR. Almost every HR function faces disruption by technology. Transformations can take place in the areas of talent acquisition, performance management, learning and development, employee feedback, employee wellness, and so forth. They can enhance employee engagement, corporate culture, employee wellness, and performance and productivity in organizations.

As a result, the HR organization has to be innovative, experimental, and technology-savvy. These new ways of thinking create demand for a new set of skills and capabilities for HR professionals to survive in the era of disruptive technology. In Hong Kong (and elsewhere), although a considerable proportion of organizations was aware of HR technology and understood that it would be beneficial to them, many felt that they lagged behind in adopting the HR technology. Opinions were divided on their preparedness to drive technology adoption in HR. Few believed they had the resources and capabilities since cost was cited as the major barrier hindering organizations to acquire the technology (70 per cent of Hong Kong respondents). For those who leveraged technology in their organizations, they were mainly used to achieve operational efficiency instead of making change, providing better decisions, or taking a more strategic HR role. Payroll or compensation and benefits were the major functions for using HR technology. And a mere one-fifth of the organizations had adopted a learning experience platform or ATS. In other words, the overall level of implementation was low across the board in Hong Kong.

Based on the maturity model for digital disruption with four levels of digital literacy developed by the first author,[32] we may suggest that Hong Kong's HR is still at the early stage of digital maturity—that is level 1, 'exploring digital' (for automation), or level 2, 'doing digital' (extending current capabilities)—with 'reactive and procedural' or 'functional and fragmented' HR activities.[33] We understand that most of the companies adopting HR technology are large multinational companies which have more resources or follow best practice from the headquarters. Otherwise, HR technology is used for routine operational purposes. So our HR people are not 'disruptors'. We have not yet found evidence of thinking creatively, asking more questions, or pushing vendors or organizations to new management models in order to transform HR or change the company culture. To remain competitive and help improve business performance, our discussion in this chapter warrants HR professionals in Hong Kong and elsewhere to think where and how they can fit into the trend of digital transformation.

Review Questions

1. What is meant by disruptive technology and digital transformation? How should HR respond to the wave of change? What are the objectives of adopting the HR technology?
2. Describe the evolution of HR technologies and the associated HR focuses.
3. Discuss an example how HR technology can disrupt an HR function or process nowadays.
4. What are the differences between VR and AR? Discuss how they can be used in different HR functions.
5. How would you evaluate the pace of adopting HR technology in Hong Kong? What are the drivers and obstacles in the implementation?
6. What roles can Hong Kong's HR play in the era of disruptive technology? How can the HR professionals equip themselves for their digital transformation in the near future?

Notes

1. Great thanks should be given to Josh Bersin, a retired principal and founder of Bersin and Associates, which has been acquired by Deloitte. Some details of this chapter are based on his articles: Bersin, J. (2016). *HR technology disruptions for 2017: Nine trends reinventing the HR software market*. Oakland: Deloitte. Retrieved from https://www2.deloitte.com/content/dam/Deloitte/us/Documents/human-capital/us-hc-disruptions.pdf.
   Bersin, J. Lead author. (2017). *HR technology disruptions for 2018: Productivity, design and intelligence reign*. Oakland: Deloitte. Retrieved from http://marketing.bersin.com/rs/976-LMP-699/images/HRTechDisruptions2018-Report-100517.pdf
2. Bower, Joseph L., and Christensen, Clayton M. (1995, January–February). Disruptive technologies: Catching the wave. *Harvard Business Review*, 43–53.
3. Rubio, E. (2017, Dec. 12). *The case for disruptive innovation in human resources*. Retrieved from https://www.linkedin.com/pulse/case-disruptive-innovation-human-resources-enrique-rubio-csm-cspo
4. Solis, B., and Littleton, A. (2015). *Research report: The 2017 state of digital transformation*. Altimeter. Retrieved from https://marketing.prophet.com/acton/media/33865/altimeter--the-2017-state-of-digital-transformation
5. Woolnough, R. (2017, Nov. 17). Digital transformation: How can HR help to make this a reality? *Personnel Today*. Retrieved from https://www.personneltoday.com/hr/digital-transformation-can-hr-help-make-reality/
6. Spence, A. (n.d.). *Scoop.it!* Retrieved from https://www.scoop.it/i/hr-management
7. Bersin, J. (2016, July 18). *The HR software market reinvents itself*. Retrieved from www.forbes.com/sites/joshbersin/2016/07/18/the-hr-software-market-reinvents-itself/#277e25ea4930
8. HKIHRM. (2017, Nov.). *2017 HKIHRM topical study—Survey on adoption of technology in HR management*. Hong Kong: HKIHRM.
9. Cloud computing refers to keeping data on vendors' servers operating on the Internet or 'in the cloud,' instead of on a company's computers.
10. In Hong Kong examples of companies for payroll outsourcing are IPL, ADP, Tricor, Delken, Links International, etc.
11. Bersin, J. Lead author. (2017). *HR technology disruptions for 2018: Productivity, design and intelligence reign*. Oakland: Deloitte. Retrieved from http://marketing.bersin.com/rs/976-LMP-699/images/HRTechDisruptions2018-Report-100517.pdf
12. Bersin, J. (2015, February 24). *Becoming irresistible: A new model for employee engagement*. Deloitte Review Issue 16. Retrieved from https://www2.deloitte.com/insights/us/en/deloitte-review/issue-16/employee-engagement-strategies.html
13. Bersin, J. (2015, August 26). Feedback is the killer app: A new market and management model emerges. *Forbes*. Retrieved from https://www.forbes.com/sites/joshbersin/2015/08/26/employee-feedback-is-the-killer-app-a-new-market-emerges/#61a785d45edf
14. Blended learning is an education program (formal or non-formal) that combines online media with traditional classroom methods. The 70-20-10 Model for learning and development is used to describe the optimal sources of learning. It holds that individuals obtain 70 per cent of their knowledge from job-related experience, 20 per cent from interactions with others, and 10 per cent from formal training.
15. Bersin, J. Lead author. (2017). *HR technology disruptions for 2018: Productivity, design and intelligence reign*. Oakland: Deloitte. Retrieved from http://marketing.bersin.com/rs/976-LMP-699/images/HRTechDisruptions2018-Report-100517.pdf
16. Harris, S., and Spencer, E. (2016). *Sierra-Cedar 2016–2017 Survey HR systems survey* (19th annual ed.). Retrieved from https://www.sierra-cedar.com/wp-content/uploads/sites/12/2016/10/Sierra-Cedar_2016-2017_HRSystemsSurvey_WhitePaper.pdf
17. Deloitte Consulting LLP. (2016). *Deloitte Global Human Capital Trends survey data*. Retrieved from https://www2.deloitte.com/content/dam/Deloitte/global/Documents/HumanCapital/gx-dup-global-human-capital-trends-2016.pdf

18. Facebook gives employees big money to move closer to work. (2015, Dec. 18). *Fortune*. Retrieved from http://fortune.com/2015/12/17/facebook-employees-money-to-move
19. A 'trust network' is a network of people who share substantial interests in common, and who have a high level of trust in one another that permits them to undertake risky joint activities. Interested readers may read this website: https://www.trustnetworks.com/
20. IBM. (n.d.). *IBM Watson career coach for career management*. Retrieved from https://www.ibm.com/talent-management/career-coach
21. IBM. (n.d.). *IBM Watson Recruitment*. Retrieved from https://www.ibm.com/talent-management/hr-solutions/recruiting-software
22. Bersin, J. (2016). *HR technology disruptions for 2107: Nine trends reinventing the HR software market*. Oakland: Deloitte. Retrieved from https://www2.deloitte.com/content/dam/Deloitte/us/Documents/human-capital/us-hc-disruptions.pdf

    Bersin, J. Lead author. (2017). *HR technology disruptions for 2018: Productivity, design and intelligence reign*. Oakland: Deloitte. Retrieved from http://marketing.bersin.com/rs/976-LMP-699/images/HRTechDisruptions2018-Report-100517.pdf
23. Quantified self: Self knowledge through numbers: http://quantifiedself.com
24. Johnson, Richard D., and Gueuta, Hal G. (2011). *Transforming HR through technology: The use of E-HR and HRIS in organizations*. Retrieved from https://www.shrm.org/hr-today/trends-and-forecasting/special-reports-and-expert-views/Documents/HR-Technology.pdf
25. Guenole, N., Ferrar, J., and Feinzig, S. (2017). *The power of people: Learn how successful organizations use workforce analytics to improve business performance*. Indianapolis: Pearson.

    Bondarouk, T., Ruel, H.J. M., and Parry, E. (2017). (Eds.). *Electronic HRM in the smart era: The changing of managing people*. Bingley: Emerald.
26. Ferrar, J. (2017, Nov. 21). *6 skills for people analytics success*. Retrieved from https://www.visier.com/clarity/six-skills-people-analytics-success/
27. Stephan, M., Uzawa, S., Volini, E., Walsh, B., and Yoshida, R. (2016, Feb. 29). *Digital HR: Revolution, not evolution*. Retrieved from https://dupress.deloitte.com/dup-us-en/focus/human-capital-trends/2016/digital-hr-technology-for-hr-teams-services.html
28. Faragher, J. (2018, February 7). *HR needs to improve people analytics skills to gain credibility*. Personnel Today. Retrieved from https://www.personneltoday.com/hr/hr-needs-to-improve-people-analytics-skills-to-gain-credibility/
29. Mazor, A., Stephan, M., Walsh, B., Schmahl, H., Schmahl, Hendrik., and Valenzuela, Jaime. (2015, February 27). *Reinventing HR: An extreme makeover*. Retrieved from https://dupress.deloitte.com/dup-us-en/focus/human-capital-trends/2015/reinventing-hr-human-resources-human-capital-trends-2015.html
30. HKIHRM. (2017, November). *2017 HKIHRM topical study—Survey on adoption of technology in HR management*. Hong Kong: HKIHRM.
31. Wright, A.D. (2011, August 15). *Cloud computing and security: How safe is HR data in the cloud?* Retrieved from https://www.shrm.org/resourcesandtools/hr-topics/technology/pages/cloudsecurity.aspx
32. Level 1—'exploring digital' (for automation); Level 2—'doing digital' (extending current capabilities); Level 3—'becoming digital' (unify and synchronize activities); Level 4—'being digital' (integrate new models into work). Bersin, J. Lead author. (2017). *HR technology disruptions for 2018: Productivity, design and intelligence reign*. Oakland: Deloitte. Retrieved from http://marketing.bersin.com/rs/976-LMP-699/images/HRTechDisruptions2018-Report-100517.pdf
33. Bersin, J. Lead author. (2017). *HR technology disruptions for 2018: Productivity, design and intelligence reign*. Oakland: Deloitte. Retrieved from http://marketing.bersin.com/rs/976-LMP-699/images/HRTechDisruptions2018-Report-100517.pdf

10
Managing Organizational Change in Hong Kong

The Role of Human Resource Management for Success

Victor M. T. Ng, Derek K. H. Cheng, Emily Guohua Huang, and Michael N. Young

> **LEARNING OUTCOMES**
>
> By the end of this chapter, the readers should be able to
> - describe the organization development approach and various models to manage organizational change;
> - analyse the role and importance of HRM in managing change;
> - identify issues and factors that can affect the success of a cross-border acquisition in Hong Kong; and
> - understand the implications to the organizations and HR professionals regarding change management.

Introduction

W. G. Pollard (1911–1989) famously argued, 'Without change there is no innovation, creativity, or incentive for improvement. Those who initiate change will have a better opportunity to manage the change that is inevitable.'[1] Nowadays, it is commonplace for an organization to be constantly undergoing some sort of change. Most of these changes are due to some variables, internal or external, that require the organizations to respond in order to stay productive and competitive. However, organizational change programmes often fail to achieve their desired results. Thus, discovering how to implement successful organizational change has become a major challenge for organizational leaders.

Ignoring or neglecting the people aspect of change would often result in resistance to change—and in most situations, change failure. Through a case study of acquisition in the banking industry in Hong Kong, this chapter highlights the importance of managing the human resource aspect of an organizational change. It discusses the pivotal role that HR professionals are expected to play in the process of managing change. For illustrating effective management of change, this chapter follows a generic approach, referred to as organization development, entailing three main sequential steps: (1) the identification of critical success factors for the intended organizational change; (2) the diagnosis of potential people management risks and problems; and (3) the design of suitable strategies and tactics for mitigating risks and preventing problems.[2]

In the literature, there are many published change management models prescribing ways to implement change programmes. Examples are Kotter's 8-step model, McKinsey's 7S framework, Galpin's 9-step model, and Luecke's 7-step model, and many others.[3] Box 10.1 illustrates the eight steps as suggested by Kotter for leading organizational change. Although these models are not discussed here (as they have been adequately covered elsewhere), it is worth noting that understanding different models and the ways of applying them may help increase the chance of successful change management.

HRM in Focus—Box 10.1

Kotter's 8-step Model for Leading Change

- Establishing sense of urgency
- Creating a vision
- Developing political support
- Generating buy-in
- Implementing change
- Evaluating change
- Making small wins
- Institutionalizing

Adapted from Kotter, J. P. (2012). *Leading change*. Boston: Harvard Business School Press.

Organizational Change

Some scholars suggest that organizations must change or die.[4] Organizational change is aimed to make an organization adapt to the environment, to improve its performance, to renew itself, or most probably a combination of all three of them.[5]

Organizational change comes in many forms and sizes. While change can be made in the markets served, products produced, and services delivered by an organization, it can be manifested in the organization's leadership, strategies, culture, structure, systems, processes, and tasks.[6] While organizational change is typically organization-wide, it may happen to a department, a team, or a single individual. However, whatever level it is, the change should have non-trivial impact on the overall organizational performance to be regarded as meaningful organizational change.[7]

Nowadays, organizations frequently undergo change. The American Management Association reported that more than 80 per cent of the US firms were implementing one or more large-scale change initiatives and about one-half of the responding firms said that they were in the midst of three or more organizational change programmes.[8] And there is a general consensus that the rates of change, in all organizations and in all industries, have not been as fast as in today's environment.[9]

No matter what the forms, sizes, rates, and aims of organizational change are, embracing change is now deemed an important part of organizational life and a necessity for business prosperity.[10] Drucker declared that 'everybody has accepted by now that change is unavoidable' and 'change is the norm.'[11] Whether one likes it or not, change has already been taken as a constant, and it is certain that organizational change will not go away for the foreseeable future.[12]

Past experiences of organizational change

There is no sign that the pace of organizational change will slow down any time in the near future. Instead, the pace will likely become even faster in the upcoming decade as the competition in most industries heightens.[13] Nevertheless, although of high importance, leading or managing organizational change is not at all a well-understood aspect of being a contemporary organizational leader.[14] Most, if not all, organizations are confronted with a major challenge in leading change effectively. As revealed by a US Bureau of National Affairs survey, a significant number of the responding companies considered change to be their real challenge and major concern.[15]

Similarly, organizational change has been described as chaotic.[16] The findings of relevant studies have indicated that the failure rates associated with organizational change are high.[17] About 70 per cent of organizational change initiatives have failed to achieve the original objectives.[18] In their bestselling book *The Dance of Change*, Senge and his co-authors described the challenge, 'Most change initiatives fail . . . and even without knowing the statistics most of us know firsthand that change programmes fail.'[19]

The extant literature reports many examples of failure in managing change. Various researchers have found in their studies that, instead of increasing competitiveness, many companies undergoing downsizing or delayering ended up with lower profit margins and poorer returns on assets and equities than those that did not do so. Only about 20 to 50 per cent of organizations engaging in downsizing achieved anticipated objectives of improved productivity, higher investment returns, reduced costs, and increased profits. Business results got worse because of problems such as insufficient manpower or resources, poor-quality services, increased costs in using less-effective agency staff, temporary contract staff, or even the wrong mix of skills, which were the direct consequences of poorly managed change programmes of downsizing and delayering.

Similarly, various studies in Hong Kong have found problematic organizational changes. A study by Chiu unveiled three Hong Kong companies' TQM attempts.[20] Run by local Chinese business owners/top managers, those three companies found implementing TQM daunting tasks. Besides being crippled by some questionable motives, the TQM initiatives fell at the hurdle of mismatch in management style. In particular, many Chinese managers felt threatened by the idea of delegating authority that was a key theme in driving TQM. There were also barriers regarding the employees' cultural passivity to change, their non-commitment towards new behaviours needed in TQM, as well as the management's lack of communication and sharing of information with the employees about the change. Along with the poor change management by the nominal TQM steering committees, the change programmes in those three companies quickly ran into trouble and were silently abandoned. Another study by Wimalasiri and Kouzmin also found that the adoption of employee involvement initiatives in Hong Kong was slower than that of their US counterparts.[21] The researchers noted that most organizations in their Hong Kong sample just used the programmes as morale boosters instead of productivity or quality improvement. Nonetheless, owing to overwhelming pressure on short-term performance, lack of transparency, resistant culture, indifferent middle management, or inadequate performance rewards, benefits of the employee involvement programmes were mostly unrealized.

Downsizing experiences in Hong Kong have not been any better. Admittedly, business firms have constantly restructured throughout the history of Hong Kong. Coupled with economic downturns, downsizing activities peaked respectively in the late 1990s and 2000s. The 'downsizing syndrome in Hong Kong', as Chu and Ip called it, can be viewed as part of the universal process of globalization of modern economies, which has caused firms in many parts of the world to undergo delayering in order to become leaner and faster in providing products and services.[22] In search of agility and flexibility to enhance competitiveness, firms in Hong Kong have long begun to benchmark against their Western counterparts and jump on the downsizing bandwagon. There were, however, constant reports of unpleasant incidents in both large and small businesses that reckless decisions of restructuring or downsizings were made disregarding the feelings of the staff. As observed by Chu and Ip, the inequity perceived by the majority of downsized employees was high. There was no prior consultation or communication to explain the reasons for downsizing. The companies did not assist those downsized employees in looking for new employment at all. Only a very few employers promised to give preference to the affected employees should hiring open up in the future. After downsizing, the companies did little to help the survivors, who often had to carry heavier workload without proper training or retraining. Only a limited number of them were encouraged, motivated, or reassured to perform their duties. Both casualties and survivors suffered a lot in most downsizing activities, indeed. Evidently, without proper management of the organizational change accompanying downsizing, demonstrations, strikes, and lawsuits were not uncommon while company profits were not boosted.

Even though the high rates of failure of organizational change programmes both in the West and Hong Kong are astonishing, organizational change is not doomed to fail. The studies of organizational change have drawn great attention from scholars, researchers, and practitioners, and there are voluminous academic or commercial publications discussing the causes of high failure from organizational change and prescribing ways to implement successful change programmes. In the change literature, there is already consensus recognizing poor change management as one important cause of change failure. Specifically, most failure cases of change boil down to the mismanagement of the human aspect of the change. Undoubtedly, if an organizational change programme is not well managed, its chances of success are slim no matter how well intentioned it may be. When an organization fails to change in necessary ways or deliver the expected change outcomes, the costs of failure may be very high.[23] The Harvard Business School found that organizational change cost Fortune 100 corporations on average $1 billion dollars each between 1980 and 1995.[24] In today's business environment, the capability to adapt, improve, and change successfully is highly regarded as a competitive advantage. As such, it is crucial for companies to understand how to better manage change.[25]

Role of HRM in change management

HR professionals can have a lot to contribute in managing change. For example, an organization looking for a lower overhead cost may undertake a major restructuring that can drastically change the way in which employees are organized and their work coordinated, as well as the nature of the relationships they develop. Aiming to better align with its new business strategy, an organization may mandate a change of culture that necessitates employees to uphold a new set of values and exhibit a new pattern of work behaviours. Development or launching of new products in an organization may require the installation and commissioning of new work systems, processes, and tasks that employees are totally unfamiliar with. In these or other similar situations of change, it should not be overemphasized that the involvement and competence of HR can be crucial in making (or breaking) the intended change.

At the strategic level, HR can help better manage change by pointing to the top managers, change leaders, and other decision makers important people issues pertinent to an organizational change, identifying proper management of these people issues as a critical success factor of the change, and recommending strategies to manage or even avoid such people issues. As a classic example here, given that cultural change is the deepest change of all kinds that will likely meet with the greatest employee resistance, HR professionals knowledgeable in change management should ensure top managers or change leaders intending to change an organization's culture are making well-informed decisions.[26] In contrast, when the decision makers have no intention at all to change the culture but their planned change, if proceed, will alter or somehow disturb the culture albeit unintentionally, HR professionals in such cases should step up and advise the decision makers to adjust or avoid the change. Besides the strategic level, HR can also contribute at the operational level. A host of practices within the HR domain are available to facilitate organizational change. When duly deployed, these HR practices can help employees get ready for and subsequently adapt to the change. If properly executed, they can help keep employees productive, motivated, satisfied, and committed even when they are subject to drastic organizational change.

To help prepare employees for organizational change, HR can start right when a person is hired. When a new person is hired, HR can make the person aware that the organization is going through change and that he or she will be expected to participate with opinions and ideas on how to make things better. HR can also help company leaders make change by working with them to define new job descriptions that arise as a result of the change, specify the kinds of skills that will be needed for these new jobs, and then work to match the best people to these jobs. Despite the popularity of the traditional focus of recruitment and selection process on matching people to specific well-defined jobs, some have suggested that the process should be shifted to one where emphasis is placed on finding and selecting people who have the necessary attributes to be able to adjust readily to changing roles.[27] Thus, if adopted, this HR resourcing strategy can help build a highly flexible workforce capable of adapting swiftly to organizational change.

HR can help with change by providing employee training and management development. Most of the time, training is required to facilitate change. Whether the change entails a new system, process, software, or an overhaul in customer service, the employees need to be well-trained for the change. HR can design and deliver programmes that are effective in training employees in the new way of doing things. With effective training, HR can facilitate change by closing any knowledge or skills gaps that may arise as a result of the change. Training is also useful in the ongoing process of cultural development as a means of employee socialization whereby cultural values and norms are inculcated.[28] Also, when organizational change renders certain kinds of jobs redundant, HR can offer to help people who lose their jobs this way with some retraining or relocation programmes. Furthermore, coaching, mentoring, counselling or other employee supportive programmes may need to be made available in midst of drastic organizational change to help employees adjust to or cope with the change.

While it is beyond the scope of this chapter to review the many theories and research findings on motivation available in the literature, what has clearly been established is that rewards can motivate employees to behave in a way in which they may not otherwise behave. Rewards may be defined as either financial or non-financial, and internal or external. And, although what motivates one person may be of no interest to another, the right mix of rewards is well known to be effective incentives for promoting change in general and developing a strong culture in particular.[29] Successful implementation of change is often seen as dependent on providing the right rewards because change can only be sustained where improved performance or new behaviour desired by the organization is enabled and reinforced with rewards. In practice, HR can enhance employees' adoption of change by putting in place an incentive plan to publicly reward those who take the time and effort to embrace the change, especially those who do it with a good attitude and get other employees on board.

Performance management can be viewed as an HR management system aiming to improve organizational performance by improving the performance of individual employees through appraising employees, developing employees, and rewarding employees.[30] When accompanied with goal cascading, performance management can be effective in communicating downward an organization's mission, vision, and strategies, as well as linking its business objectives to individual employees' performance goals. As such, good performance management practice can be very powerful in shaping employee behaviour in such a way to support an organization's needed change. It can also be tailored to appraise employees' espoused values and thus have significant capacity to facilitate changing of an organization's culture. It can all start by aligning employee goals to the new values, behaviours, or performance as needed by the organization. The extent of achievement of these employee goals is then measured and monitored continuously. And, formal and informal feedback should be provided in due course to employees regarding their performance on achieving the stated goals, and reward and developmental decisions should be made accordingly.[31]

Open communication and employee involvement typically used to promote positive employee relations can be particularly important in facilitating change. Specifically, it should be critical to communicate effectively with employees to help them see the rationale behind a change because ignorance or misunderstanding is often observed to be the main barrier to successful change.[32] Communication is never too much for organizational change. All available communication channels (e.g. public speeches, meetings, presentations, social events, intranet, emails, posters, and slogans) may be used. And employees should be given ample opportunities to express their opinions and views throughout the change process. In any form of organizational change, involvement of employees in decision-making should not be ignored. Instead, the employees' voices should be heard as much as possible because employee involvement in designing and implementing change—for example, in the form of consultation—can be effective in gaining their buy-in to the intended change.[33] Many advocates of quality management, continuous improvement, and other similar change initiatives see employee involvement as a condition for success.[34]

Mergers and acquisitions

As noted at the beginning of this chapter, companies can have many different types of organizational change. As a kind of inter-organizational change entailing two or more firms combined to form a new entity, mergers and acquisitions (M&A) may represent the most challenging organizational change to be managed successfully as the content and process issues associated with M&As are far more complex, sensitive, and difficult to manage than are often imagined.

There are many reasons for firms to merge or acquire. In essence, M&As are assumed to be the fastest ways to grow. Additionally, firms can attain increased market and financial power; cost reduction owing to economies of scale, resource sharing, and redundancy elimination; or access to unique talent, competencies, and technologies not otherwise accessible, among various other potential synergetic advantages of M&As. In view of the amount of upside gains as well as the size of investments in money, time, and other resources associated with M&As, a lot is usually at stake for the firms undertaking such an organizational change, let alone the negative consequences in case of failure to manage the change well. Again, not unexpectedly, the track record of M&As is bad. Various studies have estimated that about 50 to 75 per cent of M&As failed to achieve their stated objectives.[35] Only 15 per cent of M&As in the US achieved objectives in terms of share value, return on investment, and post-combination profitability; more than half ruined shareholder value instead.[36] Notorious examples of failed M&As were between AOL and Time Warner as well as Daimler and Chrysler.

As mentioned earlier, like any other kinds of organizational change, M&As are not doomed to fail. While some studies have attributed failures of M&As to legal, financial, or operational issues, there is converging evidence that people issues are as crucial to the success of M&As as other issues. Arguably, in order to improve chances of success, firms undertaking M&As should invest time and money not only in their due diligence to assess strategic fit, evaluate financial integrity, consider possible market and customer reactions, and contemplate product roadmaps but also in understanding the possible impacts of their M&A activities on people and doing the right things to mitigate such impacts. Unfortunately, reports have indicated that only 35 per cent of senior HR executives are involved in M&A activities.[37]

An M&A Case Study in Hong Kong's Banking Industry

Hong Kong's status as an international financial centre has been built over the course of thirty years. In the early 1980s Hong Kong transitioned from an industrial economy to a post-industrial economy, with the finance and service industries as her pillars. During the 1980s Hong Kong moved from a monolithic banking system to a three-tier system comprising licensed banks, restricted licence banks, and deposit-taking companies.

During that time, Hong Kong met a massive influx of Western financial institutions. Besides injecting investment funds, these global financial institutions brought to Hong Kong Western corporate culture, leadership, management philosophies, and banking practices. Across those twenty years, the lending business in Hong Kong grew by more than fifteenfold. Right after the handover of Hong Kong's sovereignty from Great Britain to China in 1997, however, the banking industry faced the 1997 Asian financial crisis. Hong Kong endured deflation and economic downturn for the subsequent six years. In 2003 the outbreak of severe acute respiratory syndrome (SARS) dragged the economy to its lowest level, when the GDP shrank by 5 per cent in aggregate over six years. During this prolonged recession, banks in Hong Kong explored new ways of generating revenue by offering such non-traditional services such as risk management, mutual funds, insurance, foreign currency derivatives, and investment consultancy. After the extinguishment of SARS in 2003, Hong Kong received various support policy-wise from China that facilitated cross-border business between Hong Kong and China. With more Hong Kong businesses investing in mainland China, mainland enterprises started to expand to Hong Kong and regarded Hong Kong as a well-developed platform and stepping stone for their further expansion internationally. Specifically, the presence of mainland banks in Hong Kong increased significantly through three acquisitions and mergers during the period from 2004 to 2008.

The acquisition

In the mid-2000s a Chinese state-owned regional bank (Bank A) reached an agreement with a foreign-funded international financial institution to acquire its wholly owned subsidiary licensed bank (Bank B) in Hong Kong. Being the most profitable and the largest subsidiary of its parent bank outside the US, Bank B operated retail and commercial banking in Hong Kong for over forty years. For Bank A, the acquisition was considered highly important as it was a critical milestone for further expanding its business overseas. Moreover, it was the first time Bank A had ever conducted a cross-border acquisition in the fifty years since its establishment in China.

Right after the acquisition, Bank A pronounced that Bank B's well-developed platform, business model, and talents would play a major role in its future business expansion both in Hong Kong and in other Asian countries. In the pronouncement, Bank A commended highly Bank B's existing culture, leadership, structure, and goodwill in the local market. Despite what was pronounced by Bank A, however, the reality was that Bank B was renamed as Bank A (Asia), with immediate effect upon its being acquired. Simultaneously, Bank A (Asia) was asked to change its business strategy to a very aggressive one. And, nine months later, Bank A appointed a team of mainland Chinese senior executives to join Bank A (Asia) and oversee two-thirds of its business operations. During the same period, the performance of Bank A (Asia) took a deep dive. Within three years of the acquisition, Bank A (Asia) recorded that around 40 per cent of the original employees had left the bank, much higher than the annual voluntary attrition rate of 5 per cent before the acquisition. It was noted that the majority of leavers were managers or officer grades. In particular, the CEO left one year after the acquisition, with several key senior executives following suit in the subsequent months.

Among other dissatisfactions to the post-acquisition performance of Bank A (Asia), Bank A was very disappointed to see the extraordinary employee turnover happening at the acquired bank and started to realize that talent retention and motivation should be considered as a critical success factor to its acquisition of Bank B. Bank A reasoned that the rapid deterioration of business of Bank A (Asia) might have stemmed from its serious loss of talented employees. While admitting that it was something that should have been done much earlier when planning for the acquisition, Bank A solicited the professional service of two external HR consultants (Consultants) so as to learn more about the people issues that had embedded inside its acquisition activities. Even though the process of the employees making their individual decisions to leave the newly acquired bank could be complex, Bank A figured that they really needed to understand such complexities and the nuances of the individual leavers' experiences so that appropriate measures could be adopted for its future acquisitions in other Asian countries like Singapore, Taiwan, Malaysia, Indonesia, and Thailand.

At the request of Bank A, the Consultants began to study the post-acquisition experiences of those employees who chose to leave Bank A (Asia). The study was designed in such a way to put more emphasis on those leavers who had been recognized as good performers as they were supposed to be the most valuable human resource assets having significant influence to the continuity and on-going concerns of the acquired bank. Among other research methods, the Consultants interviewed a sample of such leavers. The interviews revealed that the acquisition brought to the acquired bank significant change in organizational culture, leadership style, employee identity, and business strategy, although formal structure remained unchanged.

Organizational culture

The employees in Bank A (Asia) experienced an imminent disruption to the organization's enduring culture regarding power distance. Being one of the first researchers to examine what culture looks like in different countries, Hofstede coined the term 'power distance'.[38] Put in an organizational context, power distance represents the extent to which the less powerful members of organizations accept and expect that power is distributed unequally. According to Hofstede, Western firms tend to have low power distance culture whereas Chinese firms are typically high power-distanced. Being influenced by its Western parent bank and Western leaders coming from its parent bank and stationing in Hong Kong, Bank B had developed over the years before the acquisition a low power distance culture under which employee participation and empowerment were the norms. However, such a culture was haphazardly disrupted by the acquisition. Along with the acquisition by Bank A, renaming from Bank B to Bank A (Asia), and moving in of mainland Chinese senior executives, the employees of Bank A (Asia) found that the head office of Bank A and the new leaders from mainland China decided and acted in a high power-distanced way, which was totally incompatible with these employees' pre-existing low power distance culture (Box 10.2 elaborates a power distance culture). Naturally, the employees of Bank A (Asia) resented and resisted Bank A's disturbance or disruption to these employees' deep-rooted organizational culture (Box 10.3 shows an exhibit of possible reaction to organizational change). By referring to Lewin's theory of change and relevant research studies, the Consultants noted that such resentment and resistance can be overt or covert in nature and may frequently include job quitting.[39]

HRM in Focus—Box 10.2

Power Distance Culture

Hofstede's work has been focusing on national cultural values and is widely regarded as the most famous and systematic study in the area. Being one of the first researchers to examine what culture looks like in different countries, Hofstede coined the term 'power distance'. According to Hofstede, power distance ranges from high to low, and indicates the extent to which people are willing to accept unequal power distribution among different statuses/rankings.

In an organization having high power distance, there is substantial unequal distribution of power among different statuses. In high power distance culture, people at large pay more respect to higher-status persons and consider that power is high-status persons' sole privilege.

A low power distance culture is one in which there is little unequal distribution of power among statuses. In low power distance culture, people generally consider it important to treat others as equal, disregarding their status, and expect that power be generously shared.

A high-power distance culture may be characterized as follows:
- Inequality is not disturbing
- Everyone has a place
- People should depend on a leader
- The powerful are entitled to privileges
- The powerful should not hide their power
- Authoritarian management
- Limited communication/feedback
- Centralized decision-making

Adapted from Hofstede, G. (1980). *Culture's consequences: International differences in work-related values.* Beverly Hills, CA: Sage.

Hofstede, G. (1984). *Culture's consequences: International differences in work-related values.* Beverly Hills: Sage. Hofstede, G. (2001). *Culture's consequences: Comparing values, behaviours, institutions, and organizations across nations* (2nd ed.). Thousand Oaks, CA: Sage.

Hofstede, G., Hofstede, G. J., & Minkov, M. (2010). *Cultures and organizations: Software of the mind* (3rd ed.). New York: McGraw-Hill.

HRM in Focus—Box 10.3

A Continuum of Reaction to Change

A continuum of reaction to change from resistance to positive acceptance of the change.

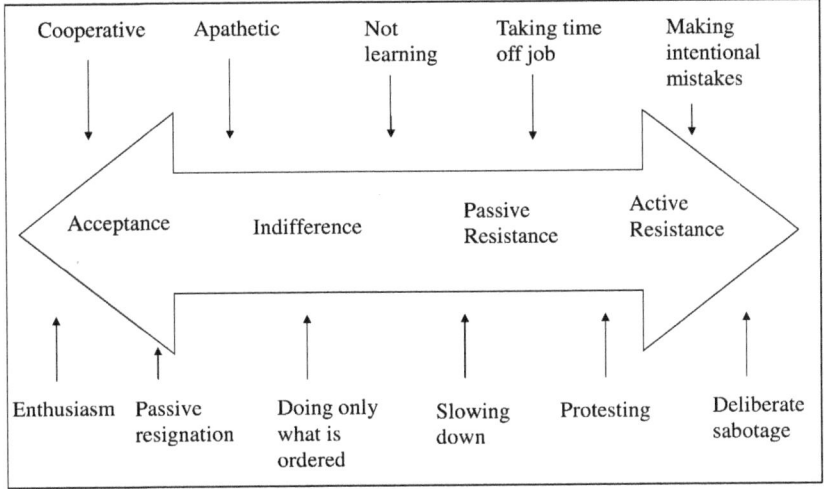

Adapted from Judson, A. S. (1991). *Changing behaviour in organizations: Minimizing resistance to change*. Cambridge, MA: Blackwell.

Leadership style

Closely associated with the change in organizational culture, the Consultants' study showed that there was also drastic change in leadership style. Employees at Bank A (Asia) generally disliked that the mainland executives acted in their mainland 'official' values and ways of doing things. For example, before the acquisition, the prevalent leadership style had been open with two-way communication and led from the heart. But then it was changed to top-down management after the acquisition. According to the employees, their previous leaders were transparent, caring, responsive, and pragmatic, whereas the new leaders were generally considered as followers, subjective, unwilling to provide directions, and unresponsive.

Identity

Furthermore, the findings showed a general consideration that working in Bank A (Asia) was inferior to working in Bank B. Since employees were not familiar with Chinese banks, they had feelings of inferior identity just like changing their jobs to smaller and less-famous banks. Specifically, the brand name of Bank A (Asia) was much weaker than that of Bank B. Front-line employees were the most worried group having great concern on the customers' perception towards Bank A (Asia) as they found its weaker brand name negatively impacting their efforts to keep old customers and acquire new customers. Moreover, the employees' reluctance to accept the new identity of working in a Chinese bank rather than a more reputable foreign bank was magnified when similar negative comments came not only from their customers but also from their peers, ex-colleagues, friends, relatives, and families. The Consultants also found that the leaving employees had a strong desire indeed to carry their pre-acquisition identity, which turned out to be a crucial factor affecting their decisions to stay or not.

Business strategy

In fact, the business strategy changed soon after the acquisition, which was very stressful for the employees. Previously, Bank B focused on top 20 per cent income earners of the Hong Kong population. However, immediately after the acquisition, Bank A (Asia) started a new business strategy and expanded its business segment to cover also the middle-income class. As a result, the workload increased significantly when the number of employees grew comparatively slowly, since it took substantial time to recruit the new needed headcount and train up the new recruits. As the new strategy was implemented in haste, many new products and services were launched within a very short time without proper planning and organizing. Given the weak commitment to the new employer after the acquisition, many employees felt that it was not worthwhile to stay, especially when they were put under much heavier workload that threatened to become harmful to their health. Coupled with the fact that the new employer did not attempt to make any special effort to motivate the employees to work harder so they might handle the extra workload, more and more employees quickly became tempted to quit.

Recommendations by the Consultants

By implementing the actions suggested below, the Consultants contended that a great majority of the people-related issues, concerns, and challenges arising from the acquisition of Bank B could have been dealt with appropriately. Even though hindsight could not change what had already happened, the Consultants believed that Bank A could convert its experience into foresight that would yield better results in future acquisitions.

Talent retention

The Consultants revealed that people issues associated with the acquisition were either mostly ignored or poorly managed, resulting in significant employee turnover. In particular, Bank A did not identify talent retention as a critical success factor of the acquisition and take adequate measures to ensure it. In order to achieve continual success of the bank like it had done before the acquisition, the Consultants recommended that Bank A should retain as many of Bank B's highly competent workforce as possible, especially its management personnel—including top managers, middle managers, and supervisors—to work continuously in Bank A (Asia) and that it should seek to maintain high morale. To this end, the Consultants suggested Bank A provide within a period of not less than two years after the completion of the acquisition that all retained employees of Bank A (Asia) would be offered compensation packages no less favourable than those they had previously received at Bank B.

Bank A offered retention bonuses to key employees who stayed for twelve months after the acquisition. The Consultants noted that, while these employees in Bank A (Asia) generally welcomed the retention bonus, they mostly adopted a 'wait-and-see' tactic, and many of them chose to leave right after receiving their retention bonus. That said, the retention bonus served to delay employees' leaving but not increase their organizational commitment per se. As such, the Consultants maintained that Bank A should not only provide retention bonus but also take other effective talent retention measures.

Naturally, as news of the acquisition spread, headhunters would promptly show up to lure a number of high-performing employees at Bank A (Asia) with attractive package offered by competitors, prompting high turnover of talent particularly among those front-line business-generating staff. Therefore, the Consultants suggested Bank A put in place a counteroffer policy to 'salvage' some of them from leaving. Yet the Consultants reiterated that such a policy should be handled cautiously and tactfully. The counteroffers made should be ensured not far beyond reasonable market levels and not be fallen prey to salary blackmails.

The consultants recommended that the professional service of an external turnover ombudsman should be solicited for counselling intended leavers. The ombudsman could help reduce leaving by inviting prospective leavers to consider all the factors of changing employer and avoid making hasty decisions before taking stock of the positive aspects of their current job and the potential negative aspects that might come with working a new job.

Drawing on various research findings, the Consultants noted that resistance to change most often came when employees felt the change was being done 'to them' rather than 'with them'. To this end, the Consultants proposed a participative approach to change management. Specifically, employees or their representatives in Bank A (Asia) should be involved in the design, consultation, and implementation of any change in, for example, strategies, policies, systems, or practices should such change be deemed unavoidable and necessary to the acquisition.

Bank A appointed a team of personnel from mainland China to join Bank A (Asia) to execute or oversee some change associated with the acquisition. To facilitate this, the Consultants recommended that dedicated team-building activities should be conducted to encourage cooperation between the new mainland employees and the existing Hong Kong employees, without which they might remain two divided, if not opposing, groups of employees working at Bank A (Asia). The Consultants noted that enhanced social acquaintance and relationship via timely and thoughtful team-building activities can effectively promote mutual understanding, trust, knowledge transfer, and joint problem-solving between these two groups of employees, which would also help reduce any resentment, change resistance, and voluntary turnover of the existing Hong Kong employees.

Consultants also recommended the offering to employees of Bank A (Asia) training programmes at Bank A's mainland offices so as to reinforce their understanding about Bank A's business and operation in the mainland banking market. When viewed as a part of the talent retention effort, such cross-border learning opportunities could help keep employees at Bank A (Asia) by having them experience in real life the strengths, capabilities, networks, and other positive aspects of Bank A. The Consultants contended that seeing something would be far better than merely hearing about it.

Apart from the aforementioned talent retention measures directly targeting the employees, the Consultants proposed launching a large-scale customer retention programme to keep Bank B's customers with Bank A (Asia). The Consultants argued that proactive and widely covered promotional programmes lasting, for example, for the first six months immediately after the acquisition could gain customers' continual support and eventually help build the employees' confidence in doing their jobs, which would contribute indirectly to these employees' retention and probably their organizational commitment as well.

A sense of continuity

Bank A continued to use Bank B's existing organizational structure. But the Consultants considered such preservation efforts inadequate. Given the outstanding business performance of Bank B before its acquisition, the Consultants recommended Bank A also preserve Bank B's existing organizational culture, leadership style, brand name, business strategy, and management systems and practices, which the Consultants viewed as Bank B's competitive advantages. The Consultants argued that it should make good business sense for Bank A to make its best efforts to preserve them as wholly as possible in Bank A (Asia). By so doing, on the one hand, Bank A could immediately capitalize on Bank B's competitive advantages that in actual practice would be difficult to develop from scratch or imitate by others. On the other hand, Bank A could readily establish a sense of continuity among the employees of Bank A (Asia) that would increase the chances of successful talent retention. The Consultants argued that such a sense of continuity could minimize not only these employees' perception of significant adverse change brought by the acquisition but also feelings of inferiority or frustration that might otherwise arise should Bank A fail to preserve the existing ways of conducting business.

As a consequence, the Consultants recommended that Bank A's head office and new employees coming from mainland China should receive intensive training to raise their awareness of the low power distance culture at Bank A (Asia). And since these new employees were mostly in the leadership capacities, they should be trained to practise a participative leadership style. The Consultants noted that Bank B's brand name actually carried so much valuable goodwill that it was unwise for Bank A not to keep using it for at least three more years after the acquisition. Within the first one to two years after the acquisition, little or no change should be made to the winning strategy that Bank B had already proved effective. Similarly, the existing management systems and work practices at Bank B represented its decades of progressive organizational learning that, according to the Consultants, should be treasured and allowed to operate as they had been, unless some legal or regulatory compliance situation prevented it. Should Bank A want to impose on Bank A (Asia) new policies and procedures for the sake of tightening internal control, the Consultants suggested such change should be limited to only crucial items in order not to create any perception of distrust.

Communication

Communication made by Bank A regarding the acquisition was inadequate in the sense that it left employees a lot of ambiguity and anxiety about their future prospects and possibly significant change of their way of doing things in the workplace. Inadequate communication increased resentment and resistance to change from employees and caused their loss of commitment and trust in the acquisition. The Consultants recommended that Bank A should adopt an all-out approach to provide employees with honest, open, and timely information about the content and process of the acquisition through both formal and informal communication channels.

Among other things, an open letter should be issued to all the employees on the first day of the public announcement of the acquisition. It should provide specific information about how the acquisition would affect the employees. Such information should include but not limit to the aforesaid matters about retaining talent and preserving a sense of continuity, which the Consultants considered to be the employees' most serious area of concern. Additionally, the vision for Bank A (Asia) should be succinctly expressed. Strategic objectives like doubling the business size and branch network in Hong Kong in five years and leveraging Bank A (Asia) as the platform to carry out offshore development in other Asian markets would help generate buy-in of the employees. Furthermore, Bank A should show the employees some concrete facts about its strengths, especially in terms of financial capability, credit rating, and range of product and services provided to stimulate positive attitudes about acquisition. Bank A should go on to clearly explain how it would couple its strengths with Bank B's proven and successful business model and management expertise to realize such strategic objectives and make the vision come true.

Human resource management

The findings further revealed that there was a general lack of awareness of the significant role that HR professionals should play in managing the change associated with the acquisition. The HR professionals did not get themselves involved in the M&A process by advising top management as subject-matter experts on such pertinent HRM issues as potential cultural incompatibility, strategy, and leadership conflict, as well as talent loss and attrition. While the acquisition of Bank B by Bank A could be broadly divided into three phases of pre-acquisition, during-acquisition, and post-acquisition, the Consultants argued that senior HR executives of both Bank A and Bank B, together with some external professional consultants, should have been heavily involved in all three phases of the acquisition to help diagnose and address the issues of organizational culture, formal structure, strategies, key management systems, processes, and talent needs and retention. All these issues should be taken seriously as they would have a significant impact on the success of people management at the resultant Bank A (Asia).

Implication and Conclusion on HRM in Organizational Change

So far, the importance of managing organizational change and how to go about doing it have been duly discussed. This chapter will conclude with a discussion on the role that HR professionals have to play when an organization is undergoing change. In a survey across a wide range of industries and organizational levels by Baran, Filipkowski, and Stockwell, most of the 547 HR professionals in organizational change revealed their roles as 'change agent' and 'consultant', with only a small portion viewed their roles as limited or not very important.[40] According to the Society for Human Resource Management's Competency Model, dealing with, managing, or leading change is an important part of what HR professionals should be doing, at least at the mid-level of one's HR career. Similarly, HKIHRM's HR Professional Standards Model clearly states that change management is a part of what HR professionals need to know and practise at the professional and strategic levels.

From the perspective of strategic HRM, HR professionals in the role of change maker or change agent should be operating at the highest level within the organization and as early as possible in organizational change. This ensures that HR professionals have due opportunities to share their expertise in change management with top management and contribute in the identification of critical success factors for the intended organizational change, diagnosis of potential people management risks and problems, and design of suitable strategies and tactics for mitigating risks and preventing problems. Also, at the operational level, conventional HRM practices—such as recruitment and selection, training and development, compensation and benefits, and performance management and employee relations—can assist in managing change effectively. Through providing suitable appraisal, rewards, knowledge / skills, or communication, HR can support the needed change in work behaviours, leadership styles, and organizational culture, in addition to securing and retaining talent. Furthermore, HR can help employees cope with organizational change by making available stress management programmes or social support groups within and outside the organization. Otherwise, people would avoid engaging in change activities which they believe exceed their coping capability.[41] Kotter specifically suggested providing support as a key method for neutralizing employees' resistance to change.[42]

Organizational change inherently disrupts employees' status quo and drives them out of their comfort zone, as change often brings different ways of doing things, unfamiliar work situations, risks of incompetence or poor performance, and uncertainties of the future; which often cause typical employees to feel anxious, stressful, or even fearful about change. As such, employees tend to evaluate workplace change negatively and exhibit resistance to change.[43] Generally speaking, employees' resistance to change is the key driving force behind maintaining the status quo, and hindering successful implementation of change.[44] Drawing on Lewin's theory of change, Armenakis and his associates proposed that one effective way to reduce employees' resistance is to increase their readiness for change—that is, to prepare or make ready them for organizational change by shaping their attitudes towards organizational change in such a way that they start to hold positive views about the need for organizational change and come to believe that such changes are beneficial for themselves and the wider organization.[45] Along the same vein, a recent empirical study showed that high-commitment HRM practices can elicit employees' positive attitude, motivation, and even commitment towards organizational change, which are deemed crucial psychological determinants to successful change implementation.[46]

Taken together, HRM is indeed pivotal in the management of organizational change. Any omission of HRM strategically or operationally (or both, in the worst-case scenario) seriously undermines an organization's effectiveness in managing its needed change. If an organization does not manage change well, its change programme is doomed to fail. And, while not launching a needed change is already problematic enough, it is important to note that a change failure can be even more problematic than not launching a needed change at all. This is because a failed change can bring all sorts of negative consequences. Possibly, an organization may need to confront such added problems as absolute chaos, staff turnover, ballooning costs, losing customers, or other adverse consequences in the aftermath of its failed change, besides merely missing its desirable objectives planned in the outset of the change. Given that organizational change is inevitable or a must, an organization's capacity to manage change well can be its competitive advantage for beating its competitors,[47] and this chapter has argued that effective HRM significantly contributes to such a competitive advantage.

While HR professionals should know their roles in managing organizational change, it is worth mentioning here that increasingly studies have been published in the literature about the notion of devolvement of HRM activities to line managers.[48] In particular, various researchers have highlighted the advantages associated with such HRM devolvement as enhanced employee commitment and, ultimately, business performance.[49] It is thus advisable that HR professionals aim to devolve to line managers or attempt to share with them the ownership of change management in organizations. In this regard, appropriate training should be provided to ensure that line managers are also competent enough in managing organizational change.[50]

Review Questions

1. In the case of Bank A, what were the critical success factors for its acquisition of Bank B? Explain the main causes of its change failure.
2. A retention bonus scheme was put in place at Bank A (Asia) for retaining its key employees but subsequently proved to be of limited use. Can you suggest a workable retention bonus scheme in terms of its amount, target employees, and awarding mechanism that can effectively boost employee organizational commitment at Bank A (Asia)?
3. This chapter points out that 'employees or their representatives in Bank A (Asia) should be involved in the design, consultation, and implementation of any change in, for example, strategies, policies, systems, or practices should such change be deemed unavoidable and necessary to the acquisition.' Can you give some examples of such unavoidable and necessary changes in the acquisition?
4. This chapter contains a lot of recommendations from the Consultants hired by Bank A about what it 'should do'. Do you think those recommendations were valid to the situation of Bank A (Asia)? Discuss whether the recommendations would be valid to any acquisition situation in the banking industry or in any industry.
5. Describe an organizational change that you experienced in the past. How did you feel about the change? Was the change successful? Why yes / no? How did the organization deal with the human dimensions of the change?
6. As a HR professional, what roles do you play in managing organizational change? How can you effectively facilitate the change process in an organization?

Notes

1. W. G. Pollard (1911–1989) was a nuclear physicist, priest, author, teacher, and founder of the Oak Ridge Institute of Nuclear Studies. For the quote, see, for example, Granville, M. (2010). *The exceptional leader: A quick guide to personal branding and leadership development.*

Bloomington: AuthorHouse. For the bio of Pollard, see, for example, William G. Pollard – Founder of ORAU. Retrieved July 8, 2018, from https://www.orau.org/about-orau/history/william-pollard.aspx

2. Anderson, D. L. (2010). *Organization development: The process of leading organizational change*. Thousand Oaks: Sage Publications. Cummings, T. G., & Worley, C. G. (2005). *Organization development and change* (8th ed.). Mason: South-Western.

3. Kotter, J. P. (2012). *Leading change*. Boston: Harvard Business School Press. Waterman, R. H., Jr., Peters, T. J., and Phillips, J. R. (1980). Structure is not organization. *Business Horizons, 23*(3), 14–26. Galpin, T. (1996). *The human side of change: A practical guide to organization redesign*. San Francisco: Jossey-Bass. Luecke, R. (2003). *Managing change and transition*. Boston: Harvard Business School Press.

4. See for example, Deutschman, A. (2007). *Change or die*. New York: HarperCollins.

5. Barr, P. S., Stimpert, J. L., and Huff, A. S. (1992). Cognitive change, strategic action, and organizational renewal [Special issue]. *Strategic Management Journal, 13*, 15–36. Boeker, W. (1997). Strategic change: The influence of managerial characteristics and organizational growth. *Academy of Management Journal, 40*(1), 152–170. Child, J., and Smith, C. (1987). The context and process of organizational transformation—Cadbury Limited in its sector. *Journal of Management Studies, 24*(6), 565–593. De Meuse, K. P., Marks, L., and Dai, G. (2010). Organizational downsizing, mergers and acquisitions, and strategic alliances: Using theory and research to enhance practice. In S. Zedeck (Ed.), *APA handbook of industrial and organizational psychology* (pp. 729–768). Washington: American Psychological Association. Gordon, S. S., Stewart, W. H., Sweo, R., and Luker, W. A. (2000). Convergence versus strategic reorientation: The antecedents of fast-paced organizational change. *Journal of Management, 26*, 911–945. Jones, G. R. (2013). *Organizational theory, design, and change* (7th ed.). Harlow: Pearson. Keck, S. L., and Tushman, M. L. (1993). Environmental and organizational context and executive team structure. *Academy of Management Journal, 36*(6), 1314–1344. Leana, C. R., and Barry, B. (2000). Stability and change as simultaneous experiences in organizational life. *Academy of Management Review, 25*(4), 753–759. Tidd, J., Bessant, J., and Pavitt, K. (2009). *Managing innovation: Integrating technological, market and organizational change* (4th ed.). Chichester: John Wiley.

6. Burke, W. W., and Litwin, G. H. (1992). A causal model of organizational performance and change. *Journal of Management, 18*, 523–545.

7. Daft, R. L. (1995). *Organization theory and design* (5th ed.). St. Paul: West Group.

8. Peak, M. H. (1996). An era of wrenching corporate change: New challenges and opportunities arise for American businesses, according to the members of AMA's councils. *Management Review, 85*(7), 45–49.

9. Balogun, J., and Hope Hailey, V. (2004). Exploring strategic change (2nd ed.). London: Prentice Hall. Burnes, B. (2004). *Managing change: A Strategic approach to organizational dynamics* (4th ed.). Harlow: Prentice Hall. Carnall, C. A. (2003). *Managing change in organizations* (4th ed.). Harlow: Prentice Hall. Kotter, J. P. (2012). *Leading change*. Boston: Harvard Business School Press. Luecke, R. (2003). *Managing change and transition*. Boston: Harvard Business School Press. Moran, J. W., and Brightman, B. K. (2001). Leading organizational change. *Career Development International, 6*(2), pp. 111–118. Okumus, F., and Hemmington, N. (1998). Barriers and resistance to change in hotel firms: An investigation at unit level. *International Journal of Contemporary Hospitality Management, 10*(7), pp. 283–288. Paton, R. A., and McCalman, J. (2000). *Change management: A guide to effective implementation* (2nd ed.). London: SAGE Publications. Senior, B. (2002). *Organizational change* (2nd ed.). London: Prentice Hall.

10. Burnes, B. (2004). *Managing change: A Strategic approach to organizational dynamics* (4th ed.). Harlow: Prentice Hall. Luecke, R. (2003). *Managing change and transition*. Boston: Harvard Business School Press. Okumus, F., and Hemmington, N. (1998). Barriers and resistance to change in hotel firms: An investigation at unit level. *International Journal of Contemporary Hospitality Management, 10*(7), pp. 283–288.

11. Drucker, P. F. (1999). *Management challenges for the 21st century* (p. 73). New York: HarperCollins.
12. Berquist, W. (1993). *The postmodern organization: Mastering the art of irreversible change*. San Francisco: Jossey-Bass.
13. Kotter, J. P. (2012). *Leading change*. Boston: Harvard Business School Press. Kotter, J. P. (2014). *Accelerate: Building strategic agility for a faster-moving world*. Boston: Harvard Business Review Press.
14. Armenakis, A. A., and Harris, S. G. (2002). Crafting a change message to create transformational readiness. *Journal of Organizational Change Management, 15*(2), 169–183.
15. Vakola, M., and Nikolaou, I. (2005). Attitudes towards organizational change: What is the role of employees' stress and commitment? *Employee Relations, 27*, 160–174.
16. Burke, W. W., and Litwin, G. H. (1992). A causal model of organizational performance and change. *Journal of Management, 18*, 523–545. Pritchett, P. (1996). *Resistance: Moving beyond the barriers to change*. Dallas: Pritchett & Associates.
17. See for example, Appelbaum, S. H., and Wohl, L. (2000). Transformation or change: Some prescriptions for health care organizations. *Managing Service Quality, 10*(5), 279–298. Beer, M., Eisenstat, R. A., and Spector, B. (1990). Why change programs don't produce change. *Harvard Business Review, 68*(6), 158–166. Bibler, R. S. (1989). *The Arthur Young management guide to mergers and acquisitions*. New York: Wiley. Burnes, B. (2004). *Managing change: A Strategic approach to organizational dynamics* (4th ed.). Harlow: Prentice Hall. Elving, W. J. L. (2005). The role of communication in organizational change. Corporate Communications: *An International Journal, 10*(2), 129–138. Porras, J. I., and Robertson, P. J. (1992). Organizational development: Theory, practice, research. In M. D. Dunnette, and L. M. Hough (Eds.), *Handbook of organizational psychology* (2nd ed., Vol. 3, pp. 719–822). Palo Alto: Consulting Psychology Press.
18. Balogun, J., and Hope Hailey, V. (2004). *Exploring strategic change* (2nd ed.). London: Prentice Hall. Beer, M., and Nohria, N. (2000). *Breaking the code of change*. Cambridge: Harvard Business School Press. Burke, W. W., & Biggart, N. (1997). Interorganizational relations. In D. Druckman, J. E. Singer, and H. Van Cott (Ed.), *Enhancing organizational performance* (pp. 120–149). Washington: National Academies Press. Furman, J. L., and McGahan, A. M. (2002). Turnarounds. *Managerial and Decision Economics, 23*, 283–300.
19. Senge, P., Kleiner, A., Roberts, C., Ross, R., Roth, G., and Smith, B. (1999). *The dance of change: The challenges to sustaining momentum in learning organizations* (p. 5). New York: Doubleday.
20. Chiu, R. K. (1999). Employee involvement in a total quality management programme: problems in Chinese firms in Hong Kong. *Managerial Auditing Journal, 14*(1/2), 8–11.
21. Wimalasiri, J. S., and Kouzmin, A. (2000). A comparative study of employee involvement initiatives in Hong Kong and the USA. *International Journal of Manpower, 21*(8), 614–634.
22. Chu, P., and Ip, O. (2002). Downsizing in the internet industry: The Hong Kong experience. *Leadership & Organization Development Journal, 23*(3), 158–166.
23. Gamal, I., and MaLaughlin, C. W. (1991). Organizational change: Blessing or burden? *Personnel Administer, 34*(8), 94–95. Moravec, M. (1995). From reengineering for revitalization. *Executive Excellence, 12*(2), 18–19.
24. Jacobs, M. (1998). A strategic approach to a changing world. *Credit Union Magazine, 64*(9), 17–21.
25. Szamosi, L. T., and Duxbury, L. (2002). Development of a measure to assess organizational change. *Journal of Organizational Change Management, 15*(2), 184–201.
26. Burke, W. W. (2008). *Organization change: Theory and practice* (2nd ed.). Sage Publications.
27. Offermann, L. R., and Gowing, M. K. (1993). Personnel selection in the future: The impact of changing demographics and the nature of work. *Personnel Selection in Organizations, 1*, 385–417.
28. Robbins, S. P., and Judge, T. A. (2019). *Organizational behaviour* (18th ed.). Upper Saddle River, NJ: Pearson.

29. ThornHill, A., Lewis, P., Millmore, M., and Saunders, M. N. K. (2000). *Managing change: A human resource strategy approach*. England: Pearson Education.
30. Armstrong, M. (2017). *Armstrong's handbook of performance management: An evidence-based guide to delivering high performance* (6th ed.). Kogan Page.
31. Aguinis, H. (2012). *Performance management* (3rd ed.). Boston, MA: Pearson.
32. Kotter, J. P. (2012). *Leading change*. Boston: Harvard Business School Press.
33. Kotter, J. P. (2012). *Leading change*. Boston: Harvard Business School Press.
34. Wilkinson, A., Marchington, M., Goodman, J., and Ackers, P. (1992). Total quality management and employee involvement. *Human Resource Management Journal, 2*(4), 1–20.
35. Marks, M. L. (2002). *Charging back up the hill: Workplace recovery after mergers, acquisitions and downsizings*. San Francisco: Jossey-Bass. Marks, M. L., and Mirvis, P. H. (2001). Making mergers and acquisitions work: Strategic and psychological preparation. *The Academy of Management Executive, 15*(2), 80–92. Nahavandi, A., and Malekzadeh, A. R. (1993). Leader style in strategy and organizational performance: An integrative framework. *Journal of Management Studies, 30*(3), 405–425.
36. Haebeck, M. H., Kroger, F., and Trum, M. R. (2000). *After the mergers: Seven rules for successful post-merger integration*. New York: Prentice Hall.
37. Giles, P. (2000). The importance of HR in making your merger work. *Workspan*, August, 16–20. Liberatore, M. D. (2000). HR's relative importance in mergers and acquisitions. *Human Resource Executive, 2*, 48.
38. Hofstede, G. (1980). *Culture's consequences: International differences in work-related values*. Beverly Hills: Sage Publications. Hofstede, G. (2001). *Culture's consequences: Comparing values, behaviours, institutions, and organizations across nations* (2nd ed.). Thousand Oaks: Sage Publications.
39. Lewin, K. (1947). Frontiers in group dynamics. *Human Relations, 1*(2), 143–153. Lewin, K. (1951). *Field theory in social science*. New York: Harper & Row. Lapointe, L., and Rivard, S. (2005). A multilevel model of resistance to information technology implementation. *MIS Quarterly, 29*(3), 461–491. Neves, P. (2009). Readiness for change: Contributions for employee's level of individual change and turnover intentions. *Journal of Change Management, 9*(2), 215–231. Oreg, S. (2006). Personality, context, and resistance to organizational change. *European Journal of Work and Organizational Psychology, 15*(1), 73–101.
40. Baran, B. E., Filipkowski, J., and Stockwell, R. (2017). Human resource management professionals' views of organizational change. In *Academy of Management Proceedings* (Vol. 2017, No. 1, p. 11381). Briarcliff Manor: Academy of Management. Retrieved July 16, 2018, from https://doi.org/10.5465/ambpp.2017.11381abstract
41. Bandura, A. (1982). Self-efficacy mechanism in human agency. *American Psychologist, 37*(2), 122–147.
42. Kotter, J. P. (2012). *Leading change*. Boston: Harvard Business School Press.
43. Carnall, C. A. (2003). *Managing change in organizations* (4th ed.). Harlow: Prentice Hall.
44. Bouckenooghe, D. (2010). Positioning change recipients' attitudes toward change in the organizational change literature. *Journal of Applied Behavioural Science, 46*, 500–531. Bovey, W. H., and Hede, A. (2001). Resistance to organizational change: The role of cognitive and affective processes. *Leadership and Organization Development Journal, 22*, 372–382. Del Val, M. P., and Fuentes, C. M. (2003). Resistance to change: A literature review and empirical study. *Management Decision, 41*, 148–155.
45. Armenakis, A. A., Harris, S. G., and Mossholder, K. W. (1993). Creating readiness for organizational change. *Human Relations, 46*(6), 681–702.
46. Chang, S, Way, S. A., and Cheng, K. H. D. (2017). The elicitation of frontline, customer contact, hotel employee innovative behaviour: Illuminating the central roles of readiness for change and absorptive capacity. *Cornell Hospitality Quarterly*. DOI: 10.1177/19389655177349
47. Burnes, B. (2009). *Managing change: A strategic approach to organizational dynamics* (5th ed.). Harlow, UK: Pearson Education. Pettigrew, A., and Whipp, R. (1993). *Managing change for competitive success*. Oxford: Blackwell. Prastacos, G., Söderquist, K., Spanos, Y., and Van

Wassenhove, L. (2002). An integrated framework for managing change in the new competitive landscape. *European Management Journal*, 20(1), 55–71. Szamosi, L. T., and Duxbury, L. (2002). Development of a measure to assess organizational change. *Journal of Organizational Change Management*, 15(2), 184–201. Tuominen, K. (2000). *Managing change: Practical strategies for competitive advantage*. Milwaukee: ASQ Quality Press.

48. Larsen, H. H., and Brewster, C. (2003). Line management responsibility for HRM: What is happening in Europe? *Employee Relations*, 25(3), 228–244. Renwick, D. (2003). Line manager involvement in HRM: An inside view? *Employee Relations*, 25(3), 262–280. Storey, J. (1995). *Human resource management: A critical text (First edition)*. London: Routledge.

49. Cunningham, I., and Hyman, J. (1999). Devolving human resource responsibilities to the line: Beginning of the end or new beginning for personnel? *Personnel Review*, 28(1/2), 9–27. Hutchinson, S. and Purcell, J. (2003). *Bringing policies to life: The vital role of front line managers in people management*. London: CIPD. Thornhill, A., and Saunders M. N. K. (1998). What if line managers don't realize they're responsible for HR? Lessons from an organization experiencing rapid change. *Personnel Review*, 27(6), 460–476.

50. Maxwell, G. A., and Watson, S. (2006). Perspectives on line managers in human resource management: Hilton International's UK hotels. *The International Journal of Human Resource Management*, 17(6), 1152–1170.

11
Challenges and Future for Human Resource Management in Hong Kong

Anna P. Y. Tsui

> **LEARNING OUTCOMES**
>
> By the end of this chapter, readers should be able to
> - understand the change drivers in Hong Kong business;
> - identify the challenges to HRM in Hong Kong;
> - understand the future implications to HR professionals in Hong Kong; and
> - develop the future skills and competencies of HR professionals in Hong Kong.

Introduction

In this concluding chapter, we look at the challenges to HRM and their future implications in Hong Kong. Challenges arise from globalization and economic forces, sociocultural changes in the society, political-legal impacts, and new technologies. They provoke change to the business strategies in terms of use of technology, organizational structure, work force changes, and HR process. As a consequence, HR strategies and activities also need to undergo transformations in order to support these business changes. This requires transformation of HR in terms of its basic skills and competencies.[1] An overview of these new skills is examined at the end of the chapter.

HR Challenges and Future Implications

Challenge from economic factors

The emergence of a knowledge economy has placed new demands on Hong Kong organizations. The old assumptions underlying traditional HR processes could not be effective with the new service economy. For instance, old HR practices suppose that jobs should be narrowly defined, supervisors should control workers, and efficiency should be emphasized. Short-term results are to be achieved.[2] In contrast, knowledge organizations stress that employees' knowledge and skills have a major impact on organizational success. Jobs should be designed more broadly so as to encourage innovation, autonomy, continuous improvement, and participation in decision-making. Therefore, broad-based recruiting is required in the near future in order to uncover skilled applicants, and job designs should emphasize autonomy and participation. Team-based structures are also encouraged while learning, and development for new skill development should cater with new business needs.[3] In addition, employee retention is important as the skills of knowledge workers are not substitutable.[4] To manage knowledge workers effectively, management's challenge is to unleash their professional knowledge and creativity. They need to emphasize responsibility rather than controlling their efforts. But many Hong Kong companies are now run like the stereotypical Chinese family businesses. Such a hierarchically authoritarian management style could hamper the development towards a knowledge-based economy.[5]

Regarding Hong Kong's economic structure, for many years, it has been dominated by four pillar industries—namely, the financial services, trading and logistics, producer and professional services, and the tourism sector. Their combined GDP contribution was once at a peak of 60.3 per cent in 2007. But since then, it has dropped to less than 56.6 per cent in 2016. Currently, the four pillar industries together employ over 1.7 million people, or almost half (46.9 per cent in 2016) of the total labour force. As an initiative to diversify the local industry structure, the then chief executive identified 'Six Industries' as top priorities for further development: cultural and creative industries, medical services, education services, innovation and technology, testing and certification services, and environmental industries. In 2016, the six industries together contributed 8.9 per cent of the GDP and 12.7 per cent of total employment, which slightly rose from 8.0 per cent of GDP and 11.3 per cent of total employment in 2009.[6] Nevertheless, the four pillar industries are still the key driving force of economic growth. We reckon that Hong Kong's economic prosperity is strongly connected to its manpower growth. But according to government statistics, Hong Kong is projected to undergo a continuing labour shortage if the local economy expanding at a rate of 4 per cent. On the other hand, Hong Kong may record a labour surplus if the local economy slows down owing to fluctuations of the outside economies.[7]

Meanwhile, Hong Kong is also facing other economic concerns. The costs of business operation, mainly office rental and staff expenses, in Hong Kong remain high, with the shortage in office supply, skilled, and front-line workers. Hong Kong has been continuously ranked as one of the most expensive cities in the world. This factor may drive business away from Hong Kong. Quite a number of Asia-Pacific regional offices have moved out of Hong Kong to Shanghai and Singapore, for a number of reasons. One is the relatively high costs of operation mainly incurred by office rental and staff costs.[8] This remains a constant struggle for businesses operating in Hong Kong where they are consciously working to save costs while striving to maintain high standards.

The China factor

The economic (and political) development of Hong Kong is closely linked to China. As we pointed out in Chapter 2, Hong Kong's economy has benefited from its motherland in terms of labour supply. And the China factor has attracted many multinationals to Hong Kong in order to tap the huge China market for their products. They also have a significant impact on local HRM.[9] Now, China's economy has been growing steadily and has become the number-one consumer market and manufacturer globally. Mainland Chinese is the top customer source in Hong Kong's retail segment. And Chinese companies form the majority in the Hong Kong stock market. In recent years, Chinese firms set up their headquarters or companies in the territory to pursue their international expansion plans. In Chapter 2 we recognize that they expand quickly and serve the engine of growth in the economy. They offer attractive compensation packages to their employees. But their HR practices are yet to be strategic. The management style could be directive and hierarchical. Some Hong Kong employees may find difficulties working in the Chinese companies. Employee turnover rate is high.[10] As a result of the above economic changes, we draw some future implications for HR professionals in Hong Kong:

- HR department should have a thorough review of their processes and practices in organizations so as to match with the shifted requirements of a knowledge organization.
- HR professionals should continue to train and retrain their employees for different skills in order to reflect changing business needs, competition, and increasing globalization.
- HR professionals have to drive the process of continuous review of functional efficiency and effectiveness with appropriate prioritization, standardization, or outsourcing to different countries.
- Increased specialization may reduce the exposure of HR professionals to a wider spectrum of HRM functions. And some HR activities can be outsourced. But HR professionals have to become strategic business partners. They have to learn to speak the right language with business, build trustworthy relationships with their business partners, and further develop their business acumen.
- HR should help their employees adapt to different business and management styles, including those of mainland Chinese origins.
- HR also plays a coordinating and facilitation role in the cross-border activities. They may help establish Chinese HR offices and oversee or coordinate their operations through centralized or decentralized HR policies and systems.

Challenge of sociocultural factors

Despite the transformation of Hong Kong to a service economy, the current government policies on education, youth, economic, immigration, and manpower planning are not aligned. There is a general lack of front-line and skilled workers in many industries. Indeed, skill mismatch is one of the major causes of talent shortage in Hong Kong. For instance, the tertiary education in Hong Kong is viewed as academic and theoretical. There is a large gap between the graduate competencies and those required by the employers. Many industries experience skill mismatch, like the construction and private banking industries. A lack of employability skills at school, insufficient workplace training, and a lack of graduates' long term job commitment are the major reasons leading to skill mismatch. The gap between academic education and business competencies has resulted in significantly higher training costs for industries.[11] In effect, the shortage of skilled labour and experienced managers has discouraged business development plans. Many organizations have now become aware of the growing importance of maintaining good relationship with former employees of all ages. This is because they may rejoin the company or engage again in another form of business partnership after departing from the companies.

Thus, as the current recruitment sources become saturated, organizations are forced to be more open-minded and creative in adopting various platforms for recruiting. As one of the strategies adopted to unleash the potential workforce, Hong Kong's HR professionals in general welcome the government to extend the retirement age of newly hired civil servants from 60 to 65, as people live longer and medical costs may not be affordable for retirees. Some organizations also encounter challenges to building a succession pipeline for middle managers because of the manpower shortage. In accordance with a recent research on retirement age, nearly 80 per cent of HR professionals in Hong Kong believe that raising retirement age is an effective measure to alleviate pressure in Hong Kong's manpower shortage.[12]

But the above groups of people have posed challenges for HRM in Hong Kong. Organizations are now staffed by members of multiple generations of different work values, attitudes, and behaviours. We note from Chapter 2 that the young generations in Hong Kong are more individualistic and look for work-life balance. While employment loyalty is not their priority, fast-track success, achievement or higher salary often could be. For HR, employee engagement has therefore become more critical than retention of the young workforce. They need to increase flexible work arrangements, allow part-time work, and provide a more supportive environment. HR is also confronted with more complex reward and compensation systems towards multiple generations and workforce of different backgrounds.

In parallel, we note that Hong Kong organizations are faced with major shifts in the composition of the workforce. The population will be older and more ethnically diverse. Research studies, however, consistently show that diversity increases innovation and creativity.[13] And changes in generational and ethnic diversity create opportunities for Hong Kong's HR to utilize the many talents and skills. Hong Kong's HR professionals thus need to expand their labour resource pool including the younger ethnic minorities for employment. Apart from providing on-the-job or language skills training, they should nurture emotional connections of these minorities with their Hong Kong employee counterparts and help develop a sense of loyalty in the workplace. Successful diversity management is critical for companies to compete in the global markets. Thanks to the recent government promotional efforts and introduction of anti-discrimination laws, Hong Kong has lived up to its reputation as Asia's world city. It has topped the list in Asia for workplace inclusion and diversity.[14]

The following implications are drawn for HR professionals in the near future:

- HR professionals have to think beyond the traditional recruitment and retention, succession planning, and learning and development strategies. There should be a stronger emphasis on positive engagement experience. The succession-planning cycle needs to be shortened and split into a few more stages in view of the high staff turnover.

- Employee engagement is more challenging with the multiple generations, ethnic backgrounds, and qualifications among the same workforce.
- HR should have more sophisticated talent acquisition strategies, such as the use of employment branding and enhancing candidate and employee experience. The HRM cycle should also start earlier during pre-graduation and extend to post-retirement.
- HR departments should develop a workplace diversity policy with measures to hire people based on ability rather than unfair discriminatory factors.

Challenge from political and legal factors

As discussed before, since its handover to China in 1997, Hong Kong's development in most areas has been tied to China's, for better and for worse. Though the general public of Hong Kong is glad to see China's improvement in economic development and political stability, the general societal atmosphere in Hong Kong has been somewhat mixed. While some industry sectors (such as tourism and retail industries) are welcoming mainland tourists as their key customers, some Hong Kong residents consider the mainland immigrants and visitors as intruders to the quality of their daily living. And many Hong Kong people have made demonstrations on the street to voice their dissatisfaction over various contentious issues. Many Hong Kong people identify themselves as Hong Kongers rather than Chinese citizens. Someone has argued that 'Hong Kong has returned in name, but not in substance'.[15] Another prominent person warned of the threat to the city as China's top financial centre since the tensions over electoral reform.[16] It is apparent that Hong Kong is facing a critical juncture in its political development.

In fact, Hong Kong's human resource arena is not immune to political issues. To address the challenges as a result of demographic changes, the chief executive proposed a number of measures to unleash the potential of the local labour force and recruit overseas talent and professionals. But in response, four police associations expressed their disagreement about extending the retirement ages of new recruits, though the suggestion does not apply to the existing civil servants.[17] At the same time, there have been prolonged debates among professional associations and political parties on imported labour, statutory minimum wage and standard working hours, maternity/paternity leave, elimination of the offset mechanism of Mandatory Provident Fund against the long-service and severance payments, collective bargaining rights, definition of 'continuous contract of employment' (the so-called 418 working hours requirement), to name a few. Also, the legal status of the 'gig workers' could be uncertain.[18] We also note that strikes and labour actions nowadays are increasingly backed by trade unions in a more organized fashion.

Therefore, Hong Kong's labour scene is not entirely free from problems and unrest. It is prone to social protests by different interest and pressure groups. While progressing towards advanced capitalism, Hong Kong has an imbalanced economic growth, skewing towards certain economic sectors like property development and finance. This problem is exacerbated by inflation and the high property and rental prices in the city. Wealth is now concentrated in the hands of a few privileged groups. Low pay, however, persists among a sizeable portion of the working class, and there are many people who live below the poverty line. Hong Kong's Gini coefficient, a measure of income disparity, is one of the highest in the world.[19] The massification of higher education has resulted in a large number of university graduates. Many of them have to move down to jobs of lesser pay and responsibilities, such as retail sales or clerical posts. Injustices in the distribution of life opportunities and economic deprivation have caused a series of protests in the past decade. Demonstrations and public assemblies are common on weekends and major public holidays. They helped fuel the event of the Occupy Central movement in 2014. And regarding the recent wave of emigration, many of the emigrants are affluent middle class with professional and managerial backgrounds. Their departure from Hong Kong could cause challenges to the local talent supply and managerial resource capabilities of businesses.

In addition, we notice that there is a shortage of HRM professional representatives or lobbyists in the Hong Kong government organs and committees. In many cases, their practical findings on the draft laws and legislation have not been considered carefully by the government. In order to minimize the impact of possible loopholes or misunderstandings, HR organizations and professionals should engage in more active participation with the government bodies, employers' associations, employees, and trade unions on proposed legislative and regulatory changes. More extensive lobbying or discussion before implementations of those policies is required. Possible future implications of the above on HR professionals are specified below:

- HR professionals should keep abreast of the political environment and changes at local and international levels. They should be capable of taking risk management or drafting a contingency plan for business.
- HR professionals need to be internal advisers to the top management team's strategic discussions on the development of political and other environmental scanning factors.
- HR should develop skills in dealing with unionism and more active labour movements.
- HR professionals should have a good understanding of the law and provide business with any update on legislation and regulation development.
- It is important to enhance HRM presence in the process of drafting, consulting, and communicating new labour-related laws and legislation in different public or private organizations.
- With the diversified sources of employees, HR professionals should have a broad understanding of the employment laws of other countries, like China and other Asian countries, in order to avoid any legal complications. There should also be an increased need to engage external legal advisers in handling more complicated and sensitive employee issues.

Impact of HR technology

We note from Chapter 9 that Hong Kong organizations are aware of the importance to adopt a more sophisticated data analysis methodology (big data) and human resource information system (HRIS). By leveraging HR data, they help redefine the employee experience and make work more productive, real-time, engaging, and rewarding. HR professionals can identify the key competencies for job positions, and thus target the right candidates without going through tedious selection processes. Big data also allows

HR professionals to gain a deep understanding of the organizational culture—from how an individual performs to how departments interact to how well the corporate values are thriving within the organization. However, promotion of its benefits to a wider audience is needed as only a few organizations in Hong Kong are actually using big data at the moment. A study regarding Hong Kong HR directors' recruitment preferences revealed that only about 24 per cent of the respondents reported using social media to source candidates, 18 per cent used it to communicate with them, and 12 per cent checked online profiles for behaviour and suitability. These figures were much lower than their Asian counterparts in mainland China, Singapore, and Japan. Though some organizations leveraged social media as a successful employer branding tool, they did not utilize or realize this as an effective recruitment tool in Hong Kong.[20]

And in theory, technology should facilitate the role of HR as business partner. HR has the opportunity to revolutionize organizations through new digital platforms, technologies, tools, apps, and analytics while outsourcing low value-added activities. A more strategic HR department demands a new workplace with a suitable digital strategy that aligns with the needs of the HR department and the business growth. On the other hand, technological change could lead to displacement and deskilling of the workforce and reshape the pattern of skill requirements in the workplace. The impact of technological change on employment opportunities has long been an area of debate in management research. In the past, most of the studies have examined the potential impacts of technology in the workforce in developed economies, especially the Anglo-Saxon countries between the 1970s and 1990s.[21] Recently, studies have been extended to developing Asian economies, like China and ASEAN countries. For example, it is argued that more than 60 per cent of manufacturing workers in Indonesia and 73 per cent in Thailand are at risk of losing their jobs to automation. The growing use of automation technology such as sewing robots affect 86 per cent of textile workers in Vietnam and 88 per cent in Cambodia.[22] In Hong Kong, though an early study did not identify any adverse effect on work and work behaviour of workers because of new technology,[23] we have noticed a shift from traditional modes of production and a low-skill-based economic structure towards a more knowledge-based economy since the 1980s. New jobs are created while old jobs are replaced. These knowledge-based jobs demand new skills, knowledge, and competencies, which are probably filled by the younger generation rather than those displaced from production lines and low-end service jobs. As we argued before, this could be a serious problem where our education system has not provided enough skilled candidates to meet the exigencies of the modern workforce. The current rise of the Greater Bay Area integration initiative could put even more jobs at stake as more industry shifts will take place. But despite the fact that the government has established bodies like the Employees Retraining Board and the Continuing Education Fund to teach and upgrade labour skills, the number of vocational courses does not meet the market demand or needs from thousands of unemployed and low-income people.[24]

The following summarizes future HR implications in response to the aspect of HR technology transformation.

- HR should develop a strategic mindset envisioning the manpower and workforce changes inside and outside the organization. While they should understand the business requirements that would affect the internal workforce in terms of number and skill mix, they should also examine the issue in a macroenvironmental context that would lead to changes in workforce supply and their skills/quality in the labour market.

- HR should evaluate whether the HR digital transformations are effective (to business performance), apart from realizing the benefit of gaining efficiency. Some questions need to be asked: Does e-recruiting attract talented and diverse applicants who can perform successfully in organizations? Does the use of e-selection help organizations hire the most talented applicants? Is e-learning as effective as normal classroom training?[25]
- HR should consider and evaluate the use of social media, cognitive assessments (e.g. artificial intelligence, natural language processing, predictive algorithms, and self-learning tools) and other HR technologies and analytics for various HR practices.
- A new form of employee engagement may arise. For example, an organization may redesign the concept of physical office space and working hours and scale back face-to-face dialogue in favour of on-line communication and social media.
- HR may strengthen HRM reporting and data analysis and develop internal superusers to generate quality data. Evidence-based HR proposals with statistical evidence will help businesses make better decisions.
- HR and employees' understanding of ordinances and statutory regulations related to data protection and release of personal data is required.
- HR may look into outsourcing opportunities of low-value-added activities such as recurring, transactional and administrative tasks like payroll, leave, and benefits management.

The Future for Our Local HRM Professionals

Existing HR literature has reflected a well-placed emphasis on the transformation of HR from an administrative function to a core business function that contributes to organizational effectiveness. The convergence of various environmental and organizational factors has served as impetuses for the shift.[26] Some researchers separate the transformation of HR into three general waves:

- Wave 1—the administrative wave of HR with traditional administrative HR activities and services;
- Wave 2—the HR practices wave with the design of innovative HR practices in people management, rewards management, communication and organizational policies; and
- Wave 3—the HR strategy wave that HR practices are aligned to the business strategy.[27]

But we argue that the destination of HR in Hong Kong should not end with Wave 3. As we discuss above, HR can move from connecting to the business to connecting to the broader business context in which a business operates (i.e. Wave 4). In other words, HR professionals should shift from an inside/outside to an outside/inside approach. Early on, HR emerged as a profession using an inside/outside approach. Under the outside/inside approach, HR professionals should, however, not only create value by serving employees, redesigning HR practices, or making them more efficient. They should create value by making sure that HR services inside the company align with the expectations outside the organization as well. An example could be being the employer of choice the customers/candidates would choose. Organizations can build on their strengths that will strengthen others. Then, every HR practice can be further transformed by noticing the value created for those outside the company. Not only would it position HR to respond to strategy, but it would help shape and re-create HR with a full partnership role through serving employees and managers as well as meeting expectations of external stakeholders, including customers, investors, and the community. It moves HR from an inside/outside approach with a focus on HR responding to organizational challenges to more fully participating in business strategy development and adding value towards a broader business environment. Ulrich and Dulebohn have proposed three major issues to address the move of HR to an outside/inside approach: HR's relationship to the business; HR's targets or outcomes to meet for its work with respect to individuals, organizational and leadership; and the domains for HR investments.[28] This idea could be instructive to HR professionals in Hong Kong as we see that HR should monitor business contexts and stakeholders and align their works with external contextual factors, apart from the current discussion of HR's strategic fits within their business. But this could be an ambitious agenda for our HR in the future.

We now end with a summary of some important knowledge and skills for HR professionals in Hong Kong in the future. In a more demanding work environment nowadays, HR professionals must master a sound knowledge base. Working as 'business partners', they should understand the underpinning theory, models, and techniques for managing various HR functions, developing appropriate systems and structures (e.g. high-performance work system, teams, and the associated rewards systems), promoting employee learning, and creating opportunities for consultation and participation. They should be able to apply their knowledge synergistically to have an impact on organizational outcomes. HR professionals are expected to understand the business, its internal and external environments, the opportunities and challenges it faces, its customers, competitors and other internal or external stakeholders. Identifying, communicating, and reinforcing organizational priorities and values would be necessary. HR strategy should therefore be embedded in organizational strategy and integrated with other strategic frameworks, such as marketing and finance.

In order to develop knowledge in these areas and the associated professional competencies, HR professionals need to continually update their professional and theoretical knowledge and be aware of practices in the industry and other organizations. We discuss in Chapter 1 some professional standards established by HKIHRM for continuous HR career development. The Education Bureau of the Hong Kong SAR government, in collaboration with local senior HR professionals, has also proposed a qualification framework with competency standards of the HRM sector with the objective of providing a similar platform for practitioners to pursue continuous and lifelong learning.[29] This initiative is welcome by local HR professionals, and employers should encourage hiring of their professional HR people meeting the standards and competencies specified in the framework.

Regarding HR skills and competencies, there is already much discussion in the current literature.[30] We also discuss some relevant ones to Hong Kong in Chapter 1 and various chapters. Here, we highlight the importance of several skills. First are the change management skills. Probably, they top the priority list for HR working towards the 'business partner' model as we need to overcome resistance and maximize solutions. HR has to anticipate the response of employees and pre-empt negative reactions by communicating the opportunities and challenges involved in pursuing new approaches to work. Designing, implementing, and rewarding mechanisms for engaging in organizational change are encouraged. Another related skill is developing future leaders. This requires making the right selection decisions and creating developmental opportunities to foster right leadership attributes. As a consequence, HR professionals have to make contributions at a strategic level as coaches. Coaching support to senior management is necessary. HR therefore needs to be agile at providing honest and constructive feedback, challenging existing mindsets, and providing a context for senior managers to explore alternatives and question the viability of current practices. HR professionals need to build alliances across the organization to encourage joint problem-solving. It may involve creating different career paths that allow movement across organizational boundaries and hierarchies. Finally, HR professionals should be adept at marketing their contributions and persuading line managers to involve them as equal partners in the management team. This may require political acumen, combined with an ability to focus on high-profile strategic initiatives that would be noticed by the senior managers. In other words, personal characteristics and charisma of the HR professionals can have significant impact on the willingness of others to involve the HR team in the strategic decision-making process.

In sum, the above discussion has presented unprecedented challenges as well as opportunities for Hong Kong's HR professionals to help at the level of business strategy formulation, execution, and achievement of business results. They need to have a strong understanding of HR, business, competitors, and internal and external environments. And we note ample job opportunities in this field. Educated and experienced human resource managers will be in high demand across a wide range of industries. However, in such a turbulent environment and with the impact of HR technologies, the HR field is becoming more demanding. Table 11.1 provides some information about Hong Kong employers' demands of HR capabilities in the market. As we note from Chapter 9, HR professionals are often noted for lacking digital or data literacy. Discussion of failures, pains, or even outsourcing (if not removal) of HR is noted elsewhere. And many business leaders do not believe that HR has a reputation to support business.[31] Is our HR going to adapt or perish? Massive reskilling and change of mindsets are required in order to achieve new HR capabilities.

Conclusion

The perspectives and insights provided by this chapter and contributors of various chapters of this book combine to create a vision for the future of HRM in Hong Kong. It should be challenging but promising. By addressing the issues and concerns, we hope to assist this field in both understanding the future and meeting its challenges.

Table 11.1: HR capabilities demanded by Hong Kong employers

Technical Skills	Soft Skills
1. Regional talent acquisition	1. Driving and managing change
1. Regional compensation and benefits	2. Drive for results
2. Stakeholder engagement	3. Innovative thinking
3. HR shared services	4. Learning agility
4. HR analytics	5. Critical thinking
	6. Negotiation and influencing skills
	7. Stakeholder engagement
	8. Resilience
	9. Digital literacy
	10. Data literacy

Source: Hudson (2016). *Human resources Hong Kong market trends*. Retrieved from https://hudson.hk/insights/infographics/market-trends/human-resources

Review Questions

1. Among the major challenges to HRM in Hong Kong, which one is the easiest and which is the most difficult factor for HR professionals?
2. Based on your own experience (or a company you are familiar with), identify one HR challenge you have encountered. Discuss the ways your company and HR can cope with it.
3. Discuss the ways how your company's HR can move from an inside/outside to the outside/inside approach suggested in this chapter. Identify the opportunities and threats for HR when evolving to this stage.
4. Identify one required attribute (knowledge, skills, attitudes, or something else) for HR professionals in Hong Kong in the future. Discuss how they can be achieved.

Further References

Susskind, R., and Susskind, D. (2017). *The future of the professions: How technology will transform the work of human experts*. London: Oxford University Press.

West, Darrell M. (2018). *The Future of Work: Robots, AI, and automation*. New York: Brookings Institution Press.

Ford, Martin. (2016). *Rise of the robots: Technology and the threat of a jobless future*. New York: Basic Books.

Kessler, S. (2018). *Gigged: The end of the job and the future of work*. New York: St. Martin's Press

Morgan, J. (2014). *The future of work: Attract new talent, build better leaders, and create a competitive organization*. Hoboken, NJ: Wiley.

Kochan, Thomas A., and Dyer, L. (2017). *Shaping the future of work: A handbook for action and a new social contract*. Cambridge: MIT Press.

Notes

1. Hong Kong SAR Government. (2017, March 14). *Specification of competency standards (SCS) of the HRM sector (Consultation version)*. Retrieved from https://www.hkqf.gov.hk/filemanager/hrm/common/SCSconsultation/HRM percent20SCS percent20(draft percent20March percent202017).pdf
2. Trice, H. M., and Beyer, J. M. (1993). *The cultures of work organizations*. New York: Prentice-Hall.
3. Stone, Diana L., and Deadrick, Diana L. (2015). Challenges and opportunities affecting the future of human resource management. *Human Resource Management Review, 25*, 139–145.
4. Barney, Jay B., and Wright, Patrick, M. (1997). *On becoming a strategic partner: The role of human resources in gaining competitive advantage* (Working Paper 97-09). Ithaca, Centre for Advanced Human Resource Studies, Cornell University. Retrieved from https://digitalcommons.ilr.cornell.edu/cgi/viewcontent.cgi?referer=https://www.google.com/&httpsredir=1&article=1149&context=cahrswp
5. Hempel, Paul S. (n.d.). *Managing knowledge workers: Can Hong Kong learn from Taiwan?* Retrieved from https://www.cb.cityu.edu.hk/mgt/document/Applied percent20Articles/Applied percent20Articles/Hempel percent20-percent20Knowledge percent20Workers.pdf
6. Census and Statistics Department, HKSAR Government. (2018, May). *Hong Kong monthly digest of statistics. Feature article: The four key industries and other selected industries in the Hong Kong economy*. Retrieved from https://www.statistics.gov.hk/pub/B71805FB2018XXXXB0100.pdf
7. Hong Kong SAR Government. (2017, March 14). *Specification of competency standards (SCS) of the HRM sector (Consultation version)*. Retrieved from https://www.hkqf.gov.hk/filemanager/hrm/common/SCSconsultation/HRM percent20SCS percent20(draft percent20March percent202017).pdf
8. Wong, M. (2018, November 20). Hong Kong losing competitive edge to Singapore, Shanghai, and has yet to face worst of trade war impact, poll finds. *South China Morning Post*. Retrieved from https://www.scmp.com/business/companies/article/2174201/hong-kong-losing-competitive-edge-singapore-shanghai-and-has-yet
9. England, J. (1989). *Industrial relations and law in Hong Kong*. Hong Kong: Oxford University Press. Tsui, A., Lai, K. T., and Wong, Isabella, H. M. (2009). The development and current state of HRM in Hong Kong. In A. Tsui and K. T. Lai (Eds.), *Professional practices of HRM in Hong Kong: Linking HRM to organizational success* (pp. 11–26). Hong Kong: HKU Press. Chan, A., and Man, D. (2014). Human resource management in Hong Kong. In Arup Varma and Pawan S. Budhwar (Eds.), *Managing human resource in Asia-Pacific* (pp. 82–96). London: Routledge.
10. Ngai, Joe. (2017, November 30). Want to work for a Chinese company? Make sure you understand this first. *South China Morning Post*. Retrieved from https://www.scmp.com/business/article/2122316/want-work-chinese-company-make-sure-you-understand-first
11. Hong Kong SAR Government. (2017, March 14). *Specification of competency standards (SCS) of the HRM sector (Consultation version)*. Retrieved from https://www.hkqf.gov.hk/filemanager/hrm/common/SCSconsultation/HRM percent20SCS percent20(draft percent20March percent202017).pdf
12. Hong Kong Institute of Human Resource Management. (2015, May). *2015 Retirement age poll by Hong Kong Institute of Human Resource Management*. Hong Kong: HKIHRM.
13. Van Knippenberg, D., De Dreu, C. K., and Homan, A. C. (2004). Work group diversity and group performance: An integrative model and research agenda. *Journal of Applied Psychology, 89*(6), 1008.
14. Wong, A. (2015, September 15). Hong Kong has Asia's most diverse and inclusive workplaces. *HumanResources*. Retrieved from http://www.humanresourcesonline.net/hong-kong-asias-diverse-inclusive-workplaces

15. Abdoolcarim, Z. (2007, June 7). Hong Kong's future: Sunshine, with clouds. *TIME*. Retrieved from http://content.time.com/time/specials/2007/article/0,28804,1630244_1630240_1630206,00.html
16. Yam, Joseph. (2014). 《居安思危》 Hong Kong: Enrich.
17. Siu, P., and Chan, S. (2014, August 4). Police unions say plan for raising retirement age discriminates against current officer. *South China Morning Post*. Retrieved from https://www.scmp.com/news/hong-kong/article/1566099/police-unions-say-plan-raising-retirement-age-discriminates-against
18. Bullock, P., and McCormack, U. (2017, October). Legal implications of 'gig economy' for employment. *Human Resource* (pp. 37–38). Hong Kong: HKIHRM.
19. Zero means completely equal distribution. It was recorded at 0.539, being the highest in the past four decades. Census and Statistics Department. (2017, June 9). Census and Statistics Department announces results of study on household income distribution in Hong Kong. Retrieved from http://www.censtatd.gov.hk/press_release/pressReleaseDetail.jsp?pressRID=4180&charsetID=1
20. Anand, P. (2012, November). Hong Kong HR Directors favour traditional recruitment. *Human Resources* (pp. 4–5). Hong Kong: HKIHRM.
21. Braverman, H. (1974). *Labour and monopoly capital: The degradation of work in the Twentieth Century*. New York: Monthly Review Press. Scarbrough, H., and Corbett, J. Martin (1992). *Technology and organization: Power, meaning, and design*. London: Routledge.
22. Kim, S. H. and Cooke, F. L. (2018). The future of human resource management in Asia in a world of change. In F. L. Cooke and S. H. Kim (Eds.), *Routledge handbook of human resource management in Asia* (pp. 415–430). Oxford: Routledge. Chang, J. L., and Huynh, P. (2016). *ASEAN in transformation. The future of jobs at risk of automation*. Retrieved from https://www.ilo.org/wcmsp5/groups/public/---ed_dialogue/---act_emp/documents/publication/wcms_579554.pdf
23. Poon, T. (1992). Western technology in Chinese context: New technologies and the organization of work in Hong Kong. In Jane Marceau (Ed.), *Reworking the world* (pp. 205–238). New York: De Gruyter.
24. Lai, Gary. (2019, January 19). As industries shift, retraining Hong Kong's workers is key to staying competitive. *South China Morning Post*. Retrieved from https://www.scmp.com/comment/insight-opinion/hong-kong/article/2182855/industries-shift-retraining-hong-kongs-workers-key
25. Some studies indicate that e-recruiting attracts greater number of applicants, but not higher quality of applicants. Stone, D. L., Lukaszewski, K. M., and Isenhour, L. C. (2005). E-recruiting: Online strategies for attracting talent. In H. G. Gueutal and D. L. Stone (Eds.), *The brave new world of eHR: Human resource management in the digital age* (pp. 22–53). San Francisco: Jossey Bass. In addition, it may not help increase workforce diversity since older applicants, ethnic minorities, and women are less likely to use e-recruiting. McManus, M. A., and Ferguson, M. W. (2003). Biodata, personality, and demographic differences of recruits from these sources. *International Journal of Selection and Assessment*, 11, 175–183. Also, attractiveness of website was not related to applicants' motivation to apply for jobs. Instead, e-recruiting increases administrative and transaction costs, while appealing to job hoppers with unfavourable backgrounds. Stone, D. L., Lukaszewski, K. M., and Isenhour, L. C. (2005). E-recruiting: Online strategies for attracting talent. In H. G. Gueutal and D. L. Stone (Eds.), *The brave new world of eHR: Human resource management in the digital age* (pp. 22–53). San Francisco: Jossey Bass. And MSS and ESS have shifted the responsibilities from HR to managers and employees.
26. Roehling, Mark V. et al. (2005). The future of HR management: Research needs and directions. *Human Resource Management*, 44(2), 207–216.
27. Ulrich, D., and Dulebohn, James H. (2015). Are we there yet? What's next for HR? *Human Resource Management Review*, 25, 188–204.

28. Ulrich, D., and Dulebohn, James H. (2015). Are we there yet? What's next for HR? *Human Resource Management Review, 25*, 188–204.
29. Hong Kong SAR Government. (2017, March 14). *Specification of competency standards (SCS) of the HRM sector (Consultation version)*. Retrieved from https://www.hkqf.gov.hk/filemanager/hrm/common/SCSconsultation/HRM percent20SCS percent20(draft percent20March percent202017).pdf
30. Buckley, F., and Monks, K. (2004). The implications of meta-qualities for HR roles. *Human Resource Management Journal, 14*, 41–56. Ulrich, D., Brockbank, W., Yeung, A. K., and Lake, D. G. (1995). Human resource competencies: An empirical assessment. *Human Resource Management, 34*, 473–496.
31. See for example, Mazor, A., Stephan, M., Walsh, B., Schmahl, Hendrik., and Valenzuela, Jaime. (2015, February 27). Reinventing HR: An extreme makeover. *Deloitte Insights*. Retrieved from https://www2.deloitte.com/insights/us/en/focus/human-capital-trends/2015/reinventing-hr-human-resources-human-capital-trends-2015.html. Mehta, S. (2017). Adapt or perish: Why HR is going to extinct? Retrieved from https://blog.bonus.ly/adapt-or-perish-why-hr-is-going-extinct/

Index

ability, 54, 57, 63, 66, 83
ability test, 54, 62, 63, 66, 73, 74
acquisition, 172, 191, 197–199, 201–205, 207
administration, 20, 27, 30, 31, 171
administrative expert, 2
adverse impact, 74, 110
ageing, 4, 14, 16, 35, 161
ageing population, 14, 16, 35, 161
algorithms, 2, 24, 28, 117, 174, 181, 219
American Society for Training and Development (ASTD), 90
analytics, 2, 3, 4, 10, 14, 27, 29, 31, 32, 41, 43, 44, 171, 172, 174, 176, 179, 180, 181, 182, 184, 185, 187, 218, 219, 222
  predictive analytics, 182, 183
anti-discrimination ordinances, 35, 74, 157–158, 163, 215
applicant tracking system, 2, 30, 45, 174, 184
application forms, 73
  online application forms, 73
application service provider (ASP), 28
aptitude tests, 54, 62, 64, 66, 72, 73
artificial intelligence (AI), 2, 3, 28, 44–46, 68, 84, 171, 178, 181, 219
Asia Pacific Federation of Human Resource Management (APFHRM), 7
assessment centre, 19, 21, 30, 67–73
Association for Talent Development (ATD), 90
attitudes, 4, 16, 22, 91, 164, 165, 205, 206, 215
augmented reality (AR), 3, 29, 95, 171, 178

base/basic pay/salary, 23

benefits, 5, 6, 11, 16, 19, 20, 21, 26, 30, 130, 131, 132, 133, 144, 145, 146, 147, 150, 153, 156, 157, 1581, 160, 161, 164, 166, 171, 172, 184, 187, 188, 194, 206, 219, 222
benefits administration, 20
bias, 64, 67, 111, 112, 113, 124, 175, 180
big data, 24, 41, 42–44, 91, 97, 98, 100, 105, 118, 174, 217, 218
big data analytics, 41
bonus, 23, 110, 112, 115, 129, 130, 132, 133, 139, 140, 141, 176
  discretionary bonuses, 21, 135, 139–140
  retention bonus, 203
British Psychological Society (BPS), 65, 70
business partner, 9, 137, 166, 214, 218, 220, 221
business partnership, 5, 8, 133, 215
business strategy, 131, 132, 133, 134, 164, 195, 198, 199, 202, 204, 219, 220, 221

California Personality Inventory (CPI), 65
candidate experience, 2, 43, 44, 57, 69, 80
career opportunities, 23, 130, 166
central tendency, 113
certification, 180, 213
change agent, 2, 100, 205, 206
change management, 94, 185, 191–207
Chartered Institute of Personnel and Development (CIPD), 7, 164
chatbot, 2, 28, 53, 174, 181, 185
cheating, 61
  candidate cheating, 65–67
China factor, 213–214
cloud, 3, 44, 171, 172, 173, 174, 175, 182
cloud computing, 28, 30, 185, 187

coaches, 32, 70, 71, 72, 76–79, 196, 221
coaching, 3, 10, 21, 33, 56, 61, 65, 98, 101, 103, 108, 116, 119, 123, 125, 130, 173, 176, 177, 181, 196
    interview coaching, 57
collective bargaining, 34, 160–161, 163, 216
commissions, 55
commitment, 2, 15, 21, 26, 76, 82, 124, 125, 142, 147, 164, 202, 203, 204, 205, 206, 207, 214
    emotional commitment, 164
    rational commitment, 164
communication, 164–166, 167, 196, 200, 204–205, 219
company board, 5–7, 9
compa-ratio, 111, 115, 136, 138
compensation and benefits, 5, 6, 11, 130, 132, 166, 171, 184, 188, 206, 222
competency/competencies, 2, 3, 8, 64, 67, 71, 74, 117, 123, 220
    Competency Model, 206
    Competency Standards, 8
    competency-based interview, 73
    core competencies, 96, 101, 102, 104
competency framework, 7, 64, 101
Computer Adaptive Testing (CAT), 63
Confederation of Trade Unions (CTU), 36, 157
consistency, 66, 67, 71, 112, 117
consultants, 25, 76, 101, 104, 144, 176, 182, 187, 199, 201, 202, 203, 204, 205
continuous contract of employment, 153–154, 216
continuous contract, 153
contract for service, 154
contract of service, 154
contracting out, 156
contractors, 15, 36, 101, 155
critical incident, 125
Cross-Industry Training Advisory Committee (CITAC), 8
crossvergence, 16
culture, 15–18, 214–216
    Chinese culture, 34, 113, 114

data protection, 219
data security, 185
database, 28, 48, 174
development centre, 67–73, 76, 77
digital transformation, 170–188

digitization, 91, 95, 97, 98, 100, 102
Disability Discrimination Ordinance, 157
discrimination, 85, 111, 158, 163, 166, 167
disputes, 20, 35, 36, 152, 163
    labour disputes, 11, 35, 152, 163, 162–164
disruptive HR technology, 3–4
disruptive innovation, 170
disruptive technology, 170–188
diversity, 14, 15, 16, 42, 84, 145, 215, 216
    workforce diversity, 4, 14
drivers of change, 91

e-compensation, 30
e-learning, 30, 176, 177, 204, 219
e-performance management, 30
e-recruiting, 30
e-selection, 30
electronic human resource management (e-HRM), 29, 30
employee advocate, 2, 4
employee champion, 2, 166
employee engagement, 4, 6, 11, 110, 115, 117, 119, 122, 152, 153, 163, 164–166
employee referral, 15, 20, 53
employee relations, 6, 9, 11, 152–167
employee self-service (ESS), 31, 173, 182
employee wellness, 11, 145, 147–149, 187
Employees' Compensation Ordinance (Chapter 282), 153, 154
employer branding, 2, 21, 30, 69, 75, 218
employment branding, 216
employment brands, 173, 176
employment contracts, 34, 35, 158, 159
Employment Ordinance, 34, 35, 146, 153, 154, 155, 156, 160, 161, 163
employment relations, 11, 34, 35–36, 152
Enterprise Resource Planning (ERP) system, 28, 172
extrinsic rewards, 17, 130
evidence-based approach, 4, 32, 219

Facebook, 28, 46, 47, 50, 52, 53, 56, 172, 179
facial expression, 45, 85
faking, 66, 67, 80
family status, 35, 158
    Family Status Discrimination Ordinance, 157
favouritism, 109, 113
Federation of Trade Unions (FTU), 36

feedback, 69, 116–117, 76–77, 121
fixed pay, 133
forced ranking, 110, 112, 115, 122
functional expert, 2
Fundamental Interpersonal Relationship Orientation (FIRO), 65

game-based assessment, 79, 174
gamification, 10, 52, 68, 79–84, 175
gamified assessment, 79–85
Generation X, 17, 51, 100
Generation Y, 17
Generation Z, 17, 49, 50, 80, 146, 181
gig economy, 155, 181
globalization, 4, 10, 14, 16, 19, 49, 51, 144, 194, 212, 214
Graduate and Managerial Assessment (GMA), 63
graphic rating scale, 125
group discussions, 72, 73, 101

halo effect, 114, 127
health and safety, vii, 29, 35, 148, 159, 163, 178
hierarchy, 22, 124
High Performance Work System, 2
Hofstede, 113, 126, 199, 200, 210
Hogan Assessment, 64
holidays
  public holidays, 156, 217
  statutory holidays, 153, 156
Hong Kong Institute of Human Resource Management (HKIHRM), viii, 7
Hong Kong Management Association (HKMA), 7, 13
Hong Kong People Management Association (HKPMA), 7
Hong Kong Psychological Society, viii
horn effect, 113
HR analytics, 32, 39, 58, 171, 179, 182, 187, 222
HR audit, 209
HR Business Partner, viii, 5, 6, 9, 13, 133, 137
HR career ladder, 8, 13
HR certification system, 213
HR competency/competencies, 2
HR dashboard, 31, 32
HR leader, 2
HR magazine, 7
HR portals, 19, 28
HR Professional Standards Model, 7, 206
HR reports, 31
HR roles, 3, 52, 92, 225
HR strategy/strategies, 9, 12, 13, 19, 25, 166, 212, 219, 220
HR technology, vii, 3, 9, 10, 11, 14, 27, 171, 172, 179, 182–190, 217, 218
human capital developer, 2
human capital management, 2
human resource department, 42, 93, 94
human resource information system (HRIS), 5, 11, 143, 217
human resource management profession (HRM profession), 9, 13, 217, 219
human resource management professionals (HRM professionals), 9, 219
  strategic human resource management (strategic HRM), 39
  traditional and short-term HRM, 141, 194, 213
hygiene factors, 152

identity, 37, 45, 158, 168, 199, 201, 202
incentive, 110, 115, 130, 133, 141, 142, 191, 196
industrial/organizational psychology, viii, 87, 88, 126, 127, 128, 208, 209, 210
industrial relations, ix, 34, 37, 223
information system, 5, 11, 29, 99, 118, 143, 217
information technology, 27, 106, 210
inherent requirements, 144
Instagram, 28, 46, 47
institutional permissiveness, 34
institutional theory, vii, 19, 34
insurance, 65, 77, 142, 147, 158, 160, 181, 198
internet, 25, 28, 29, 30, 82, 87, 96, 141, 174, 187, 189, 209
internship, 26, 44, 55, 56
interventionary HR, 2
interviewing, 10, 44, 45, 49, 58, 84, 85, 86, 173, 174
  digital interviewing, 45, 84
  video interviewing, 58, 84, 85, 86, 173
intrinsic rewards, 17, 125, 129, 130

job analysis, 74
job description, 24, 26, 195

job evaluation system, 19
job satisfaction, 4, 26, 164
job specification, 8, 223, 225

Kirkpatrick Four-level Training Evaluation, 99
knowledge workers, 4, 10, 14, 16, 38, 213, 223
knowledge-based economy, 4, 16, 37, 213, 218

Labour Advisory Board (LAB), 167, 168, 169
Labour Department, viii, 13, 35, 36, 162, 163, 167, 168, 169
labour disputes, viii, 11, 35, 152, 162, 163, 164
labour laws, 35, 40
labour market, 16, 19, 20, 24, 34, 35, 62, 159, 219
labour shortage, 16, 161, 213
Labour Tribunal, 35, 162, 163, 169
Labour Tribunal Ordinance, 35, 162, 163, 169
law/laws, 9, 10, 11, 14, 33, 34, 35, 36, 37, 40, 51, 128, 145, 152–169, 171, 194, 215, 217, 223
leadership, vii, viii, ix, x, 3, 4, 10, 15, 22, 54, 60, 61, 67, 69–79, 86, 94, 95, 98, 101, 102, 104, 119, 120, 124, 133, 164, 165, 175, 192, 198, 199, 201, 204, 205, 206, 207, 209, 210, 220, 221
leadership assessment, viii, ix, 10, 71, 73, 74, 75, 76, 77, 78, 79, 86
learning, v, vi, 2, 3, 9, 10, 12–14, 16, 24, 28, 29, 30, 41, 43, 44, 54, 68, 76, 79, 90–106, 120, 131, 142, 171–182, 184, 185, 187, 188, 203, 204, 213, 215, 219, 220, 222
learning analytics, 3, 106
learning and development, 90–106
learning and development officer, 102, 103
learning experience platforms, 177, 184
learning management system, 30, 98, 99, 106, 177
leave
  annual leave, 129, 145, 150, 153
  maternity leave, 125, 146, 150, 151, 156
  paternity leave, 35, 145, 146, 150, 151, 153, 216
  sick leave, 153, 155
legal compliance, 13, 27, 83, 93, 95, 102, 135, 152, 157, 172, 180, 204
legal environment, 4, 5
leniency, 113
LinkedIn, 6, 13, 28, 44, 46, 47, 49, 51, 53, 56, 58, 87, 97, 106, 172, 174, 176, 177, 178, 179, 189
long service payments, 153, 160

machine learning, 2, 24, 28, 43, 45, 68, 181
mainland Chinese companies, 20
Management by Objectives (MBO), 125
management of change, 191
manager self-service (MSS), 31
Mandatory Provident Fund Scheme (MPF), 31, 153, 155, 160, 161
Mandatory Provident Fund Schemes Ordinance (MPFSO), 153, 155, 160, 161
manpower, 7, 193, 209, 213, 214, 215, 218
manpower and cost planning, 214
manpower planning, 214
manufacturing, ix, 4, 12, 16, 20, 33, 72, 218
market position, 133, 138
Massive Open Online Courses (MOOC), 177
maximum performance, 62, 66, 86
measurement, 42, 64, 78, 82, 116, 183
mergers, ix, 20, 197, 198, 208, 209, 210
mergers and acquisitions, ix, 20, 197, 198, 208, 209, 210
merit increase, 112, 134, 135, 136, 138
merit pay, 110, 111, 115
microlearning platforms, 177
millennials, 16, 17, 37, 38, 49, 50, 51, 58, 59, 80, 100, 101, 119, 151, 181
Minimum Wage Commission, 34, 147, 168
Minimum Wage Ordinance, 34, 157, 166
Minnesota Multiphasic Personality Inventory (MMPI), 65
Minor Employment Claims Adjudication Board, 35, 162, 169
mobile learning, 30, 95, 176
mobile platforms, 98, 173
mobile technology, 119, 185
motivational distortion, 66
multinational corporations (MNC), viii, 16, 19, 20, 172
Myers Briggs Type Indicator (MBTI), 65

natural language processing, 2, 1 81, 219
networks, 26, 28, 44, 47, 165, 172, 173, 180, 190, 203
non-interventionary HR, 34, 87, 127
norms, 63, 64, 67, 112, 196, 199

Occupational Personality Questionnaire (OPQ), 64
online personality test, 66, 73
online platform, 46, 48, 96
Oracle, 28, 29, 172, 174, 175, 177, 180
organizational changes, ix, 193
organizational culture, 6, 62, 124, 199, 201, 204, 205, 206, 218
organizational development, 94, 101, 209
organizational performance, 2, 3, 32, 108, 192, 196, 208, 209, 210
organizational structure, 24, 27, 94, 105, 204, 212
outsourcing, 30, 36, 105, 106, 160, 189, 214, 218, 219, 221

pay differentiation, 135, 136
pay-for-performance plans, 3, 121, 123, 133, 135, 138, 143
   delinking pay to performance, 122
   linking pay to performance, 122
pay mix, 133
payment in lieu of notice, 162
payroll, 20, 26, 30, 134, 138, 172, 184, 188, 189, 219
people analytics, 172, 182, 185, 190
people management, 2, 7, 22, 96, 98, 101, 136, 164, 171, 173, 192, 205, 306, 211, 219
performance appraisal, 7, 10, 20, 30, 31, 107–118, 122–128, 132, 137, 142
performance management system (PMS), 107–128
performance management cycle, 107, 108, 109, 123, 126
performance feedback, 113, 122
performance ratings, 111, 113, 116–122, 126–128, 135, 137, 139, 140, 144, 149
performance-related pay (PRP), 128
performance standards, 113, 116, 124, 125
personal credibility, 183, 187, 190
Personal Data (Privacy) Ordinance, 82, 100, 185
personality questionnaires, 62–66, 72, 86

personality tests, 66, 73
person-job match, 48, 49
person-organization match, 24, 45, 48, 49, 78, 136, 193, 195, 214
personnel management (PM), 165
planning, 3, 6, 12, 13, 16, 24, 28, 30, 32, 51, 52, 67, 69, 73, 75, 76, 86, 96, 97, 100, 101, 120, 135, 147, 150, 172, 179, 184, 199, 202, 214, 215
platform as a service (PAAS), 173
political environment, 10, 33, 166, 217
power distance, 113, 124, 199, 200, 204
predictive, 2, 32, 43, 63, 64, 174, 179, 181, 182, 183, 185
predictive analytics, 182, 183
predictive hiring, 174
pregnancy, 156, 163
programme
   online programme, 95, 99, 100, 102, 103
   virtual programme, 98, 99, 100, 101, 103, 104
Project Oxygen, 32
psychometric tests, vii, 10, 21, 30, 61, 63, 65, 73, 85, 86
public holidays, 156, 217
pulse surveys, 175, 176

Qualification Framework (QF), 8, 220

Race Discrimination Ordinance, 157
ranking, 110, 112, 115, 119, 121, 125, 200
rater bias, 113
ratingless, 121, 125–126
Raven's Progressive Matrices, 63
reaction, 75, 77, 81, 99, 121, 197, 199, 201, 221
reasoning tests, 63
recency effect, 113
recognition, 7, 20, 34, 54, 121, 130, 131, 134, 141–142, 149, 165, 176, 181
recruiting, 10, 27, 30–32, 42, 44, 46, 48, 52–53, 57, 134, 157, 172, 174, 177, 182, 213, 215, 219
recruitment, 2, 10–11, 15, 20–21, 24, 26, 28–29, 41–43, 45–48, 50–58, 61, 63–69, 74–75, 79–86, 94, 131, 157, 171, 173–174, 176, 180–181, 187, 195, 206, 215, 218
recruitment platform, 45, 48, 174
redundancy, 28, 156, 160, 197

re-engineering, 97
reference checks, 174
referral, 15, 20, 25–26, 53, 174
reliability, 117
remuneration, 129, 131–133, 145, 154
resource-based, 19
resources, 1, 5, 19, 22, 27–29, 44, 53, 55–56, 68, 92–97, 115, 120, 145, 164, 177, 188, 193, 197
rest day, 153
retention, 11, 44, 75–76, 134–135, 138, 143, 164, 179–180, 187, 199, 202–205, 207, 213, 215
retirement, 11, 16, 31, 34–35, 100, 146, 156, 159, 161, 215–216
retirement age, 16, 35, 100, 161, 215–216
retirement schemes, 16
return on investment (ROI), 83, 197
rewards, 3, 9–11, 17, 23–24, 108–109, 111, 117–118, 120–122, 125–126, 129–144, 146, 148–149, 154, 165, 194, 196, 206, 219–220
rewards management, 10–11, 23, 109, 118, 129, 219
rewards management strategies, 11
   total rewards strategies, 9–10, 129, 133–134, 144, 149
robotic process automation, 2, 181–182
robots, 28, 218

SAP, 28, 172–173, 177, 180
scores, 32, 67, 69, 113
service economy, 212, 214
severance payments, 216
Sex Discrimination Ordinance, 157
simulations, 3, 67, 71–72, 178
skills, 2–3, 9–10, 12, 16, 22, 27–28, 30, 32, 54, 57, 62, 71, 78–83, 90–91, 93, 95–98, 101–105, 109, 116, 134–135, 143, 149, 164, 170–171, 174–175, 177–179, 182–183, 187, 193, 196, 206, 212–215, 217–222
Small and Medium Enterprises (SME), 19–20, 25, 27, 49, 100, 115, 157
social desirability, 66
social media, 28, 30, 41, 46–48, 50, 52–54, 56–58, 82, 144, 164, 182, 218–219
Society of Human Resource Management (SHRM), 2, 53
software as a service (SaaS), 23, 28, 172

Specification of Competency Standards (SCS), 8
stack ranking, 112
staffing, 171
standard working hours, 35, 158–159, 167, 216
start-ups, 23–27, 37, 41, 49, 52, 84, 171
statutory holidays, 153, 156
strategy, 5, 7, 32, 44, 72, 101, 120, 130, 131–135, 142, 149, 164, 180, 195, 198–199, 202, 204–205, 218–221
strategic HR roles, 6, 188, 206, 218
strategic human resource management, 2
strategic partner, 12
strictness, 113
strike, 4, 35–36, 194, 216
subcontractors, 35
succession planning, 3, 6, 73, 75, 86, 184, 215
surveys, 7, 31–32, 101, 152, 164–165, 171, 175–176

talent, 2, 4, 5, 6, 9–11, 20–21, 24, 26–27, 29, 32, 41–48, 50–54, 56–58, 61–62, 65, 67, 72–73, 77–81, 83–86, 90–91, 94, 97, 101, 118, 120, 122–123, 130, 132–135, 138, 144, 149, 171–177, 181, 183–184, 187, 197–199, 202–206, 214–217, 219, 222
talent acquisition, 2, 5, 9–11, 43–44, 46–47, 50–51, 57–58, 65, 138, 171, 173–174, 184, 187, 216, 222
talent assessment, 9–10, 61–62, 67, 73, 79–80, 83–85, 174
talent management, 2, 6, 65, 67, 118, 123, 149, 171–173, 177, 184
talent retention, 11, 134, 199, 202, 203–204
talent shortage, 214
team management, 171, 173, 176, 181
teams, 3, 5, 27, 31, 53, 81, 93, 95, 119, 142, 147, 149, 172–173, 180, 182, 220
technological environment, 27
technology, 3–4, 9–11, 14–16, 24–32, 41, 49–50, 52, 56–57, 62, 68, 80, 82, 84–86, 95, 97–98, 100–101, 103–104, 118–119, 121, 134, 146, 164, 170–174, 179, 182–188, 212–213, 217–218
total quality management (TQM), 193
total rewards, 3, 9–10, 118, 129–134, 136–138, 141, 143–144, 146, 148–149

total rewards management, 118, 129
total rewards philosophy, 130–132, 149
total rewards principles, 131–133
total rewards programme, 143
total rewards strategies, 9–10, 129, 133–134, 144, 149
touchpoints, 119
trade unions, 11, 34, 36, 157, 159–161, 163, 167, 216–217
training, 3, 7–8, 10–11, 16, 19–20, 30, 42, 54, 69, 90–105, 109–110, 113–114, 116, 123–125, 158, 171–172, 176–178, 180, 194–196, 203–204, 206–207, 214–215, 218–219
training and development (T&D), 3, 7, 10, 11, 19, 69, 90–91, 104–105, 110, 124, 171, 206
training budget, 95
training curriculum, 97
training delivery, 102, 104
training evaluation, 99
training needs assessment/analysis (TNA), 98
training officer, 101–102
turnover, 4, 11, 23, 29, 32, 179–180, 198, 202–203, 207, 214–215
typical performance, 62, 66, 108–110, 115, 126

unfair dismissal, 153, 155, 162, 166–167
unions, 11, 20, 34–36, 157, 159–161, 163, 167, 216–217
university, 22, 25, 29, 44, 51, 54, 56, 58, 94, 217
unlawful dismissal, 155, 163

validation, 64, 66
validity, 64, 67–68, 73–74, 85
value, 1, 4–5, 7, 9, 16–18, 24, 32, 43, 47, 50, 52, 54, 56, 61, 64–65, 67, 70, 73–74, 77, 80, 82, 90, 92, 94, 96, 98, 101–102, 107, 113, 122–124, 130–133, 136, 138, 141–145, 148–149, 158, 165, 167, 170–171, 177, 182, 195–197, 200–201, 215, 218–220
variable pay, 133, 135, 141, 145
variation, 139–140
variety, 15, 26–27, 42, 67, 96, 108, 147, 155, 174
velocity, 42

virtual reality (VR), 3, 29, 68, 95, 103, 171, 177–178
vitality curve, 112
volume, 42–44, 52, 80, 140, 143

wages, 34–35, 156–160, 162–163
war for talent, 4, 10, 42–43, 57, 172
web-based, 27, 29–31, 182
websites, 29, 31, 48, 58, 144
Workday, 28, 172, 175, 177, 179, 180–181
workers, 1, 4, 10, 14, 16, 20, 35, 36, 49, 52, 53–54, 56, 101, 116, 148, 153, 155–156, 159–161, 164–165, 180–181, 212–214, 216, 218
workforce diversity, 4, 14
working hours, 11, 35, 51, 55, 156, 158, 159, 162–163, 165, 167, 216, 219
work-life balance, 4, 17, 19, 51, 100, 130, 134, 145, 148, 159, 215
work schedules, 78
work stoppage, 35
World Federation of People Management Associations (WFPMA), 7

YouTube, 28, 177
youngsters, 17, 34

www.ingramcontent.com/pod-product-compliance
Ingram Content Group UK Ltd.
Pitfield, Milton Keynes, MK11 3LW, UK
UKHW051850210426

5322IPUK00025B/642